Lecture Notes in Computer Science　　10533

Commenced Publication in 1973
Founding and Former Series Editors:
Gerhard Goos, Juris Hartmanis, and Jan van Leeuwen

More information about this series at http://www.springer.com/series/7408

Nina Yevtushenko · Ana Rosa Cavalli
Hüsnü Yenigün (Eds.)

Testing Software and Systems

29th IFIP WG 6.1 International Conference, ICTSS 2017
St. Petersburg, Russia, October 9–11, 2017
Proceedings

 Springer

Editors
Nina Yevtushenko 🆔
Tomsk State University
Tomsk
Russia

Hüsnü Yenigün 🆔
Sabanci University
Istanbul
Turkey

Ana Rosa Cavalli 🆔
SAMOVAR, CNRS, Télécom SudParis
Paris-Saclay University
Paris
France

ISSN 0302-9743   ISSN 1611-3349   (electronic)
Lecture Notes in Computer Science
ISBN 978-3-319-67548-0   ISBN 978-3-319-67549-7   (eBook)
DOI 10.1007/978-3-319-67549-7

Library of Congress Control Number: 2017952861

LNCS Sublibrary: SL2 – Programming and Software Engineering

Printed on acid-free paper

This Springer imprint is published by Springer Nature
The registered company is Springer International Publishing AG
The registered company address is: Gewerbestrasse 11, 6330 Cham, Switzerland

Preface

This volume contains the proceedings of the 29th International Conference on Testing Software and Systems, ICTSS 2017. The conference was held in St. Petersburg, Russia, during October 9–11, 2017.

The conference has a long history. In the past five years, ICTSS has been held in Graz (Austria), Dubai and Sharjah (United Arab Emirates), Madrid (Spain), Istanbul (Turkey), and Aalborg (Denmark). During the period from 2007 to 2009, the conference was held as part of the International Conference on Testing of Communicating Systems (TESTCOM) and FATES in Tallinn (Estonia), Tokyo (Japan), and Eindhoven (the Netherlands). Before that, between 2000 and 2006, TESTCOM was held in Ottawa (Canada), Berlin (Germany), Sophia Antipolis (France), Oxford (UK), Montreal (Canada), and New York City (USA). During the period from 1997 to 1999, the conference was called the International Workshop on Testing of Communicating Systems (IWTCS) and was held on Cheju Island (South Korea), in Tomsk (Russia), and in Budapest (Hungary). Between 1988 and 1996, the conference was known as the International Workshop for Protocol Test Systems (IWPTS). Nine workshops took place in Vancouver (Canada), Berlin (Germany), McLean (USA), Leidschendam (the Netherlands), Montreal (Canada), Pau (France), Tokyo (Japan), Evry (France), and Darmstadt (Germany).

The topics of this volume cover model-based testing, test derivation and monitoring, fault localization, and system testing including real-time systems. In total, 41 papers were submitted and the Program Committee selected 18 regular and 4 short papers for presentation at the conference. The accepted papers form the contents of the proceedings.

We are grateful to the authors of submitted papers, invited speakers, and Steering and Program Committee members for their valuable contributions, and particularly to Robert M. Hierons, the Steering Committee chair, for his help and guidance. We acknowledge the use of EasyChair for the conference management and thank the IFIP and WG 6.1 chair, Jean-Bernard Stefani, for his help. We also thank Springer for publishing the proceedings, and the Tomsk State University, the Institut Mines-Télécom/Télécom SudParis, and Sabanci University for their support.

October 2017

Nina Yevtushenko
Ana Rosa Cavalli
Hüsnü Yenigün

Organization

ICTSS 2017 was organized by Tomsk State University in cooperation with the International Federation for Information Processing (IFIP).

Steering Committee

Robert M. Hierons   Brunel University London, UK (Chair)
Andreas Ulrich   Siemens AG, Germany
Ana Rosa Cavalli   SAMOVAR, CNRS, Télécom SudParis,
                           Paris-Saclay University, France
Franz Wotawa   Technische Universität Graz, Austria
Natalia Kushik   SAMOVAR, CNRS, Télécom SudParis,
                           Université Paris-Saclay, France
Khaled El–Fakih   American University of Sharjah, United Arab Emirates
Nina Yevtushenko   Tomsk State University, Russia
Mercedes G. Merayo   Universidad Complutense de Madrid, Spain
Edgardo Montes de Oca   Montimage, France

Conference Chairs

General Chairs

Nina Yevtushenko   Tomsk State University, Russia
Ana Rosa Cavalli   SAMOVAR, CNRS, Télécom SudParis,
                           Paris-Saclay University, France
Hüsnü Yenigün   Sabanci University, Turkey

Industrial Chair

Masaki Suzuki   KDDI Research, Inc., Japan

Publicity Chair

Jorge López   SAMOVAR, CNRS, Télécom SudParis,
                           Université Paris-Saclay, France

Program Committee

Harald Altinger   Audi AG, Ingolstadt, Germany
Sergey Baranov   St. Petersburg Institute for Informatics and Automation
                           of the Russian Academy of Sciences, Russia
Mario Bravetti   University of Bologna, Italy
Ana Rosa Cavalli   SAMOVAR, CNRS, Télécom SudParis,
                           Paris-Saclay University, France

Additional Referees

Local Organizing Committee

Nina Yevtushenko   Tomsk State University, Russia
Stanislav Mikoni   St. Petersburg Institute for Informatics
                        and Automation of the Russian Academy of Sciences,
                        St. Petersburg, Russia
Natalia Aseeva   Monomax Company, St. Petersburg, Russia

Sponsoring Institutions

International Federation for Information Processing (IFIP), Laxenburg, Austria
Tomsk State University, Russia

Contents

Model Based Testing

Test Derivation Methods

Safety and Security Testing

Model Based Testing

Fragility-Oriented Testing with Model Execution and Reinforcement Learning

Tao Ma[1(✉)], Shaukat Ali[1], Tao Yue[1,2], and Maged Elaasar[3]

[1] Simula Research Laboratory, P.O. Box 134, 1325 Lysaker, Norway
{taoma,shaukat,tao}@simula.no
[2] University of Oslo, P.O. Box 1072, 0316 Blindern, Norway
[3] Carleton University, 1125 Colonel by Dr., Ottawa, ON K1S5B6, Canada
melaasar@gmail.com

Abstract. Self-healing is becoming an essential behavior of smart Cyber-Physical Systems (CPSs), which enables them to recover from faults by themselves. Such behaviors make decisions autonomously at runtime and they often operate in an uncertain physical environment making testing even more challenging. To this end, we propose Fragility-Oriented Testing (FOT), which relies on model execution and reinforcement learning to cost-effectively test self-healing behaviors of CPSs in the presence of environmental uncertainty. We evaluated FOT's performance by comparing it with a Coverage-Oriented Testing (COT) algorithm. Evaluation results show that FOT significantly outperformed COT for testing nine self-healing behaviors implemented in three case studies. On average, FOT managed to find 80% more faults than COT and for cases when both FOT and COT found the same faults, FOT took on average 50% less time than COT.

Keywords: Cyber-Physical Systems · Uncertainty · Self-healing behaviors · Model execution · Reinforcement learning

1 Introduction

Self-healing is becoming an important functionality of smart Cyber-Physical Systems (CPSs) [1]. With such functionality, a Self-Healing CPS (SH-CPS) has the ability to recover from faults and adapt its behavior accordingly. Given that uncertainty is inherent in CPSs since such systems operate in highly unpredictable physical environment [2], self-healing behaviors of an SH-CPS must deal with uncertainty gracefully. By uncertainty, we mean *"the lack of knowledge of which value an uncertain factor will take at a given point of time during execution"* [3]. In this paper, we limit our scope to uncertain factors related to sensing (e.g., noise) and actuation (e.g. deviation) of SH-CPSs as a starting point.

To check the correctness of self-healing behaviors of SH-CPSs in the presence of uncertainty, a cost-effective testing method is required. In this paper, we propose a

This research was funded by the MBT4CPS project (grant no. 240013/O70).

N. Yevtushenko et al. (Eds.): ICTSS 2017, LNCS 10533, pp. 3–20, 2017.
DOI: 10.1007/978-3-319-67549-7_1

Fragility-Oriented Testing (FOT) algorithm to ensure that self-healing behaviors properly handle environmental uncertainty. The core idea of FOT is using *fragility* (i.e., a measure indicating how near an SH-CPS is to fail in a given state) as a heuristic for revealing faults. Based on this heuristic, we use model execution and reinforcement learning to explore various execution paths of the SH-CPS and simulate uncertainty in its physical environment to cost-effectively find faults.

A traditional model-based testing (MBT) approach generates test cases from test models with a test strategy and executes them on a system in separate steps. In contrast, FOT tests a system with a test strategy that dynamically incorporates information during execution to decide the next test execution step. From the execution information, FOT uses a reinforcement learning method to identify transitions that have high possibilities to reveal a fault, i.e., lead to a state with the highest fragility. Accordingly, FOT adapts its transition selection policy to favor these transitions for test execution with the aim to cost-effectively find faults.

We evaluated FOT by testing nine self-healing behaviors in three case studies. We conducted one experiment per self-healing behavior and compared cost (measured as time to find a fault) and effectiveness (measured as the number of faults found) of FOT as opposed to Coverage-Oriented Testing (COT) [4]. Each self-healing behavior was tested under 10 environmental uncertainties. Evaluation results show that FOT significantly outperformed COT in five out of nine experiments in terms of finding faults. On average, FOT found 80% more faults and spent 50% less test execution time to find a fault than COT. Note that COT was used as a naive baseline to be compared with FOT and comparison with more sophisticated comparable algorithms is required in the future.

Our key contributions: (1) proposing a reinforcement learning based testing algorithm to cost-effectively find faults in SH-CPSs under uncertainty, (2) defining *fragility* as the heuristic to guide the reinforcement learning algorithm, (3) evaluating FOT (by comparing with COT) in terms of cost-effectiveness for testing nine self-healing behaviors implemented in three real case studies. We organize the paper as follows. Section 2 presents the background, Sect. 3 presents the running example, and the FOT is presented in Sect. 4. Section 5 presents an evaluation, Sect. 6 summarizes related work, and Sect. 7 concludes the paper.

2   Background

This section discusses Executable Test Model (ETM) and Dynamic Flat State Machine (DFSM), the key models used in FOT, in Sects. 2.1 and 2.2. Section 2.3 briefly summarizes a test model execution framework – TM-Executor.

2.1   Executable Test Model (ETM)

A CPS can be seen as a set of networked physical units, working together to monitor and control physical processes. A physical unit can be further decomposed into sensors, actuators, and controllers. A controller monitors and controls physical processes via sensors and actuators, which are functional behaviors. As a specific type of CPSs, an

SH-CPS monitors fault occurrences and adapts its behavior if a fault is detected with self-healing behaviors. As the objective of a self-healing behavior is to restore functional behaviors, both *expected* functional and self-healing behaviors need to be captured for testing. Previously, we proposed a UML-based modeling framework, called MoSH [3], which allows creating an Executable Test Model (ETM) for an SH-CPS Under Test (SUT). The ETM consists of a set of UML state machines annotated with dedicated stereotypes from the MoSH profiles.

The set of state machines captures expected functional and self-healing behaviors of the SUT: $SM = \{sm_1, \ldots, sm_n\}$, where each state machine sm_i has MoSH stereotype applied. A sm_i has a set of states $S_{sm_i} = \{s_{sm_i1}, \ldots, s_{sm_is}\}$ and transitions $T_{sm_i} = \{t_{sm_i1}, \ldots, t_{sm_it}\}$. A state s_{sm_ij} ($s_{sm_ij} \in S_{sm_i}$) is defined by a *state invariant* O_{sm_ij}, which is specified as a constraint in OCL[1] constraining one or more state variables. When s_{sm_ij} is active, its corresponding state invariant should be satisfied. A transition t_{sm_ik} ($t_{sm_ik} \in T_{sm_i}$) is defined as a tuple $t := (s_{src}, s_{tar}, op, g)$, where s_{src} and s_{tar} are the source and target states of t. op denotes an operation call event that can trigger the transition[2] and the operation represents a testing API used to control the SUT. g signifies the transition's guard, an OCL constraint. It restricts input parameter values that can be used to invoke the operation for firing the transition. By conforming to the fUML[3] and Precise Semantics Of UML State Machines(PSSM)[4] standards, the specified state machines are executable. Thus the test model is called an Executable Test Model.

2.2 Dynamic Flat State Machine (DFSM)

Test execution with concurrent and hierarchical state machines is computationally expensive and complex. Since statically flattening state machines may lead to state explosion, we implemented an algorithm to dynamically and incrementally flatten UML state machines into a DFSM during test execution. A DFSM has a set of states $\mathbb{S} = \{s_1, s_2, \ldots, s_n\}$ and a set of transitions $\mathbb{T} = \{t_1, t_2, \ldots, t_m\}$. Each state s_i in $\mathbb{S}$ is constituted by states s_{sm_ij} from each sm_i, denoted as $s_i = s_{sm_1i} \wedge s_{sm_2j} \wedge \ldots \wedge s_{sm_nk}$. Accordingly, the conjunction of all constituents' state invariants $[o_{sm_1i} \wedge o_{sm_2j} \wedge \ldots \wedge o_{sm_nk}]$ forms the state invariant of s_i, denoted as o_i. Meanwhile, the set of transitions connecting the DFSM states is captured by $\mathbb{T}$. Each transition t_i belonging to $\mathbb{T}$ is uniquely mapped to a transition t_{sm_xj} in a state machine sm_x, expressed as $t_i = t_{sm_xj}$. While the ETM is being executed, the DFSM of the ETM is dynamically constructed. FOT uses the DFSM to learn the value of firing each transition and find the optimal transition selection policy to cost-effectively find faults. Thus, we mainly use DFSM to explain FOT.

---

[1] http://www.omg.org/spec/OCL/2.4.

[2] Though call, change and signal event occurrences can all be triggers to model expected behaviors, only transitions having call event occurrences as triggers can be activated from the outside. A change event or a signal event is only for the SUT's internal behaviors, which cannot be controlled for testing.

[3] http://www.omg.org/spec/FUML/1.2.1.

[4] http://www.omg.org/spec/PSSM/1.0/Beta1.

2.3 Test Model Execution Framework

We developed a testing framework called TM-Executor [3] in our previous work, which executes the ETM and the SUT at the same time. Via testing APIs, state variable values are queried from the SUT and used by TM-Executor to evaluate state invariants of the active state. If an invariant is evaluated false, it means that the SUT fails to behave consistently with the ETM and a fault is detected.

The execution of an ETM results in the execution of the SUT. During the execution, TM-Executor dynamically and incrementally derives a DFSM from the set of concurrent state machines in the ETM. As aforementioned, a transition's trigger *op* and guard *g* specify which operation to invoke with which input parameter values to make the SUT and the ETM transit from one state to another. While an operation is being invoked, an operation call event is generated, which drives the execution of the ETM. Meanwhile, the operation is executed to call a corresponding testing API, which makes the SUT enter the next state.

Two kinds of testing APIs for controlling the SUT can be specified as a transition's trigger *op*. One is functional control operation, which instructs the SUT to execute a nominal functional operation. Second is fault injection operation, which introduces a fault in the SUT, based on which, TM-Executor controls when and which faults to be injected to the SUT to trigger its self-healing behaviors.

3 Running Example

We will use a running example of an Unmanned Aerial Vehicle control system (i.e., ArduCopter[5]) to illustrate FOT. It has two physical units, i.e., copter and Ground Control Station (GCS). With the GCS, users remotely control the copter using a number of flight modes. During the flight, the copter is constantly affected by environmental uncertainties such as wind speed and direction, measurements noise from the GPS, accelerometer, and compass. This poses an extra challenge to the self-healing behaviors of the copter. *Collision avoidance* is one of the self-healing behaviors. Due to improper flight control (operational fault), the copter may approach another aircraft. In such case, the copter automatically adapts the velocity and orientation (i.e., the angles of rotations in roll, pitch, and yaw) of the flight to avoid a collision. We build an ETM to specify the expected collision avoidance behavior along with related functional behaviors. Figure 1 presents a partial simplified DFSM corresponding to the ETM; while, the complete ETM is presented in [5]. We take one path (bold transitions in Fig. 1: $t1 \rightarrow t2 \rightarrow t3 \rightarrow t4 \rightarrow t11 \rightarrow t12 \rightarrow t16 \rightarrow t18$) to explain test execution.

Starting from the *Initial* state, the DFSM directly enters *Stopped*, as there is no trigger on $t1$. From *Stopped*, TM-Executor fires $t2$ by calling the functional control operation *start* to launch the SUT. As a result, *Started* becomes active. To make the copter enter state *Lift*, TM-Executor invokes operation *throttle* with a valid value of input parameter *thr* obtained by solving guard constraint *[thr > 1600 and thr < 2000]* via constraint solver EsOCL [6]. Then, the copter takes off and reaches the *Lift* state. In

---

[5] http://ardupilot.org/copter/.

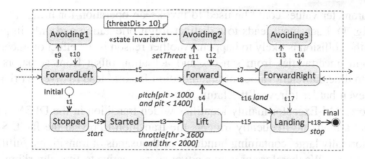

Fig. 1. A Simplified DFSM for ArduCopter

the *Lift* state, TM-Executor needs to choose one of the two outgoing transitions to be triggered. Assuming t4 is chosen, it is triggered by invoking *pitch* with a valid value of *pit* satisfying *[pit > 1000 and pit < 1400]*. This invocation triggers the copter to move forward. In the *Forward* state, TM-Executor either changes the copter's movement (i.e., firing t5, t7, or t16) or invokes the fault injection operation *setThreat*, which simulates that an aircraft is approaching from the left behind of the copter to trigger the collision avoidance behavior. Here the second option is adopted. Triggered by this, the collision avoidance behavior controls the copter to fly away from the aircraft. When the distance between them (*threatDis*) is over 1000 meters (not shown in Fig. 1), the collision threat is avoided and the copter's flight mode changes back to the previous one. Hence, t12 is traversed[6]. Then TM-Executor chooses to trigger t16, followed by firing t18, to stimulate that the copter passes through the *Landing* state and reaches the final state.

In parallel to the execution, TM-Executor periodically obtains the values of the SUT's state variables through testing APIs and repeatedly uses these values to evaluate the active state's invariant, using a constraint evaluator DresdenOCL [7]. If an invariant is evaluated to be false, then a fault is detected.

The decision to which transition to be triggered determines if a fault can be found by executing the ETM and the SUT. From specifications, we know that there is a fault in the collision avoidance behavior when an aircraft is approaching from −45° and the copter is flying to the forward left, the collision avoidance behavior has to reverse the copter's orientation to make the two aerial vehicles fly away. Since reversing the orientation takes more time than other orientation adjustments, the copter, in this case, flies closer to the approaching aircraft. Due to noisy sensor data and inaccurate actuations, a collision does have a chance to occur in this condition.

To detect the fault leading to the collision, the fault injection operation *setThreat* needs to be invoked in state *ForwardLeft*, i.e., t9 must be activated. However, activating t9 once may not be sufficient to find the fault. One reason is that a large number

---

[6] When a collision is avoided, the copter is back to the flight mode. Hence, no testing API needs to be invoked to trigger t12. When the flight mode is changed back, a corresponding change event is generated by TM-Executor to activate the transition. As this event is from inside, we do not capture it in DFSM.

of input parameter values could be used to invoke an operation for firing a transition, e.g., t4 (Fig. 1). Each input leads to a distinct flight orientation and only in particular situations, the collision is likely to happen. Another reason is the effect of uncertainties. Measurement uncertainties from sensors and actuation offset from actuators change from time to time. Different values of the uncertain factors[7] lead to diverse orientations, making it even harder to reveal the fault.

Therefore, TM-Executor mainly identifies which transition in the DFSM will most likely reveal a fault and frequently triggers the transition to reveal the fault. Since the DFSM is normally large, containing hundreds or thousands of transitions, fulfilling this task is non-trivial. We therefore present a novel cost-effective testing algorithm, FOT. It uses a reinforcement learning method to learn values of firing each transition, which helps TM-Executor to cost-effectively find faults.

4 Fragility-Oriented Testing Under Uncertainty

In this section, we present details of the testing algorithm FOT (Sect. 4.1) and three uncertainty generation strategies (Sect. 4.2), which together enable TM-Executor to cost-effectively find faults in the SUT under uncertainty. Section 4.3 describes the implementation of FOT and the uncertainty generation strategies.

4.1 Testing Algorithm

Definition 1. The fragility of the SUT in a given state expressed as $F(\mathbb{s})$, is a real value between 0 and 1. It describes how close (distance wise) the state invariant of $\mathbb{s}$ is to be *false*, where 1 means that the state invariant is *false* and 0 means that it is far from being violated. We therefore define $F(\mathbb{s})$ as follows:

$$F(\mathbb{s}) = 1 - dis(\neg \mathbb{o}) \tag{1}$$

where $\neg \mathbb{o}$ is the negation of state $\mathbb{s}$'s invariant $\mathbb{o}$ and $dis(\neg \mathbb{o})$ is a distance function (adopted from [6]) that returns a value between 0 and 1 indicating how close the constraint $\neg \mathbb{o}$ is to be true. For instance, in the running example, if the SUT is currently in state *Avoiding2* and the value of state variable *threatDis* is 15, then the distance of invariant "*threatDis > 10*" to be false can be calculated as $dis(\neg(threatDis > 10)) = \frac{(15-10)+1}{(15-10)+1+1} = 0.86$[8]. The closer the distance is to zero, the higher the possibility the invariant is to be violated, i.e., the SUT failing in the state. Hence, $1 - dis(\neg \mathbb{o})$ is used to define the fragility of the SUT in state $\mathbb{s}$.

Definition 2. The T-value of a transition expressed as $T(\mathbb{t})$, is a real value between 0 and 1. It states the possibility that a fault can be revealed after firing the transition. With

---

[7] Uncertain factor is a feature (e.g., a parameter) whose value is uncertain due to lack of knowledge.

[8] The distance function of greater operator is: $dis(x > y) = (y - x + k)/(y - x + k + 1), when\, x \leq y$, where k is an arbitrary positive value. Here we set k = 1. More details are in.

an assumption that the more fragile the SUT is, the higher the chance a fault can be revealed, we define the T-value of a transition as the discounted highest fragility of the SUT after firing the transition:

$$T(\mathfrak{t}) = \max_{s \in \mathbb{S}_{next}} \{\gamma^n \cdot F(s)\} \tag{2}$$

where γ ($0 \leq \gamma < 1$) is a discount rate; n is the number of transitions between s and $\mathfrak{t}$'s target state; and $\mathbb{S}_{next}$ is a set of states that can be reached from $\mathfrak{t}$'s source state via a path in the DFSM. As for testing, revealing faults via a short path is preferable, we penalize the fragility of a state by multiplying γ^n, if traversing at least n transitions is required to reach the state from $\mathfrak{t}$'s target state. For example, in Fig. 1, to obtain the T-value of $\mathfrak{t}4$, we calculate the discounted fragility of each state in $\mathbb{S}_{next}$. For the fragility of *Avoiding1*, it needs to be discounted by γ^2, since at least two transitions $\mathfrak{t}5$ and $\mathfrak{t}9$ are required to connect the *Avoiding1* state to $\mathfrak{t}4$'s target state *Forward*. Clearly, when γ equals 0, only the fragility of $\mathfrak{t}$'s target state is considered. While, γ approaching 1 makes a state to be reached more important.

Overview. The objective of FOT is to find the optimal transition selection policy to cost-effectively find faults. To achieve this objective, FOT tries to learn transitions' T-values during the execution of the SUT. Each transition's T-value indicates the possibility that a fault will be revealed after firing the transition. When transitions' T-values are learned, by simply firing the transition with the highest T-value, FOT can manage to cost-effectively find faults. The pseudocode of FOT is presented below with in total 17 lines (L1–L17).

At the beginning, all transitions' T-values are unknown. As every transition has a possibility to reveal a fault, we initialize an estimated T-value of each transition with the highest one (L1, L2). This encourages the algorithm to extensively explore uncovered transitions. After that, iterations of test execution and the learning process begin. At each iteration, the execution of the ETM as well as the SUT starts from the initial state (L4) and terminates at a final state (L5). During the execution, a DFSM is dynamically constructed (L6) to enable the continuous calculation of T-values. Whenever, the SUT enters a state s, FOT selects one of the outgoing transitions of s according to their estimated T-values (L7, L8) and makes TM-Executor trigger the selected transition (L9). As the transition is fired, the system moves from s to s'. If the state invariant of s' is not satisfied, then a fault is detected (L12–L15). Otherwise, FOT evaluates the fragility of the SUT in s' (L16), i.e., $\mathbb{F}(s')$, and uses $\mathbb{F}(s')$ to update estimated T-values. Since it is possible to reach s' via numerous transitions, finding all these transitions and updating their T-values are computationally impractical for an ETM with hundreds of transitions. Thus FOT only updates the estimated T-value of the last triggered transition (L17). Since $\mathbb{F}(s')$ is not a constant value, the upper bound of $\mathbb{F}(s')$ is used to update the T-value. As the iteration of the execution proceeds, the estimated T-values are continuously updated and getting close to their true values. In this way, the T-values are learned from the execution and the learned T-values direct FOT to cost-effectively find faults. Note that testing budget determines the maximum number of iterations. If it is too small, FOT may not able to find faults. The details of T-value learning and transition selection policy are explained next.

Algorithm 1 FOT(TMExecutor executor, ETM etm, int maxIteration):
 Input *executor* is TM-Executor, the testing framework
     etm is the Executable Test Model
     maxIteration is the maximum iteration number
 Begin
   1 for each transition in etm
   2 transition.Tvalue ← 1   // initialize T-values of transitions
   3 for i=1 to maxIteration
   4 etm.Start()
   5 **while** etm.ReachFinalState() is false
   6   dfsm ← EnrichDFSM(etm) // dynamically construct the DFSM
   7   reachedTransitions ← dfsm.activeState.outgoingTransitions
   8   selectedTransition ← SoftmaxSelect(reachedTransitions) //select transition
   9   executor.Trigger(selectedTransition)
   11 stateInvariant ← selectedTransition.target.invariant
   12 **if** executor.Evaluate(stateInvariant) is false
   13   LogFaultDetected(selectedTransition)
   14   dfsm.Remove(selectedTransition)
   15   **break**
   16 fragility ← executor.DistanceToViolation(stateInvariant)
   17 executor.UpdateTvalue(selectedTransition, fragility)
          // revise the T-value of selectedTransition
 End

T-Value Learning. Before executing the SUT and the ETM, the T-value $T(\mathfrak{t})$ of every transition is unknown. We adopt a reinforcement learning approach to learn $T(\mathfrak{t})$ from execution. A fundamental property of $T(\mathfrak{t})$ is that it satisfies a recursive relation, which is called the Bellman Equation [8], as shown in the formula below:

Recursive relation between $T(\mathfrak{t})$ and $\mathbb{T}_{suc}$:

$$T(\mathfrak{t}) = \max\left\{ F(\mathfrak{s}_{tar}), \gamma \cdot \max_{\mathfrak{t}_{suc}\in\mathbb{T}_{suc}} T(\mathfrak{t}_{suc}) \right\} \tag{3}$$

where $\mathfrak{s}_{tar}$ is the target state of transition $\mathfrak{t}$; $\mathbb{T}_{suc}$ represents a set of direct successive transitions whose source state is $\mathfrak{s}_{tar}$. This equation reveals the relation between the T-values of a transition and its direct successive transitions. It states that the T-value of $\mathfrak{t}$ must equal to the greater of two values: the fragility of $\mathfrak{t}$'s target state ($F(\mathfrak{s}_{tar})$) and the maximum discounted T-value of $\mathfrak{t}$'s direct successive transitions $\left(\gamma \cdot \max_{\mathfrak{t}'\in\mathbb{T}_{suc}} T(\mathfrak{t}')\right)$. Given a DFSM, $T(\mathfrak{t})$ is the unique solution to satisfy Eq. (3). So, we try to update the estimate of each T-value to make it get increasingly closer to satisfy Eq. (3). When Eq. (3) is satisfied by the estimated T-values for all transitions, it implies that the true $T(\mathfrak{t})$ is learned.

Inspired by Q-learning [8], a reinforcement learning method, FOT uses the estimated T-value $ET(\mathfrak{t})$ to approximate $T(\mathfrak{t})$, i.e., the true T-value. $ET(\mathfrak{t})$ is updated in the following way to make it approach $T(\mathfrak{t})$.

$$ET(\mathfrak{t})' = max\left\{ F(\mathsf{s}_{tar}), \gamma \cdot \max_{\mathfrak{t}_{suc} \in \mathbb{T}_{suc}} ET(\mathfrak{t}_{suc}) \right\} \tag{4}$$

where $ET(\mathfrak{t})'$ denotes the updated estimate of $\mathfrak{t}$'s T-value and $ET(\mathfrak{t}_{suc})$ represents the current estimated T-value of a successive transition.

Equation (4) enables FOT to iteratively update $ET(\mathfrak{t})$. Once a transition $\mathfrak{t}$ is triggered, the fragility of the SUT in $\mathfrak{t}$'s target state $F(\mathsf{s}_{tar})$ can be evaluated using Eq. (1). Using Eq. (4), $ET(\mathfrak{t})$ can be updated whenever a fragility is obtained. As proved in [8], as long as the estimated T-values are continuously updated, $ET(\mathfrak{t})$ will converge to the true T-value: $T(\mathfrak{t})$.

However, the fragility of the SUT in a state dynamically changes, due to the variation of test inputs and environmental uncertainty. To deal with this, we use the bootstrapping technique [9] to predict the distribution of the fragility and select the upper bound of its 95% interval as the value for $F(\mathsf{s}_{tar})$, to update the estimated T-value. Thus $ET(\mathfrak{t})$ is iteratively updated by the following equation:

$$ET(\mathfrak{t})' = max\left\{ Upper[F(\mathsf{s}_{tar})], \gamma \cdot \max_{\mathfrak{t}_{suc} \in \mathbb{T}_{suc}} ET(t_{suc}) \right\} \tag{5}$$

where $Upper[F(\mathsf{s}_{tar})]$ is the upper bound of $F(\mathsf{s}_{tar})$'s 95% confidence interval.

Softmax Transition Selection. To cost-effectively find faults, FOT should extensively explore different paths in a DFSM. Meanwhile, the covered high T-value transitions should be exploited (triggered) more frequently to find faults, as a high T-value implies a high possibility to reveal faults. Hence, in FOT, we use a softmax transition selection policy to address the dilemma of exploration and exploitation by assigning a selection probability to a transition proportional to the transition's T-value. The selection probability is given below (from [8]):

$$\mathrm{Prob}(\mathfrak{t}'_{out}) = e^{ET(\mathfrak{t}'_{out})/\tau} / \sum_{\mathfrak{t}_{out} \mathbb{T}_{out}} e^{ET(\mathfrak{t}_{out})/\tau} \tag{6}$$

where $Prob(\mathfrak{t}'_{out})$ denotes the selection probability of an outgoing transition $\mathfrak{t}'_{out}$; $ET(\mathfrak{t}'_{out})$ is the estimated T-value; $\mathbb{T}_{out}$ represents the set of all outgoing transitions under the current DFSM state, and τ is a parameter, called temperature [10]. τ is a positive real value from 0 to infinity. A large τ causes transitions to be equally selected, whereas, a small τ causes high T-value transitions to be selected much more frequently than transitions with lower T-values.

At the beginning, all transitions' estimated T-values $(ET(\mathfrak{t}))$ are initialized to 1, thus initially transitions have equal probability to be selected. As testing proceeds, $ET(\mathfrak{t})$ is continuously updated using Eq. (5). Directed by $ET(\mathfrak{t})$, the softmax policy assigns a high selection probability to transitions that leads to states with high fragilities. As a result, more fragile states will be exercised more frequently. Note that this doesn't preclude covering the less fragile states. In addition, loops in the ETM are also covered depending on fragilities of states involved in a loop.

4.2   Uncertainty Generation Strategies

Since SH-CPSs typically operate in an uncontrolled environment [2] and are constantly affected by various environmental uncertainties, e.g., measurement uncertainties from sensors and actuation deviation from actuators. Effects of these uncertainties on SH-CPSs' behaviors should be explicitly considered and tested.

In our previous work [3], we adopted three levels of uncertainty from [11] and provided modeling notions to explicitly capture uncertainties that affect the behaviors of SH-CPSs. Table 1 presents a summary of the three uncertainty levels, with their definitions, methods for specification, and generation mechanisms.

For level 1 uncertainty, at a given point of time, the value of an uncertain factor is a single value with a margin of error, such as the precision of a digital compass. Based on its specification, its precision can be determined with a margin of error. The determined value and the margin of error are specified as an interval. By selecting a value from the interval, level 1 uncertainty can be simulated.

Level 2 uncertainty signifies the situation that an uncertain factor has alternative values with known probabilities, like the measurement error of an accelerometer. By statistically analyzing samples of the measurement error, the probability distribution of the measurement error can be obtained. Based on the distribution, a value can be generated for the uncertain factor to simulate level 2 uncertainty.

For level 3 uncertainty, an uncertain factor also has multiple possible values, while only ranked likelihoods rather than probabilities of the possible values are known. In this case, possibility distribution is used to capture the ranked likelihoods. For instance, wind speed and direction are level 3 uncertainties, since the probability of each possible value is unknown due to limited knowledge and we can only compare their likelihood. To simulate level 3 uncertainty, the possibility distribution is first transformed to an equivalent probability distribution [12], from which the value of the uncertain factor is generated.

Based on testers' domain knowledge, relevant environmental uncertainties can be explicitly modeled at the three levels (see [3] for further details). By simulating the uncertainties based on the specification, effects of uncertainties are reflected in the testing environment, which enables SH-CPSs to be tested under uncertainties.

4.3   Implementation

We implemented the FOT algorithm and the three uncertainty generation strategies in TM-Executor. Figure 2 presents its three packages: software in the loop testing (light gray), uncertainty generation (dark gray), and FOT (white).

TM-Executor tests the software of an SH-CPS in a simulated environment. During testing, sensor data is computed by simulation models in simulators. Based on the simulated data, the software generates actuation instructions to control the system. Uncertainties are added to simulators' inputs and outputs to simulate the effects of uncertainties. Based on uncertainty specification, an uncertainty generator generates the values of uncertain factors whenever sensor data or actuation instructions are transferred between the software and simulators. By using the values to modify simulators'

Table 1. Uncertainty level, definition, specification and generation

Level	Definition	Specification	Generation
1	"A determined value with a margin of error" [13]	Interval	Derive an uncertainty value from the interval
2	A set of possible values with known probability for each value [13]	Probability distribution	Generate an uncertainty value according to the probability distribution
3	A set of possible values with known likelihood for each value [13]	Possibility distribution	Transform the possibility distribution to an equivalent probability distribution [12]. Based on it, generate an uncertainty value

inputs and outputs, the specified uncertainties are introduced into the testing environment.

The SUT and its ETM are executed together by an execution engine, which is deployed in Moka [14], a UML model execution platform. During the execution, the engine dynamically derives a DFSM from the ETM and used it to guide the execution. Meanwhile, the active state's state invariant is checked by a test inspector (using DresdenOCL [7]). The inspector evaluates the invariant with the actual values of the state variables, which are updated by the execution engine via testing APIs (Sect. 2.3). If the invariant is evaluated to be false, a fault is detected. Otherwise, the inspector calculates the fragility of the SUT in the current state, using Eq. (1). Taking fragility as input, the FOT algorithm updates its estimate of T-value (Eq. (5)) and uses the softmax policy to select the next transition. Next, the test driver generates a valid test input with EsOCL [6], a search-based test data generator, for firing the selected transition. The execution engine takes this input to invoke the corresponding operation, causing the ETM and the SUT to enter the next state. In this way, T-values are learned from iterations of execution and the learned T-values direct FOT to cost-effectively find faults.

5   Evaluation

We aim to evaluate the cost-effectiveness of FOT by comparing it with a Coverage Oriented Testing (COT) algorithm to test nine self-healing behaviors in three real SH-CPSs under 10 uncertainties, by answering two research questions: **RQ1:** Is FOT more effective than COT in terms of fault revelation? **RQ2:** Compared with COT, does FOT incur less cost to find a fault?

5.1   Case Studies and Test Configuration

We used three open source SH-CPSs for evaluation: (1) ArduCopter is a fully featured copter control system supporting 18 flight modes to control a copter and has five

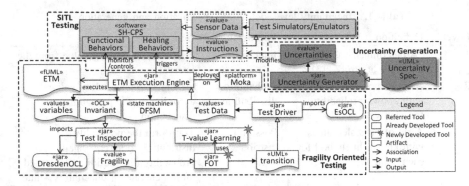

Fig. 2. SH-CPS testing framework

self-healing behaviors; (2) ArduRover[9] is an autopilot system for ground vehicles having two self-healing behaviors to avoid obstacle and handle the disruption of control link; (3) ArduPlane[10] is an autonomous plane control system having two self-healing behaviors to avoid collision and address network disruption. Test execution was performed with software in the loop simulators, including GPS, barometer, accelerometer, gyro meter, compass, and servo simulators. Nine fault injection operations were implemented in the simulators to trigger the nine self-healing behaviors to test them in the presence of uncertainty. More details can be found in [5]. The system specification includes 10 uncertainties related to the sensors and actuators and details are presented in Table 2.

Table 2. Identified uncertainties from the three case studies

Uncertainty	Level	Specification	Uncertainty	Level	Specification
Wind direction	3	Possibility Categorical Distribution	Servos Bias	2	Probability normal distribution
Wind velocity			Barometer altitude noise		
GPS location noise	2	Probability Normal Distribution	Barometer climb rate noise		
GPS velocity noise			Accelerometer noise		
GPS location drift			Compass noise		

5.2   Experimental Design and Execution

Table 3 is the experiment design. We implemented COT [4] and used it as the comparison baseline. It selects a transition with a likelihood that is reverse proportional to the total number of times that the transition has been fired plus one, to explore

---

[9] http://ardupilot.org/rover/.

[10] http://ardupilot.org/plane/.

Table 3. Experiment design

RQ	Comparison	Case study		#Runs	Metric	Statistical test
		Name	#Self-healing behaviors			
1	FOT vs. COT	ArduCopter	5	10	NDF	Fisher's exact test, odds ratio
2		ArduPlane	2		TFF	Vargha and Delaney's $\hat{A}_{12}$
		ArduRover	2			Welch's t-test

uncovered transitions as many as possible. For FOT, we set discount rate γ to 0.99 and temperature τ to 0.2.

The nine self-healing behaviors were tested independently (i.e., nine experiments). We specified expected functional and self-healing behaviors as ETMs, whose statistics are shown in Table 4. The last row of Table 4 presents twice the time taken by COT to cover all transitions of an ETM. We chose this time as the maximum test execution time for each ETM. To reduce randomness, we run each experiment 10 times for both algorithms.

Table 4. Descriptive statistics of ETMs

Statistics	ArduCopter					ArduRover		ArduPlane	
	ETM1	ETM2	ETM3	ETM4	ETM5	ETM6	ETM7	ETM8	ETM9
#States	64	60	70	64	36	58	54	79	40
#Transitions	440	268	286	440	106	306	303	347	104
Max. Exe. Time (mins)	744	472	562	740	276	960	756	914	290

To answer RQ1, we used *Number of Detected Faults* (NDF) to evaluate the effectiveness of the algorithms in terms of finding faults and is calculated as $NDF = \sum_{i=1}^{10} n_i$, where n_i is the number of detected faults in the ith run of an experiment. Note that it is the first time the three case studies are tested under uncertainties. Thus, the total number of real faults was unknown. For RQ2, we define *Time to Find Fault* (TFF, i.e., the time (in minutes) that FOT/COT spent to find a fault) to assess the cost of finding faults. TFF_i represents the TFF for the ith run of an experiment and the average TFF of an experiment is $\overline{TFF} = \frac{\sum_{i=1}^{m} TFF_i}{m}$, where m is the number of runs out of ten, that a fault was detected.

Following the guidelines in [15], we conducted the Fisher's exact test to check the significance of results and used the odds ratio as the effect size measure for the results of RQ1, as they are dichotomous data, i.e., faults found or not. Since data to answer RQ2 are continuous, i.e., the time to find a fault, we applied the Vargha and Delaney's $\hat{A}_{12}$ statistics to measure the effect size. To check the significance of the results, we first performed the Shapiro-Wilk test to test the normality of the two TFF samples. The calculated p-values corresponding to the two algorithms are 0.26 and 0.48, which are greater than 0.05 suggesting that the samples do not strongly depart from normality. Based on this, we performed the Welch's t-test to check the significance of RQ2's results, because the two *TFF* samples have unequal variances as results of the F-test revealed.

5.3   Evaluation Results

Table 5 shows results for RQ1. Within the fixed time, FOT and COT detected the same fault for SH1. FOT was able to find faults in five other self-healing behaviors, while COT failed for the rest. Note that both FOT and COT achieved 100% transition coverage and thus we do not compare them based on this measure.

For SH1, the Fisher's exact test calculated a p-value of 0.474 (greater than 0.05) suggesting no significant difference between COT and FOT. The obtained odds ratio was 3.67 indicating that FOT is likely to find more faults than COT. Both FOT and COT didn't detect any fault in SH4, SH5, and SH6, which might be due to two reasons: 1) No faults in these behaviors, 2) Neither algorithm covered a particular path with specific test input and uncertainty values that could reveal faults. For the other five behaviors, COT failed to detect any faults, while FOT succeeded in all the cases suggesting that FOT is significantly better than COT.

Since COT only detected a fault in SH1, only the *TFFs* for SH1 are used to answer RQ2. On average, FOT could find a fault within 142 min, while COT required 282 min to find a fault (Table 5). We conducted the Welch's t-test and the result (p-value = 0.043) showed that COT took significantly more time than FOT to find a fault. In addition, the result of $\hat{A}_{12} = 0.875$ suggests that, in most cases, COT is expected to spend more time than FOT to find a fault.

5.4   Discussion

We obtained three key observations. First, due to the effect of uncertainties, self-healing behaviors might fail to timely detect faults or improperly adapt system behaviors. For instance, because of sensors' measurement uncertainties, the copter could not accurately capture its location, orientation, and velocity. When the copter was

Table 5. Number of detected faults in 10 runs

Alg.	Metrics	ArduCopter					ArduRover		ArduPlane	
		SH1	SH2	SH3	SH4	SH5	SH6	SH7	SH8	SH9
COT	*NDF*	8	0	0	0	0	0	0	0	0
	TFF(mins)	282	–	–	–	–	–	–	–	–
FOT	*NDF*	10	7	6	0	0	0	8	10	5
	TFF(mins)	142	247	415	–	–	–	548	468	208

about to collide with another vehicle, inaccurate measurements sometimes caused the copter incorrectly adjust its orientation, leading to a collision. Therefore, it is necessary to test self-healing behaviors in the presence of environmental uncertainties. To build such a testing environment, we generate uncertainties according to interval, probability or possibility distributions. Though this may not be the optimal strategy, it provides a preliminary solution for this problem. Second, a typical objective of a coverage-based testing approach is to achieve full coverage, e.g., 100% transition coverage. However, this is not sufficient to reveal a fault in self-healing behaviors under uncertainty, as demonstrated by the experiment result. Since transitions have different possibilities to reveal a fault, the ones with high possibility should be tested more frequently to cost-effectively find faults. Third, for testing SH-CPSs under uncertainty, FOT is more cost-effective than COT in terms of a number of detected faults and time spent to reveal a fault. On average, FOT found 80% more faults and when both algorithms managed to find a fault, FOT took 50% less time than COT. This is because FOT used execution information to dynamically learn transitions' T-values, which indicates the possibility of revealing a fault when firing transitions; COT only used coverage information to direct test execution.

5.5   Threats to Validity

Conclusion validity is concerned with factors that affect the conclusion drawn from the outcome of experiments. Because of random transition selection used by FOT and COT, randomness in the results is the most probable conclusion validity threat. To reduce this threat, all the experiments were repeated 10 times. We applied two statistical tests and two effect size measures to evaluate statistical differences and magnitude of improvement. In addition, the variation in simulated uncertainties may be another conclusion validity threat. However, we simulated the same sequence of uncertainties for both algorithms. We fixed the maximum test execution time for both of the algorithms. This measure was taken to remove the **internal validity threat** that different settings might favor one algorithm over the other. However, more experiments with other settings in terms of test execution time are required to further strengthen the current conclusion. **External validity threats** concern the generalization of the experiment results. We tested nine self-healing behaviors of three real case studies. However, additional case studies are needed to further generalize the results. With respect to **construct validity threats**, we used the number of detected faults and the time required to detect a fault as the evaluation metrics, which are comparable across both of the algorithms.

6   Related Work

Model-Based Testing (MBT) has shown good results of producing effective test suites to reveal faults [16]. For a typical MBT approach, abstract test cases are generated from models first, e.g., using structural coverage criteria (e.g., all state coverage) [17, 18]. Generated abstract test cases are then transformed into executable ones, which are executed on the SUT. To reduce the overhead caused by test cases generation, researchers proposed to combine test generation, selection, and execution into one process [19, 20]. De Vries et al. [19] created a testing framework, with which the SUT is modeled as a labeled transition system. By parsing this model, test inputs are generated on the fly to perform conformance testing. This approach aims to test all paths belonging to this model. However, if loops exist or the specified model is large, additional mechanisms are required to reduce the state space. Larsen et al. [20] proposed a similar testing tool for embedded real-time systems. It uses the timed I/O transition system as the test model, and test inputs are randomly generated from the model on the fly for testing.

Different from the existing works, FOT relies on the model execution of ETMs to facilitate the testing of SH-CPSs under uncertainty. During the execution, FOT applies a reinforcement learning technique to learn transitions' T-values, which direct FOT to cost-effectively find faults. Besides, FOT focuses on testing self-healing behaviors in the presence of environmental uncertainty, which is not covered by existing works. The first reinforcement learning based testing algorithm was proposed in [4]. It uses frequencies of transitions' coverage as the heuristics of reinforcement learning. By learning frequencies, the algorithm tries to equally explore all transitions. However, a long-term reward is not realized in this approach. Groce et al. [21] created a framework to simplify the application of reinforcement learning for testing, which uses coverage as the heuristic and relies on SARSA(λ) [8] for calculating long term rewards. Similarly, Araiza-Illan et al. [22] used coverage as the reward function to test human-robot interactions with reinforcement learning. Due to uncertainty, achieving the full transition coverage is insufficient to find faults in self-healing behaviors. Thus, we propose to use fragility instead of coverage as the heuristic.

7   Conclusion

This paper presents a new testing algorithm, Fragility Oriented Testing (FOT), for testing self-healing behaviors of SH-CPSs under uncertainty. It applies model execution and a reinforcement learning method to learn each transition's T-value, which indicates the possibility to reveal a fault after firing the transition. Accordingly, FOT focuses on exercising transitions with high T-values to cost-effectively find faults. To evaluate FOT, we tested nine self-healing behaviors in three case studies. The results showed that FOT significantly outperformed COT for five out of nine self-healing behaviors in terms of faults finding. On average, FOT discovered 80% more faults than COT. When both algorithms succeeded to find a fault, FOT on average took 50% less time than COT. In the future, we plan to conduct more experiments and integrate more advanced reinforcement learning algorithms to further enhance the algorithm's fault detection capability.

References

1. Bures, T., Weyns, D., Berger, C., et al.: Software engineering for smart cyber-physical systems–towards a research agenda: report on the first international workshop on software engineering for smart CPS. ACM SIGSOFT Softw. Eng. Notes **40**(6), 28–32 (2015). ACM
2. Lee, E.A.: Cyber physical systems: design challenges. In: 11th IEEE International Symposium on Object and Component-Oriented Real-Time Distributed Computing (ISORC), pp. 363–369. IEEE (2008)

3. Ma, T., Ali, S., Yue, T.: Modeling healing behaviors of cyber-physical systems with uncertainty to support automated testing. In: Simula Research Lab Technical report 2016-08 (2016). https://www.simula.no/publications/modeling-healing-behaviors-cyber-physical-systems-uncertainty-support-automated-testing

4. Veanes, M., Roy, P., Campbell, C.: Online testing with reinforcement learning. In: Havelund, K., Núñez, M., Roşu, G., Wolff, B. (eds.) FATES/RV -2006. LNCS, vol. 4262, pp. 240–253. Springer, Heidelberg (2006). doi:10.1007/11940197_16

5. Ma, T., Ali, S., Yue, T.: Fragility-oriented testing with model execution and reinforcement learning. In: Simula Research Lab Technical report 2017-05 (2017). https://www.simula.no/publications/fragility-oriented-testing-model-execution-and-reinforcement-learning

6. Ali, S., Iqbal, M.Z., Arcuri, A., et al.: Generating test data from OCL constraints with search techniques. IEEE Trans. Softw. Eng. **39**(10), 1376–1402 (2013). IEEE

7. Demuth, B., Wilke, C.: Model and object verification by using Dresden OCL. In: Proceedings of the Russian-German Workshop Innovation Information Technologies: Theory and Practice, Ufa, Russia, pp. 687–690. Citeseer (2009)

8. Sutton, R.S., Barto, A.G.: Reinforcement Learning: An Introduction. MIT Press, Cambridge (1998)

9. Mooney, C.Z., Duval, R.D., Duval, R.: Bootstrapping: A Nonparametric Approach to Statistical Inference. Sage, London (1993)

10. Anzai, Y.: Pattern Recognition and Machine Learning. Elsevier, Amsterdam (2012)

11. Walker, W.E., Lempert, R.J., Kwakkel, J.H.: Deep uncertainty. In: Gass, S.I., Fu, M.C. (eds.) Encyclopedia of Operations Research and Management Science, pp. 395–402. Springer, New York (2013). doi:10.1007/978-1-4419-1153-7_1140

12. Dubois, D., Prade, H., Sandri, S.: On possibility/probability transformations. In: Lowen, R., Roubens, M. (eds.) Fuzzy Logic. Theory and Decision Library (Series D: System Theory, Knowledge Engineering and Problem Solving), vol. 12. Springer, Dordrecht (1993). 10.1007/978-94-011-2014-2_10

13. Ma, T., Ali, S., Yue, T.: Conceptually understanding uncertainty in self-healing cyber-physical systems. In: Simula Research Lab Technical report 2016-07 (2016). https://www.simula.no/publications/conceptually-understanding-uncertainty-self-healing-cyber-physical-systems

14. Tatibouet, J.: Moka – a simulation platform for Papyrus based on OMG specifications for executable UML. In: EclipseCon, OSGI (2016)

15. Arcuri, A., Briand, L.: A practical guide for using statistical tests to assess randomized algorithms in software engineering. In: 33rd International Conference on Software Engineering (ICSE), pp. 1–10. IEEE (2011)

16. Enoiu, E.P., Cauevic, A., Sundmark, D., et al.: A controlled experiment in testing of safety-critical embedded software. In: IEEE International Conference on Software Testing, Verification and Validation (ICST), pp. 1–11. IEEE (2016)

17. Utting, M., Pretschner, A., Legeard, B.: A taxonomy of model-based testing approaches. Softw. Testing, Verification Reliabil. **22**(5), 297–312 (2012)

18. Grieskamp, W., Hierons, R.M., Pretschner, A.: Model-based testing in practice. In: Dagstuhl Seminar Proceedings. Schloss Dagstuhl-Leibniz-Zentrum fuer Informatik (2011)

19. de Vries, R.G., Tretmans, J.: On-the-fly conformance testing using SPIN. Int. J. Softw. Tools Technol. Transf. (STTT) **2**(4), 382–393 (2000). Springer

20. Larsen, Kim G., Mikucionis, M., Nielsen, B.: Online testing of real-time systems using Uppaal. In: Grabowski, J., Nielsen, B. (eds.) FATES 2004. LNCS, vol. 3395, pp. 79–94. Springer, Heidelberg (2005). doi:10.1007/978-3-540-31848-4_6

21. Groce, A., Fern, A., Pinto, J., et al.: Lightweight automated testing with adaptation-based programming. In: IEEE 23rd International Symposium on Software Reliability Engineering (ISSRE), pp. 161–170. IEEE (2012)
22. Araiza-Illan, D., Pipe, A.G., Eder, K.: Intelligent agent-based stimulation for testing robotic software in human-robot interactions. In: Proceedings of the 3rd Workshop on Model-Driven Robot Software Engineering. ACM (2016)

Fault-Based Testing for Refinement in CSP

Ana Cavalcanti[1] and Adenilso Simao[2]($\boxtimes$)

[1] University of York, York, UK
ana.cavalcanti@york.ac.br
[2] University of São Paulo, São Carlos, Brazil
adenilso@icmc.usp.br

Abstract. The process algebra CSP has been studied as a modeling notation for test derivation. Work has been developed using its trace and failure semantics, and their refinement notions as conformance relations. In this paper, we propose a procedure for online test generation for selection of finite test sets for traces refinement from CSP models, based on the notion of fault domains, that is, focusing on the set of faulty implementations of interest. We investigate scenarios where the verdict of a test campaign can be reached after a finite number of test executions. We illustrate the usage of the procedure with a small case study.

1 Introduction

Model-based testing (MBT) has received increasing attention due to its ability to improve productivity, by automating test planning, generation, and execution. The central artifact of an MBT technique is the model. It serves as an abstraction of the system under test (SUT), manageable by the testing engineers, and can be processed by tools to automatically derive tests. Most notations for test modeling are based on states; examples are Finite State Machines, Labelled Transition Systems, and Input/Output Transition Systems. Many test-generation techniques are available for them [7,11,21,25]. Other notations use state-based machines as the underlying semantics [12,16].

CSP [24] has been used as a modelling notation for test derivation. The pioneering work in [20] formalises a test-automation approach based on CSP. More recently, CSP and its model checker FDR [10] have been used to automate test generation with ioco as a conformance relation [19]. A theory for testing for refinement from CSP has been fully developed in [4].

Two sets of tests have been defined and proved to be exhaustive: they can detect any SUT that is non-conforming according to traces or failures refinement. Typically, however, these test sets are infinite. A few selection criteria have been explored: data-flow and synchronisation coverage [5], and mutation testing [1] for a state-rich version of CSP. The traditional approaches for test generation from state-based models have not been studied in this context.

Even though the operational semantics of CSP defines a Labelled Transition System (LTS), applying testing approaches based on states in this context is

© IFIP International Federation for Information Processing 2017
Published by Springer International Publishing AG 2017. All Rights Reserved
N. Yevtushenko et al. (Eds.): ICTSS 2017, LNCS 10533, pp. 21–37, 2017.
DOI: 10.1007/978-3-319-67549-7_2

challenging: (i) not every process has a finite LTS, and it is not trivial to determine when it has; (ii) even if the LTS finite, in may not be deterministic; (iii) for refinement, we are not interested in equivalence of LTS; and (iv) to deal with failures, the notion of state needs to be very rich.

Here, we present a novel approach for selection of finite test sets from CSP models by identifying scenarios where the verdict of a campaign can be reached after a finite number of test executions. We adopt the concept of fault domain from state-based methods to constrain the possible faults in an SUT [22]. Fault-based testing is more general than the criteria above, since the test engineering can embed knowledge about the possible faults of the SUT into a fault domain to guide generation and execution [13]. We define a fault domain as a CSP process that is assumed to be refined by the SUT. With that, we establish that some tests are not useful, as they cannot reveal any new information about the SUT.

In addition, we propose a procedure for online generation of tests for traces refinement. Tests are derived and applied to the SUT and, based on the verdict, either the SUT is cast incorrect, or the fault domain is refined.

We present some scenarios where our procedure is guaranteed to provide a verdict after a finite number of steps. A simple scenario is that of a specification with a finite set of traces: unsurprisingly, after that set is exhaustively explored our procedure terminates. A more interesting scenario is when the SUT is incorrect; our procedure also always terminates in this case.

We have also investigated the scenario where the set of traces of the specification is infinite, but that of the SUT is finite and the SUT is correct. A challenge in establishing termination is that, while when testing using Mealy and finite state machines every trace of the model leads to a test, this is not the case with CSP. For example, for traces refinement, traces of the specification that lead to states in which all possible events are accepted give rise to no tests. After such a trace, the behavior of the SUT is unconstrained, and so does not need to be tested. Another challenge is that most CSP fault domains are infinite.

Our approach is similar to those adopted in the traditional finite state-machines setting, but addresses these challenges. We could, of course, change the notion of test and add tests for all traces. A test that cannot fail, however, is, strictly speaking, just a probe. For practical reasons, it is important to avoid such probes, which cannot really reveal faults.

The contributions of this paper are: (1) the introduction of the notion of fault domain in the context of a process algebra for refinement; (2) a procedure for online testing for traces refinement validated by a prototype implementation; and (3) the characterization of some scenarios in which the procedure terminates.

Next, in Sect. 2 we present background material: fault-based testing, and CSP and its testing theory. Section 3 casts the traditional concepts of fault-based testing in the context of CSP. Our procedure is presented in Sect. 4. Termination is studied in Sect. 5. Section 6 describes a prototype implementation of our procedure and its use in a case study. Finally, we conclude in Sect. 7.

2   Preliminaries

In this section, we describe the background material to our work.

2.1   CSP: Testing and Refinement

CSP is distinctive as a process algebra for refinement. In CSP models, systems and components are specified as reactive processes that communicate synchronously via channels. A prefixing $a \rightarrow P$ is a process that is ready to communicate by engaging in the event a and then behaves like P. The external choice operator $\square$ combines processes to give a menu of options to the environment.

Example 1. The process *Counter* uses events *add* and *sub* to count up to 2.

$Counter = add \rightarrow Counter1$
$Counter1 = add \rightarrow Counter2 \,\square\, sub \rightarrow Counter$
$Counter2 = sub \rightarrow Counter1$

*Counter*1 offers a choice to increase (*add*) or decrease (*sub*) the counter. $\square$

Other operators combine processes in internal (nondeterministic) choice, parallel, sequence, and so on. Nondeterminism can also be introduced by interleaving and by hiding internal communications, for example.

There are three standard semantics for CSP: traces, failures, and failure-divergences, with refinement as the notion of conformance. As usual, the testing theory assumes that specifications and the SUT are free of divergence, which is observed as deadlock in a test. So, tests are for traces or failures refinement.

We write $P \sqsubseteq_T Q$ when P is trace-refined by Q; similarly, for $P \sqsubseteq_F Q$ and failures-refinement. In many cases, definitions and results hold for both forms of refinement, and we write simply $P \sqsubseteq Q$. In all cases, $P \sqsubseteq Q$ requires that the observed behaviours of Q (either its traces or failures) are all possible for P.

The CSP testing theory adopts two testability hypothesis. The first is often used to deal with a nondeterministic SUT: there is a number k such that, if we execute a test k times, the SUT produces all its possible behaviours. (In the literature, it appears in [14,15,25], for example, as fairness hypothesis or all-weather assumption.) The second testability hypothesis is that there is an (unknown) CSP process SUT that characterises the SUT.

The notion of execution of a test T is captured by a process $Execution_{SUT}^S(T)$ that composes the SUT and the test T in parallel, with all their common (specification) events made internal. Special events in T give the verdict: *pass*, *fail*, or *inc*, for inconclusive tests that cannot be executed to the end because the SUT does not have the trace that defines the test.

The testing theory also has a notion of successful testing experiment: a property $passes_\sqsubseteq(S, SUT, T)$ defines that the SUT passes the test T for specification S. A particular definition for $passes_\sqsubseteq(S, SUT, T)$ typically uses the definition of $Execution_{SUT}^S(T)$, but also explains how the information arising from it is used to achieve a verdict. For example, for traces refinement, we have the following.

$$passes_T(S, SUT, T) \cong \forall\, t : traces\; [\![Execution^S_{SUT}(T)]\!] \bullet last(t) \neq fail$$

For a definition of $passes_\sqsubseteq(S, SUT, T)$ and a test suite TS, we use the notation $passes_\sqsubseteq(S, SUT, TS)$ as a shorthand for $\forall\, T : TS \bullet passes_\sqsubseteq(S, SUT, T)$.

In general, for a given definition of $passes_\sqsubseteq(S, SUT, T)$, we can characterise exhaustivity $Exhaust_\sqsubseteq(TS)$ of a test suite TS as follows.

Definition 1. *A test suite TS satisfies the property $Exhaust_\sqsubseteq(S, TS)$, that is, it is exhaustive for a specification S and a conformance relation $\sqsubseteq$ exactly when, for every process P, we have $S \sqsubseteq P \Leftrightarrow passes_\sqsubseteq(S, P, TS)$.*

Different forms of test give rise to different exhaustive sets. We use $Exhaust_\sqsubseteq(S)$ to refer to a particular exhaustive test suite for S and $\sqsubseteq$.

For a trace $\langle a_1, a_2, \dots \rangle$ with events a_1, a_2, and so on, and one of its forbidden continuations a, that is, an event a not allowed by the specification after the trace, the traces-refinement test $T_T(\langle a_1, a_2, \dots \rangle, a)$ is given by the process $inc \to a_1 \to inc \to a_2 \to \dots \to pass \to a \to fail$. In alternation, it gives an inc verdict and offers an event of the trace to the SUT, until all the trace is accepted, when it gives the verdict $pass$, but offers the forbidden continuation. It is accepted, the verdict is $fail$. The exhaustive test set $Exhaust_T(S)$ for traces refinement includes all tests $T_T(t, a)$ formed in this way from the traces t and forbidden continuations a of the specification.

Example 2. We consider the specification $S_1 = a \to b \to S_1$. The exhaustive test set for S_1 and traces refinement is sketched below.

$$\{\, pass \to b \to fail \to STOP, inc \to a \to pass \to a \to fail \to STOP,$$
$$inc \to a \to inc \to b \to pass \to b \to fail \to STOP, \dots\} \qquad \square$$

In [3], it is proven that $Exhaust_{\sqsubseteq_T}(S, Exhaust_T(S))$.

2.2 Fault-Based Testing

The testing activity is constrained by the amount of resources available. Some criteria is needed to select a finite subset of finite tests. Fault-based criteria consider that there is a fault domain, modelling the set of all possible faulty implementations [13,22]. They restrict the set of required tests using the assumption that the SUT is in that domain [26]. Testing has to consider the possibility that the SUT can be any of those implementations, but no others [17].

For Finite State Machines (FSMs), many test-generation techniques assume that the SUT may have a combination of initialisation faults (that is, the SUT initialises in a wrong state), output faults (that is, the SUT produces a wrong output for a given input), transfer faults (that is, a transition of the SUT leads to the wrong states), and missing or extra states (that is, the set of states of the SUT is increased or decreased). Therefore, for a specification with n states, it is common that the fault domain is defined denotationally as "the set of FSMs (of a given class) with no more than m states, for some $m \geq n$" [7,9,11]. In this case, all faults above are considered, except for more extra states than $m - n$.

Fault domains can also be used to restrict testing to parts of the specification that the tester judges more relevant. For instance, some events of the specification can be trivial to implement and the tester may decide to ignore them. An approach for modelling faults of interest, considering FSMs, is to assume that the SUT is a submachine of a given non-deterministic FSM, as in [13]. Thus, the parts of the SUT that are assumed to be correct can be easily modelled by a *copy* the specification; the faults are then modelled by adding extra transitions with the intended faults. Fault domains can also be modelled by explicitly enumerating the possible faulty implementations, known as mutants [8]. Thus, tests can be generated targetting each of those mutants, in turn.

In the next section, we define fault domains by refinement of a CSP process.

3   Fault-Based Testing in CSP

For CSP, we define a fault domain as a process $FD \sqsubseteq SUT$; it characterises the set of all processes that refine it. We use the term fault domain sometimes to refer to the CSP process itself and sometimes to the whole collection of processes it identifies. In the CSP testing theory, the specification and SUT are processes over the same alphabet of events. Accordingly, here, we assume that a fault domain FD uses only those events as well.

The usefulness of the concept of fault domain is illustrated below.

Example 3. For S_1 in Example 2, we first take just $FD_1 = RUN(\{a, b\})$ as a fault domain. For any alphabet A, the process $RUN(A)$ repeatedly offers all events in A. So, with FD_1, we add no extra information, since every process that uses only channels a and b trace refines FD_1. A more interesting example is $FD_2 = a \rightarrow (a \rightarrow FD_2 \ \square \ b \rightarrow FD_2)$. In this case, the assumption that $FD_2 \sqsubseteq_T SUT$ allows us to eliminate the first and the third tests in Example 2, because an SUT that refines FD_2 always passes those tests.   □

In examples, we use traces refinement as the conformance relation, and assume that we have a fixed notion of test. The concepts introduced here, however, are relevant for testing for either traces or failures refinement.

It is traditional in the context of Mealy machines to consider a fault domain characterised by the size of the machines, and so, finite. Here, however, if a fault domain FD has an infinite set of traces, it may have an infinite number of refinements. For traces refinement, for example, for each trace t, a process that performs just t refines FD. So, we do not assume that fault domains are finite.

Just like we define the notion of exhaustive test set to identify a collection of tests of interest, we define the notion of a complete test set, which contains the tests of interest relative to a fault domain.

Definition 2. *For a specification S, and a fault domain FD, we define a test set $TS : \mathbb{P} \, Exhaust_{\sqsubseteq}(S)$ to be complete, written $Complete_{\sqsubseteq}^{S}(TS, FD)$, with respect to FD if, and only if, for every implementation I in FD we have*

$$\neg (S \sqsubseteq I) \Rightarrow \exists \, T : TS \bullet \neg \, passes_{\sqsubseteq}(S, I, T)$$

This is a property based not on the whole of the fault domain, but just on its faulty implementations. For traces refinement, the exhaustive test set is given by $Exhaust_T(S)$ and the verdict by $passes_T(S, SUT, T)$ defined in Sect. 2.1.

If FD is the bottom of the refinement relation $\sqsubseteq$, then a complete test set TS is exhaustive. It is direct from Definition 2 the fact that a complete test set is a subset of the exhaustive test set and, therefore, unbiased, that is, it does not reject correct programs. We also need validity: only correct programs are accepted. This is also fairly direct as established in the theorem below.

Theorem 1. *Provided $FD \sqsubseteq SUT$, we have that*

$$\exists\, TS : \mathbb{P}\, Exhaust_\sqsubseteq(S) \bullet complete(TS, FD) \wedge passes_\sqsubseteq(S, SUT, TS)$$

implies $S \sqsubseteq SUT$.

Proof

$$\exists\, TS : \mathbb{P}\, Exhaust_\sqsubseteq(S) \bullet complete(TS, FD) \wedge passes_\sqsubseteq(S, SUT, TS)$$

$$= \exists\, TS : \mathbb{P}\, Exhaust_\sqsubseteq(S) \bullet \qquad\qquad\qquad\qquad \text{[Definition 2]}$$
$$(\neg\, (S \sqsubseteq SUT) \Rightarrow \exists\, T : TS \bullet \neg\, passes_\sqsubseteq(S, SUT, T)) \wedge$$
$$passes_\sqsubseteq(S, SUT, TS)$$

$$= \exists\, TS : \mathbb{P}\, Exhaust_\sqsubseteq(S) \bullet \qquad \text{[predicate calculus and definition of \emph{passes}]}$$
$$(passes_\sqsubseteq(S, SUT, TS) \Rightarrow S \sqsubseteq SUT) \wedge passes_\sqsubseteq(S, SUT, TS)$$

$$\Rightarrow (S \sqsubseteq SUT) \qquad\qquad\qquad\qquad\qquad\qquad \text{[predicate calculus]}$$

$$\square$$

Finally, if an unbiased test is added to a complete set, the resulting set is still complete. Unbias follows from inclusion in the exhaustive test set.

An important set is those of the useless tests for implementations in the fault domain. The fact that we can eliminate such tests from any given test suite has an important practical consequence.

Definition 3

$$Useless_\sqsubseteq(S, FD) = \{ T : Exhaust_\sqsubseteq(S) \mid passes_\sqsubseteq(S, FD, T) \}$$

Since FD passes the tests in $Useless_\sqsubseteq(S, FD)$, all implementations in that fault domain also pass those tests, provided $passes_\sqsubseteq(S, P, T)$ is monotonic on P with respect to refinement. This is proved below.

Lemma 1. *For every I in FD, and for every $T : Useless_\sqsubseteq(S, FD)$, we have $passes_\sqsubseteq(S, I, T)$, if $passes_\sqsubseteq(S, P, T)$ is monotonic on P with respect to $\sqsubseteq$.*

Proof

$FD \sqsubseteq I$

$\Rightarrow passes_{\sqsubseteq}(S, FD, T) \Rightarrow passes_{\sqsubseteq}(S, I, T)$ [monotonicity of $passes$]

$= T \in Useless_{\sqsubseteq}(S, FD) \Rightarrow passes_{\sqsubseteq}(S, I, T)$ [definition of $Useless_{\sqsubseteq}(S, FD)$]

$\square$

Example 4. We recall that the definition for $passes_T(S, SUT, T)$ is monotonic, as shown below, where we consider processes P_1 and P_2 such that $P_1 \sqsubseteq_T P_2$.

$Execution_{P_1}^S(T) = (P_1 \,[\![\, \alpha S \,]\!]\, T) \backslash \alpha S$ [definition of $Execution$]

$\Rightarrow Execution_{P_1}^S(T) \sqsubseteq_T (P_2 \,[\![\, \alpha S \,]\!]\, T) \backslash \alpha S$

               [monotonicity of CSP operators with respect to refinement]

$= Execution_{P_1}^S(T) \sqsubseteq_T Execution_{P_2}^S(T)$ [definition of $Execution$]

$\Rightarrow traces\,[\![Execution_{P_2}^S(T)]\!] \subseteq traces\,[\![Execution_{P_1}^S(T)]\!]$ [definition of $\sqsubseteq_T$]

$\Rightarrow (\forall\, t : traces\,[\![Execution_{P_1}^S(T)]\!] \bullet last(t) \neq fail) \Rightarrow$ [predicate calculus]
$\quad (\forall\, t : traces\,[\![Execution_{P_2}^S(T)]\!] \bullet last(t) \neq fail)$

$= passes_T(S, P_1, T) \Rightarrow passes_T(S, P_2, T)$ [definition of $passes_T$]

$\square$

Typically, it is expected that the notions of $passes_{\sqsubseteq}(S, P, T)$ are monotonic on P with respect to the refinement relation $\sqsubseteq$: a testing experiment that accepts a process, also accepts its correct implementations.

It is important to note that there are tests that do become useless with a fault-domain assumption. This is illustrated below.

Example 5. In Example 3, the first and third tests of the exhaustive test set are useless as already indicated. For instance, we can show that FD_2 passes the first test $T_1 = pass \rightarrow b \rightarrow fail \rightarrow STOP$ as follows.

$Execution_{FD_2}^{S_1}(T_1)$

$= (FD_2 \,[\![\, \{a, b\} \,]\!]\, T_1) \setminus \{a, b\}$ [definition of $Execution$]

$= (pass \rightarrow (FD_2 \,[\![\, \{a, b\} \,]\!]\, b \rightarrow fail \rightarrow STOP)) \setminus \{a, b\}$

               [step law of parallelism]

$= pass \rightarrow (FD_2 \,[\![\, \{a, b\} \,]\!]\, b \rightarrow fail \rightarrow STOP) \setminus \{a, b\}$ [step law of hiding]

$= pass \rightarrow STOP \setminus \{a, b\}$ [step law of parallelism]

$= pass \rightarrow STOP$ [step law of hiding]

So, $traces\,[\![Execution_{FD_2}^{S_1}(T_1)]\!] = \{\langle\rangle, \langle pass \rangle\}$, none of which finish with $fail$. $\square$

4   Generating Test Sets

To develop algorithms to generate tests based on a fault domain, we need to consider particular notions of refinement, and the associated notions of test and verdict. In this paper, we present an algorithm for traces refinement (Fig. 1).

A particular execution of the test can result in the verdicts *inc*, *pass* or *fail*. Due to nondeterminism in the SUT, the test may need to be executed multiple times, resulting in more than one verdict. We assume that the test is executed as many times as needed to observe all possible verdicts according to our testability hypothesis. So, for a test T and implementation SUT, we write $verd_{SUT}(T)$ to denote the set of verdicts observed when T is executed to test SUT.

If $fail \in verd_{SUT}(T)$, the SUT is faulty (if T is in $Exhaust_\sqsubseteq(TS)$). In this case, we can stop the testing activity, since the SUT needs to be corrected. Otherwise, we can determine additional properties of the SUT, considering the test verdicts. The SUT is a black box, but combining the knowledge that it is in the fault domain and has not failed a test, we can refine the fault domain.

If $fail \notin verd_{SUT}(T)$, both *inc* and *pass* bring relevant information. We consider a test $T_T(t, a)$, and recall that the SUT refines the fault domain FD. If $pass \in verd_I(T_T(t, a))$, then $t \in traces[\![SUT]\!]$, but $t \frown \langle a \rangle \notin traces[\![SUT]\!]$. Thus, the fault domain can be updated, since we have more knowledge about the SUT: it does not have the trace $t \frown \langle a \rangle$. Otherwise, if $verd_I(T_T(t, a)) = \{inc\}$, the trace t was not completely executed, and hence the SUT does not implement t. We can, therefore, update the fault domain as well.

In both cases, we include in the fault domain knowledge about traces not implemented. Information about implemented traces is not useful: given the definition of traces refinement, it cannot be used to reduce the fault domain.

Given a fault domain FD and a trace t, such that $t \notin traces[\![SUT]\!]$, we define a new fault domain as follows. First, we define a process $NOTTRACE(t)$, which tracks the execution of each event in t, behaving like the process $RUN(\Sigma)$ if the corresponding event of the trace does not happen. If we get to the end of t, then $NOTTRACE(t)$ prevents its last event from occurring. It, however, accepts any other event, and, at that point, also behaves like $RUN(\Sigma)$.

$$NOTTRACE(\langle a \rangle) = \square\, e : \Sigma \setminus \{a\} \bullet e \to RUN(\Sigma)$$
$$NOTTRACE(\langle a \rangle \frown t) = a \to NOTTRACE(t)$$
$$\square$$
$$(\square\, e : \Sigma \setminus \{a\} \bullet e \to RUN(\Sigma))$$

Formally, if the monitored trace is a singleton $\langle a \rangle$, then a is blocked by the process $NOTTRACE(\langle a \rangle)$. It offers in external choice all events except a: those in the set Σ of all events minus $\{a\}$. If a different event e happens, then $\langle a \rangle$ is no longer possible and the monitor accepts all events. If the monitored trace is $\langle a \rangle \frown t$, for a non-empty t, then, if a happens, we monitor t. If a different event e happens, then $\langle a \rangle \frown t$ is no longer possible and the monitor accepts all events.

We notice that $NOTTRACE$ is not defined for the empty trace, which is a trace of every process, and that, as required, $t \notin traces[\![NOTTRACE(t)]\!]$.

On the other hand, for any trace s that does not have t as a prefix, we have that $s \in traces \, [\![NOTTRACE(t)]\!]$. To obtain a refined fault domain $FDU(t)$, we compose FD in parallel with $NOTTRACE(t)$.

$$FDU(t) = FD \, [\![\Sigma]\!] \, NOTTRACE(t)$$

The parallelism requires synchronisation on all events and, therefore, controls the occurrence of events as defined by $NOTTRACE(t)$. So, the fault domain defined by $FDU(t)$ excludes processes that perform t.

```
 1: procedure TESTGEN(S, FD_init, SUT)
 2:     FD ← FD_init
 3:     failed ← false
 4:     TS ← ∅
 5:     while ¬ (S ⊑_T FD) ∧ ¬ failed do
 6:         Select a shortest t ∈ (traces [[FD]] ∩ traces [[S]]) \ TS
 7:         if initials(FD/t) \ initials(S/t) ≠ ∅ then
 8:             Select a ∈ initials(FD/t) \ initials(S/t)
 9:             verd ← ApplyTest(SUT, T_T(t, a))
10:             if fail ∈ verd then
11:                 failed ← true
12:             else if pass ∈ verd then
13:                 FD ← FDU(FD, t ⌢ ⟨a⟩)
14:             else                              ▷ that is, verd = {inc}
15:                 FD ← FDU(FD, t)
16:             end if
17:         else                      ▷ that is, initials(FD/t) \ initials(S/t) = ∅
18:             TS ← TS ∪ {t}
19:         end if
20:     end while
21:     return ¬ failed
22: end procedure
```

Fig. 1. Procedure for test generation

Since $t \notin traces \, [\![SUT]\!]$ and $FD \sqsubseteq_T SUT$, then $FDU(t) \sqsubseteq_T SUT$. Thus, we have $FD \sqsubseteq_T FDU(t) \sqsubseteq_T SUT$. If the fault domain trace refines the specification S, we have that $S \sqsubseteq_T FD \sqsubseteq_T SUT$; thus, we can stop testing, since $S \sqsubseteq_T SUT$.

Based on these ideas, we now introduce a procedure $TestGen$ for test generation. It is shown for a specification S, an implementation SUT, and an initial fault domain FD_{init}. In the case that there is no special information about the implementation, the initial fault domain can be simply $RUN(\Sigma)$.

$TestGen$ uses local variables $failed$, to record whether a fault has been found as a result of a test whose execution gives rise to a $fail$ verdict, and FD, to record the current fault domain. Initially, their values are **false** and FD_{init}. A variable TS records the set of traces for which tests are no longer needed, because all its forbidden continuations, if any, have already been used for testing.

The procedure loops until it is found that the specification is refined by the fault domain or a test fails. In each iteration, we select a trace t that belongs both to the specification and the fault domain (Step 6). A trace of the specification that is not of the fault domain is guaranteed to lead to an inconclusive verdict, as it is necessarily not implemented by the SUT.

Next, we check whether t has a continuation that is allowed by the fault domain FD, but is forbidden by S. If it has, we choose one of these forbidden continuations a (Step 8). If not, t is not (or no longer) useful to construct tests, and is added to TS. A forbidden continuation a of S that is also forbidden by FD is guaranteed to be forbidden by the SUT. So, testing for a is useless.

The resulting test $T_T(t, a)$ is used and the set of verdicts $verd$ is analysed as explained above, leading to an update of the fault domain. The value returned by the procedure indicates whether the SUT trace refines S or not.

Example 6. We consider as specification the *Counter* from Example 1. A few tests for traces refinement obtained by applying $T_T(t, a)$ to the traces t of *Counter* are sketched below in order of increasing length.

$T_T(\langle \rangle, sub) = pass \rightarrow sub \rightarrow fail \rightarrow STOP$
$T_T(\langle add, sub \rangle, sub) = inc \rightarrow add \rightarrow inc \rightarrow sub \rightarrow pass \rightarrow sub \rightarrow fail \rightarrow STOP$
$T_T(\langle add, add \rangle, add) = inc \rightarrow add \rightarrow inc \rightarrow add \rightarrow pass \rightarrow add \rightarrow fail \rightarrow STOP$
$T_T(\langle add, add, sub, add \rangle, add) =$
    $inc \rightarrow add \rightarrow inc \rightarrow add \rightarrow inc \rightarrow sub \rightarrow inc \rightarrow add \rightarrow pass \rightarrow add \rightarrow fail \rightarrow STOP$
$T_T(\langle add, add, sub, sub \rangle, sub) = \ldots$

This is, of course, an infinite set, arising from an infinite set of traces. We note, however, that there are no tests for a trace that has one more occurrence of *add* than *sub*, since, in such a state, *Counter* has no forbidden continuations.

The verdicts depend on the particular SUT; we consider below one example: $SUT = add \rightarrow add \rightarrow STOP$. We note that, at no point, we use our knowledge of the SUT to select tests. That knowledge is used just to identify the result of the tests used in our procedure.

In considering $TestGen(Counter, SUT, RUN(\Sigma))$, the first test we execute is $T_T(\langle \rangle, sub)$, whose verdict is *pass*. So, we have $\langle sub \rangle \notin traces[\![SUT]\!]$, and the updated fault domain is $FD_1 = NOTTRACE(\langle sub \rangle) = add \rightarrow RUN(\Sigma)$. The parallelism with the fault domain $RUN(\Sigma)$ does not change $NOTTRACE(\langle sub \rangle)$.

Counter is not refined by FD_1, which after the event *add* has arbitrary behaviour. The next test is $T_T(\langle add, sub \rangle, sub)$, whose verdict is *inc*. Thus, we have that $\langle add, sub \rangle \notin traces[\![SUT]\!]$. Now, the fault domain is FD_2 below.

$$FD_2 = FD_1 \,[\![\, \Sigma \,]\!]\, NOTTRACE(\langle add, sub \rangle)$$
$$= (add \rightarrow RUN(\Sigma)) \,[\![\, \Sigma \,]\!]\, (sub \rightarrow RUN(\Sigma) \,\square\, add \rightarrow add \rightarrow RUN(\Sigma))$$
$$= add \rightarrow add \rightarrow RUN(\Sigma)$$

The next test is $T_T(\langle add, add \rangle, add)$ with verdict *pass*. Thus, FD_3 is the process $add \rightarrow add \rightarrow sub \rightarrow RUN(\Sigma)$. Next, $T_T(\langle add, add, sub, add \rangle, add)$ gives verdict *inc*, and we get $FD_4 = add \rightarrow add \rightarrow sub \rightarrow sub \rightarrow RUN(\Sigma)$ when we update the fault domain. Finally, $T_T(\langle add, add, sub, sub \rangle, sub)$ has verdict inc as well. So, $FD_5 = add \rightarrow add \rightarrow sub \rightarrow STOP$ is the new domain. Since $Counter \sqsubseteq_T FD_5$, the procedure terminates indicating that SUT is correct.

Our procedure, however, may never terminate. We discuss below some cases where we can prove that it does.

5   Generating Test Sets: Termination

A specification that has a finite set of (finite) traces is a straightforward case, since it suffices to test with each trace and each forbidden continuation. Our procedure, however, can still be useful, because useless tests may be used if the fault domain is not considered. Our procedure can reduce the number of tests.

In this scenario, our procedure terminates because, for any maximal trace t of the specification (that is, a trace that is not a prefix of any other of its traces), all events are forbidden continuations. Thus, once t is selected and all tests derived from the forbidden continuations are applied, either we find a fault, or the fault domain is refined to a process that has no traces that extends t.

When all maximal traces of the specification are selected (and the corresponding tests are applied), if no test returns a *fail* verdict, no trace of the fault domain extends a maximal trace of the specification. Thus, if no test returns a *fail* verdict, any trace of the fault domain is a trace of the specification and the procedure stops indicating success, since, in this case, $S \sqsubseteq_T FD$.

We now discuss a scenario where the specification does not have a finite set of traces, but the SUT does. Once a trace t is selected, if the set of events, and, therefore, forbidden continuations is finite, with the derived tests, we can determine whether or not the SUT implements any of the forbidden continuations. Moreover, if no *pass* verdict is observed, t itself is not implemented.

We note that if the SUT is incorrect, that is, it does not trace refine the specification, the procedure always terminates.

Lemma 2. *If $\neg (S \sqsubseteq_T SUT)$, then $TestGen(S, FD_{init}, SUT)$ terminates (and returns false), for any fault domain FD_{init} and finite SUT.*

Proof. By $\neg (S \sqsubseteq_T SUT)$, there exists a trace $s \in traces [\![SUT]\!] \setminus traces [\![S]\!]$. Let t be the longest prefix of s that is a trace of S, that is, the longest trace in $pref(s) \cap traces [\![S]\!]$, which gives rise to the shortest test that reveals an invalid prefix of s. Let a be such that $t \frown \langle a \rangle \in traces [\![SUT]\!] \setminus traces [\![S]\!]$. We know that a is a forbidden continuation of t, since $t \in traces [\![S]\!]$, but $t \frown \langle a \rangle \notin traces [\![S]\!]$. Moreover, since $traces [\![SUT]\!] \subseteq traces [\![FD]\!]$, it follows that $t \frown \langle a \rangle \in traces [\![FD]\!]$; hence $a \in initials(FD/t) \setminus initials(S/t)$. Thus, there exists a test $T_T(t, a)$ which, when applied to the SUT produces a *fail* verdict.

Since t is the longest trace in $pref(s) \cap traces [\![S]\!]$, tests generated for any prefix of t do not exclude t from the traces of the updated fault domain. Moreover, the event a remains in $initials(FD/t) \setminus initials(S/t)$, since no tests for traces longer than t are applied before t. Therefore, the test $T_T(t, a)$ is applied (unless a test for a trace of the same length of t is applied and the verdict is *fail*, in which case the result also follows). In this case, $TestGen(S, FD_{init}, SUT)$ assigns *true* to the variable *failed*, since the verdict is *fail* and terminates with $\neg$ *failed*, that is, *false*.   □

Now we consider the case when the SUT is correct and finite. For some specifications, like the *Counter* from Example 1 the procedure terminates, but not for all specifications as illustrated below.

Example 7. We consider $UNBOUNDED = a \rightarrow UNBOUNDED \,\square\, b \rightarrow STOP$, the initial fault domain $FD_{init} = RUN(\Sigma)$, where $\Sigma = \{a, b\}$, and the SUT $STOP$. In $TestGen(UNBOUNDED, SUT, RUN(\Sigma))$, the first trace we choose is $\langle\rangle$, for which there is no forbidden continuation, and so, no test. The next trace is $\langle a \rangle$, for which again there is no forbidden continuation. For $\langle b \rangle$, the events a and b are forbidden continuations; the test $T_T(\langle b \rangle, a)$ results in an *inc* verdict. Thus, the fault domain is updated to $FD_1 = FDU(FD_{init}, \langle b \rangle)$ below.

$$FD_1 = FD_{init} \,[\![\, \Sigma \,]\!]\, NOTTRACE(\langle b \rangle)$$
$$= RUN(\Sigma) \,[\![\, \Sigma \,]\!]\, a \rightarrow RUN(\Sigma)$$
$$= a \rightarrow RUN(\Sigma)$$

As expected, $\langle b \rangle$ is not a trace of the fault domain anymore and no further tests are generated for it: it is never again selected in Step 6.

The next trace we select is $\langle a, a \rangle$, for which there is no forbidden continuation. Then, we select $\langle a, b \rangle$, with forbidden continuations a and b. $T_T(\langle a, b \rangle, a)$ is executed with an *inc* verdict. The next fault domain is $FD_2 = FDU(FD_1, \langle a, b \rangle)$.

$$FD_2 = FD_1 \,[\![\, \Sigma \,]\!]\, NOTTRACE(\langle a, b \rangle)$$
$$= (a \rightarrow RUN(\Sigma)) \,[\![\, \Sigma \,]\!]\, (b \rightarrow RUN(\Sigma) \,\square\, a \rightarrow a \rightarrow RUN(\Sigma))$$
$$= a \rightarrow a \rightarrow RUN(\Sigma)$$

In fact, the refined fault domains are always of the form

$$a \rightarrow a \rightarrow ... \rightarrow a \rightarrow RUN(\Sigma)$$

This is because there is no test generated for a trace $\langle a \rangle^k$, for $k \geq 0$. So, the procedure does not terminate. This happens for any correct SUT with respect to the specification $UNBOUNDED$. For an incorrect SUT, the procedure terminates.   □

Example 8. We now consider *Counter* and why our procedure stops for its correct finite implementations. First, we note that our procedure uses traces of increasing length for deriving and applying tests, and for a finite SUT, there is a k such that all traces of the SUT are shorter than k. We consider a trace $t \in traces\,[\![Counter]\!]$ of length k. There are three possibilities for $Counter/t$. If $Counter/t = Counter$ or $Counter/t = Counter2$, we have *initials*(*Counter*/t) $\neq \Sigma$ and, thus, there is a test $T_T(t, a)$ for a forbidden *sub* or *add*. The verdict for this test is *inc* because the SUT has no trace of the length of t and the fault domain is updated, removing t as a trace of the fault domain and, thus, as a possible trace of the *SUT*. If *Counter*/t = *Counter*1, we have that *initials*(*Counter*/t) = Σ and no test can be derived from t. However, for each trace s, such that $t \frown s \in$ *traces* [[*Counter*]], s starts with either *add* or *sub*. In either case, a test will be generated, since *Counter*/$t \frown \langle add \rangle$ = *Counter*2 and *Counter*/$t \frown \langle sub \rangle$ = *Counter*1, for which there are tests, as seen before. For those tests, the verdict is *inc*, the fault domain is similarly updated, and the traces $t \frown \langle add \rangle$ and $t \frown \langle sub \rangle$ are removed. The fact that t for which *Counter*/t = *Counter*1 cannot be arbitrarily extended just to traces without tests is the key property required for the procedure to terminate.

For some specifications, like *UNBOUNDED*, there may be no tests for an unboundedly long trace. In this case, a correct *SUT* does not fail and, in spite of this, no test is applied that prunes the fault domain. □

To characterise the above termination scenario, we introduce some notation.

Given traces r and t, we say that r is a prefix of t, denoted $r \leq t$ if there exists s, such that $r \frown s = t$. A prefix is proper, denoted $r < t$, if $s \neq \langle \rangle$. We say that t is a (proper) suffix of r if, and only if, r is a (proper) prefix of t. We denote by *pref*(t) all prefixes of t, that is, *pref*(t) = $\{s : \Sigma^* \mid s \leq t\}$, and by *ppref*($t$), all proper prefixes of t, that is, *ppref*(t) = *pref*(t) $\setminus \{t\}$. Similarly, we denote by *suff*(t) the set of all suffixes of t.

For a process S and $k \geq 0$, we define the set *traces* $[[S]]_k$ of the traces of S of length k. Formally, *traces* $[[S]]_k = \{t : traces [[S]] \mid \#t = k\}$. Another subset *hfc*($S, FD$) of traces of S includes those for which there is at least a forbidden continuation that takes into account the fault domain. Formally, *hfc*(S, FD) = $\{t : traces [[S]] \mid initials(FD/t) \setminus initials(S/t) \neq \emptyset\}$. Importantly, for each $t \in$ *hfc*(S, FD), there exists at least one test $T_T(t, a)$ for a forbidden continuation a that is allowed by the fault domain. Finally, given a set of traces Q, we denote by *minimals*(Q) the set of traces of Q that are not a proper prefix of another trace in Q. Formally, *minimals*(Q) = $\{t : Q \mid \neg \exists s : Q \bullet t < s\}$.

We use *hfc*(S, FD) to define conditions for termination of the procedure.

Lemma 3. *For a specification S and a fault domain FD_{init}, if for any finite set of traces $P \subseteq traces [[S]]$, there exists a $k \geq 0$, such that, for each $r \in traces [[S]]_k$, we have that there is a prefix of r that is not in P and has a forbidden continuation, that is, $((pref(r) \setminus P) \cap hfc(S, FD_{init})) \neq \emptyset$, then $TestGen(S, FD_{init}, SUT)$ terminates for any finite SUT.*

Proof. If $\neg (S \sqsubseteq_T SUT)$, by Lemma 2, the procedure terminates.

We, therefore, assume that $S \sqsubseteq_T SUT$, and so *traces* $[[SUT]] \subseteq$ *traces* $[[S]]$. Finiteness of the *SUT* means that *traces* $[[SUT]]$ is finite. Let $k \geq 0$ be such that, for each $r \in$ *traces* $[[S]]_k$, we have $((pref(r) \setminus traces [[SUT]]) \cap hfc(S, FD_{init})) \neq \emptyset$. This k is larger than the size of the largest trace of *SUT*, since otherwise *pref*(r) $\setminus$ *traces* $[[SUT]]$ is empty, and it exists because *traces* $[[SUT]]$ is finite.

Let now $Q = (pref(traces \llbracket S \rrbracket_k) \setminus traces \llbracket SUT \rrbracket) \cap hfc(S, FD_{init})$ and let $M = minimals(Q)$. Let $p \in traces \llbracket SUT \rrbracket$. Let $r \in traces \llbracket S \rrbracket_k$ be such that $p \leq r$. There is at least an $s \in pref(r)$, such that $p \leq s$ and $s \in hfc(S, FD_{init})$ because $((pref(r) \setminus traces \llbracket SUT \rrbracket) \cap hfc(S, FD_{init})) \neq \emptyset$. Without loss of generality, assume that s is the shortest such a trace. Thus, $s \in M$ and $p \in pref(M)$, since $p \leq s$. It follows that $traces \llbracket SUT \rrbracket \subseteq pref(M)$ since p is arbitrary.

For each $t \in M$, there exists $a \in initials(FD_{init}/t) \setminus initials(S/t)$, since $t \in hfc(S, FD_{init})$ and from the definition of $hfc(S, FD_{init})$. Then, if the test $T_T(t, a)$ is applied to the SUT, the verdict is inc, since $t \notin traces \llbracket SUT \rrbracket$ because $t \in M \subseteq Q$ and $Q \cap traces \llbracket SUT \rrbracket = \emptyset$. In this case, the fault domain is updated so that t is not a trace of the fault domain anymore.

Thus, if all tests derived for each $t \in M$ are applied, we obtain a fault domain FD such hat $traces \llbracket FD \rrbracket \subseteq pref(M)$. As all traces in M have length at most k, eventually, all traces in M are selected (unless the procedure has already terminated) and the tests derived for those traces are applied. As $pref(M) \subseteq Q \subseteq hfc(S, FD_{init}) \subseteq traces \llbracket S \rrbracket$, it follows that $traces \llbracket FD \rrbracket \subseteq traces \llbracket S \rrbracket$, that is, $S \sqsubseteq_T SUT$. $TestGen(S, FD_{init}, SUT)$ then terminates, with $failed = false$, and the result is $true$.

$\square$

One scenario where the conditions in Lemma 3 hold is if there is an event in the alphabet which is not used in the model. In this case, that event is always a forbidden continuation and thus a test is generated for all traces. Even though this can be rarely the case for a specification at hand, the alphabet can be augmented with a special event for the purpose, guaranteeing that the procedure terminates. Such an event would act as a *probe* event. As said before, in practice, it is best to avoid probes since the tests that they induce can reveal no faults.

6   Tool Support and Case Studies

We have developed a prototype tool that implements our procedure. The tasks related to the manipulation of the CSP model, such as checking refinement, computing forbidden continuations, determining verdicts, and so on, are handled by FDR. The tool is implemented in Ruby. It submits queries (assert clauses) to FDR and parses FDR's results in order to perform the computations required by the procedure. Specifically, FDR is used in two points:

1. for checking whether the specification refines the fault domain (Line 5). It is a straightforward refinement check in FDR;
2. for computing initials and forbidden continuations (Lines 7 and 8). For instance, to compute the complement of $initials(S/t)$, we invoke FDR to check $S \sqsubseteq_T TTHENANY(t)$, where S is compared to the process $TTHENANY(t)$ that performs t and then any event e from Σ. It is defined as follows.

$$TTHENANY(\langle\rangle) = \Box\, e : \Sigma \bullet e \rightarrow STOP$$
$$TTHENANY(\langle a \rangle \frown t) = a \rightarrow TTHENANY(t)$$

If t is a trace of S, counterexamples to this refinement check provide traces $t \frown \langle e \rangle$, where e is not in the set $initials(S/t)$. Thus, we obtain $initials(S/t)$ by considering the events in Σ for which no such counterexample exists.

Currently, our prototype calls FDR many times from scratch. As a future optimization, we will incorporate the caching of the internal results of the FDR, to speed up posterior invocations with the same model.

We have used our prototype to carry out two case studies, the Transputer-based sensor for autonomous vehicles in [23], and the Emergency Response System (ERS) in [2]. The sensor is part of an architecture where each sensor is associated with a Transputer for local processing and can be part of a network of sensors. The ERS allows members of the public to identify incidents requiring emergency response; it is a system of operationally independent systems (a Phone System, a Call Center, an Emergency Response Unit, and so on). The ERS ensures that every call is sent to the correct target. It is used in [18] to assess the deadlock detection of a prototype model checker for *Circus*.

For each case study, we have randomly generated 1000 finite SUTs with the same event alphabet. The experimental results confirm what we expected from the lemmas of the previous section. Namely, all incorrect SUTs are identified and the procedure terminates for all finite SUTs identified in Lemma 3. The prototype tool and the CSP model for the sensor, the ERS and other examples are in http://www.github.com/adenilso/CSP-FD-TGen. The data for the SUTs used in this case study is also available.

7   Conclusions

In this paper, we have investigated how fault domains can be used to guide test generation from CSP models. We have cast core notions of fault-domain testing in the context of the CSP testing theory. For testing for traces refinement, we have presented a procedure which, given a specification and a fault domain, it tests whether an SUT trace refines the fault domain. If the SUT is incorrect, the procedure selects a test that can reveal the fault. In the case of a correct SUT, we have stated conditions that guarantee that the procedure terminates.

There are specifications for which the procedure does not terminate. We postulate that for those specifications, there is no finite set of tests that is able to demonstrate the correctness of the SUT. Finiteness requires extra assumptions about the SUT. We plan to investigate this point further in future work.

The CSP testing theory also includes tests for *conf*, a conformance relation that deals with forbidden deadlocks; together, tests for *conf* and traces refinement can be used to establish failures refinement. Another interesting failures-based conformance relation for testing from CSP models takes into account the asymmetry of controllability of inputs and outputs in the interaction with the SUT [6]. It is worth investigating how fault domains can be used to generate finite test sets for these notions of conformance.

Acknowledgements. The authors would like to thank the partial financial support of the following entities: Royal Society (Grant: NI150186), FAPESP (Grant: 2013/07375-0). The authors also are thankful to Marie-Claude Gaudel, for the useful discussion in an early version of this paper.

References

1. Alberto, A., Cavalcanti, A.L.C., Gaudel, M.-C., Simao, A.: Formal mutation testing for Circus. IST **81**, 131–153 (2017)
2. Andrews, Z., et al.: Model-based development of fault tolerant systems of systems. In: SysCon, pp. 356–363, April 2013
3. Cavalcanti, A., Gaudel, M.-C.: Testing for refinement in CSP. In: Butler, M., Hinchey, M.G., Larrondo-Petrie, M.M. (eds.) ICFEM 2007. LNCS, vol. 4789, pp. 151–170. Springer, Heidelberg (2007). doi:10.1007/978-3-540-76650-6_10
4. Cavalcanti, A.L.C., Gaudel, M.-C.: Testing for refinement in Circus. Acta Informatica **48**(2), 97–147 (2011)
5. Cavalcanti, A., Gaudel, M.-C.: Data flow coverage for Circus-based testing. In: Gnesi, S., Rensink, A. (eds.) FASE 2014. LNCS, vol. 8411, pp. 415–429. Springer, Heidelberg (2014). doi:10.1007/978-3-642-54804-8_29
6. Cavalcanti, A., Hierons, R.M.: Testing with inputs and outputs in CSP. In: Cortellessa, V., Varró, D. (eds.) FASE 2013. LNCS, vol. 7793, pp. 359–374. Springer, Heidelberg (2013). doi:10.1007/978-3-642-37057-1_26
7. Chow, T.S.: Testing software design modeled by finite-state machines. IEEE Trans. Softw. Eng. **4**(3), 178–187 (1978)
8. El-Fakih, K.A., et al.: FSM-based testing from user defined faults adapted to incremental and mutation testing. Program. Comput. Softw. **38**(4), 201–209 (2012)
9. Fujiwara, S., von Bochmann, G.: Testing non-deterministic state machines with fault coverage. In: FORTE, North-Holland, pp. 267–280 (1991)
10. Gibson-Robinson, T., Armstrong, P., Boulgakov, A., Roscoe, A.W.: FDR3 — a modern refinement checker for CSP. In: Ábrahám, E., Havelund, K. (eds.) TACAS 2014. LNCS, vol. 8413, pp. 187–201. Springer, Heidelberg (2014). doi:10.1007/978-3-642-54862-8_13
11. Hierons, R.M., Ural, H.: Optimizing the length of checking sequences. IEEE TC **55**(5), 618–629 (2006)
12. Huang, W., Peleska, J.: Exhaustive model-based equivalence class testing. In: Yenigün, H., Yilmaz, C., Ulrich, A. (eds.) ICTSS 2013. LNCS, vol. 8254, pp. 49–64. Springer, Heidelberg (2013). doi:10.1007/978-3-642-41707-8_4
13. Koufareva, I., Petrenko, A., Yevtushenko, N.: Test generation driven by user-defined fault models. In: Csopaki, G., Dibuz, S., Tarnay, K. (eds.) Testing of Communicating Systems. ITIFIP, vol. 21, pp. 215–233. Springer, Boston (1999). doi:10.1007/978-0-387-35567-2_14
14. Luo, G., et al.: Test selection based on communicating nondeterministic finite-state machines using a generalized Wp-method. IEEE TSE **20**(2), 149–162 (1994)
15. Milner, R.: A Calculus of Communicating Systems. LNCS, vol. 92. Springer, Heidelberg (1980). doi:10.1007/3-540-10235-3
16. Moraes, A., et al.: A family of test selection criteria for timed input-output symbolic transition system models. SCP **126**, 52–72 (2016)
17. Morell, L.J.: A theory of fault-based testing. IEEE TSEg **16**(8), 844–857 (1990)

18. Mota, A., Farias, A., Didier, A., Woodcock, J.: Rapid prototyping of a semantically well founded *Circus* model checker. In: Giannakopoulou, D., Salaün, G. (eds.) SEFM 2014. LNCS, vol. 8702, pp. 235–249. Springer, Cham (2014). doi:10.1007/978-3-319-10431-7_17

19. Nogueira, S., Sampaio, A.C.A., Mota, A.C.: Test generation from state based use case models. FACJ **26**(3), 441–490 (2014)

20. Peleska, J.: Test automation for safety-critical systems: industrial application and future developments. In: Gaudel, M.-C., Woodcock, J. (eds.) FME 1996. LNCS, vol. 1051, pp. 39–59. Springer, Heidelberg (1996). doi:10.1007/3-540-60973-3_79

21. Petrenko, A., Yevtushenko, N.: Testing from partial deterministic FSM specifications. IEEE TC **54**(9), 1154–1165 (2005)

22. Petrenko, A., et al.: On fault coverage of tests for finite state specifications. Comput. Netw. ISDN Syst. **29**(1), 81–106 (1996)

23. Probert, P.J., Djian, D., Hu, H.: Transputer architectures for sensing in a robot controller: formal methods for design. Concurr. Pract. Exp. **3**(4), 283–292 (1991)

24. Roscoe, A.W.: Understanding Concurrent Systems. Springer, London (2011). doi:10.1007/978-1-84882-258-0

25. Tretmans, J.: Test generation with inputs, outputs, and quiescence. In: Margaria, T., Steffen, B. (eds.) TACAS 1996. LNCS, vol. 1055, pp. 127–146. Springer, Heidelberg (1996). doi:10.1007/3-540-61042-1_42

26. Yu, Y.T., Lau, M.F.: Fault-based test suite prioritization for specification-based testing. Inf. Softw. Technol. **54**(2), 179–202 (2012)

Effective Infinite-State Model Checking by Input Equivalence Class Partitioning

Niklas Krafczyk and Jan Peleska[(⊠)]

Department of Mathematics and Computer Science,
University of Bremen, Bremen, Germany
{niklas,jp}@cs.uni-bremen.de

Abstract. In this paper, it is shown how a complete input equivalence class testing strategy developed by the second author can be effectively used for infinite-state model checking of system models with infinite input domains but finitely many internal state values and finite output domains. This class of systems occurs frequently in the safety-critical domain, where controllers may input conceptually infinite analogue data, but make a finite number of control decisions based on inputs and current internal state. A variant of Kripke Structures is well-suited to provide a behavioural model for this system class. It is shown how the known construction of specific input equivalence classes can be used to abstract the infinite input domain of the reference model into finitely many classes. Then quick checks can be made on the implementation model showing that the implementation is not I/O-equivalent to the reference model if its abstraction to observable minimal finite state machines has a different number of states or a different input partitioning as the reference model. Only if these properties are consistent with the reference model, a detailed equivalence check between the abstracted models needs to be performed. The complete test suites obtained as a by-product of the checking procedure can be used to establish counter examples showing the non-conformity between implementation model and reference model. Using various sample models, it is shown that this approach outperforms model checkers that do not possess this equivalence class generation capability.

Keywords: Input equivalence class partition testing · Infinite-state model checking · Kripke Structures

1 Introduction

Motivation. Model checking of infinite-state systems is an important research field. Notable examples are Timed Automata, where physical time represents a model or meta variable with uncountable domain [3] and the more general Hybrid Systems, where also real-valued observables are taken into account [8]. Other approaches investigate model checking in presence of unbounded data structures, we cite here [6] as a representative of many results achieved in this area.

© IFIP International Federation for Information Processing 2017
Published by Springer International Publishing AG 2017. All Rights Reserved
N. Yevtushenko et al. (Eds.): ICTSS 2017, LNCS 10533, pp. 38–53, 2017.
DOI: 10.1007/978-3-319-67549-7_3

The close relationship between infinite state model checking and testing has been observed, for example, in [18], where a complete testing method for verifying real-time systems against Time Automata models has been presented.[1]

In this paper, we show how results from model-based testing of reactive systems can inspire approaches to infinite-state model checking.

Main contribution. We present a new algorithm for checking I/O-equivalence of systems with infinite input domains, but finite domains for internal state variables and outputs. It applies to both deterministic and nondeterministic systems, whose behavioural semantics can be expressed by I/O-state transitions systems, a specific variant of Kripke Structures. The algorithm exploits a new method for calculating input equivalence classes, that has originally been developed for constructing complete test suites for systems of this type [10]. While an algorithm for calculating these classes for deterministic models has been published in [9], the algorithm presented in this paper can handle nondeterministic systems.

It is shown that for I/O-equivalence checking problems of reference and implementation models in this domain, the new algorithm clearly outperforms conventional model checkers, because the latter need to operate on an explicit discretisation of the input space, whereas the new algorithm presented here only needs to check a significantly smaller number of input equivalence classes. Moreover, the new method is very effective for constructing counter examples in case of failing equivalence checks, since these examples are simply given by failing test cases.

To our best knowledge, this approach to checking systems with infinite input domains is new: other authors using equivalence partition techniques of the input space used more general classes, at the cost of losing the completeness of the method [19].

Overview. The equivalence calculation method and the resulting model checking algorithm are described in Sect. 2. In Sect. 3, several model checking experiments are described, comparing the implementation of the method presented here against the well-established FDR3 model checker for the CSP process algebra. Section 4 presents the conclusions.

2   Method

In this section we describe how to calculate the input equivalence class partitioning of a given model described in Sect. 3 and how we use this input equivalence class partitioning to check two models for I/O-equivalence.

---

[1] Recall that a test suite is called complete if it guarantees to accept every implementation conforming to a given reference model and to reject every non-conforming implementation, provided that its true behaviour is represented by a model from a well-defined fault domain.

2.1 State Space Representation

Our approach is based on *state transition systems (STS)* described as triples $(\mathcal{S}, \underline{s}, \mathcal{R})$ where $\mathcal{S}$ is the possibly infinite state space, $\underline{s} \in \mathcal{S}$ is the initial state and $\mathcal{R} \subseteq \mathcal{S} \times \mathcal{S}$ the transition relation. Furthermore, we assume that all states in $\mathcal{S}$ are reachable from the initial state via the transition relation and require that the properties of *I/O-state transition systems (IOSTS)* apply which we specify as follows:

- Every state $s \in \mathcal{S}$ is a valuation function $s : \mathcal{V} \to \mathcal{D}$, mapping variables v from a finite set of symbols $v \in \mathcal{V}$ to their values $s(v)$ in the domain $\mathcal{D}$.
- The set $\mathcal{V}$ of variable symbols can be partitioned into disjoint sets of input variables, internal state variables, and output variables. Let $I \subseteq \mathcal{V}$ be the set of input variables. Then D_I is the set of all input vectors which is the cross product of the domains of all input variables in I. From now on, the set of input variables is referred to as I, the set of internal state variables as M, and the set of output variables as O.
- The state space of an IOSTS can be partitioned into two sets of states S_Q and S_T which are the sets of the so-called *quiescent* and *transient* states, respectively. Transient and quiescent states are characterised as follows.

$$\forall (s_q, s) \in S_Q \times S_Q : (s_q, s) \in \mathcal{R} \Rightarrow s|_{M \cup O} = s_q|_{M \cup O} \tag{1}$$

$$\forall (s_t, s) \in S_T \times \mathcal{S} : (s_t, s) \in \mathcal{R} \Rightarrow s|_I = s_t|_I \tag{2}$$

$$\forall (s_q, s) \in S_Q \times S_T : (s_q, s) \in \mathcal{R} \Rightarrow \exists x \in I : s(x) \neq s_q(x) \tag{3}$$

Here, $s|_X, X \subseteq \mathcal{V}$ denotes the restriction of the valuation function s to the set of variables symbols $v \in X$. Thus, no internal state or output variable may change over a transition from a quiescent state, no input variables may change over a transition from a transient state, and every transient state reached by a transition from a quiescent state needs to evaluate at least one input variable differently. If the latter were not the case, S_Q and S_T would not be disjoint.
- The initial state is contained in S_Q.

An IOSTS describes the behaviour of a state-based system. From the outside view, only input variables influence the state of the system and only output variables are observable. States in partition S_Q of the state space are stable states where the system waits for new inputs. States in partition S_T of the state space are transient states. A system performing some sort of calculation would wait in a quiescent state for the inputs to the calculation. If the inputs allow for the calculation to be performed, the internal state variables and output variables are modified in a sequence of transient states. The calculation is finished when a quiescent state is reached, allowing for the outputs to be observed. Inputs are changed by modifying the input variables. The possible modifications to the input variables are defined by the transition relation as follows: An input vector c can be applied to the system if for the new state $s' = s \oplus \{x \mapsto c\}$ the condition $(s, s') \in \mathcal{R}$ holds. The set of all input vectors allowed in state s is defined as $C(s) = \{c \in D_I \mid \exists x : (s, s \oplus \{x \mapsto c\}) \in \mathcal{R}\}$.

If the condition $\forall s \in S_Q : C(s) = \mathcal{D}_I$ holds for every state of S_Q of an IOSTS, that IOSTS is called *completely specified*. An IOSTS is free of livelocks if there is no reachable infinite sequence of transitions between transient states linked by the transition relation.

Let $S = (\mathcal{S}, \underline{s}, \mathcal{R})$ be an IOSTS as defined above. Then, the partitioning of $S_Q \subseteq \mathcal{S}$ induced by the equivalence relation $s \sim_{MO} s' \iff \forall v_{mo} \in M \cup O : s(v_{mo}) = s'(v_{mo})$ with $s, s' \in S_Q$ is called the *MO partitioning*. All states evaluating all internal state and output variables in the same way are members of the same partition. Here, such a partitioning is named $\mathcal{A} = \mathcal{A}_0, \ldots, \mathcal{A}_n$ and it is finite, as the domains of all internal state and output variables are finite. Every member of $\mathcal{A}$ is called a *state class*. The state class containing the initial state of the IOSTS under consideration is called $\mathcal{A}_0$. For mapping a state to the corresponding state class, the shorthand $MO : \mathcal{S} \to \mathcal{A}$ is introduced.

For any IOSTS free of livelocks, every quiescent state s of that IOSTS can be mapped to a set of quiescent states that are reachable by a finite, possibly empty sequence of only transient states for every input vector $c \in C(s)$. Let s/c be this mapping for state s and input vector c. The case where $(s \oplus \{x \mapsto c\}) \in S_Q$ holds is trivial. If, however, $(s \oplus \{x \mapsto c\}) \in S_T$ holds, the set of quiescent states the state s maps to under input vector c can be determined by unrolling the transition relation. If, for any s and any c, $|s/c| > 1$, the IOSTS is called *nondeterministic*.

2.2 Input Equivalence Class Partitioning

When checking a pair of livelock free IOSTS for I/O-equivalence, we may have to deal with a possibly infinite input domain. In our approach we partition the input domain into a finite number of input equivalence classes as presented by [10]. For every pair s_1, s_2 of states in the same state class of the MO partitioning of an IOSTS, and for every input vector in every element $\mathcal{I}_i$ of such an input equivalence class partitioning (IECP) $\mathcal{I}$, the state classes of the reachable quiescent states are identical: $\forall s_1, s_2 \in \mathcal{S} : \forall \mathcal{I}_i \in \mathcal{I} : \forall c \in \mathcal{I}_i : MO(s_1) = MO(s_2) \implies \{MO(s'_1)|s'_1 \in s_1/c\} = \{MO(s'_2)|s'_2 \in s_2/c\}$. To obtain such an IECP, first the input equivalence classes of every state class are calculated. An algorithm to do so is given in Sect. 2.2.1, taking nondeterminism into account. Given these IECPs for every state class, the final IECP is given as every non-empty intersection of input equivalence classes containing exactly one element from each of the calculated IECPs of every state class for which an algorithm is given in Sect. 2.2.2.

For illustration purposes, the approach is applied to the system described by the SysML state machine shown in Fig. 1. This model has one integer input variable x and one output variable m. Initially, the output m is 0, meaning that no alarm is active. If the input value x exceeds a threshold max, m is set to 2, triggering an alarm which will only be ceded after x is equal to or drops below another threshold max - delta. However, if the input value is equal to max, the behaviour of the described system is non-deterministic: either, the alarm is triggered and the system progresses as described before, or a state is entered

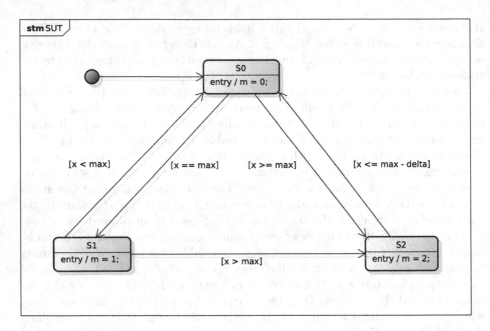

Fig. 1. SysML model of an alarm system reacting to input changes.

where there is no full alarm but maybe a message is sent to a security company to check on the secured object (these possibilities are not shown in the model). For this state to be left into the idle state where there is no alarm, the input may simply drop by an arbitrary amount. However, if it rises further, a full alarm is triggered.

2.2.1 Input Equivalence Classes for State Classes

Let $g_{i,j}$ be the condition on the input variables describing all input vectors for which there is a possibly empty sequence of only transient states terminated by a quiescent state for every state in state class $\mathcal{A}_i$ ending in state class $\mathcal{A}_j$: $\forall c \in \mathcal{D}_I : c \models g_{i,j} \iff \forall s \in \mathcal{A}_i : \exists s' \in \mathcal{A}_j : s' \in s/c$. Furthermore, let G be the set of all such conditions for the MO partitioning of an IOSTS, where the set of satisfying input vectors is not empty, i.e. where there is at least one input vector allowing the transition from one state class into another. Finally, let G_i be a subset of G where $g_{i,\ell} \in G_i \iff \forall s \in \mathcal{A}_i : \exists c \in \mathcal{D}_I : s/c \in \mathcal{A}_\ell$, that is, G_i contains all conditions applicable to transitions emanating from state class $\mathcal{A}_i$. Then, for a given G_i, Algorithm 1 calculates a set M_i of tuples of conditions:

$$M_i = \{(p, n) \in \mathbb{P}(G_i) \times \mathbb{P}(G_i) \mid$$
$$(\models \bigwedge_{p_k \in p} p_k \wedge \bigwedge_{n_k \in n} \neg n_k)$$
$$\wedge (\forall g \in G_i : \models \bigwedge_{p_k \in p} p_k \wedge g \iff g \in p \cup n)\}$$

Every tuple in M_i describes an input equivalence class for state class $\mathcal{A}_i$.

Transferring this to our example, we first derive the state classes $\mathcal{A}$. In the given model, every SysML state corresponds to a state class as every state maps to a separate state class in the MO partitioning. Thus, $\mathcal{A}_0$ corresponds to S0. The other state class counterparts to the SysML states may be chosen arbitrarily. We chose $\mathcal{A}_1$ to be equivalent to state S1 and $\mathcal{A}_2$ to state S2. Then, the formulas in Fig. 2 are the elements of G.

$$g_{0,0} \equiv x < max \qquad g_{0,1} \equiv x = max \quad g_{0,2} \equiv x \geq max$$
$$g_{1,0} \equiv x < max \qquad g_{1,1} \equiv x = max \quad g_{1,2} \equiv x > max$$
$$g_{2,0} \equiv x \leq max - delta \qquad\qquad g_{2,2} \equiv x > max - delta$$

Fig. 2. Expressions in G, representing all conditions on the input variables for transitions from one state class to the other to occur.

For every state class, G_i is calculated, its elements are given by the ith line of expressions in Fig. 2.

Algorithm 1 first calculates all satisfiable subsets of G_i for every state class $\mathcal{A}_i$. As the IOSTS under consideration can be nondeterministic, there may be subsets with more than one member. The classes of a partitioning are disjoint, thus an IECP cannot contain overlapping elements, i.e. multiple classes containing the same input vector. Thus, for every satisfiable subset of G_i which is also a subset of another satisfiable subset of G_i, the difference to all supersets is added as negated terms to form an input equivalence class if the resulting conjunction is satisfiable.

For G_0 from our example, the sets

$$\{g_{0,0}\}, \{g_{0,1}\}, \{g_{0,2}\}, \{g_{0,0}, g_{0,1}\}, \{g_{0,0}, g_{0,2}\}, \{g_{0,1}, g_{0,2}\}$$

and

$$\{g_{0,0}, g_{0,1}, g_{0,2}\}$$

are tested for satisfiability. As neither $g_{0,0} \wedge g_{0,1}$ nor $g_{0,0} \wedge g_{0,2}$ is satisfiable, supersets of $\{g_{0,0}, g_{0,1}\}$ and $\{g_{0,0}, g_{0,2}\}$ do not have to be checked for satisfiability, as these will never be satisfiable either. The sets of expressions satisfiable under conjunction are the singleton sets and $\{g_{0,1}, g_{0,2}\}$. The latter is introduced due to the non-determinism of the described system in the case of x == max. In this example, the satisfiable subset $\{g_{0,2}\}$ of G cannot be an input equivalence class, since the set of input vectors described would not be disjoint from the set described by $\{g_{0,1}, g_{0,2}\}$. However, $g_{0,2} \wedge \neg g_{0,1}$ is satisfiable, allowing $\mathcal{A}_2$ to be reached deterministically by a set of input vectors which now represent one input equivalence class. As $g_{0,1} \wedge \neg g_{0,2}$ is not satisfiable, neither $g_{0,1}$ nor $g_{0,1} \wedge \neg g_{0,2}$ represents an input equivalence class. Thus, the input equivalence classes of the system are given as follows:

Input: Set G of transition conditions.
Input: Set I of indexes of state classes: $\{n \in \mathbb{N} \mid n < |\mathcal{A}|\}$
Output: Set M of IECPs M_i.
$M \leftarrow \emptyset$;
for $i \in I$ **do**
$\quad G_i \leftarrow \{g_{i,j} \in G \mid \forall s \in \mathcal{A}_i : \exists c \in \mathcal{D}_I : c \models g_{i,j} \wedge s/c \in \mathcal{A}_j\}$;
$\quad$ satset $\leftarrow$ `CalculateSatisfiableSubsets`$(G_i, \emptyset)$;
$\quad M_i \leftarrow \emptyset$;
$\quad$ **for** $p \in$ satset **do**
$\quad\quad\mid$ super $\leftarrow \{s \in$ satset $\mid p \subsetneq s\}$;
$\quad\quad\mid n \leftarrow (\bigcup_{s \in \text{super}} s) \setminus p$;
$\quad\quad\mid$ **if** $\models \bigwedge_{m_i \in p} m_i \wedge \bigwedge_{n_i \in n} \neg n_i$ **then**
$\quad\quad\mid\quad \lfloor\ M_i \leftarrow M_i \cup \{(p,n)\}$;
$\quad M \leftarrow M \cup \{M_i\}$;
return M;
function *CalculateSatisfiableSubsets(G_x, E_x)*
$\quad$ **if** $G_x = \emptyset$ **then**
$\quad\quad \lfloor$ **return** $\{E_x\}$;
$\quad M_x \leftarrow \emptyset$;
$\quad U \leftarrow \emptyset$;
$\quad$ **for** $g_x \in G_x$ **do**
$\quad\quad\mid U \leftarrow U \cup \{g_x\}$;
$\quad\quad\mid$ **if** $\models \bigwedge_{e \in E_x} e \wedge g_x$ **then**
$\quad\quad\mid\quad \lfloor\ M_x \leftarrow M_x \cup$ `CalculateSatisfiableSubsets`$(G_x \setminus U, E_x \cup \{g_x\})$;
$\quad$ **return** M_x;

Algorithm 1. Algorithm calculating every state class' input equivalence classes.

$$M_0 = \{((\{g_{0,0}\}, \{\}), (\{g_{0,2}\}, \{g_{0,1}\}), (\{g_{0,1}, g_{0,2}\}, \{\})\}$$
$$M_1 = \{((\{g_{1,0}\}, \{\}), (\{g_{1,1}\}, \{\}), (\{g_{1,2}\}, \{\})\}$$
$$M_2 = \{((\{g_{2,0}\}, \{\}), (\{g_{2,2}\}, \{\})\}$$

In previous implementations, $|p| + |n| = |G_i|$ held for every element $m \in M_i$ as every element of G_i appeared in m in either identical or negated form. In contrast to this, our approach possibly results in smaller descriptions of input equivalence classes, where $|p| + |n| \leq |G_i|$, which has practical ramifications: for large sizes of $|G_i|$, instantiating and solving the resulting input equivalence classes using an SMT solver shows significant speedups. Furthermore, our approach exploits the fact that $\forall p, q \in \mathbb{P}(P) : (p \subseteq q \wedge \not\models \bigwedge_{p_i \in p} p_i) \implies \not\models \bigwedge_{q_i \in q} q_i$ holds for arbitrary sets P of first order logic formulae and may thus show significant speedups in contrast to checking every subset of G_i for satisfiability.

2.2.2 Input Equivalence Classes for IOSTS

Given the IECP for every state class, we can calculate the IECP over all state classes by calculating all non-empty intersections ϕ of input equivalence classes containing exactly one input equivalence class from every state class. In other words, the IECP is a non-empty subset $\mathcal{M}$ of $M_0 \times \ldots \times M_{|\mathcal{A}|-1}$, where every element describes a set of first order logic expressions whose conjunction is satisfiable:

$$\forall \phi \in \mathcal{M} := \bigwedge_{(p,n) \in \phi} \left(\left(\bigwedge_{p_j \in p} p_j \right) \wedge \left(\bigwedge_{n_k \in n} \neg n_k \right) \right) \tag{4}$$

To calculate all ϕ efficiently, Algorithm 2 is used. Similar to Algorithm 1, every satisfiable ϕ has to be found. Otherwise, the partitioning would be incomplete, as parts of the input domain were not covered by the result. Again, parts of the search space $M = M_0 \times \ldots \times M_{|\mathcal{A}|-1}$ not containing a solution can be left out. If for a set P the fact could be established that the conjunction of its elements is not satisfiable, conjunctions with further expressions will not be satisfiable as well. The number of elements in M of which P is a subset is

$$\prod_{i=|P|} |\mathcal{A}| - 1 |M_i| \tag{5}$$

Input: Set $M = \{M_0, \ldots, M_{|\mathcal{A}|-1}\}$ of IECPs of all state classes
Output: IECP of the IOSTS under consideration
function *CalculateSatisfiableSubsets(M_x, E_x)*
    if $M_x = \emptyset$ **then**
       return $\{E_x\}$;
    $\Phi_x \leftarrow \emptyset$;
    $M_i \leftarrow \underset{m_x \in M_x}{argmin}(|m_x|)$;
    for $(p,n) \in M_i$ **do**
       $exp \leftarrow \left(\bigwedge_{p_i \in p} p_i \right) \wedge \left(\bigwedge_{n_j \in n} \neg n_j \right)$;
       if $\models exp \wedge \bigwedge_{e \in E_x} e$ **then**
          $\Phi_x \leftarrow \Phi_x \cup$ `CalculateSatisfiableSubsets`$(M_x \backslash M_i, E_x \cup \{exp\})$;
    return Φ_x;
return *CalculateSatisfiableSubsets(M, $\emptyset$)*;

Algorithm 2. Algorithm calculating the IECP.

---

assuming the elements of P were picked by ascending index of the elements of M. This number is maximal if $|P|$ is as small and all M_i as large as possible, or if the following condition holds $\forall 0 \leq j < |P| : \forall |P| \leq k < |\mathcal{A}| : |M_j| \leq |M_k|$.

To be able to ignore as large parts of the search space as possible, sorting the elements of M by cardinality, picking a P of size ℓ out of the first ℓ elements of M and checking it for satisfiability is beneficial. If P is satisfiable, then ℓ should be increased and a new P picked until either $\ell = |\mathcal{A}|$ or a conjunction of the elements of P is not satisfiable. In the former case, P describes an input equivalence class, in the latter a different P shall be picked. Algorithm 2 describes a possible implementation. In our example, first an order for the M_i is determined, beginning with the smallest set, which is M_2. For each of its elements, every element of the next M_i in order, e.g. M_0, is picked and the conjunction checked for satisfiability. If that is satisfiable, every conjunction with every element of M_1 would be checked. This way, all IECP are found, which are listed in Fig. 3.

$$\Phi_0 = g_{0,0} \wedge g_{1,0} \wedge g_{2,0} \equiv x \leq max - delta$$
$$\Phi_1 = g_{0,0} \wedge g_{1,0} \wedge g_{2,2} \equiv x > max - delta \wedge x < max$$
$$\Phi_1 = g_{0,1} \wedge g_{1,1} \wedge g_{2,2} \equiv x = max$$
$$\Phi_1 = g_{0,2} \wedge g_{1,2} \wedge g_{2,2} \wedge \neg g_{0,1} \equiv x > max$$

Fig. 3. Input equivalence classes of the alarm system example.

2.3   Checking for Input/Output Equivalence

Two IOSTS are *I/O-equivalent*, if they produce the same language of input/output traces. To check two IOSTS for I/O-equivalence, we first calculate the IECP for both. In [10] the authors show how to derive FSMs or, more precisely, transductors from these IECP which are I/O-equivalent iff the same holds for the corresponding IOSTS. In short, these transductors are constructed as follows: Let S_1, S_2 be a pair of IOSTS to be checked for I/O-equivalence with a known bijective mapping for their input and output variables, i.e. for every input and output variable of S_1 there is a corresponding variable in S_2. Furthermore, let $\mathcal{A}_{S_1}, \mathcal{A}_{S_2}$ be the MO partitionings and $\mathcal{I}_{S_1}, \mathcal{I}_{S_2}$ be the IECPs for both IOSTS. Then, $T_1 = (Q_1, \underline{q}_1, \Sigma_{I,1}, \Sigma_{O,1}, R_1), T_2 = (Q_2, \underline{q}_2, \Sigma_{I,2}, \Sigma_{O,2}, R_2)$ are the corresponding transductors, where every state in the state space Q_1 has a corresponding state class in $\mathcal{A}_{S_1}$, and every input symbol in the input alphabet $\Sigma_{I,1}$ has a corresponding input space partition in $\mathcal{I}_{S_1}$. The initial state $\underline{q}_1 \in Q_1$ maps to the state class containing the initial state of S_1. T_1's output alphabet $\Sigma_{O,1}$ results from the output vectors in the state classes $\mathcal{A}_{S_1}$ where every distinct output vector is assigned an output symbol in $\Sigma_{O,1}$. The transition relation R_1 is constructed according to the transition relation of S_1. T_2 is constructed accordingly.

For a word composed of symbols from the input alphabet, each transductor produces a set of output traces. Only for non-deterministic IOSTS, this set may contain more than one trace. Every element of that set represents a possible response of the system for the applied input trace.

Minimising the transductor allows the input alphabet to be partitioned. Two input symbols x_1, x_2 are equivalent and thus elements of the same partition element iff for every transition $(q, x_1, y, q') \in R_m$ there is a transition $(q, x_2, y, q') \in R_m$, where R_m is the transition relation of the minimised transductor. Merging all input space partitions corresponding to an element of a set of equivalent input symbols results in the coarsest IECP for the corresponding IOSTS.

After calculating the coarsest IECP using T_1 and T_2 described above, two further transductors $\bar{T}_1, \bar{T}_2$ can be derived as described above, now using the coarsest IECPs to construct the input alphabets. These are I/O-equivalent, i.e. their languages are equal, iff S_1 and S_2 are I/O-equivalent. Using a test method which is complete regarding I/O-equivalence, a test suite can be calculated, consisting of a set of input words. $\bar{T}_1$ and $\bar{T}_2$ are I/O-equivalent if and only if they produce the same set of output words for every input word of the test suite. However, if for one input word the sets of output words differ, a counterexample has been found. The counterexample consists of the input word and the symmetric difference of the sets of output words produced by $\bar{T}_1$ and $\bar{T}_2$. Naturally, the shortest counterexample can be found effectively by executing the test suite sorted by the length of the input words in ascending order. As a prerequisite for the calculation and execution of a common test suite, a bijective mapping between the input symbols of $\bar{T}_1$'s and $\bar{T}_2$'s input alphabets has to be known. This requires that the input alphabets are of the same size and that for every input equivalence class partition of the coarsest IECP of S_1 there is a congruent input equivalence class partition in the coarsest IECP of S_2. If this is not the case, S_1 and S_2 are known to not be I/O-equivalent as shown in [16]. To calculate a common test suite nonetheless, the intersection of both coarsest IECPs can be used as the coarsest common IECP, allowing $\bar{T}_1$ and $\bar{T}_2$ to be constructed with the same IECP. This is necessary if a counterexample has to be calculated.

3 Case Study and Quantitative Evaluation

3.1 General Evaluation Approach

To evaluate the described approach, a case study involving models with varying complexity and state space size has been performed. Each model was represented as a SysML state machine [14]. Its behavioural semantics was specified by associating an IOSTS transition relation with the state machine, as described in [9]. Errors were injected into each model M by applying mutation operators, this resulted in mutant models $M_1, M_2, \ldots$. Each pair (M, M_i) has been checked by means of the I/O-equivalence checking approach described in the previous section. Additionally, each model M and each mutant M_i has been represented using the CSP process algebra [17], so that the FDR3 model checker [7] could be used to check I/O-equivalence by means of CSP trace equivalence. For each equivalence check, the performance of our equivalence checker was compared to that of FDR3.

3.2   Models Used

For our case study, five models have been selected, two of these were already described in previous publications [11].

3.2.1   Airbag Controller

The most complex model used for our case study describes the behaviour of an airbag controller and is described in the following section as an example of the complexity our approach can handle. This model has two floating point inputs s1 and s2, describing the acceleration measured by the acceleration sensors the airbag controller is evaluating, and two Boolean output values, fire and defect, which are set to *true* iff the airbag should be triggered or the sensors are regarded as defect, respectively. Furthermore, there is a Boolean input variable *clk* that toggles iff there is a new pair of input values to be processed.

If the system is not defect, and if the airbag has not been triggered, the controller waits for a new pair of input values. Such a pair will be checked for plausibility first. A difference of more than 5% is considered to be implausible. For a pair of plausible input values the following relation holds: $s1 \in [s2 \cdot 0.95, s2 \cdot 1.05]$. An internal integer counter variable plausibleCtr is set to zero if this is not the case. Also, another internal integer counter variable errCtr is incremented. If afterwards the relation errCtr ≥ 3 holds, the system is regarded as defect, thus defect is set to *true* and the controller halts, otherwise, the next pair of input values is awaited. However, if the sensor values are plausible, plausibleCtr is incremented and the relation plausibleCtr ≥ 3 checked. If it holds, errCnt is reset to zero. In any case of plausible sensor values, the sensor values are compared to a threshold, in our model this is the floating point value 3.0. If one of the values does not exceed the threshold, another internal integer counter variable crashCnt is reset to zero, and the next pair of values awaited. However, if both exceed the threshold, crashCnt is incremented. If this counter equals 3 after the increment, this is considered as a trustworthy crash indication; thus the output fire is set to *true*, and the system halts. Figure 4 shows a SysML state machine describing this behaviour.

3.2.2   Further Models

Table 1 summarises the properties of all models used for the case study. Apart from the number of input variables, output variables and size of state space after applying our approach, it lists an approximation of the input domain size.

For SysML models, the size calculation $|\mathcal{D}_I|$ of the input domain is based on the lower and upper bounds of each input variable type and the number of distinct representable values between these bounds. As CSP only admits data types based on integral numbers, all variables representing floating point numbers had to be approximated as integer variables using one of two methods:

1. Two integers modelling one floating point number, where one models the integral part, and the other the fractional part.
2. Scaling all floating point numbers in a model by the same factor sufficiently large to allow for discarding the fractional part.

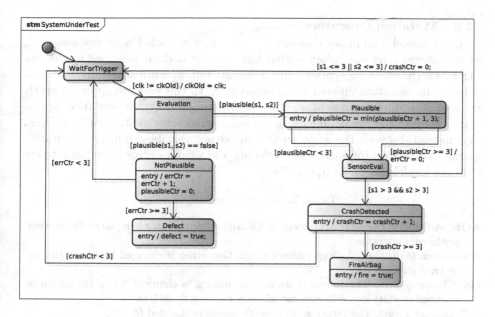

Fig. 4. SysML state machine describing the behaviour of an airbag controller.

Due to these changes, all models using floating point numbers show different input space sizes for SysML and CSP models. The size of the CSP model input space is denoted by $|\mathcal{D}_{I,\text{CSP}}|$.

Table 1. Model input and state space size for the original models used for the case study.

Model	$|\mathcal{V}_I|$	$|\mathcal{V}_O|$	$|\mathcal{D}_I|$	$|\mathcal{D}_{I,\text{CSP}}|$
alarm1	1	1	2×10^2	2×10^2
alarm2	1	1	1.1×10^9	2×10^2
csm	2	3	1.4×10^{18}	3.3×10^{12}
turn_ind	4	3	8.8×10^9	10^3
airbag	3	2	2.4×10^{18}	2.5×10^5

Model *alarm1* is the simple alarm system used in the examples above, *alarm2* is a more complex variant of *alarm1*. Model *csm* specifies a ceiling speed monitor for a train control system; it is described in [4]. Model *turn_ind* describes a turn indication controller for cars, taking left/right flashing and emergency flashing into account; it is a simplified version of the complete model described in [15].

3.2.3 Mutation Operators

For every model used in our case study – from now on called *reference model* – a set of mutated *implementation models* has been created. At least one implementation was chosen to be syntactically different, but semantically equivalent, and at least one mutation differed in its behaviour. To this end, we applied exactly one mutation operator out of a set of commonly used syntax mutation operators [1, 2, 13] to the SysML reference model, guaranteeing syntactically different implementations with the same input and output variables. Thirteen mutation operators described in Table 2 were selected and used for error injection into the reference models, as far as applicable.

Table 2. Mutation operators.

AOR *Arithmetic Operator Replacement.* An arithmetic operator is replaced by another arithmetic operator.

AS *Associativity Shift.* An expression's evaluation order is changed by bracketing or re-bracketing.

CS *Change Source.* The source state of a transition is changed, i.e. a transition is changed to start in a different but already existing SysML state.

CT *Change Target.* The target state of a transition is changed (s. *CS*).

EN *Expression Negation.* A first order logic expression is negated.

LOR *Logic Operator Replacement.* A logic operator is replaced by another logic operator.

REEA *REplace Entry Action.* A SysML state's entry action is arbitrarily modified but not removed.

RETA *REplace Transition Action.* A transition's action is arbitrarily modified but not removed.

RMEA *ReMove Entry Action.* A SysML state's entry action is removed.

RMTA *ReMove Transition Action.* A transition's action is removed.

ROR *Relational Operator Replacement.* A relational operator is replaced by another relational operator.

SGF *Set Guard False.* The guard condition of a transitions is set to false, effectively removing the transition.

SGT *Set Guard True.* The guard condition of a transition is set to true.

3.2.4 CSP Models

The CSP models were manually created by translating SysML reference models and implementations into CSP, taking into account the discretisation of floating point input variables as described above.

3.3 Results

Every SysML reference model and each associated implementation were checked for I/O-equivalence using the method described in this paper. The test suites used to check the transductors for I/O-equivalence as described in Sect. 2 were calculated using the *W-Method* [5, 20]. The corresponding CSP reference and implementation models were checked for trace equivalence using the FDR3 model checker. Each check was limited to 40 GBytes of RAM and 2 h execution time (wallclock time).

Regarding the correctness of the checks, both our model checking method and the FDR3 tool detected the same I/O-equivalence violations, as was expected.

For the *alarm1* model, the FDR3 tool was approximately 70 times slower than our checker and needed approximately 11 times more memory. These factors are calculated as the averages of all 10 checks performed for the alarm1 model and its 10 mutated implementations.

For the *alarm2* model, the FDR3 tool was approximately 22 times slower and needed 7 times more memory. This value was calculated from 11 mutations checked against the reference model.

For all model pairs derived from the models *csm*, *turn_ind* and *airbag*, the CSP model checker was not able to complete the calculation within the resource limits set, while our checker completed these checks with durations from 27 s to 1217 s. The average checking time needed by our checker was 365 s.

All performance measurements described here included the time for abstracting the original model to its finite state machine and the time for creating a counter example in case of failures. A detailed tabular view documenting all checks and comparisons performed is given in [12].

4   Conclusion

We have presented a new algorithm for I/O-equivalence checking of models with infinite input domains but finite domains for internal state and outputs. The underlying method has been based on a new complete input equivalence class testing strategy previously developed by the second author and his research group.

Our approach clearly outperforms the FDR3 model checker. The cause is easy to understand, since FDR3 does not implement the equivalence class construction techniques that were available for our checker. As a consequence, FDR3 needed to explore the models by explicitly checking a very large number of input values instead of restricting the investigation to small numbers of input classes. This comparison shows that the input equivalence class construction method advocated in this paper can be a valuable extension to other model checking tools as well. Additionally, the results presented here are another example of the closeness between testing and model checking methods.

The algorithms needed for abstracting a nondeterministic I/O-state transition system to its finite state machine have exponential worst case complexity. Future work will focus on mitigating this problem by means of further distributing the algorithms involved on multiple threads and CPU cores.

References

1. Aichernig, B.K., Brandl, H., Jöbstl, E., Krenn, W.: Model-based mutation testing of hybrid systems. In: de Boer, F.S., Bonsangue, M.M., Hallerstede, S., Leuschel, M. (eds.) FMCO 2009. LNCS, vol. 6286, pp. 228–249. Springer, Heidelberg (2010). doi:10.1007/978-3-642-17071-3_12
2. Aichernig, B.K., Lorber, F., Ničković, D.: Time for mutants — model-based mutation testing with timed automata. In: Veanes, M., Viganò, L. (eds.) TAP 2013. LNCS, vol. 7942, pp. 20–38. Springer, Heidelberg (2013). doi:10.1007/978-3-642-38916-0_2
3. Alur, R., Madhusudan, P.: Decision problems for timed automata: a survey. In: Bernardo, M., Corradini, F. (eds.) SFM-RT 2004. LNCS, vol. 3185, pp. 1–24. Springer, Heidelberg (2004). doi:10.1007/978-3-540-30080-9_1
4. Braunstein, C., Haxthausen, A.E., Huang, W., Hübner, F., Peleska, J., Schulze, U., Vu Hong, L.: Complete model-based equivalence class testing for the ETCS ceiling speed monitor. In: Merz, S., Pang, J. (eds.) ICFEM 2014. LNCS, vol. 8829, pp. 380–395. Springer, Cham (2014). doi:10.1007/978-3-319-11737-9_25
5. Chow, T.S.: Testing software design modeled by finite-state machines. IEEE Trans. Softw. Eng. (SE) **4**(3), 178–186 (1978)
6. Dingel, J., Filkorn, T.: Model checking for infinite state systems using data abstraction, assumption-commitment style reasoning and theorem proving. In: Wolper, P. (ed.) CAV 1995. LNCS, vol. 939, pp. 54–69. Springer, Heidelberg (1995). doi:10.1007/3-540-60045-0_40
7. Gibson-Robinson, T., Armstrong, P., Boulgakov, A., Roscoe, A.W.: FDR3: a parallel refinement checker for CSP. Int. J. Softw. Tools Technol. Transf. **18**(2), 149–167 (2016). http://dx.doi.org/10.1007/s10009-015-0377-y
8. Henzinger, T.A., Ho, P., Wong-Toi, H.: HYTECH: a model checker for hybrid systems. STTT **1**(1–2), 110–122 (1997). https://doi.org/10.1007/s100090050008
9. Huang, W., Peleska, J.: Complete model-based equivalence class testing. STTT **18**(3), 265–283 (2016). http://dx.doi.org/10.1007/s10009-014-0356-8
10. Huang, W., Peleska, J.: Complete model-based equivalence class testing for nondeterministic systems. Form. Asp. Comput. **29**(2), 335–364 (2017). http://dx.doi.org/10.1007/s00165-016-0402-2
11. Hübner, F., Huang, W., Peleska, J.: Experimental evaluation of a novel equivalence class partition testing strategy. In: Blanchette, J.C., Kosmatov, N. (eds.) TAP 2015. LNCS, vol. 9154, pp. 155–172. Springer, Cham (2015). doi:10.1007/978-3-319-21215-9_10
12. Krafczyk, N.: Äquivalenzprüfung für Zustandstransitionssysteme mittels Eingabeäquivalenzklassenpartitionierung. Master's thesis, University of Bremen, November 2016
13. Krenn, W., Schlick, R., Tiran, S., Aichernig, B., Jobstl, E., Brandl, H.: MoMut: UML model-based mutation testing for UML. In: 2015 IEEE 8th International Conference on Software Testing, Verification and Validation (ICST), pp. 1–8. IEEE (2015)
14. Object Management Group: OMG Systems Modeling Language (OMG SysML), Version 1.4. Technical report, Object Management Group (2015). http://www.omg.org/spec/SysML/1.4
15. Peleska, J., et al.: A real-world benchmark model for testing concurrent real-time systems in the automotive domain. In: Wolff, B., Zaïdi, F. (eds.) ICTSS 2011. LNCS, vol. 7019, pp. 146–161. Springer, Heidelberg (2011). doi:10.1007/978-3-642-24580-0_11

16. Peleska, J., Huang, W.: Model-based testing strategies and their (in)dependence on syntactic model representations. In: Beek, M.H., Gnesi, S., Knapp, A. (eds.) FMICS/AVoCS -2016. LNCS, vol. 9933, pp. 3–21. Springer, Cham (2016). doi:10. 1007/978-3-319-45943-1_1
17. Roscoe, A.W.: Understanding Concurrent Systems. Springer, London (2010). doi:10.1007/978-1-84882-258-0
18. Springintveld, J., Vaandrager, F., D'Argenio, P.: Testing timed automata. Theor. Comput. Sci. **254**(1–2), 225–257 (2001)
19. Sulzmann, M., Zechner, A.: Model checking DSL-generated C source code. In: Donaldson, A., Parker, D. (eds.) SPIN 2012. LNCS, vol. 7385, pp. 241–247. Springer, Heidelberg (2012). doi:10.1007/978-3-642-31759-0_18
20. Vasilevskii, M.P.: Failure diagnosis of automata. Kibernetika (Transl.) **4**, 98–108 (1973)

Using Robustness Testing to Handle Incomplete Verification Results When Combining Verification and Testing Techniques

Stefan Huster[✉], Jonas Ströbele, Jürgen Ruf, Thomas Kropf, and Wolfgang Rosenstiel

Department of Computer Science, University of Tübingen, Sand 14, 72076 Tübingen, Germany {huster,stroebele,ruf,kropf,rosenstiel}@informatik.uni-tuebingen.de

Abstract. Modular verification and dynamic testing techniques are often combined to validate complex software systems. Formal verification is used to cover all input spaces and program paths. However, due to the high complexity of modern software systems, they might not achieve complete verification results. Dynamic testing techniques can easily be applied to any type of software. Current approaches use them to handle incomplete verification results by validating unverified sections. This way of combining verification and testing ignores the fact that tests can only be used to show the presence of errors, but not their absence. Undiscovered errors pose the risk to trigger further errors in vulnerable code sections. Vulnerable sections are modularly verified, but depend on the guarantees of the tested code. We include robustness testing to analyse the influence of undiscovered errors. The generated robustness tests simulate failed guarantees within the tested code. The triggered response to those simulated errors helps the developer in adding additional error handling code. This makes the system more robust against undiscovered errors and guards it against uncontrolled crashes and unexpected behaviour in case of software failures. In the second part of this paper, we introduce a reference-architecture to generate and apply robustness tests. This architecture has been applied to multiple case studies and helped to identify potential errors yet undiscovered by generated test cases.

Keywords: Software verification · Robustness testing · Test vector generation

1 Introduction

Modular verification and dynamic testing techniques are often combined to validate complex software systems. Verification techniques are used to guarantee that an implementation matches its formal specification. For object oriented programs (OOPs), the specification is often defined as a set of conditions such

Published by Springer International Publishing AG 2017. All Rights Reserved
N. Yevtushenko et al. (Eds.): ICTSS 2017, LNCS 10533, pp. 54–70, 2017.
DOI: 10.1007/978-3-319-67549-7_4

as pre- and post-conditions and invariants. Modular verification techniques [1] analyse this type of specification based on a generated set of proof obligations (also known as verification goals). A proof obligation (POG) is similar to a Hoare-Triple $\{P\}$ S $\{Q\}$ [2]. The POG contains a program segment (Hoare: S), a set of assumptions (Hoare: $\{P\}$), and a guarantee (Hoare: $\{Q\}$) [3]. While considering all assumptions, the verification framework has to verify whether each possible execution of the embedded program section fulfils the defined guarantee. Assumptions made by one proof obligation must be ensured by another one. Only the validity of all proof obligations implies the correctness of the entire software system. Especially OOP concepts such as inheritance and (recursive) aggregation cause an infinite number of feasible control flows and thereby a high level of complexity. Due to this complexity, formal verification techniques are rarely capable of achieving complete verification results.

We use Listing 1.1 as running example to introduce our methodology. The listed method cannot be verified using the verification framework Microsoft Code Contracts [1]. It is part of a program to solve the Cutting Stock problem [4]. This problem is about cutting standard-sized pieces of material into pieces of specified sizes. The listed method is used to add new cutting lengths (Cut) to the current cutting layout (Bar). It checks whether the available material length is long enough to add the given piece length. It analyses the summarised lengths of all added cuts plus the required minimum space between two cuts (line 14). The value of UsedLength must always be smaller than the total material length. This is required by the invariant in line 7. Figure 1 shows how Code Contracts claims that this invariant is not guaranteed on exit. This illustrates how specifications remain unverified.

```
public bool AddCut(double cutLength)
{
    Contract.Requires(cutLength > 0);
    if ((Length - usedLength - (Cuts.Count * minspace)) < cutLength)
    {
        return false;
    }
    usedLength += cutLength;
    Cuts.Add(cutLength);
    return true;
}
```

> CodeContracts: invariant unproven: usedLength <= Length

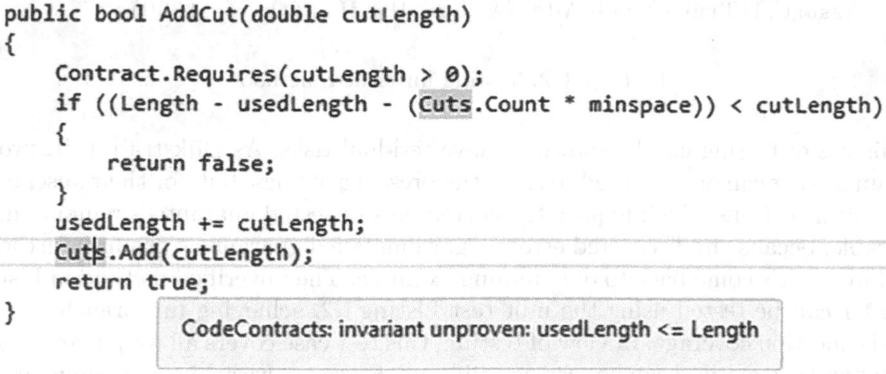

Fig. 1. Code Contracts marks unverified invariant

In such cases, where some proof obligations remain unverified, current approaches ensure the correctness of those proof obligations by exhaustive testing.

---

[1] https://www.microsoft.com/en-us/research/project/code-contracts/, Last visit June 2017.

```
1 public class Bar {
2    public double Length, UsedLength, MinSpace;
3    public List<Double> Cuts;
4    [ContractInvariantMethod]
5    private void ObjectInvariant() {
6      Contract.Invariant(UsedLength >= 0);
7      Contract.Invariant(UsedLength <= Length);
8      Contract.Invariant(Cuts != null);
9    }
10   public Bar(double length, double minSpace) {[...]}
11   public bool AddCut(double cutLength) {
12     Contract.Requires(cutLength > 0);
13     double usedSpace = Cuts.Count * MinSpace;
14     if ((Length - UsedLength - usedSpace) < cutLength) {
15       return false;
16     }
17     UsedLength += cutLength;
18     Cuts.Add(cutLength);
19     return true;
20   }
21 }
```

Listing 1.1. Code Contracts: Unverified Invariant

```
1 public void TestAddCut() {
2    Bar bar = new Bar(5000, 5);
3    bool couldAdd = bar.AddCut(1500);
4    Assert.IsTrue(couldAdd && bar.UsedLength == 1500);
5    couldAdd = bar.AddCut(5500);
6    Assert.IsTrue(!couldAdd && bar.UsedLength == 1500);
7 }
```

Listing 1.2. Testing unverified method

This use of testing can be shown to have residual risks. As Dijkstra put it, program testing can only be used to show the presence of bugs, but not their absence. Program sections which require the correctness of tested guarantees remain vulnerable, because undiscovered errors regarding failed guarantees produce further failures. Let's come back to our running example. The unverified method in Listing 1.1 can be tested using the unit test Listing 1.2, achieving full branch, path and condition coverage. In view of testing, this test case covers all major coverage rates and the method can be seen as validated. However, we achieve the same testing results when replacing line 14 by if ((Length - usedSpace)< cutLength). This would be a major bug, because this line ignores the used material length. This bug allows to add more cuts to the bar than available material space. This could be tested when executing line 4 of our test case multiple times in a row. This simple example illustrates how testing can achieve good coverage rates while missing important defects.

This paper introduces a new approach that uses robustness testing to analyse the influence of such undiscovered errors. We initialise invalid program states to simulate failed guarantees and inspect the corresponding behaviour of vulnerable program sections. Our goal is to support the developer in adding additional error handling code on critical locations in order to secure vulnerable sections against potential failures.

The remainder of this paper is structured as follows: Sect. 2 describes related work and current tools. Section 3 describes how we use robustness testing to analyse the influence of undiscovered errors. Section 4 defines one reference implementation to generate the defined type of robustness tests. Section 5 presents our results in comparison to current tools. Section 6 concludes the paper and presents future work.

2   Related Work

Several methodologies and tools already exist which combine formal verification and dynamic testing.

Christakis et al. [5–7] present a methodology that combines verification and semantic testing. Different static verification models are used together to verify the software under test in a sound way. Assumptions made by one prover, e.g. regarding numerical overflows, are ensured by another. Unverified assumptions are subsequently tested. The symbolic testing is guided to cover specifically those properties that could not been verified.

Czech et al. [8] present a method to create residual programs based on failed proof obligations. They reduce the number of required test cases, by testing only those control flows that have not been verified.

Kanig et al. [9] present an approach that uses explicit assumptions to verify ADA programs. Unverified assumptions are tested by generated test suites.

Code Contracts [10], Pex [11] and Moles [12] is the current Microsoft tool chain for software verification and symbolic test case execution. Code Contracts can be used to verify C# programs and supports contracts such as pre- and postconditions. Pex and Moles have been integrated into Visual Studio 2015 under the names IntelliTest and Fakes. Moles/Fakes is used to isolate test cases and can replace any method with a delegate. Pex iteratively applies symbolic execution to create test vectors in order to cover all branches of the method under test. The Microsoft tool chain does not provide any standard methodology to combine both tools.

In summary, all mentioned approaches try to reduce the number of required test cases by testing only unverified control flows. They try to handle incomplete verification results by achieving high test coverage on the unverified software components. No mentioned approach handled the residual risk of tested source code on vulnerable code sections. Therefore, they mark code sections as formally correct, even when those sections may contain serious errors caused by failed guarantees in tested code.

3   Methodology

The presented methodology integrates into existing workflows combining formal verification and dynamic testing techniques. Figure 2 shows an abstract illustration on how current approaches combine verification and testing. The input to those workflows is the program source code and its specification. The proof-obligation-generator analyses the source code and the specification to generate a set of proof obligations. In the second step, those proof obligations are verified by the verification backend. This step divides the set of proof obligations into a verified and unverified subset. In step 3, unverified proof obligations are further analysed by a test case generation framework. Those frameworks use symbolic execution (also known as concolic testing) to automatically create test cases and test vectors to explicitly cover control flows of unverified proof obligations.

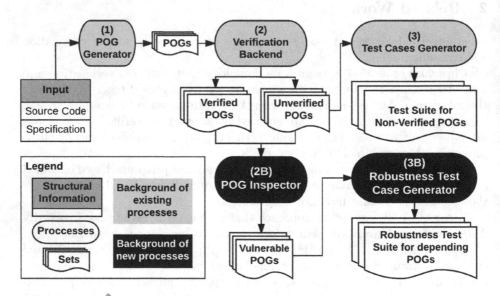

Fig. 2. Abstract workflow to combine formal verification and testing techniques

The presented methodology adds two new steps to existing workflows. In step 2B, the POG inspector analyses the dependencies between verified and unverified proof obligations in order to identify vulnerable code sections. Step 3B generates robustness tests for those vulnerable POGs. These tests simulate errors within the tested code and uncover locations where additional error handling and sanity checks are required.

This section starts by defining proof obligations, then describes how to identify vulnerable code sections, illustrates their risks and finally explains how to generate corresponding robustness tests.

3.1   Proof Obligations

We start by defining the input to our methodology and corresponding symbols to refer to the different components of object oriented programs. The input to the proof obligation inspector is a set of verified and unverified proof obligations (POG). The POGs are generated based on the source code of an object-oriented program **Prog** and its specification set $\Gamma_{\mathbf{Prog}}$. This program contains classes $c \in \mathcal{C}_{\mathbf{Prog}}$. Each class can contain methods $m \in \mathcal{M}_c$ and fields $f \in \mathcal{F}_c$. A method consists of an ordered set of statements $s \in \langle S \rangle_m$. The list of method parameters is $\bar{m}$. The specification can contain preconditions Γ_m^{pre}, postconditions Γ_m^{post}, and object invariants Γ_c^{inv}.

The proof of the overall correctness is divided into a generated set of proof obligations. Each proof obligation covers one control flow:

Definition 1 (Control Flow). *A control flow $\tilde{S} = \langle s_0, \dots, s_n \rangle$ is a set of statements $s_i \in S_m$, $m \in \mathcal{M}_c$. Between each pair of statements s_i and s_{i+1} exists one unique transition.*

Definition 2 (Proof Obligation). *The set of all generated proof obligations is Π. A proof obligation $\pi = (\Omega, \tilde{S}, \phi)$ is a triple, combining a set of assumptions (Ω), a control flow $(\tilde{S})$, and a verification goal (ϕ). We refer to the method which contains the control flow $\tilde{S}$ by m_π. Assumptions and goals are represented as boolean predicates. A proof obligation is verified iff one can show that each execution of $\tilde{S}$ validates ϕ while assuming Ω. The predicate $\Psi(\pi)$ is true iff π can be verified. A proof obligation is always generated based on a specification $\gamma \in \Gamma$, we write $\Pi(\gamma) \rightarrow \pi$.*

Let's apply this to our running example. Here we can extract two work flows and POGs: $\tilde{s}_1 = \langle s_{12}, s_{13}, s_{14}, s_{15} \rangle$ and $\tilde{s}_2 = \langle s_{12}, s_{13}, s_{14}, s_{17}, s_{18}, s_{19} \rangle$. The indexes s_i mark the global line number of the corresponding statement. The unverified invariant $\phi_1 = (UsedLength <= Length)$ is covered by two proof obligations: $\Omega_1 = \{(cutLength > 0), (CutLength! = null)\}$ in $\pi_1 = (\Omega_1, \tilde{s}_1, \phi_1)$ and $\pi_2 = (\Omega_1, \tilde{s}_2, \phi_1)$.

3.2   Identifying Vulnerable Proof Obligations

The verification framework (Step 2 in Fig. 2) divides the set of POGs Π into a set of verified POGs $\Pi^+ = \{\pi \in \Pi | \Psi(\pi)\}$ and a set of unverified POGs $\Pi^- = \{\pi \in \Pi | \neg \Psi(\pi)\}$. Modular verification techniques build their correctness proof upon dependencies between different POGs. Those dependencies must be considered when testing unverified POGs. In step 3B of Fig. 2, we identify POGs depending on unverified code. We call them vulnerable proof obligations.

Definition 3 (Vulnerable Proof Obligations). *One proof obligation $\pi_i = (\Omega_i, \tilde{s}_i, \phi_i)$ depends on a different proof obligation $\pi_j = (\Omega_j, \tilde{s}_j, \phi_j)$ iff the assumption list Ω_i contains the verification goal ϕ_j:*

$$\pi_i \vdash \pi_j \Leftrightarrow \exists \omega \in \Omega_i | \omega \equiv \phi_j \tag{1}$$

One proof obligation π_i is vulnerable iff $\pi_i \vdash \pi_j \wedge \neg \Psi(\pi_j)$. The set of all vulnerable proof obligations is defined as $\Pi^? = \{\pi_i | \pi_i \vdash \pi_j \wedge \neg \Psi(\pi_j)\}$.

```
1  public List<Bar> CreateBars(List<double> cutLengths,
       Dictionary<double, int> materials) {
2      List<Bar> cuttingLayouts = new List<Bar>();
3      foreach(double cLen in cutLengths) {
4          bool couldAdd = false;
5          foreach(Bar bar in cuttingLayouts) {
6              if(bar.AddCut(cLen)) { couldAdd = true; break; }
7          }
8          if(!couldAdd) {
9              double bfLength = Double.MaxValue;
10             foreach(double matLength in materials.Keys) {
11                 double offcut = matLength - cLen;
12                 if (offcut > 0 && offcut < bfLength - cLen &&
                        materials[matLength] > 0) {
13                     bfLength = matLength;
14                 }
15             }
16             if(bfLength < Double.MaxValue) {
17                 Bar newBar = new Bar(bfLength, 5);
18                 newBar.AddCut(cLen);
19                 cuttingLayouts.Add(newBar);
20                 materials[bfLength] -= 1;
21             }
22         }
23     return cuttingLayouts;
24  }
```

Listing 1.3. Implicit depending code

Let's have a look what dependencies and vulnerable code section we can identify in our running example. Listing 1.3 shows another code section of the Cutting Stock program. To conserve space, we list this example without its specification. This method creates different cutting layouts using the `AddCut` method. The above defined POG $\pi_2 = (\Omega_1, \tilde{s}_2, \phi_1)$ of `AddCut` requires a valid precondition. Therefore, this POG depends on all POGs covering this precondition. One of those POGs is generated based on the following control flow $\tilde{s}_3 = \langle s_2, s_3, s_4, s_5, s_6, \ldots \rangle$ for the `CreateBars` method $\pi_3 = (\Omega_3, \tilde{s}_3, (CLen > 0))$. This control flow must guarantee that the used cut length is greater than zero before calling `AddCut`. We call this an explicit dependency. There exists another kind of dependency for all control flows calling `AddCut`. These code sections depend on the invariants of `Bar`, such as π_2, even if these invariants are not explicitly addressed. This is the case because every method requires valid object states when calling their methods. We call this an implicit dependency. Such dependencies are expressed as assumptions and are handled during the POG generation. However, we remember that the POG π_2 could not be verified. Therefore, all POGs calling `AddCut` in their control flow are considered as vulnerable.

3.3   Spreading Errors - the Risk of Vulnerable Proof Obligations

The main risk is the spreading of undiscovered errors in tested code into seemingly unrelated or previously verified code sections. In such cases, errors might be difficult to find, because the error source might be hidden in the method call stack. This is illustrated in Fig. 3. The method call graph shows two methods, m_1 and m_3, both calling method m_2. The precondition γ_3 of method m_2 must be respected by both calling methods m_1 and m_3. Therefore, the precondition is covered by two POGs: π_{3a} for the control flow in m_1 and π_{3b} for the control flow in m_3. The postcondition γ_4 of m_2 is covered by the POG $\pi_4 = \Pi(\gamma_4)$. It depends on the correctness of the precondition γ_3: $\pi_4 \vdash \{\pi_{3a}, \pi_{3b}\}$. Let us assume that the POG π_{3a} can not be verified. This makes π_4 vulnerable because it now depends on an unverified POG. Errors in m_1 may cause a failed precondition γ_3, which produces errors in m_2 even though m_2 has been modularly verified. The result might be an invalid return value of m_2, which in turn may affect the code section in m_1 handling this return value. Thereby, even the postcondition γ_2 of method m_1 may fail.

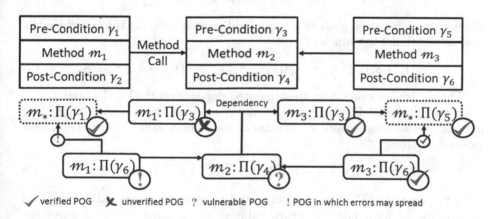

Fig. 3. Method call graph (Top) and possible POG dependency graph (Bottom)

The goal of our approach is to identify such risks by testing the method m_2 assuming that γ_3 has failed. This allows us to add additional checks to prevent such an error propagation.

3.4   Generating Robustness Tests

In general, robustness tests are used to analyse the behaviour of a program under hostile circumstances. This can be done in different ways. In some cases, it is sufficient to call a method with invalid parameter values. In other cases it is required to modify the tested code in order to simulate failures. In such a scenario, we speak of "Mocked Test Cases".

Definition 4 (Mocked Test Case). *A test case* $t \in T$ *with test vector* $\vec{t}$ *executes the control flow* $\tilde{s}$: $t \to \tilde{s}$. *A mocked test case* $t[\eta \mapsto \acute{\eta}] \to \tilde{s}$ *replaces in* $\tilde{s}$ *the symbol* η *by* $\acute{\eta}$ *before executing* $\tilde{s}$.

Definition 5 (Robustness Tests). *A robustness tests* $t \in T^?$ *is used to simulate failed guarantees by injecting invalid symbol values. We use following syntax to express the requirements on a symbol's value:* $[\![\gamma]\!]_v \to \bot$. *When evaluating* γ *using value* v, γ *must evaluate to false. Additional test oracles are defined using following syntax:* $[\![t]\!] \to \bot \ \phi$ *The evaluation of test case* t *must fulfil the boolean condition* ϕ. *Invalid symbols must be set during the test case execution and the only location to define them is within the robustness test parameter vector. Therefore it must be possible to back trace those values to the test vector. We use the right arrow syntax* $\to$ *to express this trace, e.g.* $\vec{t} \to \vec{m} \to \mathcal{F}$. *This syntax expresses that the original test vector* $\vec{t}$ *is used to fill the method parameter list* $\vec{m}$. *These parameter values* $\vec{m}$ *are used to set the class field values* $\mathcal{F}$.

We create one robustness test for each POG π_i depending on an unverified POG:

$$T^? = \{ \forall_i \pi_i = (\Omega_i, \tilde{S}_i, \phi_i) \in \Pi^? \ : \ t \to \tilde{S}_i \} \tag{2}$$

We use the verification goals of all proof obligations covering the tested control flow as additional test oracles:

$$\forall_i (t_i \to \tilde{S}_i) \in T^? \ \forall_j \pi_j = (\Omega_j, \tilde{S}_j, \phi_j) \in \Pi \ : \ [\![t_i]\!] \to \phi_j \mid \tilde{S}_i \subseteq \tilde{S}_j \tag{3}$$

The way failed guarantees are simulated depends on the POG's origin:

If the unverified POG π_i was generated to cover the precondition γ_i^{pre} of method $\acute{m}$, we must create a robustness test which calls $\acute{m}$ with parameter values $\vec{t}$ violating γ_i^{pre}:

$$\forall_j \pi_j \vdash \pi_i \mid \neg \Psi(\pi_i) : t \to \tilde{S}_j, \vec{t} \mid \ [\![\gamma_i^{pre}]\!]_{\vec{t}} \to \bot \tag{4}$$

If the unverified POG π_i was generated to cover the postcondition γ_i^{post} of method $\acute{m}$, we must inject a return value of $\acute{m}$ violating γ_i^{post}. To inject the simulated return value, we must create a mocked version $\vec{m}$ of $\acute{m}$. The mocked version uses an extended parameter list $\vec{m}$, which allows us to directly set the return value based on $\vec{t}$. We refer to the return value of $\vec{m}$ by $[\![\vec{m}]\!]$.

$$\forall_j \pi_j \vdash \pi_i \mid \neg \Psi(\pi_i) : t[\acute{m} \mapsto \vec{m}] \to \tilde{S}_j, \vec{t} \to \vec{m} \to [\![\vec{m}]\!] \mid \ [\![\gamma_i^{pos}]\!]_{[\![\vec{m}]\!]} \to \bot \tag{5}$$

If the unverified POG π_i was generated to cover an invariant γ_i^{inv} of class c_i, we must inject an invalid object instance. Therefore we must distinguish between two further cases: (1) The POG was generated based on a constructor $\acute{ctor}$. (2) The POG was generated based on a method $\acute{m}$. In the first case, the invalid object instance can be created by a mocked constructor method $\vec{ctor}$. The mocked constructor uses an extended parameter list $\vec{ctor}$, which allows us to directly set all class fields $\mathcal{F}$ based on $\vec{t}$.

$$\forall_j \pi_j \vdash \pi_i \mid \neg \Psi(\pi_i) : t[\acute{ctor} \mapsto \vec{ctor}] \to \tilde{S}_j, \vec{t} \to \vec{ctor} \to \mathcal{F} \mid \ [\![\gamma_i^{inv}]\!]_{\mathcal{F}} \to \bot \tag{6}$$

```
1 public bool AddCutMocked(double cutLength, double usedLength,
    double length) {
2   if ((Length - UsedLength - (Cuts.Count * MinSpace)) <
    cutLength)
3   { return false; }
4   UsedLength += cutLength;
5   Cuts.Add(cutLength);
6   UsedLength = usedLength;   // Inject invalid field values
7   Length = length;           // based on parameter list
8   return true;
9 }
```

Listing 1.4. Mocked method to inject simulated errors

In the second case, the invalid instance must be simulated by a mocked copy $\ddot{m}$ of $\dot{m}$. The mocked method must set all referenced class fields $\mathcal{F}$ of c_i based on its own extended parameter list $\vec{\ddot{m}}$.

$$\forall_j \ \pi_j \vdash \pi_i \mid \neg \Psi(\pi_i) : t[\ddot{ctor} \mapsto ctor] \rightarrow \tilde{S}_j, \vec{t} \rightarrow \vec{\ddot{m}} \rightarrow \mathcal{F} \mid [\![\gamma_i^{inv}]\!]_{\mathcal{F}} \rightarrow \perp \quad (7)$$

In our running example, the failed POG was generated to cover an invariant during the execution of AddBar. Therefore, we need to inject the simulated error through a mocked method, which is Listing 1.4. We have added the additional parameters $UsedLength$ and $length$ to the original parameter list. These values are used in line 6 and 7 to set the invalid object state. Now, we only need to replace calls to AddBar by calls to AddBarMocked when testing CreateBars. We can simulate the invalid object state of Bar by calling AddBarMocked, e.g. with usedLength=7000 and length=5000. The results of the robustness test will show that the created cutting layouts are invalid. Now we know that we need to add extra sanity checks to validate the correctness of cuttingLayouts before return them. This prevents undiscovered errors in AddBar from spreading into code sections where the origin of invalid cutting layouts may be difficult to find.

4   Reference-Implementation

Applying robustness tests and injecting simulated errors requires more effort than regular testing. Especially creating all required mocks is very labour intense when doing it manually. Therefore, we have implemented our methodology into a new mocking framework to face three major challenges: First, we need to ensure that every tested method is visible and accessible within the test suite. Second, we need to initialise object instances with deliberate states hosting the tested methods. Third, we must create the possibility to inject simulated errors to apply robustness testing. We meet those challenges by creating three different layers of mocked code: The first layer mocks the original source code to provide access to all class fields and methods. The second layer contains the mocked test methods to validate unverified POGs and vulnerable code sections. All steps in

Algorithm: InitList(c)

Globals: $RecursionDepth, MaxRecursion, CollectionSize$

begin

    if $RecursionDepth[c] > MaxRecursion$ **then** **return** $\{c\}$

    $IP \leftarrow \varnothing$

    $RecursionDepth[c] + +$

    foreach $f \in \mathcal{F}_c$ **do**

        if $IsSimpleType(f)$ **then** $IP = IP \cup Type(f)$

        else if $IsCollection(f)$ **then**

            for $i = 0 \rightarrow CollectionSize$ **do**

                if $HasKeyType(f)$ **then** $IP = IP \cup InitList(KeyType(f))$

                $IP = IP \cup InitList(ValueType(f))$

            end

        else $IP = IP \cup InitList(Type(f))$

    end

    $RecursionDepth[c] - -$

    return IP;

end

Algorithm 1. Algorithm to generate initialisation parameter lists

both layers can be applied automatically and do not require manual work. The third layer contains the actual test cases.

Layer 1 contains a mocked version $\overline{\text{Prog}}$ of **Prog** to make the complete code base testable. We need to consider that we do not want to test complete methods but explicit control flows of unverified POGs. Those control flows might be extracted from private or abstract methods. In $\overline{\text{Prog}}$ we set the visibility of each class field and tested method to public. We have chosen this way, because it is language independent. other solutions for accessing private symbols require language specific runtime flags or reflection APIs. We remove the abstract attribute from each tested class and method. Instead, we add an empty default implementation and a corresponding default return value to each pure abstract method so our program can be compiled. To be able to initialise every object type, we add a default constructor and a static initialisation method to each user-defined type. To create those initialisation methods, we use the recursive Algorithm 1 to inspect aggregated object types $c \in C$. The algorithm extracts a list with parameters representing the aggregated primitive values. To that end, we also create items to fill used collection types, such as Lists, Arrays or Dictionaries. The number of items are added is set with the constant $CollectionSize$. Recursively analysing the key and value types, we merge the resulting parameter lists. To prevent endless recursion steps, we track the recursion depth with the map $RecursionDepth(c \rightarrow \mathbb{N})$ until the maximum recursion depth $MaxRecursion$ has been reached.

Layer 2 contains the mocked methods and constructors to inject invalid return types and object states. Invalid return values and object states are injected by setting corresponding class fields or by creating corresponding return values, instead of computing them. We use Algorithm 1 to extract the list of required primitive types in order to manipulate or initialise the aggregated object. These extracted primitive types are added to the parameter list of the mocked method. Thereby, we can use the parameter list to explicitly control return values and object states. An example is given in Listing 1.7, in lines 6 and 7.

Layer 3 contains the actual robustness tests calling the mocked test methods in layer 2. The parameter lists of test cases in this layer combine the extended parameter lists of called mocked methods. Errors can be injected by assigning corresponding parameter values. This might require additional manual work, if the list of parameters is to long and cannot be automatically covered by a symbolic execution tool like Pex.

5   Case Studies

The real world case study 'Settings Manager' (SM) is extracted from an industrial machine control software. The case study 'Cutting Stock' (CS) is the program hosting our running example. The program creates a list of cutting layouts based on the lengths and quantities of material and pieces. The case study 'Lending Library' (LL) is a small code example to manage the rental and return of items. All three studies are implemented in C# and use Code Contracts as specification language. Table 1 summarises the main properties.

We compare our methodology with results of current verification and testing techniques. We apply Microsoft Code Contracts as formal verification framework and IntelliTest as automatic test case generation framework. To get detailed POG information, we have implemented our own POG generator based on [3,13]. The results are summarised in Table 2. To benchmark the achieved benefits, we analyse the results of the generated robustness tests, and analyse whether they triggered an error within the vulnerable code. The resulting table lists those errors as "Robustness Errors". This table also lists the automatically achieved test coverage by regular test cases on unverified proof obligations.

Table 1. Overview case studies

	Settings Manager (SM)	Cutting Stock (CS)	Lending Library (LL)
LOC	1277	634	432
Preconditions	46	32	12
Postconditions	22	19	13
Invariants	21	13	15
Proof obligations	187	115	52

```
1 public object GetValue(string targetName) { [...]
2   Contract.Requires(targetValues.ContainsKey(targetName));
3   Contract.Requires(targetScopes.ContainsKey(targetName));
4   Contract.Ensures(Contract.Result<System.Object>() != null);
5   if (!targetValues.ContainsKey(targetName))
6   { throw new UnkownTargetException("[...]"); }
7   // Exception when targetName is no key [...] }
8   SettingScope targetSope = targetScopes[targetName];
```

Listing 1.5. Vulnerable code section which can causes a software crash

5.1   Case Study: Settings Manager

We have created 187 POGs to cover all 89 single specifications. The verification framework left 4 POGs unverified, covering different preconditions. The automatically generated test suite achieved 92% branch coverage on those 4 unverified control flows. Analysing those 4 unverified POGs, we could identify 18 vulnerable proof obligations. Two of them were not sufficiently secured against undiscovered errors.

Listing 1.5 shows one of those unsecured code sections. The precondition in line 3 could not be verified for each caller. To handle this incomplete verification result, related approaches create test cases to validate the unverified caller. In addition, we use robustness tests to analyse the consequences of a failing precondition. The robustness tests created by our approach call this method with a value for *targetName* which explicitly invalidates the precondition in line 2, while respecting all other assumptions. Thereby, we discovered the potential **KeyNotFound**-Exception in line 8, which would cause a software crash. This distinguishes a robustness test from a regular test. Regular test coverage could be achieved by testing this method while respecting both preconditions, but such tests would not trigger the error in line 8. This method was programmed based on the assumption that both containers (**targetScopes** and **targedNames**) share the same keys. Therefore the programmer checked the key only for one container. After discovering this risk, the developer could add additional exception handling similar to the one in lines 5–6.

5.2   Case Study: Cutting Stock

This case study is comprised of 64 specifications, which are covered by 115 POGs. The verification framework left 7 POGs unverified (4 invariants, 2 preconditions, 1 postcondition). The automatically generated test suite achieved 94% branch coverage on those 7 unverified control flows. We could identify 23 vulnerable proof obligations.

One of them was already discussed above and used as the running example. Another unverified POG covers the postcondition of **GetFreeClamp** in Listing 1.6. This method is called by a different method **AssignClamps**, which of course depends on the validity of that postcondition. **AssignClamps** calculates the required Clamp positions for the cutting machine, which is used to produce

```
1 private Clamp GetFreeClamp(double minPos, double maxPos) {
2   Contract.Ensures(Contract.Result<Clamp>() == null || (
    Contract.Result<Clamp>().free && Contract.Result<Clamp>().
    minPos <= minPos));
3   foreach (Clamp clamp in clamps) {
4     if(clamp == null) continue;
5     if(clamp.minPos <= minPos && clamp.maxPos >= maxPos)
6     { return clamp; }
7   }
8 return null; }
```

Listing 1.6. Code section with an unverified postcondition

the generated cutting-layouts. Wrong clamp positions may cause damage to the machine, e.g. when the saw hits a wrongly positioned clamp. Therefore, we want to test the behaviour of `AssignClamps` when this postcondition fails, in order to guarantee safe error handling. The corresponding robustness test must inject an invalid return value for `GetFreeClamp` into `AssignClamps`. Our framework generates the mocked copy `GetFreeClampMocked` in Listing 1.7. In `AssignClamps`, all method calls to the original methods are replaced in order to call the mocked copy. As described in Sect. 4, the mocked method uses an extended parameter list to initialise the returned object: `free_3`, `minPos_4`, `maxPos_5`. These parameters map to the basic field values of class `Clamp`. Thereby it is possible to return a `Clamp` instance which is not null and which does not meet the defined postcondition. The analysis of this robustness test shows that the simulated error caused an invalid return value for `AssignClamps`. An invalid return value would cause invalid cutting layouts, leading to faulty production in the real world. What makes this bug particular dangerous is the absence of easily detectable errors such as exceptions or a crash. The problem would not have been detected until someone tried to produce the erroneously calculated cutting layouts. Analysing the robustness test, the developer can add an additional sanity check within `AssignClamps` and make sure that the results meet all requirements.

```
1 private Clamp GetFreeClampMocked(double minPos_1, double
    maxPos_2, bool free_3, double minPos_4, double maxPos_5) {
2   Clamp clamp = new Clamp();
3   clamp.Init(free_3, minPos_4, maxPos_5);
4   return clamp; }
```

Listing 1.7. Mocked method to inject invalid return values

5.3   Case Study: Lending Library

The smallest case study, 'Lending Library' was specified using 30 conditions, which were covered by 54 generated POGs. The verification step left 6 proof obligations unverified (3 invariants, 2 postconditions, 1 precondition). Based on those 6 unverified POGs, we could identify 12 vulnerable code sections. The corresponding robustness tests discovered 3 critical code sections where additional

```
1 public bool ReturnItem(RentalItem item) {
2   if (!item.Rented) { return false; }
3   [...] }
```

Listing 1.8. Existing checks also handle simulated errors

sanity checks were required. Now someone could wonder about the vulnerable sections where no robustness error was found. The answer is very simple. The other 9 vulnerable code sections already contained error handling code, so no additional code needed to be added. An example is given in Listing 1.8. This method requires that the given `RentalItem` is actually rented and not returned. This state is encoded as an boolean class field. The related precondition could not be verified. However, this flag is already checked in line 2 and the robustness test could not trigger any new error.

Table 2. Comparsion between both approaches

	SM	CS	LL
Unverified proof obligations	4	7	6
Autom. achieved code coverage	92%	94%	98%
Identified vulnerable code sections	18	23	12
Discovered robustness errors	2	5	3

6   Conclusion and Future Work

Our case studies have shown that automatic test frameworks already achieve high coverage rates on unverified code sections. This poses the risk that such test suites might never be checked manually by the corresponding developer to identify insufficient test cases, as shown in Listing 1.2. That makes the inspection of code sections that rely on the correctness of the tested code particularly important. Even tested methods, entirely covered, may still contain errors. Therefore, only testing unverified code sections is insufficient when combining formal verification and dynamic testing techniques. Undiscovered errors in tested code my spread into other code sections, even those sections that have been previously verified. Such errors may be hard to debug, as they might be camouflaged after having been propagated through different methods. This was demonstrated in our running example extracted from the Cutting Stock case study. These risks are not handled by current approaches.

To reduce this residual risk, we have presented a new methodology to use robustness testing to handle incomplete verification results. We extract the guarantees of unverified proof obligations and use them to create and inject simulated errors. Those errors test the behaviour of vulnerable code sections in situations when those guarantees fail. The presented reference-architecture demonstrates how robustness tests can be generated and how simulated errors can be injected. By injecting simulated errors, the developer can analyse the consequences of failed guarantees. They can add further exception handling and sanity checks to prevent the propagation of previously undiscovered errors into other methods. The software can then handle errors in a controlled way rather than defaulting to unpredictable behaviour. It could be argued that developers can always add more exception handling and state checking. But this would be very labour intense when applied for every return value and argument. Furthermore, these sanity checks must be tested as well, requiring many robustness tests to cover the corresponding program paths. The presented methodology helps the developer to localise precisely those code sections, where additional error handling is required.

Finally, one major issue regarding formal verification needs to be addressed in future work. There is still no proper way to tell whether the defined specifications are sufficient and cover all necessary requirements. When the specification is insufficient, the number of generated POGs may be too small to properly analyse dependencies between them in order to identify vulnerable sections. Future work must find more sophisticated coverage rates for specifications.

References

1. Müller, P. (ed.): Modular Specification and Verification of Object-Oriented Programs. LNCS, vol. 2262. Springer, Heidelberg (2002). doi:10.1007/3-540-45651-1
2. Hoare, C.A.R.: An axiomatic basis for computer programming. Commun. ACM **12**(10), 576–580 (1969)
3. Beckert, B., Hähnle, R., Schmitt, P.H. (eds.): Verification of Object-Oriented Software. The KeY Approach. LNCS (LNAI), vol. 4334. Springer, Heidelberg (2007). doi:10.1007/978-3-540-69061-0
4. Amor, H.B., de Carvalho, J.V.: Cutting stock problems. In: Desaulniers, G., Desrosiers, J., Solomon, M.M. (eds.) Column Generation, pp. 131–161. Springer, Boston (2005). doi:10.1007/0-387-25486-2_5
5. Christakis, M., Müller, P., Wüstholz, V.: Collaborative verification and testing with explicit assumptions. In: Giannakopoulou, D., Méry, D. (eds.) FM 2012. LNCS, vol. 7436, pp. 132–146. Springer, Heidelberg (2012). doi:10.1007/978-3-642-32759-9_13
6. Christakis, M., Müller, P., Wüstholz, V.: Guiding dynamic symbolic execution toward unverified program executions. In: Proceedings of the 38th International Conference on Software Engineering, pp. 144–155. ACM (2016)
7. Christakis, M.: Narrowing the gap between verification and systematic testing. Ph.D. thesis, National Technical University of Athens, Greece (2015)
8. Czech, M., Jakobs, M.-C., Wehrheim, H.: Just test what you cannot verify!. In: Egyed, A., Schaefer, I. (eds.) FASE 2015. LNCS, vol. 9033, pp. 100–114. Springer, Heidelberg (2015). doi:10.1007/978-3-662-46675-9_7
9. Kanig, J., Chapman, R., Comar, C., Guitton, J., Moy, Y., Rees, E.: Explicit assumptions - a prenup for marrying static and dynamic program verification. In: Seidl, M., Tillmann, N. (eds.) TAP 2014. LNCS, vol. 8570, pp. 142–157. Springer, Cham (2014). doi:10.1007/978-3-319-09099-3_11

10. Fähndrich, M.: Static verification for code contracts. In: Cousot, R., Martel, M. (eds.) SAS 2010. LNCS, vol. 6337, pp. 2–5. Springer, Heidelberg (2010). doi:10. 1007/978-3-642-15769-1_2

11. Xie, T., Tillmann, N., Lakshman, P.: Advances in unit testing: theory and practice. In: Proceedings of the 38th International Conference on Software Engineering Companion, pp. 904–905. ACM (2016)

12. Halleux, J., Tillmann, N.: Moles: tool-assisted environment isolation with closures. In: Vitek, J. (ed.) TOOLS 2010. LNCS, vol. 6141, pp. 253–270. Springer, Heidelberg (2010). doi:10.1007/978-3-642-13953-6_14

13. Huster, S., Heckeler, P., Eichelberger, H., Ruf, J., Burg, S., Kropf, T., Rosenstiel, W.: More flexible object invariants with less specification overhead. In: Giannakopoulou, D., Salaün, G. (eds.) SEFM 2014. LNCS, vol. 8702, pp. 302–316. Springer, Cham (2014). doi:10.1007/978-3-319-10431-7_25

AI for Localizing Faults in Spreadsheets

Birgit Hofer[✉], Iulia Nica, and Franz Wotawa

Graz University of Technology, Graz, Austria
{bhofer,inica,wotawa}@ist.tugraz.at

Abstract. Localizing faults in programs is considered a demanding task. A lot of effort is usually spent in finding the root cause of a misbehavior and correcting the program such that it fulfills its intended behavior. The situation is even worse in case of end user programming like spreadsheet development where more or less complex spreadsheets are developed only with little knowledge in programming and also testing. In order to increase quality of spreadsheets and also efficiency of spreadsheet development, tools for testing and debugging support are highly required. In this paper, we focus on the latter and show that approaches originating from Artificial Intelligence can be adapted for (semi-) automated fault localization in spreadsheets in an interactive manner. In particular, we introduce abstract models that can be automatically obtained from spreadsheets enabling the computation of diagnoses within a fraction of a second. Besides the basic foundations, we discuss empirical results using artificial and real-world spreadsheet examples. Furthermore, we show that the abstract models have a similar accuracy to models of spreadsheets capturing their semantics.

Keywords: Fault localization · Abstract models · Empirical evaluation

1 Introduction

Quality assurance of software and systems is an important part of development to avoid failures occurring after deployment. Activities like testing at all levels are part of all currently used development processes where experienced and educated personnel is involved. This unfortunately does not hold in spreadsheet programming where end users are developing programs, who are usually not educated in program development. In addition, in spreadsheet development it is not easy to distinguish testing from programming, and further more, the programs themselves, i.e., the equations assigned to cells, are not that visible during development. As a consequence, there is a 3–5% error rate when writing formulae in spreadsheets (see Panko [16]). Therefore, there is a need for tools supporting testing and fault localization during spreadsheet development specifically considering the end-user aspect, requiring tools that easily and transparently integrate into spreadsheet development causing a high degree of interactivity. Previously developed approaches to spreadsheet fault localization like [7] are not sufficient

© IFIP International Federation for Information Processing 2017
Published by Springer International Publishing AG 2017. All Rights Reserved
N. Yevtushenko et al. (Eds.): ICTSS 2017, LNCS 10533, pp. 71–87, 2017.
DOI: 10.1007/978-3-319-67549-7_5

due to high runtime requirements. There Hofer and colleagues reported that computing single faults including repair suggestions took 25.1 s even for smaller spreadsheets having up to 70 non-empty cells.

In this paper, we focus solely on spreadsheet fault localization aiming at improving runtime whereas not reducing the quality of diagnosis. For this purpose, we introduce abstract models that can be automatically derived from spreadsheets and used for (semi-)automated fault localization. In order to show how models can be used for fault localization, let us have a look at a small example. In Fig. 1(a) we see a spreadsheet allowing to compute payments of Mr. Green and Mrs. Jones based on their weekly working hours and their hourly rate. In Fig. 1(b) we have the same spreadsheet but with a fault in cell D2 introduced. What we immediately see is that the values of cells F2 and D4 are lower than expected. Note that in practice at least the failure in cell F2 would have been easily detected because Mr. Green would complain about the lower payment to be received for two weeks. When having a look at the equations stored (see Fig. 1(c)), the reason behind the failures becomes obvious. Instead of summing up the hours of week 1 and week 2 in cell D2 only the working hours for week 1 are considered. But how to find such a bug using the available information?

	A	B	C	D	E	F
1		week 1	week 2	Total	$/h	Gross Pay
2	Green	23	31	54	15	810
3	Jones	35	34	69	17	1173
4	Total	58	65	123		

(a) Correct version

	A	B	C	D	E	F
1		week 1	week 2	Total	$/h	Gross Pay
2	Green	23	31	23	15	345
3	Jones	35	34	69	17	1173
4	Total	58	65	92		

(b) Faulty version

	A	B	C	D	E	F
1		week 1	week 2	Total	$/h	Gross Pay
2	Green	23	31	=B2	15	=D2*E2
3	Jones	35	34	=B3+C3	17	=D3*E3
4	Total	=B2+B3	=C2+C3	=D2+D3		

(c) Equations used in faulty version

Fig. 1. A small spreadsheet example (a variant from the EUSES corpus [5])

In the following, we make use of the equations stored in the spreadsheets, their references to other cells and assumptions about the correctness of cells to localize the faulty cell. Let us, for example, assume that all cells except cell D2 are correct. In practice, we obtain this information from the spreadsheet user, who indicates his/her observations about the computed values. Additionally, we make use of the expected values for cells F2 and D4, which are 810 and 123 respectively. From the values of E2 and the expected value of F2 we can derive a value of 54 for cell D2 (Note, 54 = 810/15). When using this value and the value of cell D3 we finally receive 123 (=54 + 69), which is exactly the expected value for cell D4. Hence, D2 is a potential root cause, but are there more? We can use the same idea but in this case we assume all cells except cell F2 to be correct. In this case, we would get again a value of 92 for cell D4 when using the underlying equations. Therefore, cell F2 alone is not a candidate. When assuming F2 and D4 to be faulty, we would not be able to compute values for cells F2 and D4 and there is no contradiction when comparing these values with the expected ones. Hence, we have another root cause comprising cells F2 and D4. In most cases we are more interested in smaller explanations. In this case, we would prefer diagnosis D2 over diagnosis F2, D4.

What can we take from this brief example? First, we only considered the available equations for computing values. Second, we used assumptions about the correctness of cells. In case a cell is assumed to be correct, we used the corresponding equation. Otherwise, we ignored the equation and did not compute any value using this equation. Computing all diagnoses can be simplified done assuming all subsets of cells comprising equations to be faulty and the others to be correct, and checking whether the computable values are contradicting input values or expected output values. Unfortunately, this is computationally infeasible. In addition, equation solving is also computationally demanding, and there is a need for abstract models. An abstract model, for example, might only consider information regarding whether a certain value is smaller, equivalent, or larger than expected, or whether the value is correct or not correct. In our running example, we obtain that the value of cells F2 and D4 are both too small. When assuming cell F2 to work as expected and assuming that the cells comprising only values are correct (like done previously), we can immediately conclude that also the value of cell D2 is too small. With similar arguments than before when using the equations and real values, we are able to come up with similar diagnoses. We will discuss the abstract models in detail in the next section. The idea behind abstract models dealing with qualities instead of quantitative values comes from *Qualitative Reasoning (QR)*, which is a subfield of Artificial Intelligence (AI).

The consequences when using abstract models instead of the stored equations and values are interesting. Do we compute more diagnoses? Do the computed diagnoses always include the real fault? What is the impact of abstract models on the runtime? And finally, are there any other consequences when using real world spreadsheets? In this paper, we will discuss these questions and also give answers. In summary, the contributions of this paper are:

- Providing a solid foundation for model-based debugging of spreadsheets, which is based on previous work on model-based diagnosis [17,19].
- Introducing three different types of models where one makes use of a qualitative representation of deviations between the expected and the current spreadsheet.
- Comparing the different types of models with respect to their diagnosis accuracy and runtime.

The paper is organized as follows. First, we introduce the basic definitions of diagnosis and discuss the underlying models. Afterwards, we present the results of our experimental evaluation, where we focus on the runtime issue and the diagnosis accuracy. Finally, we conclude the paper, which includes a brief discussion on related research.

2   Basic Definitions

Wotawa [19] described the use of constraints for fault localization. Constraints are basically equations or conditions on variables that must hold in order to be satisfied. For example, the constraint $x = 2 \cdot y$ is satisfied when assigning a value of 2 to variable x and 1 to variable y. When given a set of constraints the aim of constraint solving is to provide variable assignments such that all constraints are satisfied. For a deeper introduction into constraint solving including algorithms we refer the interested reader to Dechter [4]. However, in order to be self-contained, we briefly introduce the basic concepts of constraint solving first, discuss automated diagnosis afterwards, and show how spreadsheets can be compiled into three different constraint representations for the purpose of automated fault localization.

Constraint Solving: We define a **constraint system** as a tuple (*VARS, DOM, CONS*) where *VARS* is defined as a finite set of variables, *DOM* is a function mapping each variable to its domain comprising at least one element, and *CONS* is a finite set of constraints. Without restricting generality we define a constraint c as a pair $((v_1, \ldots, v_k), tl)$ where $(v_1, \ldots, v_k)$ is a tuple of variables from *VARS*, and tl a set of tuples $(x_1, \ldots, x_k)$ of values where for each $i \in \{1, \ldots, k\}$: $x_i \in DOM(v_i)$. The set of tuples tl in this definition declares all allowed variable value combinations for a particular constraint. For simplicity, we assume a function $scope(c)$ for a constraint c returning the tuple $(v_1, \ldots, v_k)$, and a similar function $tl(c)$ returning the set of tuples tl of c.

Searching for solutions of given constraint systems is equivalent to searching for values assigned to all variables such that all constraints are satisfied. The corresponding problem is called **constraint satisfaction problem** (CSP). In order to formally define CSP we first start defining **value assignments**: Given a constraint system (*VARS, DOM, CONS*), and variable $v \in VARS$, then $v = x$ with $x \in DOM(v)$ is a single assignment of a value x to the variable v. We further define a value assignment as a set of single assignments where there is at maximum one single assignment for each variable. A constraint c with scope $(v_1, \ldots, v_k)$ fulfills a value assignment $\{\ldots, v_1 = x_1, \ldots, v_k = x_k, \ldots\}$, if there exists a tuple $(x_1, \ldots, x_k)$ in the constraint $tl(c)$. Otherwise, we say that such a value assignment contradicts the constraint.

Example 1. Cell D3 of the spreadsheet in Fig. 1(c) contains the formula B3 + C3. We model this by using the constraint $((B3, C3, D3), \{(a, b, a + b) | a, b \in \mathbb{N}\})$ where $B3$, $C3$, $D3$ are the variables representing the value of cells B3, C3, D3 respectively.

Using the definition of value assignments, we are now able to define CSPs. A CSP for a given constraint system is defined as question whether there exists a value assignment that fulfills all given constraints. If there is such a value assignment, the CSP is said to be fulfilled. Solving a constraint satisfaction problem is computationally demanding but there are efficient algorithms available, e.g. [6].

Model-Based Diagnosis: Model-based diagnosis is an AI method for computing all diagnoses from an available model of a system or in our case spreadsheet. The underlying idea is to make the assumptions about correctness of a component explicit. For each component, we add a model representing its behavior. Diagnosis becomes searching for assumptions about the correctness of certain components of a system: Which components are correct and which behave faulty so that given observations are not in contradiction with values obtained using the model?

Reiter [17] defines a **diagnosis problem** as a tuple $(COMP, SD, OBS)$ where $COMP$ is a set of components, SD a logical sentence describing the behavior of the system, i.e., the system description, and OBS a set of observations. In our case, the observations are the information we obtain from the user who indicates that a certain cell contains a wrong value while others compute the correct result. When using constraints for diagnosis, we have to slightly modify this definition. We assume a constraint representation of the system and additional constraints specifying the observations. In this context, the diagnosis problem becomes a tuple $(VARS, DOM, CONS \cup COBS)$ where $(VARS, DOM, CONS)$ is a constraint representation of a system comprising variables ab_C for every component C of the system, and $COBS$ is the constraint representation of all observations OBS.

Example 2 (Continuation of Example 1). Assuming that the values of B3 and C3 are correct, then D3 either computes the desired output or its formula is faulty. We can model this by using the following constraint where we introduced a variable ab_{D3} representing the assumption that cell D3 is faulty:

$$((ab_{D3}, B3, C3, D3), \{(F, a, b, a+b)|a, b \in \mathbb{N}\} \cup \{(T, a, b, c)|a, b, c \in \mathbb{N}\}).$$

We can create such constraints for all formula cells to represent the spreadsheet given in Fig. 1. For simplicity, in the following model, we only consider the cells D2, D3, and D4. The constraints for D2, D4 are similar to the one of D3. This set of constraints builds the system description SD. The given formula cells build the set of components $COMP$, i.e. $COMP = \{D2, D3, D4\}$. The set of observations contains the information about the correct and erroneous output as well as the input cells and their values: $OBS = \{B2 = 23, C2 = 31, B3 = 35, C3 = 34, D4 = 123\}$. The observations can be easily represented as a constraint, e.g., $((B2, B3, C2, C3, D4), \{(23, 35, 31, 34, 123)\})$.

Given a diagnosis problem a solution, i.e., a **diagnosis**, is a subset of the set of components $COMP$ so that assuming all components in a diagnosis to be faulty, allows to compute a solution for the corresponding constraint representation. Formally, a diagnosis $\Delta \subseteq COMP$ is a diagnosis if and only if the following constraint system is satisfiable, i.e., there exists a solution for:

$CONS \cup COBS \cup \{((ab_C), \{(T)|C \in \Delta\}), ((ab_C), \{(F)|C \in COMP \setminus \Delta\})\}$. There could be more than one diagnosis. We are usually focusing on minimal diagnoses only. A minimal diagnosis in our setting is a diagnosis where none of its subsets is itself a diagnosis.

Nica and Wotawa [15] introduced the ConDiag algorithm that allows computing all minimal diagnoses up to a predefined size using the constraint representation of a diagnosis problem. Algorithm 1 illustrates the pseudo-code of ConDiag. At the beginning of the algorithm, the result and the model are initialized (line 1–2). Within the loop the constraint model is constructed (line 4) bringing together the initial model M and the assumption that we are only interested in diagnoses of size i. Afterwards, in line 5 the constraint solver is called returning all diagnoses of size i. If the constraint system is satisfiable for i = 0, we terminate ConDiag and return the set comprising the empty set as results meaning that the system is fault free. In line 9 the new diagnoses are added and in line 10 a new constraint is added to the model. This constraint basically states that we are not interested in supersets of already computed diagnoses. The loop continues until we reach the maximum size. ConDiag always terminates (providing the constraint solver terminates) and computes all minimal diagnoses up to a pre-defined size n. ConDiag is also efficient. Nica et al. [14] compared ConDiag with other diagnosis algorithms showing a good overall runtime. In practice, n is usually set to 1 up to 3.

Algorithm 1. ConDiag(($VARS, DOM, CONS \cup COBS$), $COMP, n$)

Input: A constraint model ($VARS, DOM, CONS \cup COBS$) of a system having components $COMP$ and the desired diagnosis cardinality n
Output: All minimal diagnoses up to the predefined cardinality n

1: Let DS be {}
2: Let M be $CONS \cup COBS$
3: **for** $i = 0$ **to** n **do**
4:     $CM = M \cup \{|\{ab_C|C \in COMP \wedge ab_C = T\}| = i\}$
5:     $S = \mathcal{P}(\textbf{CSolver}(VARS, DOM, CM))$
6:     **if** i is 0 **and** S is {{}} **then**
7:        **return** S
8:     **end if**
9:     Let DS be $DS \cup S$.
10:     $M = M \cup \{\neg(\mathcal{C}(S))\}$
11: **end for**
12: **return** DS

Modeling for Spreadsheets: For making use of model-based diagnosis for spreadsheet fault localization, we have to provide a constraint model of the spreadsheet. For simplicity, we assume a **spreadsheet** to be a finite set of cells $\{c_1, \ldots, c_k\}$. Each cell c_i is uniquely identifiable using its row and column. Like in ordinary spreadsheet implementations we write a cell as Ar where A denotes the column using letters, and r the row using natural numbers. A cell c has a value and maybe a corresponding formula. In case c has attached a formula its value is determined by the formula. Without restricting generality, we assume every formula to be of the form c_1 op c_2 where c_1, c_2 are (references to) cells and op is an operator $+, -, /,$ or $*$. A cell with no formula attached is called an input cell. A cell that is never referenced in a formula is called an output cell.

Algorithm 2 gives the pseudo-code of a compiler that takes a spreadsheet as input and computes its corresponding constraint representation. The algorithm Compile2Model makes use of two functions $constraint_F$ and $constraint_O$ which compute the constraint representation of formulae and observations respectively. These functions depend on the used model type: We explain the functions for the three different types of models in this paper. One model directly represents the behavior of formulae (called value-based model) and serves as reference model. The other model (called dependency-based model) only considers knowledge about the correctness of values, whereas the third model (called comparison-based model) uses the deviations of cell values. The last two models are abstract models not considering the real values used in spreadsheets.

Algorithm 2. Compile2Model(SP, OBS)

Input: A spreadsheet SP and its observations OBS
Output: A constraint model

1: Let M and VAR be $\{\}$.
2: **for** all cells c in SP **do**
3:     Add c to VAR and let $DOM(c) = \mathbb{N}/\mathbb{B}/\{0,1,2\}$.
4:     **if** c has an equation attached **then**
5:         Add ab_c to VAR and let $DOM(ab_c) = \mathbb{B}$.
6:         Add $constraint_F(c)$ to M.
7:     **end if**
8: **end for**
9: Add $constraint_O(OBS)$ to M.
10: **return** (VAR, DOM, M)

In line 3, all cells of the spreadsheet are added to the set of variables VAR and are assigned an domain DOM depending on the underlying model: $DOM = \mathbb{N}$ when using the value-based model, $DOM = \mathbb{B}$ when using the dependency-based model, and $DOM = \{0,1,2\}$ when using the comparison-based model. For all cells containing equations, an additional variable ab_c is added to VAR with $DOM(ab_c) = \mathbb{B}$ and the equations are translated into constraints (lines 4–7). Finally, the constraints for the observations are added using the function $constraint_O$. The functions $constraint_F$ and $constraint_O$ for the different models are defined as follows:

- *Value-based model (VM):* The VM directly represents spreadsheets. Formulae are directly represented as constraints. Let us assume a formula c_1 *op* c_2 stored in cell c. The function $constraint_F(c)$ returns the constraint
$$((ab_c, c_1, c_2, c), \{(F, a, b, a\ op\ b)|a, b \in \mathbb{N}\} \cup \{(T, a, b, c)|a, b, c \in \mathbb{N}\}).$$
In this constraint, we distinguish the correct case where ab_c is set to false from the faulty case. In the latter case, there are no restrictions on the values of cells c, c_1, c_2. For the representation of observations, we assume to have a set $\{c_1 = v_1, \ldots, c_k = v_k\}$. In this case $constraint_O$ returns one constraint $((c_1, \ldots, c_k), \{(v_1, \ldots, v_k)\})$.
- *Dependency-based model (DM):* The DM only considers values being correct or not correct, which are represented using the numbers 1 and 0 respectively. A formula c_1 *op* c_2 for a cell c cannot be directly represented as constraint. Instead, we make use of the following idea: A formula returns a definitely correct value only if both input values are correct. In cases where we do not have fault masking, we are also able to say that a correct value computed using a formula also requires both inputs to be correct. This assumption is not always true. However, in case of using only numbers failure masking has a very low probability. More information on this improved version of the dependency-based model can be found in [8,10].
Taking the idea of dealing with correctness and incorrectness of values, we are able to define $constraint_F$ as a function returning the constraint $((ab_c, c_1, c_2, c), T_D)$ where T_D is a set comprising the following elements:

ab_{XY}	c_1	c_2	c
F	1	1	1
F	0	1	0
F	1	0	0
F	0	0	0
T	.	.	.

In this table "." stands for arbitrary values. Thus, in case of a fault all possible combinations are considered. For the observations, we define $constraint_O$ as follows: Let us assume to have a set $\{c_1 = v_1, \ldots, c_k = v_k\}$ and a function δ with the cell and its value as parameters. $\delta(c, v)$ returns 1 if c is an input cell or if the value of cell c provided when executing the spreadsheet is equivalent to v. Otherwise, δ returns 0. $constraint_O$ returns a constraint of the following form: $((c_1, \ldots, c_k), \{(\delta(c_1, v_1), \ldots, \delta(c_k, v_k))\})$.
- *Comparison-based model (CM):* CM is very similar to DM. But instead of only considering values to be correct or incorrect, we consider values to be smaller, equivalent or larger than expected represented using the numbers 0, 1, and 2 respectively. The function $constraint_E$ applied to formula c_1 *op* c_2 of cell c returns a constraint $((ab_c, c_1, c_2, c), T_D)$ where T_D is a set comprising elements depending on the underlying operator. The table for operators $+$ and $*$ is given on the right; the table for operators $-$ and $/$ is given on the left:

ab_c	c_1	c_2	c
F	1	1	1
F	0	1	0
F	1	0	0
F	0	0	0
F	2	1	2
F	1	2	2
F	2	2	2
F	0	2	1
F	0	2	0
F	0	2	2
F	2	0	1
F	2	0	0
F	2	0	2
T	.	.	.

ab_c	c_1	c_2	c
F	1	1	1
F	0	1	0
F	1	0	2
F	0	0	0
F	0	0	1
F	0	0	2
F	2	1	2
F	1	2	0
F	2	2	0
F	2	2	1
F	2	2	2
F	0	2	0
F	2	0	2
T	.	.	.

Again, "." stands for arbitrary values and in case of a fault we consider all possible combinations to be part of the constraint values. For the observations and function $constraint_O$, we make use of a similar idea than for DM. Instead of using function δ, we define a function ψ with the cell and its value as parameters. $\psi(c, v)$ returns 0 if c is not an input cell and the value computed when executing the spreadsheet is smaller than v. ψ returns 1 if c is an input cell or if the value of cell c provided when executing the spreadsheet is equivalent to v. Otherwise, ψ returns 2. Function $constraint_O$ returns a constraint of the following form: $((c_1, \ldots, c_k), \{(\psi(c_1, v_1), \ldots, \psi(c_k, v_k))\})$.

3   Experimental Evaluation

In this section, we present and discuss empirical results obtained using a class of artificially generated examples and real-world spreadsheets. The purpose of this section is to answer the questions whether the comparison-based model has a good runtime and accuracy compared with the dependency-based model and the value-based model. The latter can be seen as reference model because it is more or less a one-to-one representation of its corresponding spreadsheet. For solving the constraints, we used Minion [6], an out-of-the-box, open source constraint solver that supports arithmetic, relational, and logic constraints over Boolean and Integers.

In the **first part of the experimental evaluation**, we focused mainly on the question regarding the runtime of the different models to compute all diagnoses. Therefore, we used a parametrizable example comprising components for adding and multiplying integers, which is close to an ordinary spreadsheet for calculating sums of numbers. For the artificial example have a look at Fig. 2 where we have parameters $m, n \geq 2$. From the figure we see that we obtain $((n+4) \cdot m) - 3$ components for given parameters in total. For the experiment, we implemented an input-output values generator, which randomly assigns values to the $m \times n$ inputs $x_{i\ j}$ and computes the expected m outputs z_k, and outputs

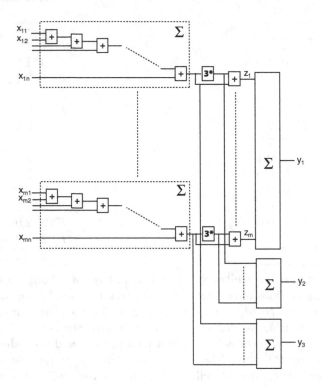

Fig. 2. Parametrizable example with $m \times n$ inputs $x_{i\ j}$, m outputs z_k, and outputs y_1, y_2, and y_3.

y_1, y_2, y_3. Furthermore, we implemented a model generator, which returns the three models and the observations directly as constraints.

In Table 1, we summarize the obtained results when running the search for single, double, and triple diagnoses on a Windows 10 Pro notebook with a Intel(R) Core(TM) i7-4500U CPU 1.80 GHz and 8 GB of RAM. For the dependency-based and comparison-based model, we carried out ten runs and give the obtained average values in the table. For the value-based model, we used only three runs due to the very high runtime requirements, especially when carrying out the computation of triple fault diagnoses. The times given in Table 1 are in milli-seconds. The table has two parts. In the upper one, the results when setting only one output to a wrong value are given. The lower part comprises the results obtained when introducing failures at two outputs.

From Table 1 we see that in case of one output to be faulty the dependency-based and the comparison-based models provide the same set of diagnoses that is substantially different from the results obtained using the value-based model. In contrast, the more abstract models are less computationally demanding. In case of two output values that are different to the expected value, the situation is different. Here, the comparison-based model provide less diagnoses than the dependency-based model. The runtime again is much better for the more

Table 1. Results for parametrizable example with V representing the value-based model, C representing the comparison-based model and D representing the improved dependency-based model. Note that Minion is called with -timelimit 1200

Model	Inputs	Comps	Runtime [ms]						Number of diagnoses					
Diag. size			V		C		D		V		C		D	
m	n		1	2	1	2	1	2	1	2	1	2	1	2
Single failure														
10	10	100	137	319	7561	916	104	66	56	2	0	99	0	99	0
10	15	150	187	707	33085	201	100	95	58	2	0	149	0	149	0
10	2	20	57	71	82	71	62	36	44	2	0	19	0	19	0
15	10	150	207	992	46995	247	97	96	71	2	0	149	0	149	0
15	2	30	87	111	195	96	95	47	44	2	0	29	0	29	0
15	20	300	357	3985	422274	536	147	299	93	2	0	299	0	299	0
2	10	20	25	56	62	58	50	37	37	1	0	19	0	19	0
2	15	30	35	49	116	60	57	32	41	1	0	29	0	29	0
2	2	4	9	29	41	49	54	35	35	1	0	3	0	3	0
2	20	40	45	61	256	64	68	41	42	1	0	39	0	39	0
2	3	6	11	38	38	88	58	40	35	1	0	5	0	5	0
20	15	300	377	4971	520498	575	154	313	96	2	0	299	0	299	0
20	2	40	117	147	527	94	92	60	47	2	0	39	0	39	0
20	20	400	477	9714	1205255	867	158	583	117	2	0	399	0	399	0
3	2	6	15	47	34	68	70	37	34	2	0	5	0	5	0
Double failure														
10	10	100	137	268	9836	110	231	89	62	0	24	90	342	99	0
10	15	150	187	573	41880	135	248	117	76	0	24	140	342	149	0
10	2	20	57	61	122	54	153	58	55	0	24	10	342	19	0
15	10	150	207	711	59066	129	1028	121	76	0	34	135	812	149	0
15	2	30	87	108	384	49	502	64	53	0	34	15	812	29	0
15	20	300	357	3000	526077	380	1741	356	115	0	34	285	812	299	0
2	10	20	25	47	70	48	45	37	42	0	3	18	6	19	0
2	15	30	35	52	116	55	56	48	50	0	3	28	6	29	0
2	2	4	9	43	35	44	49	44	49	0	3	2	6	3	0
2	20	40	45	52	249	53	62	54	48	0	3	38	6	39	0
2	3	6	11	31	43	88	199	44	35	0	3	4	6	5	0
20	15	300	377	3627	702607	426	5707	383	96	0	44	280	1482	299	0
20	2	40	117	139	1066	70	1840	69	65	0	44	20	1482	39	0
20	20	400	477	6176	1204305	581	7343	668	134	0	44	380	1482	399	0
3	2	6	15	43	41	104	99	45	40	0	10	3	20	5	0

abstract models. Figure 3 shows the runtime of diagnosis using all three models as a function of the number of components. The dependency-based and the comparison-based model provide a similar runtime behavior whereas the value-based model requires a lot more time for computing all single fault diagnoses. This hold for the case of single failures as well as for double failures.

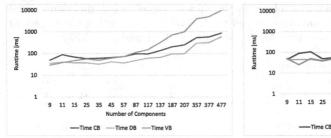
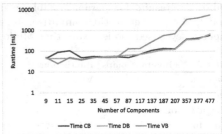

(a) Single failure at output   (b) Two failures at output

Fig. 3. Runtime using parametrizable example for computing all single fault diagnoses

In the **second part of the empirical evaluation**, we used a subset of the publicly available Integer spreadsheet corpus [3][1]. This corpus contains spreadsheets with up to three artificially seeded faults. Unfortunately, we have to exclude some of the spreadsheets from our evaluation for two reasons: First, Minion was not able to compute any solutions at all within a time limit of 20 min for some of the spreadsheets when using the value-based model. Second, our prototype does not support the conversion of IF and MAX expressions to constraints. This is not a limitation of the approach, but only a limitation of the prototype. We have used an Intel Core processor (2.90 GHz) with 8 GB RAM, a 64-bit version of Windows 8 and MINION version 1.8 for this part of the evaluation.

Table 2 shows the results for 35 faulty spreadsheets. The spreadsheets are categorized into three groups: 15 spreadsheets whose true fault is a single fault, 14 spreadsheets with a double fault as true fault and 6 spreadsheets with a triple fault as true fault. The runtime is the time Minion requires to parse and solve the given constraint system for the indicated diagnosis size (1, 2, 3). The indicated times are the arithmetic mean over 10 runs. Whenever we have indicated '0' as time, Minion required less than 0.5 ms and therefore returned 0 ms as solving time. Whenever we have indicted '-' as time, Minion's solving process exceeded a time limit of 20 min. The value-based model requires significantly more time than the dependency-based and comparison-based model and Minion could not compute double (respectively triple) fault diagnoses for 6 (respectively 7) spreadsheets. The reason for the poor runtime behavior of the value-based model lies in the different domain sizes: The abstract models restrict the variables' domains to a size of 2 (dependency-based model) respectively 3 (comparison-based model); the value-based model reasons of Integer values ranging from $-2,000$ to $50,000$. The comparison-based model and the dependency-based model have similar runtimes.

---

[1] http://spreadsheets.ist.tugraz.at/index.php/corpora-for-benchmarking/integer-corpus/.

Table 2. Results for Integer Corpus with V representing the value-based model, C representing the comparison-based model and D representing the improved dependency-based model. The solving time and the number of diagnoses are separately indicated for single (1), double (2), and triple (3) fault diagnoses. An '-' entry indicates a timeout. The entries of the columns 'Faults founds' indicate whether the model has the true fault as one of its diagnoes (Y) or only a subset of it (P). 'Obs.' provides information about the observations, where column 'F' indicates the number of observations where the computed output contradicts the expected output and 'T' indicates those where the computed output is equal to the expected one.

| Model | Runtime [ms] | | | | | | | | | Number of Diagnoses | | | | | | | | | Fault found | | | Obs. | |
| | V | | | C | | | D | | | V | | | C | | | D | | | | | | | |
Diag. Size	1	2	3	1	2	3	1	2	3	1	2	3	1	2	3	1	2	3	V	C	D	F	T
True fault = single fault																							
arith02_1_1	19156	486603	215245	1	4	3	4	3	0	13	0	0	16	0	0	16	0	0	Y	Y	Y	1	0
arith02_1_2	610	-	-	3	1	3	1	6	6	7	-	-	8	26	0	8	9	0	Y	Y	Y	1	1
arith02_1_3	490	2963	44	0	0	3	3	4	3	7	27	0	7	29	0	7	8	0	Y	Y	Y	1	1
cake_1_1	175564	-	-	10	13	16	32	32	35	44	-	-	65	0	0	65	0	0	Y	Y	Y	1	1
oscars_1_3	845	1594	1823	4	3	3	1	4	12	2	36	0	11	0	0	11	0	0	Y	Y	Y	1	1
oscars_1_4	801	91	91	3	3	1	9	0	0	10	0	0	10	0	0	10	0	0	Y	Y	Y	1	2
oscars_1_5	507	1454	6903	0	1	3	12	4	1	1	0	57	11	0	0	11	0	0	Y	Y	Y	1	1
prom_1_1	338	245	243	1	0	0	1	0	0	13	0	0	13	0	0	13	0	0	Y	Y	Y	1	1
shares_1_1	969	933	935	3	4	4	10	13	20	1	0	0	1	1	2	1	1	2	Y	Y	Y	1	11
shares_1_2	1254	1227	1226	1	3	3	13	9	13	1	0	0	1	0	0	1	0	0	Y	Y	Y	1	11
shares_1_3	1327	3179	5384	1	0	4	12	10	15	1	1	2	1	1	2	1	1	2	Y	Y	Y	1	11
shares_1_4	1591	3128	5222	3	0	4	9	9	16	1	1	2	1	1	2	1	1	2	Y	Y	Y	1	11
shares_1_5	1260	1227	1227	1	3	1	12	6	12	1	0	0	1	0	0	1	0	0	Y	Y	Y	1	11
shop_b1_1_1	529	107	107	1	3	3	10	9	6	15	0	0	15	0	0	15	0	0	Y	Y	Y	1	2
shop_b1_1_2	513	107	109	6	3	4	7	6	7	15	0	0	15	0	0	15	0	0	Y	Y	Y	1	2
Average	13717	-	-	3	3	4	9	8	10	9	-	-	12	4	0	12	1	0					
True fault = double fault																							
arith01_2_2	112	1199	63	0	3	4	3	1	0	0	36	0	1	32	0	3	15	0	Y	Y	P	2	0
arith01_2_3	136	-	-	1	3	3	4	1	1	4	-	-	4	15	0	4	6	0	P	P	P	1	1
arith02_2_1	207	5104	115	1	1	9	3	7	1	0	81	0	0	90	0	7	8	0	Y	Y	P	2	0
arith02_2_2	465	2979	-	0	3	7	1	4	1	5	24	-	7	29	0	7	8	0	P	P	P	1	1
cake_2_1	162217	-	-	13	16	16	31	37	34	43	-	-	64	0	0	64	0	0	P	P	P	1	2
cake_2_2	158977	-	-	12	15	16	35	38	35	20	-	-	65	0	0	65	0	0	P	P	P	1	1
cake_2_3	156173	-	-	10	13	13	34	32	37	17	-	-	65	0	0	65	0	0	P	P	P	1	1
oscars_2_2	504	1471	6251	1	3	4	4	4	6	1	0	48	11	0	0	11	0	0	P	P	P	1	1
prom_2_1	424	337	335	1	3	3	4	4	3	13	0	0	13	0	0	13	0	0	P	P	P	1	1
prom_2_2	341	245	245	3	3	1	1	1	3	13	0	0	13	0	0	13	0	0	P	P	P	1	1
prom_2_3	343	248	246	6	0	0	3	6	3	13	0	0	13	0	0	13	0	0	P	P	P	1	1
shop_b1_2_1	526	107	107	1	4	0	9	9	7	15	0	0	15	0	0	15	0	0	P	P	P	1	2
shop_b1_2_2	512	107	109	3	4	1	4	10	6	15	0	0	15	0	0	15	0	0	P	P	P	1	2
shop_b1_2_3	515	112	109	1	1	4	9	9	10	16	0	0	16	0	0	16	0	0	P	P	P	1	2
Average	34389	-	-	4	5	6	10	12	10	13	-	-	22	12	0	22	3	0					
True fault = triple fault																							
arith01_3_1	31	108	32	4	3	3	0	0	3	0	6	0	3	16	0	3	16	0	P	P	P	2	0
arith02_3_1	19600	451007	214501	4	4	4	3	1	3	13	0	0	16	0	0	16	0	0	P	P	P	1	0
cake_3_1	2194	837413	-	1	27	66	26	52	87	0	96	-	0	186	0	0	186	0	P	P	P	2	2
prom_3_1	340	245	246	3	3	1	7	1	3	10	3	0	13	0	0	13	0	0	P	P	P	1	1
shares_3_1	1265	1585	47272	3	3	7	10	7	26	0	0	16	0	0	17	0	0	17	Y	Y	Y	3	9
shop_b1_3_1	504	4124	352	4	20	35	9	16	41	0	240	0	0	240	0	0	240	0	P	P	P	2	1
Average	3989	215747	-	3	10	19	9	13	27	4	58	-	5	74	3	5	74	3					

The value-based model performs better than the abstract models w.r.t. their diagnostic accuracy. For 22 spreadsheets, all models compute the same single fault diagnoses. For 13 spreadsheets, value-based model computed fewer diagnoses while the abstract models have the same single fault diagnoses. For two spreadsheets, the comparison-based model computed fewer single fault diagnoses than the value-based model.

An important question is whether the models are able to detect the true fault. This information is given in Table 2 in the columns labeled 'Fault found'. An 'Y' entry indicates that the fault was reported as diagnosis; a 'P' entry indicates that only a part of the true fault (i.e. a subset) was reported as diagnosis, e.g. {D4} was reported as diagnosis, but {D4, D5} is the true fault. This is no problem per se, because all supersets of a diagnosis are also considered as diagnoses. However, the exacter a diagnosis is, the more helpful it is for spreadsheet programmers. For all spreadsheets with a single fault as true fault, the true fault has been reported as diagnosis. For two of the spreadsheets with a double fault, the value-based and the comparison-based models identified the true fault as one of the diagnoses, while the dependency-based model detected a subset as diagnosis. For all other spreadsheets with double faults, all models reported subsets of the true fault as diagnosis. All models identified the true diagnosis only for one of the triple fault spreadsheets, while they identified a subset of the true fault as diagnosis for all other triple fault spreadsheets.

The columns 'Obs.' provide information about the observations used. The 'F'-column indicates the number of non-input observations where the computed value differs from the expected value; the 'T'-column indicates the number of non-input observations where the computed value is equal to the expected value.

To summarize, the second part of the empirical evaluation shows that model-based diagnosis can be used to debug artificially created and real-life spreadsheets when an abstract model is used. Unfortunately, the value-based model requires too much runtime and therefore cannot be used in practice. The comparison-based and the dependency-based models convince by their low computation times of several milliseconds. These low computation times allow us to use these models in real-life scenarios, where a user expects to obtain the diagnosis candidates immediately after starting the diagnosis process. When comparing the diagnostic accuracy, the abstract models nearly reach the results of the value-based model. In practice, the slightly worse diagnostic accuracy is a good tradeoff for the runtime performance gain.

4   Conclusions

Using models for localizing faults in spreadsheets is not novel. Jannach and Engler [11] introduced the use of constraint solving for spreadsheet debugging for the first time. Later the same authors presented an add-on for Excel, the EXQUISITE debugging tool [12]. Abreu et al. [2] presented a similar approach. In contrast to Jannach and Schmitz's approach, this approach relies on a single test case, and directly encodes the reasoning about the correctness of cells into the CSP. Hofer *et al.* [8,10] were the first proposing to use dependency-based models for spreadsheet debugging. In contrast to this work, we – in addition – introduce a general framework for obtaining different models, discuss the comparison-based model, and present a detailed empirical evaluation comparing the different models. Other approaches to fault localization not based on model-based reasoning include Ruthruff *et al.* [18], Hofer *et al.* [9], and Abraham and Erwig [1]. For more details about quality assurance methods, we refer the interested reader to Jannach *et al.*'s survey paper [13], which provides an exhaustive overview on different techniques and methods for detecting, localizing, and repairing spreadsheets.

In this paper, we introduce a framework for fault localization based on models. In particular, we presented the underlying foundations and introduced an algorithm that allows compiling spreadsheets directly into models represented as set of constraints. Furthermore, we discussed three different types of models. The value-based model directly represents the behavior of a spreadsheet. The comparison-based model makes use of deviations between correct cell values and the actual values. The dependency-based model only distinguishes faulty from correct values occurring during computation. In addition, to the foundations and models, we presented empirical results obtained using generated examples that are parametrizable, and real-world spreadsheet programs comprising faults. The parametrizable spreadsheet has a structure and behavior close to spreadsheets occurring in practice. With the empirical evaluation we wanted to get answers to the following two questions: (1) Which model provides a good runtime performance? And, (2) whether the comparison-based model provides a good diagnosis accuracy?

From the obtained runtime results we can conclude that the dependency-based and the comparison-based model provide a good runtime performance and provide diagnoses much faster than the value-based model. With the dependency-based and the comparison-based model we are able to provide diagnosis capabilities almost at real time. Regarding diagnosis accuracy, the dependency-based and the comparison-based model are both weaker than the value-based model, which served as reference model in this case. The comparison-based model provides in some but not all cases a better diagnosis accuracy compared to the dependency-based model. This holds especially in cases where more than 1 output can be classified as faulty. Because of a similar runtime performance and a slightly better diagnosis accuracy the comparison-based model can be considered as superior to the dependency-based model.

Acknowledgments. The work described in this paper has been funded by the Austrian Science Fund (FWF) project DEbugging Of Spreadsheet programs (DEOS) under contract number I2144 and the Deutsche Forschungsgemeinschaft (DFG) under contract number JA 2095/4-1.

References

1. Abraham, R., Erwig, M.: GoalDebug: a spreadsheet debugger for end users. In: 29th International Conference on Software Engineering (ICSE), pp. 251–260 (2007)
2. Abreu, R., Hofer, B., Perez, A., Wotawa, F.: Using constraints to diagnose faulty spreadsheets. Softw. Qual. J. **23**(2), 297–322 (2015)
3. Ausserlechner, S., Fruhmann, S., Wieser, W., Hofer, B., Spork, R., Muhlbacher, C., Wotawa, F.: The right choice matters! SMT solving substantially improves model-based debugging of spreadsheets. In: 13th International Conference on Quality Software, pp. 139–148 (2013)
4. Dechter, R.: Constraint Processing. Morgan Kaufmann, San Francisco (2003)
5. Fisher, M.I., Rothermel, G.: The EUSES spreadsheet corpus: a shared resource for supporting experimentation with spreadsheet dependability mechanisms. ACM SIGSOFT Softw. Eng. Notes **30**(4), 1–5 (2005)
6. Gent, I.P., Jefferson, C., Miguel, I.: Minion: a fast, scalable, constraint solver. In: Proceedings of the 17th European Conference on Artificial Intelligence (ECAI 2006) (2006)
7. Abreu, R., Außerlechner, S., Hofer, B., Wotawa, F.: Testing for distinguishing repair candidates in spreadsheets – the mussco approach. In: El-Fakih, K., Barlas, G., Yevtushenko, N. (eds.) ICTSS 2015. LNCS, vol. 9447, pp. 124–140. Springer, Cham (2015). doi:10.1007/978-3-319-25945-1_8
8. Hofer, B., Hoefler, A., Wotawa, F.: Combining models for improved fault localization in spreadsheets. IEEE Trans. Reliab. **66**(1), 38–53 (2017)
9. Hofer, B., Perez, A., Abreu, R., Wotawa, F.: On the empirical evaluation of similarity coefficients for spreadsheets fault localization. Autom. Softw. Eng. **22**(1), 47–74 (2015)
10. Hofer, B., Wotawa, F.: Why does my spreadsheet compute wrong values? In: Proceedings of the International Symposium on Software Reliability Engineering (ISSRE), vol. 25, pp. 112–121 (2014)
11. Jannach, D., Engler, U.: Toward model-based debugging of spreadsheet programs. In: 9th Joint Conference on Knowledge-Based Software Engineering (JCKBSE 2010), pp. 252–264 (2010)
12. Jannach, D., Schmitz, T.: Model-based diagnosis of spreadsheet programs - a constraint-based debugging approach. Autom. Softw. Eng. **23**(1), 105–144 (2016). Springer
13. Jannach, D., Schmitz, T., Hofer, B., Wotawa, F.: Avoiding, finding and fixing spreadsheet errors - a survey of automated approaches for spreadsheet QA. J. Syst. Softw. **94**, 129–150 (2014)
14. Nica, I., Pill, I., Quaritsch, T., Wotawa, F.: A route to success - a performance comparison of diagnosis algorithms. In: Proceedings of the International Joint Conference on Artificial Intelligence (IJCAI) (2013)
15. Nica, I., Wotawa, F.: Condiag - computing minimal diagnoses using a constraint solver. In: Proceedings of the International Workshop on Principles of Diagnosis (DX), pp. 185–191 (2012)
16. Panko, R.R.: Thinking is bad: implications of human error research for spreadsheet research and practice. In: CoRR (2008)
17. Reiter, R.: A theory of diagnosis from first principles. Artif. Intell. **32**(1), 57–95 (1987)

18. Ruthruff, J., Creswick, E., Burnett, M., Cook, C., Prabhakararao, S., Fisher II, M., Main, M.: End-user software visualizations for fault localization. In: Proceedings of the 2003 ACM Symposium on Software Visualization (SoftVis 2003), pp. 123–132. ACM (2003)
19. Wotawa, F.: On the use of qualitative deviation models for diagnosis. In: 29th International Workshop on Qualitative Reasoning (QR), New York, July 2016

Test Derivation Methods

n-Complete Test Suites for IOCO

Petra van den Bos(✉), Ramon Janssen, and Joshua Moerman

Institute for Computing and Information Sciences,
Radboud University, Nijmegen, The Netherlands
{petra,ramonjanssen,joshua.moerman}@cs.ru.nl

Abstract. An n-complete test suite for automata guarantees to detect all faulty implementations with a bounded number of states. This principle is well-known when testing FSMs for equivalence, but the problem becomes harder for ioco conformance on labeled transitions systems. Existing methods restrict the structure of specifications and implementations. We eliminate those restrictions, using only the number of implementation states, and fairness in test execution. We provide a formalization, a construction and a correctness proof for n-complete test suites for ioco.

1 Introduction

The holy grail of model-based testing is a complete test suite: a test suite that can detect any possible faulty implementation. For black-box testing, this is impossible: a tester can only make a finite number of observations, but for an implementation of unknown size, it is unclear when to stop. Often, a so called n-complete test suite is used to tackle this problem, meaning it is complete for all implementations with at most n states.

For specifications modeled as finite state machines (FSMs) (also called Mealy machines), this has already been investigated extensively. In this paper we will explore how an n-complete test suite can be constructed for suspension automata. We use the *ioco* relation [11] instead of equivalence of FSMs.

An n-complete test suite for FSM equivalence usually provides some way to reach all states and transitions of the implementation. After reaching some state, it is tested whether this is the correct state, by observing behavior which is unique for that state, and hence distinguishing it from all other states.

Unlike FSM equivalence, ioco is not an equivalence relation, meaning that different implementations may conform to the same specification and, conversely, an implementation may conform to different specifications. In this paper, we focus on the problem of distinguishing states. For ioco, this cannot be done with simple identification. If an implementation state conforms to multiple specifications states, those states are defined to be *compatible*. Incompatible states can be handled in ways comparable to FSM-methods, but distinguishing compatible states requires more effort.

P. van den Bos and R. Janssen—Supported by NWO project 13859 (SUMBAT).

N. Yevtushenko et al. (Eds.): ICTSS 2017, LNCS 10533, pp. 91–107, 2017.
DOI: 10.1007/978-3-319-67549-7_6

In this paper, we give a structured approach for distinguishing incompatible states. We also propose a strategy to handle compatible states. Obviously, they cannot be distinguished in the sense of incompatible states. We thus change the aim of distinguishing: instead of forcing a non-conformance to either specification state, we may also prove conformance to both. As our only tool in proving this is by further testing, this is a recursive problem: during complete testing, we are required to prove conformance to multiple states by testing. We thus introduce a recursively defined test suite. We give examples where this still gives a finite test suite, together with a completeness proof for this approach. To show an upper bound for the required size of a test suite, we also show that an n-complete test suite with finite size can always be constructed, albeit an inefficient one.

Related Work. Testing methods for Finite State Machines (FSMs) have been analyzed thoroughly, and n-complete test suites are already known for quite a while. A survey is given in [3]. Progress has been made on generalizing these testing methods to nondeterministic FSMs, for example in [6,9]. FSM-based work that more closely resembles ioco is *reduction* of non-deterministic FSMs [4].

Complete testing in ioco received less attention than in FSM theory on this subject. The original test generation method [11] is an approach in which test cases are generated randomly. The method is complete in the sense that any fault *can* be found, but there is no upper bound to the required number and length of test cases.

In [8], complete test suites are constructed for Mealy-IOTSes. Mealy-IOTSes are a subclass of suspension automata, but are similar to Mealy machines as (sequences of) outputs are coupled to inputs. This makes the transition from FSM testing more straightforward.

The work most similar to ours [10] works on deterministic labeled transition systems, adding quiescence afterwards, as usual for ioco. Non-deterministic models are thus not considered, and cannot be handled implicitly through determinization, as determinization can only be done after adding quiescence. Some further restrictions are made on the specification domains. In particular, all specification states should be reachable without depending on choices for output transitions of the implementation. Furthermore, all states should be mutually incompatible. In this sense, our test suite construction can be applied to a broader set of systems, but will potentially be much less efficient. Thus, we prioritize exploring the bounds of n-complete test suites for ioco, whereas [10] aims at efficient test suites, by restricting the models which can be handled.

2   Preliminaries

The original ioco theory is defined for labeled transition systems, which may contain internal transitions, be nondeterministic, and may have states without outputs [11]. To every state without outputs, a self-loop with quiescence is added as an artificial output. The resulting labeled transition system is then determinized to create a *suspension automaton*, which is equivalent to the initial labeled transition system with respect to ioco [13]. In this paper, we will consider a slight generalization of suspension automata, such that our results hold for ioco in general: quiescent transitions usually have some restrictions, but we do not require them and we will treat quiescence as any other output. We will define them in terms of general automata with inputs and outputs.

Definition 1. *An I/O-automaton is a tuple* (Q, L_I, L_O, T, q_0) *where*

- Q *is a finite set of states*
- L_I *is a finite set of input labels*
- L_O *is a finite set of output labels*
- $T : Q \times (L_I \cup L_O) \rightharpoonup Q$ *is the (partial) transition function*
- $q_0 \in Q$ *is the initial state*

We denote the domain of I/O-automata for L_I and L_O with $\mathcal{A}(L_I, L_O)$.

For the remainder of this paper we fix L_I and L_O as disjoint sets of input and output labels respectively, with $L = L_I \cup L_O$, and omit them if clear from the context. Furthermore, we use a, b as input symbols and x, y, z as output symbols.

Definition 2. *Let* $S = (Q, L_I, L_O, T, q_0) \in \mathcal{A}$, $q \in Q$, $B \subseteq Q$, $\mu \in L$ *and* $\sigma \in L^*$. *Then we define:*

$$q \ after \ \mu = \begin{cases} \emptyset & if \ T(q, \mu) = \bot \\ \{T(q, \mu)\} & otherwise \end{cases} \qquad B \ after \ \sigma = \bigcup_{q' \in B} q' \ after \ \sigma$$

$$B \ after \ \mu = \bigcup_{q' \in B} q' \ after \ \mu \qquad out(B) = \{x \in L_O \mid B \ after \ x \neq \emptyset\}$$

$$in(B) = \{a \in L_I \mid B \ after \ a \neq \emptyset\}$$

$$q \ after \ \epsilon = \{q\} \qquad init(B) = in(B) \cup out(B)$$

$$q \ after \ \mu\sigma = (q \ after \ \mu) \ after \ \sigma \qquad Straces(B) = \{\sigma' \in L^* \mid B \ after \ \sigma' \neq \emptyset\}$$

$$S \ is \ \text{output-enabled} \ if \ \forall p \in Q : out(p) \neq \emptyset \qquad \mathcal{SA} = \{S' \in \mathcal{A} \mid S' \ is \ output\text{-}enabled\}$$

$$S \ is \ \text{input-enabled} \ if \ \forall p \in Q : in(p) = L_I \qquad \mathcal{SA}_{IE} = \{S' \in \mathcal{SA} \mid S' \ is \ input\text{-}enabled\}$$

We interchange singleton sets with its element, e.g. we write $out(q)$ instead of $out(\{q\})$. Definitions on states will sometimes be used for automata as well, acting on their initial states. Similarly, definitions on automata will be used for states, acting on the automaton with that state as its initial state. For example, for $S = (Q, L_I, L_O, T, q_0) \in \mathcal{A}$ and $q \in Q$, we may write S *after* μ instead of q_0 *after* μ, and we may write that q is input-enabled if S is input-enabled.

In this paper, specifications are suspension automata in $\mathcal{SA}$, and implementations are input-enabled suspension automata in $\mathcal{SA}_{IE}$. The ioco relation formalizes when implementations conform to specifications. We give a definition relating suspension automata, following [11], and the coinductive definition [7] relating states. Both definitions have been proven to coincide.

Definition 3. *Let* $S \in \mathcal{SA}$, *and* $I \in \mathcal{SA}_{IE}$. *Then we say that* I *ioco* S *if* $\forall \sigma \in Straces(S) : out(I \ after \ \sigma) \subseteq out(S \ after \ \sigma)$.

Definition 4. *Let* $S = (Q_s, L_I, L_O, T_s, q_0^s) \in \mathcal{SA}$, *and* $I = (Q_i, L_I, L_O, T_i, q_0^i) \in \mathcal{SA}_{IE}$. *Then for* $q_i \in Q_i$, $q_s \in Q_s$, *we say that* q_i *ioco* q_s *if there exists a coinductive ioco relation* $R \subseteq Q_i \times Q_s$ *such that* $(q_i, q_s) \in R$, *and* $\forall (q, p) \in R$:

- $\forall a \in in(p) : (q \text{ after } a, p \text{ after } a) \in R$
- $\forall x \in out(q) : x \in out(p) \land (q \text{ after } x, p \text{ after } x) \in R$

In order to define complete test suites, we require execution of tests to be *fair*: if a trace σ is performed often enough, then every output x appearing in the implementation after σ will eventually be observed. Furthermore, the implementation may give an output after σ before the tester can supply an input. We then assume that the tester will eventually succeed in performing this input after σ. This fairness assumption is unavoidable for any notion of completeness in testing suspension automata: a fault can never be detected if an implementation always chooses paths that avoid this fault.

3 Distinguishing Experiments

An important part of n-complete test suites for FSM equivalence is the distinguishing sequence, used to identify an implementation state. As ioco is not an equivalence relation, there does not have to be a one-to-one correspondence between specification and implementation states.

3.1 Equivalence and Compatibility

We first describe equivalence and compatibility relations between states, in order to define distinguishing experiments. We consider two specifications to be equivalent, denoted $S_1 \approx S_2$, if they have the same implementations conforming to them. Then, for all implementations I, we have I ioco S_1 iff I ioco S_2. For two inequivalent specifications, there is thus an implementation which conforms to one, but not the other.

Intuitively, equivalence relates states with the same traces. However, implicit underspecification by absent inputs should be handled equivalently to explicit underspecification with chaos. This is done by using chaotic completion [11]. This definition of equivalence is inspired by the relation wioco [12], which relates specifications based on their sets of traces.

Definition 5. *Let* $(Q, L_I, L_O, T, q_0) \in \mathcal{SA}$. *Define* chaos, *a specification to which every implementation conforms, as* $X = (\{\chi\}, L_I, L_O, \{(\chi, x, \chi) \mid x \in L\}, \chi)$. *Let* $Q_X = Q \cup \{\chi\}$. *The relation* $\approx \subseteq Q_X \times Q_X$ *relates all equivalent states. It is the largest relation for which it holds that* $q \approx q'$ *if:*

$$out(q) = out(q') \land (\forall \mu \in init(q) \cap init(q') : q \text{ after } \mu \approx q' \text{ after } \mu)$$
$$\land (\forall a \in in(q) \backslash in(q') : q \text{ after } a \approx \chi) \land (\forall a \in in(q') \backslash in(q) : q' \text{ after } a \approx \chi)$$

For two inequivalent specifications, there may still exist an implementation that conforms to the two. In that case, we define the specifications to be *compatible*, following the terminology introduced in [9,10]. We introduce an explicit relation for compatibility.

Definition 6. *Let* $(Q, L_I, L_O, T, q_0) \in \mathcal{SA}$. *The relation* $\Diamond \subseteq Q \times Q$ *relates all compatible* states. *It is the largest relation for which it holds that* $q \Diamond q'$ *if:*

$$(\forall a \in in(q) \cap in(q') : q \text{ after } a \Diamond q' \text{ after } a)$$
$$\wedge (\exists x \in out(q) \cap out(q') : q \text{ after } x \Diamond q' \text{ after } x)$$

Compatibility is symmetric and reflexive, but not transitive. Conversely, two specifications are *incompatible* if there exists no implementation conforming to both. When $q_1 \Diamond q_2$, we can indeed easily make an implementation which conforms to both q_1 and q_2: the set of outputs of the implementation state can simply be $out(q_1) \cap out(q_2)$, which is non-empty by definition of $\Diamond$. Upon such an output transition or any input transition, the two successor states are again compatible, thus the implementation can keep picking transitions in this manner. For example, in Fig. 1, compatible states 2 and 3 of the specification are both implemented by state 2 of the implementation.

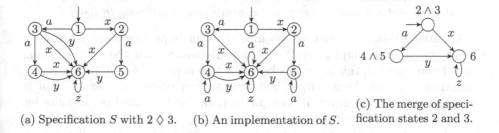

(a) Specification S with $2 \Diamond 3$.   (b) An implementation of S.   (c) The merge of specification states 2 and 3.

Fig. 1. A specification, an implementation, and a merge of two states.

Beneš et al. [1] describe the construction of *merging* specifications. For specification states q_s and q'_s, their merge is denoted $q_s \wedge q'_s$. For any implementation state q_i, it holds that q_i ioco $q_s \wedge q_i$ ioco $q'_s \iff q_i$ ioco $(q_s \wedge q'_s)$. Intuitively, a merge of two states thus only allows behavior allowed by both states. Figure 1c shows the merge of specification states 2 and 3. The merge of q_s and q'_s can be implemented if and only if $q_s \Diamond q'_s$: indeed, for incompatible states, the merge has states without any output transitions, which is denoted *invalid* in [1].

3.2   Distinguishing Trees

When an implementation is in state q_i, two incompatible specification states q_s and q'_s are distinguished by showing to which of the two q_i conforms, assuming that it conforms to one. Conversely, we can say that we have to show a non-conformance of q_i to q_s or q'_s. Generally, a set of states D is distinguished by showing non-conformance to all its states, possibly except one. As a base case, if $|D| \leq 1$, then D is already distinguished. We will construct a distinguishing tree as an input-enabled automaton which distinguishes D after reaching **pass**.

Definition 7. *Let μ be a symbol and D a set of states. Then injective(μ, D) if $\mu \in \bigcap \{in(q) \mid q \in D\} \cup L_O \wedge \forall q, q' \in D : q \neq q' \wedge \mu \in init(q) \cap init(q') \implies q$ after $\mu \neq q'$ after μ. This is extended to sets of symbols Σ as injective(Σ, D) if $\forall \mu \in \Sigma : injective(\mu, D)$.*

Definition 8. *Let $(Q, L_I, L_O, T, q_0) \in \mathcal{SA}(L_I, L_O)$, and $D \subseteq Q$ a set of mutually incompatible states. Then define $\mathcal{DT}(L_I, L_O, D) \subseteq \mathcal{A}(L_O, L_I)$ inductively as the domain of input-enabled distinguishing trees for D, such that for every $Y \in \mathcal{DT}(L_I, L_O, D)$ with initial state t_0:*

- *if $|D| \leq 1$, then t_0 is the verdict state **pass**, and*
- *if $|D| > 1$, then t_0 has either*
  - *a transition for a single input $a \in L_I$ to a $Y' \in \mathcal{DT}(L_I, L_O, D$ after $a)$ such that injective(a, D), and transitions to a verdict state **reset** for all $x \in L_O$, or*
  - *a transition for every output $x \in L_O$ to a $Y' \in \mathcal{DT}(L_I, L_O, D$ after $x)$ such that injective(x, D).*

  *Furthermore, **pass** or **reset** is always reached after a finite number of steps, and these states are sink states, i.e. contain transitions only to itself.*

A distinguishing tree can synchronize with an implementation to reach a verdict state. As an implementation is output-enabled and the distinguishing tree is input-enabled, this never blocks. If the tree performs an input, the implementation may provide an output first, resulting in **reset**: another attempt is needed to perform the input. If no input is performed by the tree, it waits for any output, after which it can continue. In this way, the tester is guaranteed to steer the implementation to a **pass**, where the specification states disagree on the allowed outputs: the implementation has to choose an output, thus has to choose which specifications (not) to implement.

For a set D of mutually incompatible states, such a tree may not exist. For example, consider states 1, 3 and 5 in Fig. 2. States 1 and 3 both lead to the same state after a, and can therefore not be distinguished. Similarly, states 3 and 5 cannot be distinguished after b. Labels a and b are therefore not injective according to Definition 7 and should not be used. This concept is similar in FSM testing [5]. A distinguishing sequence always exists when $|D| = 2$. When $|D| > 2$, we can thus use multiple experiments to separate all states pairwise.

Lemma 9. *Let $S \in \mathcal{SA}$. Let q and q' be two states of S, such that $q \not\Downarrow q'$. Then there exists a distinguishing tree for q and q'.*

Proof. Since $q \not\Downarrow q'$, we know that:

$$(\exists a \in in(q) \cap in(q') : q \text{ after } a \not\Downarrow q' \text{ after } a)$$
$$\vee (\forall x \in out(q) \cap out(q') : q \text{ after } x \not\Downarrow q' \text{ after } x)$$

So we have that some input or all outputs, enabled in both q and q', lead to incompatible states, for which this holds again. Hence, we can construct a tree with nodes that either have a child for an enabled input of both states, or children for all outputs enabled in the states (children for not enabled outputs are distinguishing trees for $\emptyset$), as in the second case of Definition 8. If this tree would be infinite, then this tree would describe infinite sequences of labels. Since S is finite, such a sequence would be a cycle in S. This would mean that $q \lozenge q'$, which is not the case. Hence we have that the tree is finite, as required by Definition 8. $\qquad\qquad\qquad\qquad\qquad\qquad\qquad\qquad\qquad\qquad\qquad\qquad\square$

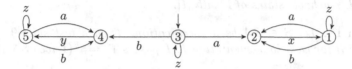

Fig. 2. No distinguishing tree exists for $\{1,3,5\}$.

3.3 Distinguishing Compatible States

Distinguishing techniques such as described in Sect. 3.2 rely on incompatibility of two specifications, by steering the implementation to a point where the specifications disagree on the allowed outputs. This technique fails for compatible specifications, as an implementation state may conform to both specifications. Thus, a tester then cannot steer the implementation to showing a non-conformance to either.

We thus extend the aim of a distinguishing experiment: instead of showing a non-conformance to any of two compatible states q_s and q'_s, we may also prove conformance to both. This can be achieved with an n-complete test suite for $q_s \wedge q'_s$; this will be explained in Sect. 4.1. Note that even for an implementation which does not conform to one of the specifications, n-complete testing is needed. Such an implementation may be distinguished, but it is unknown how, due to compatibility. See for example the specification and implementation of Fig. 1. State 2 of the implementation can only be distinguished from state 3 by observing ax, which is non-conforming behavior for state 2. Although y would also be non-conforming for state 2, this behavior is not observed.

In case that a non-conformance to the merged specification is found with an n-complete test suite, then the outcome is similar to that of a distinguishing tree for incompatible states: we have disproven conformance to one of the individual specifications (or to both).

4 Test Suite Definition

The number n of an n-complete test suite $\mathbb{T}$ of a specification S tells how many states an implementation I is allowed to have to give the guarantee that I ioco

S after passing $\mathbb{T}$ (we will define passing a test suite later). To do this, we must only count the states relevant for conformance.

Definition 10. *Let $S = (Q_s, L_I, L_O, T, q_0^s) \in \mathcal{SA}$, and $I = (Q_i, L_I, L_O, T_i, q_0^i) \in \mathcal{SA}_{IE}$. Then,*

- *A state $q_s \in Q_s$ is reachable if $\exists \sigma \in L^* : S$ after $\sigma = q_s$.*
- *A state $q_i \in Q_i$ is specified if $\exists \sigma \in Straces(S) : I$ after $\sigma = q_i$. A transition $(q_i, \mu, q_i') \in T_i$ is specified if q_i is specified, and if either $\mu \in L_O$, or $\mu \in L_I \wedge \exists \sigma \in L^* : I$ after $\sigma = q_i \wedge \sigma\mu \in Straces(S)$.*
- *We denote the number of reachable states of S with $|S|$, and the number of specified, reachable states of I with $|I|$.*

Definition 11. *Let $S \in \mathcal{SA}$ be a specification. Then a test suite $\mathbb{T}$ for S is n-complete if for each implementation $I: I$ passes $\mathbb{T} \implies (I$ ioco $S \vee |I| > n)$.*

In particular, $|S|$-complete means that if an implementation passes the test suite, then the implementation is correct (w.r.t. ioco) *or* it has strictly more states than the specification. Some authors use the convention that n denotes the number of *extra* states (so the above would be called 0-completeness).

To define a full complete test suite, we first define sets of distinguishing experiments.

Definition 12. *Let $(Q, L_I, L_O, T, q_0) \in \mathcal{SA}$. For any state $q \in Q$, we choose a set $W(q)$ of distinguishing experiments, such that for all $q' \in Q$ with $q \neq q'$:*

- *if $q \not\Diamond q'$, then $W(q)$ contains a distinguishing tree for $D \subseteq Q$, s.t. $q, q' \in D$.*
- *if $q \Diamond q'$, then $W(q)$ contains a complete test suite for $q \wedge q'$.*

Moreover, we need sequences to access all specified, reachable implementation states. After such sequences distinguishing experiments can be executed. We will defer the explicit construction of the set of access sequences. For now we assume some set P of access sequences to exist.

Definition 13. *Let $S \in \mathcal{SA}$ and $I \in \mathcal{SA}_{IE}$. Let P be a set of access sequences and let $P^+ = \{\sigma \in P \cup P \cdot L \mid S$ after $\sigma \neq \emptyset\}$. Then the distinguishing test suite is defined as $\mathbb{T} = \{\sigma\tau \mid \sigma \in P^+, \tau \in W(q_0$ after $\sigma)\}$. An element $t \in \mathbb{T}$ is a test.*

4.1 Distinguishing Experiments for Compatible States

The distinguishing test suite relies on executing distinguishing experiments. If a specification contains compatible states, the test suite contains distinguishing experiments which are themselves n-complete test suites. This is thus a recursive construction: we need to show that such a test suite is finite. For particular specifications, recursive repetition of the distinguishing test suite as described above is already finite. For example, specification S in Fig. 1 contains compatible states, but in the merge of every two compatible states, no further compatible states remain. A test suite for S needs to distinguish states 2 and 3. For this purpose, it uses an *n*-complete test suite for $2 \wedge 3$, which contains no compatible states, and thus terminates by only containing distinguishing trees.

However, the merge of two compatible states may in general again contain compatible states. In these cases, recursive repetition of distinguishing test suites may not terminate. An alternative unconditional *n*-complete test suite may be constructed using state counting methods [4], as shown in the next section. Although inefficient, it shows the possibility of unconditional termination. The recursive strategy thus may serve as a starting point for other, efficient constructions for *n*-complete test suites.

Unconditional *n*-complete Test Suites. We introduce Lemma 16 to bound test suite execution. We first define some auxiliary definitions.

Definition 14. *Let* $S \in \mathcal{SA}$, $\sigma \in L^*$, *and* $x \in L_O$. *Then* σx *is an ioco-counterexample if* S *after* $\sigma \neq \emptyset$, $x \notin out(S \text{ after } \sigma)$.

Naturally, I ioco S if and only if $Straces(I)$ contains no ioco-counterexample.

Definition 15. *Let* $S = (Q_s, L_I, L_O, T_s, q_s^0) \in \mathcal{SA}$ *and* $I \in \mathcal{SA}_{IE}$. *A trace* $\sigma \in Straces(S)$ *is short if* $\forall q_s \in Q_s : |\{\rho \mid \rho \text{ is a prefix of } \sigma \wedge q_s^0 \text{ after } \rho = q_s\}| \leq |I|$.

Lemma 16. *Let* $S \in \mathcal{SA}$ *and* $I \in \mathcal{SA}_{IE}$. *If* $I \not\text{ioco} S$, *then* $Straces(I)$ *contains a short ioco-counterexample.*

Proof. If $I \not\text{ioco} S$, then $Straces(I)$ must contain an ioco-counterexample σ. If σ is short, the proof is trivial, so assume it is not. Hence, there exists a state q_s, with at least $|I| + 1$ prefixes of σ leading to q_s. At least two of those prefixes ρ and ρ' must lead to the same implementation state, i.e. it holds that q_i^0 after $\rho = q_i^0$ after ρ' and q_s^0 after $\rho = q_s^0$ after ρ'. Assuming $|\rho| < |\rho'|$ without loss of generality, we can thus create an ioco-counterexample σ' shorter than σ by replacing ρ' by ρ. If σ' is still not short, we can repeat this process until it is. $\square$

We can use Lemma 16 to bound exhaustive testing to obtain *n*-completeness. When any specification state is visited $|I| + 1$ times with any trace, then any extensions of this trace will not be short, and we do not need to test them. Fairness allows us to test all short traces which are present in the implementation.

Corollary 17. *Given a specification* S *the set of all traces of length at most* $|S| * n$ *is an n-complete test suite.*

Example 18. Figure 3 shows an example of a non-conforming implementation with a counterexample $yyxyyxyyxyyx$, of maximal length $4 \cdot 3 = 12$.

4.2 Execution of Test Suites

A test $\sigma\tau$ is executed by following σ, and then executing the distinguishing experiment τ. If the implementation chooses any output deviating from σ, then the test gives a **reset** and should be reattempted. Finishing τ may take several

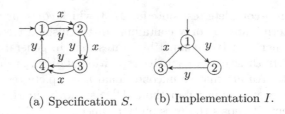

(a) Specification S.   (b) Implementation I.

Fig. 3. A specification, and a non-conforming implementation.

executions: a distinguishing tree may give a **reset**, and an n-complete test suite to distinguish compatible states may contain multiple tests. Therefore σ needs to be run multiple times, in order to allow full execution of the distinguishing experiment. By assuming fairness, every distinguishing experiment is guaranteed to termininate, and thus also every test.

The verdict of a test suite $\mathbb{T}$ for specification S is concluded simply by checking for observed ioco-counterexamples to S during execution. When executing a distinguishing experiment w as part of $\mathbb{T}$, the verdict of w is ignored when concluding a verdict for $\mathbb{T}$: we only require w to be fully executed, i.e. be reattempted if it gives a **reset**, until it gives a **pass** or **fail**. For example, if σ leads to specification state q, and q needs to be distinguished from compatible state q', a test suite $\mathbb{T}'$ for $q \wedge q'$ is needed to distinguished q and q'. If $\mathbb{T}'$ finds a non-conformance to either q or q', it yields **fail**. Only in the former case, $\mathbb{T}$ will also yield **fail**, and in the latter case, $\mathbb{T}$ will continue with other tests: q and q' have been successfully distinguished, but no non-conformance to q has been found. If all tests have been executed in this manner, $\mathbb{T}$ will conclude **pass**.

4.3 Access Sequences

In FSM-based testing, the set P for reaching all implementation states is taken care of rather efficiently. The set P is constructed by choosing a word σ for each specification state, such that σ leads to that state (note the FSMs are fully deterministic). By passing the tests $P \cdot W$, where W is a set of distinguishing experiment for every reached state, we know the implementation has at least some number of states (by observing that many different behaviors). By passing tests $P \cdot L \cdot W$ we also verify that every transition has the correct destination state. By extending these tests to $P \cdot L^{\leq k+1} \cdot W$ (where $L^{\leq k+1} = \bigcup_{m \in \{0, \cdots, k+1\}} L^m$), we can reach all implementation states if the implementation has at most k more states than the specification. For suspension automata, however, things are more difficult for two reasons: (1) A specification state may be reachable only if an implementation chooses to implement a particular, optional output transition (in which case this state is not *certainly reachable* [10]), and (2) if the specification has compatible states, the implementation may implement two specification states with a single implementation state.

Consider Fig. 4 for an example. An implementation can omit state 2 of the specification, as shown in Fig. 4b. Now Fig. 4c shows a fault not found by a test suite $P \cdot L^{\leq 1} \cdot W$: if we take $y \in P$, $z \in L$, and observe $z \in W(3)$, we do not reach the faulty y transition in the implementation. So by leaving out states, we introduce an opportunity to make a fault without needing more states than the specification. This means that we may need to increase the size of the test suite in order to obtain the desired completeness. In this example, however, a test suite $P \cdot L^{\leq 2} \cdot W$ is enough, as the test suite will contain a test with $yzz \in P \cdot L^2$ after which the faulty output $y \notin W(3)$ will be observed.

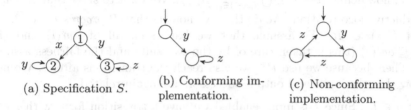

(a) Specification S.

(b) Conforming implementation.

(c) Non-conforming implementation.

Fig. 4. A specification with not certainly reachable states 2 and 3.

Clearly, we reach all states in a n-state implementation for any specification S, by taking P to be all traces in $Straces(S)$ of at most length n. This set P can be constructed by simple enumeration. We then have that the traces in the set P will reach all specified, reachable states in all implementations I such that $|I| \leq n$. In particular this will mean that P^+ reaches all specified transitions. Although this generates exponentially many sequences, the length is substantially shorter than the sequences obtained by the unconditional n-complete test suite. We conjecture that a much more efficient construction is possible with a careful analysis of compatible states and the not certainly reachable states.

4.4   Completeness Proof for Distinguishing Test Suites

We let $\mathbb{T}$ be the distinguishing test suite as defined in Definition 13. As discussed before, if q and q' are compatible, the set $W(q)$ can be defined using another complete test suite. If the test suite is again a distinguishing test suite, completeness of it is an induction hypothesis. If, on the other hand, the unconditional n-complete test suite is used, completeness is already guaranteed (Corollary 17).

Theorem 19. *Let $S = (Q_s, L_I, L_O, T_s, q_0^s) \in \mathcal{SA}$ be a specification. Let $\mathbb{T}$ be a distinguishing test suite for S. Then $\mathbb{T}$ is n-complete.*

Proof. We will show that for any implementation of the correct size and which passes the test suite we can build a coinductive ioco relation which contain the initial states. As a basis for that relation we take the states which are reached by the set P. This may not be an ioco relation, but by extending it (in two steps) we obtain a full ioco relation. Extending the relation is an instance of a so-called *up-to technique*, we will use terminology from [2].

More precisely, Let $I = (Q_i, L_I, L_O, T_i, q_0^i) \in \mathcal{SA}_{IE}$ be an implementation with $|I| \leq n$ which passes $\mathbb{T}$. By construction of P, all reachable specified implementation states are reached by P and so all specified transitions are reached by P^+.

The set P defines a subset of $Q_i \times Q_s$, namely $R = \{(q_0^i \text{ after } \sigma, q_0^s \text{ after } \sigma) \mid \sigma \in P\}$. We add relations for all equivalent states: $R' = \{(i, s) \mid (i, s') \in R, s \in Q_s, s \approx s'\}$. Furthermore, let $\mathcal{J} = \{(i, s, s') \mid i \in Q_i, s, s' \in Q_s \text{ such that } i \text{ ioco } s \wedge i \text{ ioco } s'\}$ and $R_{i,s,s'}$ be the ioco relation for i ioco $s \wedge i$ ioco s', now define $\overline{R} = R' \cup \bigcup_{(i,s,s') \in \mathcal{J}} R_{i,s,s'}$. We want to show that $\overline{R}$ defines a coinductive ioco relation. We do this by showing that R *progresses* to $\overline{R}$.

Let $(i, s) \in R$. We assume that we have seen all of $out(i)$ and that $out(i) \subseteq out(s)$ (this is taken care of by the test suite and the fairness assumption). Then, because we use P^+, we also reach the transitions after i. We need to show that the input and output successors are again related.

- Let $a \in L_I$. Since I is input-enabled we have a transition for a with i *after* $a = i_2$. Suppose there is a transition for a from s: s *after* $a = s_2$ (if not, then we're done). We have to show that $(i_2, s_2) \in \overline{R}$.
- Let $x \in L_O$. Suppose there is a transition for x: i *after* $x = i_2$ Then (since $out(i) \subseteq out(s)$) there is a transition for x from s: s *after* $x = s_2$. We have to show that $(i_2, s_2) \in \overline{R}$.

In both cases we have a successor (i_2, s_2) which we have to prove to be in $\overline{R}$. Now since P reaches all states of I, we know that $(i_2, s_2') \in R$ for some s_2'. If $s_2 \approx s_2'$ then $(i_2, s_2) \in R' \subseteq \overline{R}$ holds trivially, so suppose that $s_2 \not\approx s_2'$. Then there exists a distinguishing experiment $w \in W(s_2) \cap W(s_2')$ which has been executed in i_2, namely in two tests: a test σw for some $\sigma \in P^+$ with S *after* $\sigma = s_2$, and a test $\sigma' w$ for some $\sigma' \in P$ with S *after* σ'. Then there are two cases:

- If $s_2 \not\sqsubseteq s_2'$ then w is a distinguishing tree separating s_2 and s_2'. Then there is a sequence ρ taken in w of the test σw, i.e. w *after* ρ reaches a **pass** state of w, and similarly there is a sequence ρ' that is taken in w of the test $\sigma' w$. By construction of distinguishing trees, ρ must be an ioco-counterexample for either s_2 or s_2', but because $\mathbb{T}$ passed this must be s_2'. Similarly, ρ' disproves s_2. One implementation state can implement at most one of $\{\rho, \rho'\}$. This contradicts that the two tests passed, so this case cannot happen.
- If $s_2 \lozenge s_2'$ (but $s_2 \not\approx s_2'$ as assumed above), then w is a test suite itself for $s_2 \wedge s_2'$. If w passed in both tests then i_2 ioco s_2 and i_2 ioco s_2', and hence $(i_2, s_2) \in R_{i,s_2',s_2} \subseteq \overline{R}$. If w failed in one of the tests σw or $\sigma' w$, then i_2 does not conform to both s_2' and s_2, and hence w also fails in the other test. So again, there is a counterexample ρ for s_2' and ρ' for s_2. One implementation state can implement at most one of $\{\rho, \rho'\}$. This contradicts that the two tests passed, so this case cannot happen.

We have now seen that R progresses to $\overline{R}$. It is clear that R' progresses to $\overline{R}$ too. Then, since each $R_{i,s,s'}$ is an ioco relation, they progress to $R_{i,s,s'} \subseteq \overline{R}$. And so the union, $\overline{R}$, progresses to $\overline{R}$, meaning that $\overline{R}$ is a coinductive ioco relation. Furthermore, we have $(i_0, s_0) \in \overline{R}$ (because $\epsilon \in P$), concluding the proof. $\square$

We remark that if the specification does not contain any compatible states, that the proof can be simplified a lot. In particular, we do not need n-complete test suites for merges of states, and we can use the relation R' instead of $\overline{R}$.

5   Constructing Distinguishing Trees

Lee and Yannakakis proposed an algorithm for constructing adaptive distinguishing sequences for FSMs [5]. With a partition refinement algorithm, a splitting tree is build, from which the actual distinguishing sequence is extracted.

A splitting tree is a tree of which each node is identified with a subset of the states of the specification. The set of states of a child node is a (strict) subset of the states of its parent node. In contrast to splitting trees for FSMs, siblings may overlap: the tree does not describe a partition refinement. We define *leaves*(Y) as the set of leaves of a tree Y. The algorithm will split the leaf nodes, i.e. assign children to every leaf node. If all leaves are identified with a singleton set of states, we can distinguish all states of the root node.

Additionally, every non-leaf node is associated with a set of labels from L. We denote the labels of node D with *labels*(D). The distinguishing tree that is going to be constructed from the splitting tree is built up from these labels. As argued in Sect. 3.2, we require injective distinguishing trees, thus our splitting trees only contain injective labels, i.e. *injective*(*labels*(D), D) for all non-leaf nodes D.

Below we list three conditions that describe when it is possible to split the states of a leaf D, i.e. by taking some transition, we are able to distinguish some states from the other states of D. We will see later how a split is done. If the first condition is true, at least one state is immediately distinguished from all other states. The other two conditions describe that a leaf D can be split if after an input or all outputs some node D' is reached that already is split, i.e. D' is a non-leaf node. Consequently, a split for condition 1 should be done whenever possible, and otherwise a split for condition 2 or 3 can be done. Depending on the implementation one is testing, one may prefer splitting with either condition 2 or 3, when both conditions are true.

We present each condition by first giving an intuitive description in words, and then a more formal definition. With $\Pi(A)$ we denote the set of all non-trivial partitions of a set of states A.

Definition 20. *A leaf D of tree Y can be split if one of the following conditions hold:*

1. *All outputs are enabled in some but not in all states.*

$$\forall x \in out(D) : injective(x, D) \land \exists d \in D : d \; after \; x = \emptyset$$

2. *Some states reach different leaves than other states for all outputs.*

$$\forall x \in out(D) : injective(x, D) \land \exists P \in \Pi(D), \forall d, d' \in P :$$
$$(d \neq d' \implies \forall l \in leaves(Y) : l \cap d \; after \; x = \emptyset \lor l \cap d' \; after \; x = \emptyset)$$

3. *Some states reach different leaves than other states for some input.*

$$\exists a \in in(D) : injective(a, D) \wedge \exists P \in \Pi(D), \forall d, d' \in P :$$
$$(d \neq d' \implies \forall l \in leaves(Y) : l \cap d \text{ after } a = \emptyset \vee l \cap d' \text{ after } a = \emptyset)$$

Algorithm 1 shows how to split a single leaf of the splitting tree (we chose arbitrarily to give condition 2 a preference over condition 3). A splitting tree is constructed in the following manner. Initially, a splitting tree is a leaf node of the state set from the specification. Then, the full splitting tree is constructed by splitting leaf nodes with Algorithm 1 until no further splits can be made. If all leaves in the resulting splitting tree are singletons, the splitting tree is complete and a distinguishing tree can be constructed (described in the next section). Otherwise, no distinguishing tree exists. Note that the order of the splits is left unspecified.

Input: A specification $S = (Q, L_I, L_O, T, q_0) \in \mathcal{SA}$
Input: The current (unfinished) splitting tree Y
Input: A leaf node D from Y
1 **if** Condition 1 holds for D **then**
2     $P := \{D \text{ after } x \mid x \in out(D)\}$;
3     $labels(D) := out(D)$;
4   Add the partition blocks of P as children of D;
5 **else if** Condition 2 holds for D **then**
6     $labels(D) := out(D)$;
7   **foreach** $x \in out(D)$ **do**
8        $P :=$ the finest partition for Condition 2 with D and x;
9   Add the partition blocks of P as children of D;
10   **end**
11 **else if** Condition 3 holds for D with input a **then**
12     $P :=$ the finest partition for Condition 3 with D and a;
13     $labels(D) := \{a\}$;
14   Add the partition blocks of P as children of D;
15 **return** Y;

Algorithm 1. Algorithm for splitting a leaf node of a splitting tree.

Example 21. Let us apply Algorithm 1 on the suspension automaton in Fig. 5a. Figure 5b shows the resulting splitting tree. We initialize the root node to $\{1, 2, 3, 4, 5\}$. Condition 1 applies, since states 1 and 5 only have output y enabled, while states 2, 3 and 4 only have outputs x and z enabled. Thus, we add leaves $\{1, 5\}$ and $\{2, 3, 4\}$.

We can split $\{1, 5\}$ by taking an output transition for y according to condition 2, as 1 *after* $y = 4 \in \{2, 3, 4\}$, while 5 *after* $y = 1 \in \{1, 5\}$, i.e. 1 and 5 reach different leaves. Condition 2 also applies for $\{2, 3, 4\}$. We have that $\{2, 3\}$ *after* $x = \{2, 4\} \subseteq \{2, 3, 4\}$ while 4 *after* $x = 5 \in \{5\}$. Hence we obtain children $\{4\}$

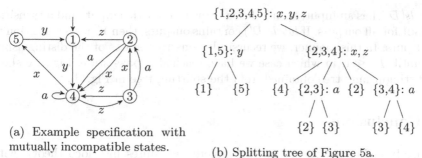

(a) Example specification with mutually incompatible states.

(b) Splitting tree of Figure 5a.

Fig. 5. Specification and its splitting tree.

and $\{2,3\}$ for output x. For z we have that 2 *after* $z = 1 \in \{1\}$ while $\{3,4\}$ *after* $z = \{3,4\} \subseteq \{2,3,4\}$, so we obtain children $\{2\}$ and $\{3,4\}$ for z.

We can split $\{2,3\}$ by taking input transition a according to condition 3, since 2 *after* $a = 4$ and 3 *after* $a = 2$, and no leaf of the splitting tree contains both state 2 and state 4. Note that we could also have split on output transitions x and z. Node $\{3,4\}$ cannot be split for output transition z, since $\{3,4\}$ *after* $z = \{3,4\}$ which is a leaf, and hence condition 2 does not hold. However node $\{3,4\}$ can be split for input transition a, as 3 *after* $a = 2$ and 4 *after* $a = 4$. Now all leaves are singleton, so we can distinguish all states with this tree.

A distinguishing tree $Y \in \mathcal{DT}(L_I, L_O, D)$ for D can be constructed from a splitting tree with singleton leaf nodes. This follows the structure in Definition 8, and we only need to choose whether to provide an input, or whether to observe outputs. We look at the lowest node D' in the split tree such that $D \subseteq D'$.

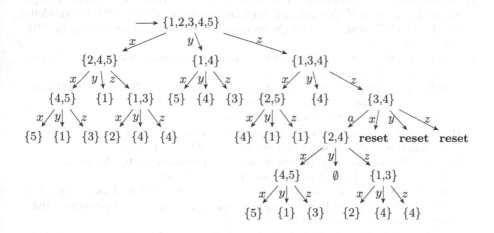

Fig. 6. Distinguishing tree of Fig. 5a. The states are named by the sets of states which they distinguish. Singleton and empty sets are the **pass** states. Self-loops in verdict states have been omitted, for brevity.

If *labels*(D') has an input, then Y has a transition for this input, and a transition to **reset** for all outputs. If *labels*(D') contains outputs, then Y has a transition for all outputs. In this manner, we recursively construct states of the distinguishing tree until $|D| \leq 1$, in which case we have reached a **pass** state. Figure 6 shows the distinguishing tree obtained from the splitting tree in Fig. 5b.

6 Conclusions

We firmly embedded theory on n-complete test suites into ioco theory, without making any restricting assumptions. We have identified several problems where classical FSM techniques fail for suspension automata, in particular for compatible states. An extension of the concept of distinguishing states has been introduced such that compatible states can be handled, by testing the merge of such states. This requires that the merge itself does not contain compatible states. Furthermore, upper bounds for several parts of a test suite have been given, such as reaching all states in the implementation.

These upper bounds are exponential in the number of states, and may limit practical applicability. Further investigation is needed to efficiently tackle these parts of the test suite. Alternatively, looser notions for completeness may circumvent these problems. Furthermore, experiments are needed to compare our testing method and random testing as in [11] quantitatively, in terms of efficiency of computation and execution time, and the ability to find bugs, preferably on a real world case study.

References

1. Beneš, N., Daca, P., Henzinger, T.A., Křetínský, J., Ničković, D.: Complete composition operators for IOCO-testing theory. In: Proceedings of the 18th International ACM SIGSOFT Symposium on Component-Based Software Engineering, pp. 101–110. ACM (2015)
2. Bonchi, F., Pous, D.: Hacking nondeterminism with induction and coinduction. Commun. ACM **58**(2), 87–95 (2015)
3. Dorofeeva, R., El-Fakih, K., Maag, S., Cavalli, A.R., Yevtushenko, N.: FSM-based conformance testing methods: a survey annotated with experimental evaluation. Inf. Softw. Technol. **52**(12), 1286–1297 (2010)
4. Hierons, R.M.: Testing from a nondeterministic finite state machine using adaptive state counting. IEEE Trans. Comput. **53**(10), 1330–1342 (2004)
5. Lee, D., Yannakakis, M.: Testing finite-state machines: state identification and verification. IEEE Trans. Comput. **43**(3), 306–320 (1994)
6. Luo, G., von Bochmann, G., Petrenko, A.: Test selection based on communicating nondeterministic finite-state machines using a generalized Wp-method. IEEE Trans. Software Eng. **20**(2), 149–162 (1994)
7. Noroozi, N.: Improving input-output conformance testing theories. PhD thesis, Technische Universiteit Eindhoven (2014)
8. Paiva, S.C., Simao, A.: Generation of complete test suites from mealy input/output transition systems. Form. Asp. Comput. **28**(1), 65–78 (2016)

9. Petrenko, A., Yevtushenko, N.: Adaptive testing of deterministic implementations specified by nondeterministic FSMs. In: Wolff, B., Zaïdi, F. (eds.) ICTSS 2011. LNCS, vol. 7019, pp. 162–178. Springer, Heidelberg (2011). doi:10.1007/978-3-642-24580-0_12

10. Simao, A., Petrenko, A.: Generating complete and finite test suite for ioco: is it possible? In: Proceedings Ninth Workshop on Model-Based Testing, MBT 2014, Grenoble, France, pp. 56–70 (2014)

11. Tretmans, J.: Model based testing with labelled transition systems. In: Hierons, R.M., Bowen, J.P., Harman, M. (eds.) Formal Methods and Testing. LNCS, vol. 4949, pp. 1–38. Springer, Heidelberg (2008). doi:10.1007/978-3-540-78917-8_1

12. Volpato, M., Tretmans, J.: Towards quality of model-based testing in the ioco framework. In: Proceedings of the 2013 International Workshop on Joining AcadeMiA and Industry Contributions to Testing Automation, pp. 41–46. ACM (2013)

13. Willemse, T.A.C.: Heuristics for ioco-based test-based modelling. In: Brim, L., Haverkort, B., Leucker, M., van de Pol, J. (eds.) FMICS 2006. LNCS, vol. 4346, pp. 132–147. Springer, Heidelberg (2007). doi:10.1007/978-3-540-70952-7_9

Multiple Mutation Testing from Finite State Machines with Symbolic Inputs

Omer Nguena Timo[1]([✉]), Alexandre Petrenko[1], and S. Ramesh[2]

[1] Computer Research Institute of Montreal, CRIM, Montreal, Canada
{omer.nguena-timo,petrenko}@crim.ca
[2] GM Global R&D, Warren, MI, USA
ramesh.s@gm.com

Abstract. Recently, we proposed a mutation-testing approach from a classical finite state machine (FSM) for detecting nonconforming mutants in a given fault domain specified with a so-called mutation machine. In this paper, we lift this approach to a particular type of extended finite state machines called symbolic input finite state machine (SIFSM), where transitions are labeled with symbolic inputs, which are predicates on input variables possibly having infinite domains. We define a well-formed mutation SIFSM for describing various types of faults. Given a mutation SIFSM, we develop a method for evaluating the adequacy of a test suite and a method for generating tests detecting all nonconforming mutants. Experimental results with the prototype tool we have developed indicate that the approach is applicable to industrial-like systems.

Keywords: Extended FSM · Symbolic inputs · Conformance testing · Mutation testing fault modelling · Fault model-based test generation · Constraint solving

1 Introduction

Detecting nonconforming implementations is a major challenge during the design and the maintenance of systems, which motivates the elaboration of innovative and efficient testing [16,23], model-checking [6] and runtime verification techniques [12]. Testing techniques [23] not only aim at exercising a system with adequate test cases to reveal failures and ideally to identify and to repair faults causing the failures. They may also target evaluating the adequacy of test cases and the generation of test cases to cover artefacts that can conceal faults [2,4,5,11], e.g., statements, branches, interfaces, requirements, mutants. Mutants which are versions of a specification of a system seeded with undesired faults can be used to generate test cases or to determine the adequacy of given test cases to reveal the faults. A fault domain can be specified with a set of mutants and test cases detecting the mutants which do not conform to the specification can be applied to detect faulty implementations of a system. Classical FSM model is often used in developing fault model based testing approaches for detecting nonconforming

© IFIP International Federation for Information Processing 2017
Published by Springer International Publishing AG 2017. All Rights Reserved
N. Yevtushenko et al. (Eds.): ICTSS 2017, LNCS 10533, pp. 108–125, 2017.
DOI: 10.1007/978-3-319-67549-7_7

implementations. Recently we proposed an approach for this model to evaluate the adequacy of test cases in a given fault domain [19] and to generate test cases detecting all nonconforming mutants [20].

In case the testers need to deal with inputs with infinite domains, the finite input alphabets which is used in classical FSM to represent the inputs of a system becomes ineffective along with FSM-based testing approaches. In the automotive applications, the behaviors of some controllers [18] depend on the truth values of predicates defined over input variables with infinite domains. Extensions of FSMs with symbolic inputs and arithmetic operations on variables have been proposed [3,14,21] to relax limitations of the classical FSM and used in developing testing methods [9,14,21]. Following the same trend, our test generation method by constraint solving from FSM in [19,20] could be enhanced to extended FSM. The work of [8] also uses an EFSM model and a mutation machine to model transition and output faults. Test generation requires (partial) unfolding of the specification, which we completely avoid. A test suite complete for used defined faults can only be generated if they satisfy certain sufficient conditions, which severely restrict types of detectable transition and output faults. Moreover, faults in transition predicates are not considered, as opposed to our approach.

In this paper, we lift the mutation testing approach from classical FSM in [19,20] to symbolic input finite state machine (SIFSM). SIFSM [21] is an extension of FSM with inputs specified with predicates on input variables possibly having infinite domains, which permits a more compact representation of data, data-flow relations and control-flow for determining outputs depending on the values of the predicates and states. Examples of realistic systems which can be specified with SIFSM can be found in [10,18]. The contribution is three-fold. First, we define mutation operations for building well-formed mutation machines specifying mutants in fault domains. New mutation operations may change predicates used in the specification or introduce new predicates. Secondly, we propose a method for evaluating the completeness of a test suite, i.e., the adequacy of a test suite to detect all nonconforming mutants. Finally we propose a method for generating complete test suites. Following the ideas in our previous work [19,20], the methods rely on building and resolving constraints specifying the mutants undetected by given test cases. However, in this work the constraints differ from those in our previous work; they are represented with Boolean expressions for expressing both undetected mutants and the input-completeness property of the mutants. The latter property is formalized with a notion of *cluster* for state. This is needed because predicates cannot be mutated independently. We evaluate the methods with a prototype tool applied to a SIFSM model of a component from the automotive domain.

The remaining of the paper is organized as follows. Section 2 introduces mutation SIFSM and mutation operations used for its creation. In Sect. 3 we present an approach for determining the mutants undetected by a test, which leads to a method for completeness checking of a given test suite in Sect. 4. In Sect. 5 we develop a method for complete test suite generation. Section 6 reports some experimental evaluation of the approach. We summarize our contributions in Sect. 7.

2 Background

2.1 Preliminaries

Let G denote the universe of *inputs* that are predicates over variables in a fixed set V for which a decision theory, e.g., an SMT solver, exists, excluding the predicates that are always *false*. G^* denotes the universe of *input sequences* and ε denotes the empty sequence. Later in the paper, a *test* is just an input sequence. Let I_V denote the set of all the valuations of the input variables in the set V, called *concrete inputs*. A set of concrete inputs is called a *symbolic input*; both, concrete and symbolic inputs are represented by predicates in G. Henceforth, we use set-theoretical operations on inputs. In particular, we say that concrete input x satisfies symbolic input g if $x \in g$. We also have that $I_V \subseteq G$. A set of inputs H is a *tautology* if each concrete input $x \in I_V$ satisfies at least one input in it, i.e., $\{x \in g \mid g \in H\} = I_V$.

We define some relations between input sequences in G^*. Given two input sequences $\alpha, \beta \in G^*$ of the same length k, $\alpha = g_1 g_2 \ldots g_k, \beta = g_1' g_2' \ldots g_k'$, we let $\alpha \cap \beta = g_1 \cap g_1' \ldots g_k \cap g_k'$ denote the sequence of intersections of inputs in sequences α and β; α and β are *compatible*, if for all $i = 1, \ldots, k$, $g_i \cap g_i' \neq \emptyset$. We say that α is a *reduction* of β, denoted $\alpha \subseteq \beta$, if $\alpha = \alpha \cap \beta$. If α is a sequence of concrete inputs as well as a reduction of β then it is called an *instance* of β; given a finite set of input sequences $E \subseteq G^*$, a set of concrete input sequences is called an instance of the set E, if it contains at least one instance for each input sequence in E.

Given a finite set of outputs O, a *trace* is a sequence of input-output pairs in $(G \times O)^*$. A trace is *concrete* if every input in it is concrete; otherwise it is *symbolic*. Given a trace $\beta \in (G \times O)^*$, the input (resp. output) projection of β, denoted $\beta_{\downarrow G}$ (resp. $\beta_{\downarrow O}$), is a sequence obtained from β by erasing symbols in O (resp. G).

We consider an extension of FSM called symbolic input finite state machine (SIFSM) [21], which operates in discrete time as a synchronous machine reading values of input variables and setting up the values of output variables. Output variables are assumed to have a finite number of valuations and form a finite output alphabet. On the other hand, the set of input valuations can be infinite.

Definition 1. *A symbolic input finite state machine* $\mathcal{S}$ *(or machine, for short) is a 5-tuple* (S, s_0, V, O, T), *where*

- S *is a finite set of* states *with the* initial *state* s_0,
- V *is a finite set of* input variables *over which inputs in* G *are defined*,
- O *is a finite set of* outputs,
- $T \subseteq S \times G \times O \times S$ *is a finite* transition relation, $(s, g, o, s') \in T$ *is a transition.*

The semantics of SIFSM is defined by a Mealy state machine with a possibly infinite input set, where the state and output sets remain finite. The set of transitions outgoing from state s is denoted by $T(s)$. We say that input g is *defined* in state s if g is the input of a transition in $T(s)$. Then, $G(s)$ denotes the sets of all the inputs defined in s. We say that transition (s, g, o, s') is *triggered* by input g' if g' is a reduction of g. Several transitions in $T(s)$ are *nondeterministic* if they can be triggered by the same input. If a set of transitions $T(s)$ includes nondeterministic transitions, the set is said to be *nondeterministic*; otherwise it is *deterministic*.

An *execution* of S from state s is a sequence of transitions $t_1 t_2 \ldots t_n$ forming a path from s in the state transition diagram of S. A *deterministic execution* is an execution such that its set of transitions is deterministic; otherwise, i.e., if for some state s and some transition in the execution there exists another transition such that both transitions belong to $T(s)$ and are triggered by an identical input, the execution is *nondeterministic*. A *symbolic trace of S in state s* is the projection of an execution from s on the input-output pairs in $(G \times O)$. A trace obtained from a symbolic trace in s by substituting every inputs by an instance of it is called a *concrete trace of S in s*. Let $Tr_S(s)$ (resp. $STr_S(s)$) denote the set of all concrete (resp. symbolic) traces of S in state s and Tr_S (resp. STr_S) denote the set of concrete (resp. symbolic) traces of S in the initial state.

We say that an input sequence *triggers* an execution of S (in state s) if it is a reduction of the input projection of a trace of the execution of S (in state s). Given an input sequence α, let $out_S(s, \alpha)$ denote the set of all output sequences which can be produced by S in response to α at state s, that is $out_S(s, \alpha) = \{\beta_{\downarrow O} \mid \beta \in STr_S(s)$ and $\alpha \subseteq \beta_{\downarrow G}\}$. We observe that $out_S(s, \alpha) = out_S(s, \gamma)$ whenever γ is a reduction of input α.

The machine S is *deterministic* (DSIFSM), if for every state s, $T(s)$ is deterministic; otherwise S is a *nondeterministic* SIFSM (NSIFSM). Clearly, a DSIFSM has only deterministic executions, while an NSIFSM can have both. State s of S is *completely specified*, if $G(s)$ is a tautology, i.e., each concrete input $x \in I_V$ satisfies at least one input defined at s. The machine S is *completely specified*, if each state is completely specified. The machine S is *initially connected*, if for any state $s \in S$ there exists an execution from s_0 to s. Henceforth, we assume that all SIFSM are initially connected and completely specified.

We adapt several relations introduced in [19, 20] for FSM to SIFSM and use trace-based definitions of the relations introduced in [21]. Given states s_1, s_2 of a SIFSM $S = (S, s_0, V, O, T)$, s_1 and s_2 are *(trace-) equivalent*, $s_1 \simeq s_2$, if $Tr_S(s_1) = Tr_S(s_2)$; s_1 and s_2 are *distinguishable*, $s_1 \not\simeq s_2$, if $Tr_S(s_1) \neq Tr_S(s_2)$; s_2 is *trace-included* into (is a reduction of) s_1, $s_2 \leq s_1$, if $Tr_S(s_2) \subseteq Tr_S(s_1)$. S is *reduced* if any pair of its states is distinguishable. Given two distinguishable states s_1 and s_2, there exists a sequence $\alpha \in G^*$ such that $out_S(s_1, \alpha) \neq out_S(s_2, \alpha)$; α is called a *distinguishing input sequence* for states s_1 and s_2, this is denoted $s_1 \not\simeq_\alpha s_2$.

We also use relations between machines. Given SIFSM $S = (S, s_0, V, O, T)$ and $P = (P, p_0, V, O, N)$, $P \leq S$ if $p_0 \leq s_0$; $P \simeq S$ if $p_0 \simeq s_0$; $P \not\simeq_\alpha S$ if $p_0 \not\simeq_\alpha s_0$ with $\alpha \in G^*$; and $P \not\simeq S$ if $P \not\simeq_\alpha S$ for some distinguishing input sequence α for p_0 and s_0. Later, we use equivalence relation between machines as a conformance relation between implementation and specification machines.

Given a NSIFSM $S = (S, s_0, V, O, T)$, a machine $\mathcal{P} = (P, p_0, V, O, N)$ is a *submachine* of S if $p_0 = s_0$, $P \subseteq S$ and $N \subseteq T$.

2.2   Mutation Machine

Let $S = (S, s_0, V, O, N)$ be a DSIFSM, called the specification machine.

Definition 2. *A NSIFSM $\mathcal{M} = (S, s_0, V, O, T)$ is a* mutation machine *of S, if S is a submachine of $\mathcal{M}$.*

Transitions of $\mathcal{M}$ that are also transitions of S are called *unaltered*, while the others, in the set $T \setminus N$, are *mutated* transitions. A transition of $\mathcal{M}$ is *suspicious* if it belongs to a nondeterministic set of transitions, let $Susp(s)$ denote the set of all suspicious transitions in state s and $Susp(\mathcal{M})$ denote the set of all suspicious transitions of $\mathcal{M}$. An unaltered transition is *trusted* if it is not suspicious; otherwise it is *untrusted* and belongs to the set $Untr(S) = Susp(\mathcal{M}) \cap N$. Given state s, a subset of $T(s)$ is called a *cluster* of s if it is deterministic and the inputs of its transitions constitute a tautology, in other words, the transitions of the cluster have a complete system of guards so that each concrete input enables a transition. Let $Z(s)$ denote the set of all clusters of s. State s is said to be *suspicious* if $|Z(s)| > 1$. We use S_{susp} to denote the set of all suspicious states of $\mathcal{M}$.

In a mutation machine, untrusted transitions can be seen as the result of applying mutation operations transforming the specification into mutants. Mutation operations may also be considered as fault seeding in the specification. For an untrusted transition to belong to a mutant, it must participate in clusters. We say that a mutation machine is *well-formed* if each of its suspicious transitions belongs to a cluster. In what follows, we consider only well-formed mutation machines.

We assume that only completely specified deterministic submachines of $\mathcal{M}$ are possible implementation machines for the specification machine S. The set of all such submachines is called a *fault domain* for S, denoted $Sub(\mathcal{M})$. If $\mathcal{M}$ is deterministic then $Sub(\mathcal{M})$ contains just S. Since each implementation machine in $Sub(\mathcal{M})$ is deterministic, each state of an implementation machine has only one cluster. The size of $Sub(\mathcal{M})$ is the product of the sizes of the clusters of the states, i.e., $|Sub(\mathcal{M})| = \prod_{s \in S} |Z(s)|$. A DSIFSM $\mathcal{P} \in Sub(\mathcal{M})$, such that $\mathcal{P} \neq S$, is called a *mutant*. Each mutant $\mathcal{P}$ has all the trusted transitions of $\mathcal{M}$ and the set of suspicious transitions $Susp(\mathcal{P})$. It holds that for all $\mathcal{P}, \mathcal{P}' \in Sub(\mathcal{M})$, if $\mathcal{P} \neq \mathcal{P}'$ then $Susp(\mathcal{P}) \neq Susp(\mathcal{P}')$.

Figure 1 presents an example of an NSIFSM which is a well-formed mutation machine with three Boolean input variables v_1, v_2 and v_3 and two outputs in $\{0, 1\}$. The mutation machine has five mutated transitions depicted with dashed lines. The solid lines represent the unaltered transitions of the specification machine. Identifiers of transitions are presented in brackets and parentheses for mutated and unaltered transition, respectively. There are eight suspicious transitions $t_5, t_6, t_7, t_8, t_9, t_{10}, t_{11}$ and t_{12}; three of them t_5, t_9 and t_{10} are untrusted.

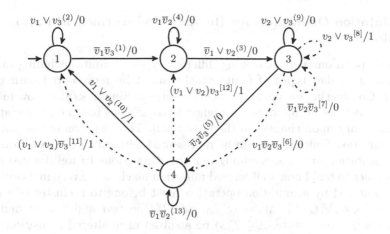

Fig. 1. A mutation SIFSM, state 1 is initial.

The states 3 and 4 are suspicious. The four clusters of state 3 are $\{t_5, t_9\}$, $\{t_5, t_8\}$, $\{t_6, t_7, t_9\}$ and $\{t_6, t_7, t_8\}$. The only two clusters for state 4 are $\{t_{10}, t_{13}\}$ and $\{t_{11}, t_{12}, t_{13}\}$. The mutation machine includes seven mutants and the specification machine. Execution $t_1t_3t_7t_5$ is nondeterministic because it includes two nondeterministic transitions t_7 and t_5. Execution $t_1t_3t_7t_6$ is deterministic and involves four mutants determined with the following sets of suspicious transitions $\{t_9, t_7, t_6, t_{10}\}$, $\{t_9, t_7, t_6, t_{11}, t_{12}\}$, $\{t_8, t_7, t_6, t_{10}\}$ and $\{t_8, t_7, t_6, t_{11}, t_{12}\}$.

Let e be an execution of $\mathcal{M}$ and $Susp(e)$ denote the set of suspicious transitions in e. We say that a (possibly nondeterministic or partially specified) submachine $\mathcal{P}$ is *involved* in e if $Susp(e) \subseteq Susp(\mathcal{P})$. An execution of any submachine of $\mathcal{M}$ is an execution of $\mathcal{M}$, but only deterministic executions of $\mathcal{M}$ are executions of submachines in $Sub(\mathcal{M})$. $\mathcal{P} \in Sub(\mathcal{M})$ is the only mutant involved in e if $Susp(e) = Susp(\mathcal{P})$.

Since the specification and mutants are completely specified and deterministic SIFSM, we use equivalence as a conformance relation for testing. A mutant $\mathcal{P}$ is *nonconforming (faulty)* if $\mathcal{P} \not\simeq S$, otherwise, it is called a *conforming* mutant. We say that a distinguishing input sequence $\alpha \in G^*$ such that $\mathcal{P} \not\simeq_\alpha S$ *detects* or *kills* the mutant $\mathcal{P}$.

The tuple $\langle S, \simeq, Sub(\mathcal{M}) \rangle$ is a fault model following [19–21]. For a given specification machine S the equivalence partitions the set $Sub(\mathcal{M})$ into conforming implementations and nonconforming ones. In this paper, we do not require the DSIFSM S to be reduced, this implies that a conforming mutant may have fewer states than the specification S; on the other hand, we assume that no fault creates new states in implementations, hence mutants with more states than the specification are not in $Sub(\mathcal{M})$.

2.3   Mutation Operations for Building Well-Formed Mutation Machines

Mutation operations permit seeding different types of faults including output, transition and other types of faults which cannot be represented with classical FSM. Considering for instance nondeterministic Simulink/Stateflow models, priorities which are automatically assigned to transitions based on the graphical layout may vary upon changes in the layout [22]. The variation of the priorities causes transition faults which can be represented with mutated transitions. We consider mutation operations adding mutated transitions to well-formed mutation machines to build new well-formed mutation machines. Every mutated transition introduced by a mutation operation must belong to a cluster of a state. Let $\mathcal{M} = (S, s_0, V, O, T)$, $\mathcal{M}' = (S, s_0, V, O, T')$ be two well-formed mutation machines, $s \in S$ be a state, $A \subseteq T(s)$ be a subset of unaltered transitions from state s in $\mathcal{M}$ and $B \subseteq T'(s)$ be a subset of mutated transitions from state s in $\mathcal{M}'$. We say that $\mathcal{M}'$ is a mutation of $\mathcal{M}$ w.r.t A and B if the following four conditions hold: $A \cap B = \emptyset$, $T' = T \cup B$, the union of the inputs of the transitions in A is equivalent to the union of the inputs of the transitions in B and there are $t \in A$ and $t' \in B$ having compatible guards but different outputs or target states. We specify a mutation operation with a tuple $(\mathcal{M}, A, B)$ such that there exists a mutation of $\mathcal{M}$ w.r.t. A and B. The set B can be obtained from the transitions in A by changing target states or outputs, merging/splitting inputs of transitions, replacing variables with default values, swapping occurrences of variables in inputs, substituting a variable for another, modifying arithmetic/-logical operations in guards. These operations introduce faults which cannot be represented in classical FSM; some of these faults are considered in [2,4,11]. Any well-formed mutation machine for a specification can be obtained by iterative application of mutation operations on the specification.

3   Boolean Expressions Specifying Mutants (un)Detected by Tests

Let $\langle \mathcal{S}, \simeq, Sub(\mathcal{M}) \rangle$ be a fault model. In the context of testing SIFSM, we consider that a test is just an input sequence. Tests detecting mutants can be determined using a distinguishing automaton obtained by composing the transitions of the specification and mutation machines as follows.

Definition 3. *Given a DSIFSM $\mathcal{S} = (S, s_0, V, O, N)$ and a mutation machine $\mathcal{M} = (S, s_0, V, O, T)$ of $\mathcal{S}$, a finite automaton $\mathcal{D} = (D \cup \{\nabla\}, d_0, G, \Theta, \nabla)$, where $D \subseteq S \times S$, ∇ is an accepting (sink) state and $\Theta \subseteq D \times G \times D$ is the transition relation is the* distinguishing automaton *for $\mathcal{S}$ and $\mathcal{M}$, if it holds that*

- *$d_0 = (s_0, s_0)$ is the initial state in D*
- *For any $(s, t) \in D$*
  - *$((s, t), g \cap h, (s', t')) \in \Theta$, if there exist $(s, g, o, s') \in N$, $(t, h, o', t') \in T$, such that $o = o'$ and $g \cap h \neq \emptyset$*

- $((s,t), g \cap h, \nabla) \in \Theta$, if there exist $(s, g, o, s') \in N$, $(t, h, o', t') \in T$, such that $o \neq o'$ and $g \cap h \neq \emptyset$

Fig. 2 presents the distinguishing automaton for the mutation and specification machines in Fig. 1. Multiple transitions are represented with a single arc labeled with multiple inputs.

An execution of $\mathcal{D}$ starting at the initial state d_0 and ending at the sink state ∇ is said to be *accepted*. The language of $\mathcal{D}$, $L_{\mathcal{D}}$ is the set of tests labeling accepted executions of $\mathcal{D}$. Any nonconforming mutant in $Sub(\mathcal{M})$ can be detected by a test in $L_{\mathcal{D}}$.

Theorem 1. *Given the distinguishing automaton $\mathcal{D}$ for $\mathcal{S}$ and $\mathcal{M}$, $\mathcal{P} \not\simeq \mathcal{S}$ for some $\mathcal{P} \in Sub(\mathcal{M})$ if and only if $\mathcal{P} \not\simeq_\alpha \mathcal{S}$ for some $\alpha \in L_{\mathcal{D}}$.*

A test $\alpha \in L_{\mathcal{D}}$ triggers several executions in the distinguishing automaton defined by executions of the specification and mutation machine $\mathcal{M}$ which are the respective projections of the distinguishing automaton's executions; a deterministic execution of $\mathcal{M}$ defining an execution of the distinguishing automaton $\mathcal{D}$ to the sink state is called α-*revealing* if it is triggered by any prefix of the test α. An α-revealing execution may belong to several mutants. As discussed above, given a deterministic execution e of $\mathcal{M}$ which has the set of suspicious transitions $Susp(e)$, a mutant $\mathcal{P}$ is involved in the execution e, if $Susp(e) \subseteq Susp(\mathcal{P})$. Since an α-revealing execution defines an accepted execution of the distinguishing automaton, each involved mutant is killed. Thus the sets of suspicious transitions in all α-revealing executions represent all the mutants killed by test α; on the other hand, it does not detect mutants which are not involved in these executions. To elaborate a mutant killing test generation procedure we need first to determine all the sets of suspicious transitions of the revealing executions for a given test. Let E_α be the finite set of α-revealing executions of $\mathcal{M}$. We use Boolean expressions for encoding of suspicious transitions of executions in E_α. A solution of a Boolean expression c over a set of variables is an assignment to *True* or *False* of every variable which makes c *True*. A solution of c can be obtained with solvers [7,13] which return *null* in case c has no solution. Given the set of suspicious transitions $Susp(\mathcal{M})$, we introduce $|Susp(\mathcal{M})|$ Boolean variables each of which represents a suspicious transition of the mutation machine. From now on we will use t to refer to both a suspicious transition and the variable which represents it. Then the conjunction $c_e \overset{\text{def}}{=} \bigwedge_{t \in Susp(e)} t$ of variables of transitions in $Susp(e)$ specifies the submachines involved in the revealing execution e. Moreover, the disjunction of conjunctions of all executions in E_α gives Boolean expression $c_\alpha \overset{\text{def}}{=} \bigvee_{e \in E_\alpha} c_e$ specifying all the submachines which are involved in all executions in E_α and killed by the test α. As usual, the disjunction over the empty set is *False* and the conjunction over the empty set is *True*. Boolean expression c_α is satisfiable whenever $E_\alpha \neq \emptyset$, since an α-revealing execution of $\mathcal{M}$ is a projection of the execution of the distinguishing machine. A witness solution of c_α provides all the variables evaluated to *True* and defines a corresponding subset of $Susp(\mathcal{M})$ which together with the trusted transitions of $\mathcal{M}$ determines (the transition relation of) a submachine of $\mathcal{M}$ involved in α-revealing executions.

Let $\alpha = (\overline{v}_1\overline{v}_2\overline{v}_3)(\overline{v}_1\overline{v}_2v_3)(\overline{v}_1\overline{v}_2\overline{v}_3)(v_1\overline{v}_2\overline{v}_3)(\overline{v}_1v_2\overline{v}_3)(v_1v_2v_3)$ be a test case. It triggers four executions in the distinguishing automaton in Fig. 2. These executions are defined by four executions of mutation machine in Fig. 1 including $e_1 = t_1t_3t_5t_{10}t_1t_3$, $e_2 = t_1t_3t_5t_{11}t_1t_3$, $e_3 = t_1t_3t_7t_5$ and $e_4 = t_1t_3t_7t_6$. The executions e_3 and e_4 are defined by the two executions to the sink state of the

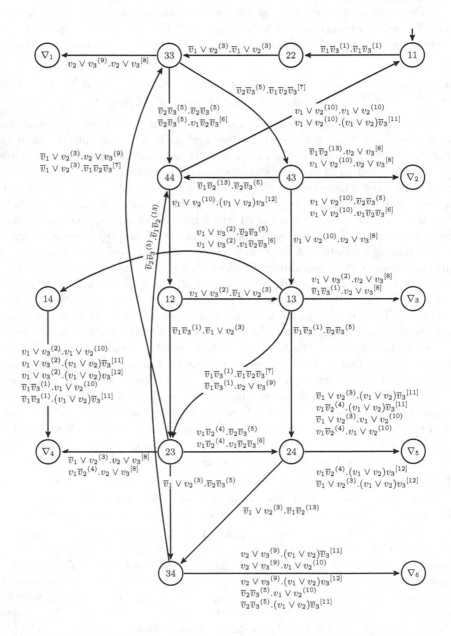

Fig. 2. The distinguishing automaton for machines in Fig. 1, state 11 is initial.

distinguishing automaton. Execution e_3 is not α-revealing because it is nondeterministic. Only execution e_4 is α-revealing and includes the two suspicious transitions in $Susp(e_4) = \{t_7, t_6\}$. Thus $c_{e_4} = t_7 t_6$ and $c_\alpha = c_{e_4}$. The solutions of c_α determine the submachines involved in e_4.

We denote by $Generate\_a\_submachine(c)$ a function which either determines such a submachine from a solution of c it obtained after calling a solver or returns *null* if c has no solution. Nondeterministic and partially specified submachines are not mutants. To exclude such submachines as well as the specification from any solution, clusters in suspicious states has to be considered.

Let s be a suspicious state, $Z(s) = \{Z_1, Z_2, \ldots, Z_n\}$ be the set of its clusters. Then the conjunction of variables of a cluster Z_i expresses the requirement that all these transitions must be present together to ensure that a submachine with the cluster Z_i is completely specified in state s. Moreover, since all mutants are deterministic, only one cluster in $Z(s)$ can be chosen, therefore, the transitions are restricted by the expressions determining clusters. Each cluster Z_i is exclusively determined by Boolean expression $z_i \stackrel{\text{def}}{=} (\bigwedge_{t \in Z_i} t) \wedge (\overline{\bigvee_{t \in Susp(s) \backslash Z_i} t})$ which permits the selection of all the suspicious transitions in Z_i and the exclusion of the remaining suspicious transitions leaving s, i.e., the exclusion of the other clusters.

Lemma 1. *Let $Z_i, Z_j \in Z(s)$ be two clusters of state s. Every solution of z_i is not a solution of z_j.*

Then each state s in S_{susp} yields the expression $c_s \stackrel{\text{def}}{=} \bigvee_{i=1}^n z_i$ of which all the solutions determine all the clusters in $Z(s)$.

Lemma 2. *Every solution of c_s determines a cluster in $Z(s)$ and every cluster in $Z(s)$ is determined by a solution of c_s.*

Each solution of $\bigwedge_{s \in S_{susp}} c_s$ determines the set of clusters of suspicious states either in the specification or in a mutant. Each such cluster in the specification has at least one untrusted transition in $Untr(\mathcal{S})$. Excluding the specification can be expressed with the negation of the conjunction of the variables of all the untrusted transitions $\overline{\bigwedge_{t \in Untr(\mathcal{S})} t}$. Any of its solutions excludes at least one cluster in the specification and therefore cannot determine the specification. The Boolean expression $c_{clstr} \stackrel{\text{def}}{=} \bigwedge_{s \in S_{susp}} c_s \wedge \overline{\bigwedge_{t \in Untr(\mathcal{S})} t}$ excludes nondeterministic and partially specified submachines and the specification, which means that c_{clstr} specifies only all mutants in the fault domain $Sub(\mathcal{M})$.

Considering the example mutation machine, we determine the Boolean expressions for the suspicious states 3 and 4. For the four clusters of state 3 $Z_{3_1} = \{t_5, t_9\}$, $Z_{3_2} = \{t_5, t_8\}$, $Z_{3_3} = \{t_6, t_7, t_9\}$ and $Z_{3_4} = \{t_6, t_7, t_8\}$ we build Boolean expressions $z_{3_1} = t_5 t_9 (\overline{t_6 t_7 t_8})$, $z_{3_2} = t_5 t_8 (\overline{t_6 t_7 t_9})$, $z_{3_3} = t_6 t_7 t_9 (\overline{t_5 t_8})$ and $z_{3_4} = t_6 t_7 t_8 (\overline{t_5 t_9})$. Then $c_3 = (z_{3_1} \vee z_{3_2} \vee z_{3_3} \vee z_{3_4})$. Similarly for state 4, we build $c_4 = (z_{4_1} \vee z_{4_2})$ where $z_{4_1} = t_{10} t_{13} (\overline{t_{11} t_{12}})$ and $z_{4_2} = t_{11} t_{12} t_{10} \overline{t_{13}}$. Finally, $c_{clstr} = c_3 \wedge c_4 \wedge (\overline{t_5} \vee \overline{t_9} \vee \overline{t_{10}})$.

A solution of $c_\alpha \wedge c_{clstr}$ defines a subset of $Susp(\mathcal{M})$ which together with the trusted transitions of $\mathcal{M}$ determines (a transition relation of) a mutant detected by α. All solutions thus determine all mutants detected by the test α. For a non-trivial mutation machine, a sheer number of killed mutants makes their enumeration impracticable. Hence, instead of determining killed mutants, we determine a (conforming or nonconforming) mutant which survives the test α. The *negation* of c_α, $\bar{c}_\alpha$ determines the transition relations of not only all mutants which survive α but also other submachines which are not mutants. Considering the running example, a partially specified submachine having the suspicious transitions t_9 and t_8 is determined by the solution of $\bar{c}_\alpha$ which assigns *True* t_9 and t_8; such a submachine is not a mutant and it does not belong to $Sub(\mathcal{M})$. To eliminate them as well as the specification, we use c_{clstr} as before. Finally, each mutant which survives test α is determined by a solution of the expression $\bar{c}_\alpha \wedge c_{clstr}$.

Theorem 2. *Test* $\alpha \in G^*$ *does not detect a mutant* $\mathcal{P}$ *if and only if there is a solution of* $\bar{c}_\alpha \wedge c_{clstr}$ *which determines* $\mathcal{P}$.

4   Checking Completeness of a Test Suite

Given a fault model $\langle \mathcal{S}, \simeq, \mathcal{M} \rangle$, a *fault subdomain* for $\mathcal{S}$, FD is a subset of $Sub(\mathcal{M})$. A *test suite*, TS is a set of tests. TS is *complete* for fault subdomain FD if it detects all the nonconforming mutants in FD. Let us define $c_{TS} \overset{\text{def}}{=} \bigvee_{\alpha \in TS} c_\alpha$, a Boolean expression which determines the submachines involved in revealing executions for the tests in TS. Procedure *Build_expression* for building c_{TS} is presented in Algorithm 1.

Let c_{fd} be a Boolean expression specifying only all mutants in a fault subdomain FD. It can be formulated as the conjunction c_{clstr} with another (possibly

---

Procedure Build_expression $(TS, \mathcal{D})$;
Input   : TS, a test suite
Input   : $\mathcal{D}$, the distinguishing automaton of mutation machine $\mathcal{M}$ and specification $\mathcal{S}$
Output : c_{TS}, a Boolean expression defining submachines of $\mathcal{M}$ involved in revealing executions for tests in TS
$c_{TS} := False$;
for   *each* $\alpha \in TS$ **do**
$\quad$ Using $\mathcal{D}$, determine E_α, the set of α-revealing executions of $\mathcal{M}$;
$\quad c_\alpha := False$;
$\quad$ **for**   *each* $e \in E_\alpha$ **do**
$\quad\quad c_e := \bigwedge_{t \in Susp(e)} t$;
$\quad\quad c_\alpha := c_\alpha \vee c_e$;
$\quad$ **end**
$\quad c_{TS} := c_{TS} \vee c_\alpha$;
end
Return c_{TS};

Algorithm 1. Building c_{TS}

always True) Boolean expression over the variables of suspicious transitions, which excludes mutants from $Sub(\mathcal{M})$ to obtain FD. A fault subdomain can always be refined with an expression specifying the mutants to be excluded. Later, in checking the completeness of a test suite for a given FD, we will be excluding conforming mutants.

Theorem 3. *Test suite TS is complete for fault subdomain FD if and only if $\overline{c_{TS}} \wedge c_{fd}$ has no solution or each of its solutions determines a conforming mutant.*

The fault domain $Sub(\mathcal{M})$ is specified with c_{clstr}, which leads to Corollary 1.

Corollary 1. *Test suite TS is complete for $Sub(\mathcal{M})$ if and only if $\overline{c_{TS}} \wedge c_{clstr}$ has no solution or each of its solutions determines a conforming mutant.*

Based on Theorem 3, checking the completeness of a test suite for a fault subdomain FD amounts to its iterative refinement by excluding conforming mutants as solutions to $\overline{c_{TS}} \wedge c_{fd}$ while no nonconforming mutant is found. In particular, the negation of the conjunction of variables of all suspicious transitions of a conforming mutant added to c_{fd} excludes it from FD. This method is formalized in Algorithm 2 which presents Procedure *Check_completeness* for checking the completeness of a test suite TS for a fault subdomain specified by the input parameter c_{fd} which is refined each time a conforming mutant is generated. The procedure *Check_completeness* also takes as inputs a test suite TS and the distinguishing automaton for the mutation and specification machines. It returns a witness test detecting a mutant surviving TS in case TS is not complete; otherwise the witness test is empty, which indicates that TS is complete. It also returns an updated expression of c_{fd} specifying a reduced fault domain which is used to generate tests that make TS a complete test suite in Sect. 5. Procedure *Check_completeness* proceeds as follows. It calls *Build_expression* for building c_{TS}, the Boolean expression which determines the submachines involved in revealing executions for tests in TS. Initialy, the fault domain is specified with the conjunction of c_{fd} with the negation of c_{TS} which determines all mutants surviving TS. The execution is iterative and each step consists in generating a mutant surviving TS, checking the conformance of the mutant and removing from the current fault domain the mutant in case it is conforming.

Procedure *Check_completeness* makes calls to *Generate_a_submachine* to select a mutant in a fault domain specified with Boolean expression c_{fd}. *Generate_a_submachine* returns *null* in case the fault domain is empty. The execution of *Check_completeness* stops when *Generate_a_submachine* returns a nonconforming mutant or *null*. In case *null* is returned, the test suite is declared complete and *Check_completeness* returns the empty test; otherwise the test suite is declared incomplete and *Check_completeness* returns a non empty witness test detecting a nonconforming mutant. In both cases *Check_completeness* returns an expression specifying the reduced fault domain at the end of the execution. In the next section, we will check the completeness of generated tests (e.g., the witness tests) for the reduced fault domains in determining complete test suites for fault domains specified with mutation machines.

Procedure Check_completeness $(c_{fd}, TS, \mathcal{D})$;
Input/Output : c_{fd} a boolean expression specifying a fault domain
Input   : TS, a (possibly empty) test suite
Input   : $\mathcal{D}$, the distinguishing automaton of $\mathcal{M}$ and $\mathcal{S}$
Output   : $\alpha \neq \varepsilon$, a test case revealing a nonconforming mutant
                   surviving the test suite; $\alpha = \varepsilon$, if TS is complete
$c_{TS} := Build\_expression(TS, \mathcal{D})$;
$c_{fd} := \overline{c_{TS}} \wedge c_{fd}$;
$c_{\mathcal{P}} := False$;
$\alpha := \varepsilon$;
repeat
$\quad \Big| \quad c_{fd} := c_{fd} \wedge \overline{c_{\mathcal{P}}}$;
$\quad \Big| \quad \mathcal{P} := Generate\_a\_submachine(c_{fd})$;
$\quad \Big| \quad$ **if** $\mathcal{P} \neq null$ **then**
$\quad \Big| \quad \Big| \quad$ Build $\mathcal{D}_{\mathcal{P}}$, the distinguishing automaton of $\mathcal{S}$ and $\mathcal{P}$;
$\quad \Big| \quad \Big| \quad$ **if** $\mathcal{D}_{\mathcal{P}}$ *has no sink state* **then**
$\quad \Big| \quad \Big| \quad \Big| \quad c_{\mathcal{P}} := \bigwedge_{t \in Susp(\mathcal{P})} t$;
$\quad \Big| \quad \Big| \quad$ **else**
$\quad \Big| \quad \Big| \quad \Big| \quad$ Set α to an input sequence in $L_{\mathcal{D}_{\mathcal{P}}}$;
$\quad \Big| \quad \Big| \quad$ **end**
$\quad \Big| \quad$ **end**
until $\alpha \neq \varepsilon$ *or* $\mathcal{P} = null$;
return (c_{fd}, α)
Algorithm 2. Checking the completeness of a test suite for a fault domain

In checking the completeness of the initial test suite $\{\alpha\}$ for the example mutation machine and test α, *Check_completeness* takes as input $c_{fd} = c_{clstr}$, $TS = \{\alpha\}$ and the distinguishing automaton in Fig. 2. Then, it determines $c_{TS} = c_\alpha = t_7 t_6$, sets $c_{fd} = \overline{c_{TS}} \wedge c_{clstr}$, $c_{\mathcal{P}} = False$ and $\alpha = \varepsilon$ and starts executing the loop. In the first iteration, the call of *Generate_a_submachine* with input c_{fd} has generated the mutant with the suspicious transitions t_8, t_{11}, t_{12}. The mutant is nonconforming and killed by the test $\beta = (\overline{v}_1 \overline{v}_3)(\overline{v}_1 \vee v_2)(v_2 \vee v_3)$ labeling a path to the sink state in the distinguishing automaton for the mutant. Then the execution of *Check_completeness* terminates with outputs c_{fd} and non empty test β, which indicates that the test suite $\{\alpha\}$ is not complete.

5   Complete Test Suite Generation

In case an initial (possibly empty) test suite does not detect all the nonconforming mutants in a fault domain, we want to generate tests which together with the initial tests constitute a complete test suite for the fault domain. This can be done iteratively by adding a new test detecting a nonconforming mutant surviving the incomplete test suite, obtaining a new test suite which in turn can be augmented in case it is not complete. This complete test suite generation method is formalized in Algorithm 3 with procedure *Complete_test_gen* which

Procedure Complete_test_gen (TS_{init}, $\langle S, \simeq, Sub(\mathcal{M})\rangle$);
Input   : TS_{init}, an initial (possibly empty) test suite
Input   : $\langle S, \simeq, Sub(\mathcal{M})\rangle$, a fault model
Output : TS, a complete test suite for $\langle S, \simeq, \mathcal{M}\rangle$
Compute c_{clstr}, the boolean expression which determines all mutants in $Sub(\mathcal{M})$;
Compute $\mathcal{D}$ the distinguishing automaton for S and $\mathcal{M}$;
$c_{fd} := c_{clstr}$;
$TS := \emptyset$;
$TS_{curr} := TS_{init}$;
repeat
$\quad$|$\quad TS := TS \cup TS_{curr}$;
$\quad$|$\quad (c_{fd}, \alpha) := Check\_completeness(c_{fd}, TS_{curr}, \mathcal{D})$;
$\quad$|$\quad TS_{curr} := \{\alpha\}$;
until ($\alpha = \varepsilon$);
return TS is complete;
Algorithm 3. Generation of a complete test suite from initial test suite TS_{init}

takes as inputs an initial test suite TS_{init} and a fault domain represented with a mutation machine. At every step, the procedure adds a current test suite to the set TS of already analyzed tests and makes a call of *Check_ completeness* to analyze the completeness of a current test suite w.r.t. a current fault domain. In case of completeness, *Check_ completeness* returns the empty test, which triggers the termination of *Complete_ test_ gen* with TS as a complete test suite for the initial fault domain; otherwise, *Check_ completeness* returns a witness test detecting a nonconforming mutant and a reduced fault domain obtained by removing the nonconforming mutant and possibly other conforming mutants, as discussed in the previous section. Then *Complete_ test_ gen* proceeds to a next iteration step after it has set the current fault domain and the current test suite to the reduced fault domain and the witness test.

Theorem 4. *Procedure* Complete_test_gen *always terminates and returns a complete test suite for the fault domain specified with a fault model.*

Procedure *Complete_ test_ gen* always terminates because the execution of its only loop always terminates. This is because the initial fault domain consisting of a finite number of mutants is reduced at every iteration step of the loop and *Check_ completeness* returns the empty test when executed with the empty fault domain as an input.

Considering the running example, Table 1 summarizes data computed in executing *Complete_ test_ gen* to generate a complete test suite from initial test suite $TS_{init} = \{\alpha\}$. The iteration step appears at the first column. Data are initialized at the end of step *init*. In each step *Complete_ test_ gen* makes a call to *Check_ completeness* which computes the executions revealed by TS_{curr} determined in the previous step and updates c_{fd}. Three iteration steps were sufficient to obtain the complete test suite $\{\alpha, \beta, \gamma\}$ having three tests for the detection of the seven nonconforming mutants, which shows that the method permits

Table 1. Execution of procedure *Complete_test_gen* with the initial test α.

	In *Check_completeness*				End of the step	
step	Revealing. Exec	$c_{TS_{curr}}$	c_{fd}	Surv. mut	TS	TS_{curr}
init	N/A	N/A	c_{clstr}	N/A	$\emptyset$	α
1	$t_1t_3t_7t_6$	t_7t_6	$c_{fd} \wedge \overline{t_7t_6}$	t_8, t_{11}, t_{12}	α	β
2	$t_1t_3t_8$	t_8	$c_{fd} \wedge \overline{t_8}$	t_9, t_{11}, t_{12}	α, β	γ
3	$t_1t_3t_5t_{12}t_3t_5t_{10}$, $t_1t_3t_5t_{10}t_1t_3t_8$	$(t_5t_{11}t_{12}) \vee (t_5t_8t_{10})$	$c_{fd} \wedge \overline{(t_5t_{11}t_{12}) \vee (t_5t_8t_{10})}$	$\emptyset$	α, β, γ	ε

$\alpha = (\overline{v}_1\overline{v}_2\overline{v}_3)(\overline{v}_1\overline{v}_2 v_3)(\overline{v}_1 v_2\overline{v}_3)(v_1\overline{v}_2\overline{v}_3)(\overline{v}_1 v_2 v_3)(v_1 v_2 v_3)$

$\beta = (\overline{v}_1\overline{v}_3)(\overline{v}_1 \vee v_2)(v_2 \vee v_3)$

$\gamma = (\overline{v}_1\overline{v}_3)(\overline{v}_1 \vee v_2)(\overline{v}_2\overline{v}_3)(v_1 v_3 \vee v_2 v_3)(\overline{v}_1\overline{v}_3)(\overline{v}_1\overline{v}_2\overline{v}_3)(v_2\overline{v}_3)$

generating fewer tests than the nonconforming mutants. Notice that we generate symbolic tests; their concrete instances should be used to execute against black box implementations. In our working example, for simplicity, all input variables are Boolean, which however, can represent comparisons of integer variables with some constants. The obtained concrete tests could then be just rewritten by replacing every Boolean variable by an instance of the corresponding comparison.

Table 2. Experimental results with the prototype tool

#Mutants	8191	163839	1105919	9400319
#Tests	14	15	18	18
Time (sec.)	30	90	100	296

6   Prototype Tool and Experimental Results

We implemented in JAVA a prototype tool consisting of three main modules. The first module for parsing mutation machines in text format was developed using ANTLR 4.1 [15]. The second module is concerned with building clusters, distinguishing automata and Boolean expressions for undetected mutants; it uses as a back-end the solver Z3 [13] for solving of non Boolean expressions obtained by combining predicates in building clusters and automata. We integrated the solver in the tool using a Z3 API. The third module is responsible of solving Boolean expressions for mutants, extracting mutants and generating new tests. The module also uses solver Z3 though it may also use a SAT solver [7] since it deals with the resolution of Boolean expressions only.

In our experiments, we use a desktop computer with the following settings: 3.4 Ghz Intel Core i7-3770 CPU, 16.0 GB of memory (RAM), Windows 7 (64 bits).

We use the prototype on an industrial-like SIFSM model obtained by transforming a Simulink/Stateflow model [18] of an automotive controller. To regulate the air quality in a vehicle, the controller sets an air source position to 0 or 1 depending on its current state and truth values of predicates on integer and Boolean input variables. The transformation required flattening and determinizing the original hierarchical Simulink/Stateflow model. The determinization is based on priorities assigned to nondeterministic transitions as it is done by Simulink [22]. We obtained a SIFSM with 13 states, 62 transitions and 22 input variables. Then we have manually introduced faults (transition faults, output faults, swapping of variables, replacing variables with constants), obtaining a mutation machine with $2^{13} - 1 = 8191$ mutants. Our tool generates, within 30 seconds, a complete test suite with 14 tests detecting the mutants. Finally, we generate complete tests from automatically generated mutation machines with a generator executing randomly selected mutation operations. Table 2 presents the numbers of mutants in the mutation machines, the number of tests in the generated complete test suites. The maximal length of the tests is 8. We observed that the test generation is fast when the mutation operations introduce a small number of nonconforming mutants, which is a realistic assumption [11] for applying our method.

7   Conclusion

We lifted the multiple mutation testing approach developed for classical (Mealy) FSM to symbolic input finite state machine (SIFSM). SIFSM extends classical FSM with predicates defined over input variables with possibly infinite domains.

We defined well-formed mutation machines for SIFSM as a fault model for compact representation of a fault domain consisting of several faulty implementations (mutants) of a specification machine. Then we defined mutation operations for building well-formed mutation machines. Based on the machine equivalence and distinguishability relations, we have defined tests detecting nonconforming mutants and developed a multiple mutation testing approach from SIFSM. The proposed approach leveraging on that developed for classical FSM includes a method for checking the completeness of test suites, i.e., their adequacy to detect all nonconforming mutants in a fault domain, and a method for complete test suite generation avoiding mutant enumeration. The novelty of the proposed approach is that it can analyze and enhance completeness of symbolic tests w.r.t. user defined fault models for a specification with infinite input domains.

The experiments with a prototype tool we have developed indicate that our methods can be applied to industrial-like models of systems.

Our current work focuses on extending the approach to FSM with outputs determined by arithmetic operations over input and output variables [17], to FSM extended with timing predicates [1, 14] and to C program.

Acknowledgements. This work is supported in part by GM, NSERC of Canada and MESI (Ministère de l'Économie, Science et Innovation) of Gouvernement du Québec.

References

1. Batth, S.S., Vieira, E.R., Cavalli, A., Uyar, M.Ü.: Specification of timed EFSM fault models in SDL. In: Derrick, J., Vain, J. (eds.) FORTE 2007. LNCS, vol. 4574, pp. 50–65. Springer, Heidelberg (2007). doi:10.1007/978-3-540-73196-2_4

2. Bessayah, F., Cavalli, A., Maja, W., Martins, E., Valenti, A.W.: A fault injection tool for testing web services composition. In: Bottaci, L., Fraser, G. (eds.) TAIC PART 2010. LNCS, vol. 6303, pp. 137–146. Springer, Heidelberg (2010). doi:10. 1007/978-3-642-15585-7_13
3. Cheng, K.T., Krishnakumar, A.S.: Automatic functional test generation using the extended finite state machine model. In: 30th ACM/IEEE Design Automation Conference, pp. 86–91 (1993)
4. Delamaro, M.E., Maldonado, J.C., Pasquini, A., Mathur, A.P.: Interface mutation test adequacy criterion: an empirical evaluation. Empir. Softw. Eng. **6**(2), 111–142 (2001)
5. DeMillo, R.A., Lipton, R.J., Sayward, F.G.: Hints on test data selection: help for the practicing programmer. Computer **11**(4), 34–41 (1978)
6. D'silva, V., Kroening, D., Weissenbacher, G.: A survey of automated techniques for formal software verification. IEEE Trans. Comput. Aided Des. Integr. Circuits Syst. **27**(7), 1165–1178 (2008)
7. Eén, N., Sörensson, N.: An extensible SAT-solver. In: Giunchiglia, E., Tacchella, A. (eds.) SAT 2003. LNCS, vol. 2919, pp. 502–518. Springer, Heidelberg (2004). doi:10.1007/978-3-540-24605-3_37
8. El-Fakih, K., Kolomeez, A., Prokopenko, S., Yevtushenko, N.: Extended finite state machine based test derivation driven by user defined faults. In: Proceedings of the 1st International Conference on Software Testing, Verification, and Validation, pp. 308–317 (2008)
9. El-Fakih, K., Yevtushenko, N., Bozga, M., Bensalem, S.: Distinguishing extended finite state machine configurations using predicate abstraction. J. Softw. Eng. Res. Dev. **4**(1), 1 (2016)
10. Huang, W., Peleska, J.: Exhaustive model-based equivalence class testing. In: Yenigün, H., Yilmaz, C., Ulrich, A. (eds.) ICTSS 2013. LNCS, vol. 8254, pp. 49–64. Springer, Heidelberg (2013). doi:10.1007/978-3-642-41707-8_4
11. Jia, Y., Harman, M.: An analysis and survey of the development of mutation testing. IEEE Trans. Softw. Eng. **37**(5), 649–678 (2011)
12. Leucker, M., Schallhart, C.: A brief account of runtime verification. J. Logic Algebraic Program. **78**(5), 293–303 (2009)
13. de Moura, L., Bjørner, N.: Z3: an efficient SMT solver. In: Ramakrishnan, C.R., Rehof, J. (eds.) TACAS 2008. LNCS, vol. 4963, pp. 337–340. Springer, Heidelberg (2008). doi:10.1007/978-3-540-78800-3_24
14. Nguena Timo, O., Rollet, A.: Conformance testing of variable driven automata. In: Proceedings of 8th IEEE International Workshop on Factory Communication Systems, pp. 241–248 (2010)
15. Parr, T.: The Definitive ANTLR 4 Reference, 2nd edn. Pragmatic Bookshelf, Dallas (2013)
16. Păsăreanu, C.S., Visser, W.: A survey of new trends in symbolic execution for software testing and analysis. Int. J. Softw. Tools Technol. Transf. **11**(4), 339–353 (2009)
17. Petrenko, A.: Checking experiments for symbolic input/output finite state machines. In: Workshops Proceedings of 9th International Conference on Software Testing, Verification and Validation, pp. 229–237 (2016)
18. Petrenko, A., Dury, A., Ramesh, S., Mohalik, S.: A method and tool for test optimization for automotive controllers. In: Workshops Proceedings of 6th IEEE International Conference on Software Testing, Verification and Validation, pp. 198–207 (2013)

19. Petrenko, A., Nguena Timo, O., Ramesh, S.: Multiple mutation testing from FSM. In: Albert, E., Lanese, I. (eds.) FORTE 2016. LNCS, vol. 9688, pp. 222–238. Springer, Cham (2016). doi:10.1007/978-3-319-39570-8_15
20. Petrenko, A., Nguena Timo, O., Ramesh, S.: Test generation by constraint solving and FSM mutant killing. In: Wotawa, F., Nica, M., Kushik, N. (eds.) ICTSS 2016. LNCS, vol. 9976, pp. 36–51. Springer, Cham (2016). doi:10.1007/978-3-319-47443-4_3
21. Petrenko, A., Simao, A.: Checking experiments for finite state machines with symbolic inputs. In: El-Fakih, K., Barlas, G., Yevtushenko, N. (eds.) ICTSS 2015. LNCS, vol. 9447, pp. 3–18. Springer, Cham (2015). doi:10.1007/978-3-319-25945-1_1
22. Scaife, N., Sofronis, C., Caspi, P., Tripakis, S., Maraninchi, F.: Defining and translating a safe subset of simulink/stateflow into lustre. In: Proceedings of the 4th ACM International Conference on Embedded Software, pp. 259–268. ACM (2004)
23. Utting, M., Pretschner, A., Legeard, B.: A taxonomy of model-based testing approaches. Softw. Test. Verification Reliab. **22**(5), 297–312 (2012)

From Passive to Active FSM Inference via Checking Sequence Construction

Alexandre Petrenko[1(✉)], Florent Avellaneda[1], Roland Groz[2], and Catherine Oriat[2]

[1] CRIM, Montreal, Canada
{Alexandre.Petrenko,Florent.Avellaneda}@crim.ca
[2] Univ. Grenoble Alpes, LIG, Grenoble, France
{Roland.Groz,Catherine.Oriat}@imag.fr

Abstract. The paper focuses on the problems of passive and active FSM inference as well as checking sequence generation. We consider the setting where an FSM cannot be reset so that its inference is constrained to a single trace either given a priori in passive inference scenario or to be constructed in active inference scenario or aiming at obtaining checking sequence for a given FSM. In each of the last two cases, the expected result is a trace representing a checking sequence for an inferred machine, if it was not given. We demonstrate that this can be achieved by a repetitive use of a procedure that infers an FSM from a given trace (identifying a minimal machine consistent with a trace) avoiding equivalent conjectures. We thus show that FSM inference and checking sequence construction can be seen as two sides of the same coin. Following an existing approach of constructing conjectures by SAT solving, we elaborate first such a procedure and then based on it the methods for obtaining checking sequence for a given FSM and inferring a machine from a black box. The novelty of our approach is that it does not use any state identification facilities. We only assume that we know initially the input set and a bound on the number of states of the machine. Experiments with a prototype implementation of the developed approach using as a backend an existing SAT solver indicate that it scales for FSMs with up to a dozen of states and requires relatively short sequences to identify the machine.

Keywords: FSM testing · Machine inference · Machine identification · Active learning · Checking experiments · Checking sequences

1 Introduction

Model-based testing from finite state models of systems, when it is only possible to interact with the system through its input/output interfaces, relies on traversing transitions of the model and being able to check that states reached after transitions in the system are consistent with those expected from the model. At the end of the test, the goal is to be able to guarantee that the system under test behaves as expected in the model. So the test must be built as a checking sequence of inputs that can uniquely identify (up to equivalence) a given model machine.

© IFIP International Federation for Information Processing 2017
Published by Springer International Publishing AG 2017. All Rights Reserved
N. Yevtushenko et al. (Eds.): ICTSS 2017, LNCS 10533, pp. 126–141, 2017.
DOI: 10.1007/978-3-319-67549-7_8

Computing a checking sequence from a finite state model dates back to the very early history of automata in computer science, starting with the work of Moore [14] and many approaches have been proposed to generate checking sequences for various types of models under various assumptions for the machine w.r.t determinism, completeness, and the existence of specific sequences for a machine such as distinguishing sequences [10], signatures [20], state identifiers [16] etc.

More recently, at the turn of the century, model-based approaches have led to an interest in inference techniques. Instead of checking whether a system behaves as specified by a model, it works the other way round: we try to build a model, called a conjecture that will predict as accurately as possible the behaviour of a system. This can be based on a corpus of given observed behaviours of the system (passive inference), or on the ability to submit test sequences (active inference). One key driver for such approaches is that experience in industrial context have shown that building and maintaining accurate and up-to-date models was complicated, and needed specific expertise. Being able to derive models automatically relieves the burden of creating and maintaining them.

Building a checking sequence can be seen as a top-down approach (from model to implementation) and inference as bottom-up approach (from implementation to conjectured model). The two are in fact closely linked: in active inference, if a sequence is built that uniquely identifies a machine, then this sequence is a checking sequence for this machine. The main difference is in the starting point: for checking sequence generation, we assume we know the (specification) machine to be identified. For inference, the machine is unknown.

In this paper, we propose an iterative approach that alternates passive inference with construction of checking experiments. Initially, an input sequence will be too short to uniquely identify a machine. But one can exhibit one of many possible conjectures that would match the observed input/output sequence (the running trace). So the idea is to build a checking experiment that will distinguish among conjectures, and which is appended to the current trace. Following this experiment, the set of potential conjectures is reduced, and the process is iterated until we get to a point where the set is reduced to a singleton, at which point the input projection of the observed trace is a checking sequence.

Interestingly, this theoretical framework had already been envisioned by J. Kella, in one of the early papers on passive inference [13]. Let us quote the end of his introduction (our comments in brackets): "When the machine has no distinguishing sequences the reducing technique can help in minimizing the length of the checking experiment by iterative construction of the experiment. An initial sequence is applied to the machine and the resulting input-output sequence is reduced [by state merging]; the result will indicate a family of machines responding in the same way. An additional sequence which eliminates nondesired machines is then applied and another reduction is performed; by repeated application of the basic iteration the sequence will reduce uniquely to the checked machine [up to the initial state]. This method of checking experiment construction was tried for some examples but there is no proof yet to whether it is more efficient than other methods [10] and whether it will converge in all cases."

Our approach shows that it is indeed possible to uniquely identify a non-resettable deterministic complete machine, while building a checking sequence for it, with no priori knowledge apart from a bound on the number of states, and the input set of the machine. Contrary to previous work [9], it does not require a characterization set or another assumption on sequences to distinguish states in the machine.

Section 2 will provide precise definitions for our formal framework, while Sect. 3 will define the inference problems and checking sequence generation in our context, i.e. from a single trace for a non-resettable machine, in relation with the state of the art. Section 4 shows how passive inference, i.e. the computation of a conjecture from a single trace can be encoded into a Boolean formula, so that a SAT solver can be used to efficiently get a conjecture. Sections 5 and 6 present our iterative approaches, showing the two sides of the coin: checking sequence generation and active inference. Section 7 presents experiments that show that the algorithms can work with middle-sized automata. Section 8 concludes.

2 Definitions

A *Finite State Machine* (FSM) M is a 5-tuple (S, s_0, I, O, T), where S is a finite set of states with an initial state s_0; I and O are finite non-empty disjoint sets of inputs and outputs, respectively; T is a transition relation $T \subseteq S \times I \times O \times S$, $(s, a, o, s') \in T$ is a transition. When we need to refer to the machine M in a state $s \in S$, we write M/s.

M is *completely specified* (complete) if for each tuple $(s, a) \in S \times I$ there exists transition $(s, x, o, s') \in T$. It is *deterministic* if for each $(s, a) \in S \times I$ there exists at most one transition $(s, a, o, s') \in T$, otherwise it is *nondeterministic*. We consider in this paper only deterministic FSMs.

An *execution* of M/s is a sequence of transitions forming a path from s in the state transition diagram of M. The machine M is *initially* connected, if for any state $s \in S$ there exists an execution from s_0 to s. M is *strongly* connected, if the state transition diagram of M is a strongly connected graph.

A *trace* of M/s is a string of input-output pairs which label an execution from s. Let $Tr(s)$ denote the set of all traces of M/s and Tr_M denote the set of traces of M/s_0. For trace $\omega \in Tr(s)$, we use s-after-ω to denote the state M reached after the execution of ω, for an empty trace ε, s-after-$\varepsilon = s$. When s is the initial state then we write M-after-ω instead of M/s_0-after-ω.

Let also $out(s, \alpha)$ be an output sequence produced by the input sequence $\alpha \in I^*$ in M/s. For input sequence α applied in state s, we let $tr_s(\alpha)$ denote the trace with the input projection α; we will omit the subscript when no confusion occurs.

Given an input sequence α, states $s, s' \in S$ are *equivalent w.r.t.* α, if $out(s, \alpha) = out(s', \alpha)$, denoted $s \cong_\alpha s'$, they are *distinguishable* by α, if $out(s, \alpha) \neq out(s', \alpha)$, denoted $s \not\cong_\alpha s'$ or simply $s \not\cong s'$. A *distinguishing* sequence of M is an input sequence α for which the output sequence produced by M in response to α identifies the state of M: for all $s, s' \in S$, $out(s, \alpha) \neq out(s', \alpha)$. A *characterization* set of M is a set input sequences such that every $s, s' \in S$, there exists a sequence α in the set such that $out(s, \alpha) \neq out(s', \alpha)$. States s and s' are equivalent if they are equivalent w.r.t. all input sequences, thus $Tr(s) = Tr(s')$, denoted $s \cong s'$. The equivalence and distinguishability relations between

FSMs is similarly defined. Two FSMs are equivalent if their initial states are equivalent. A complete FSM is *minimal*, if it has no equivalent states.

Given two FSMs $M = (S, s_0, I, O, T)$ and $M' = (S', s_0', I, O, T')$, their *product* $M \times M'$ is an FSM (P, p_0, I, O, H), where $p_0 = (s_0, s_0')$ is such that P and H are the smallest sets satisfying the following rule: If $(s, s') \in P$, $(s, x, o, t) \in T$, $(s', x, o', t') \in T'$, and $o = o'$, then $(t, t') \in P$ and $((s, s'), x, o, (t, t')) \in H$.

Lemma. *If M and M' are complete machines then they are equivalent iff the product $M \times M'$ is complete in the input set I.*

Two complete FSMs $M = (S, s_0, I, O, T)$ and $M' = (S', s_0', I, O, T')$ are called *isomorphic* if there exists a bijection $f: S \to S'$ such that $f(s_0) = s_0'$ and for all $a \in I$, $o \in O$, and $s \in S$, $f(s\text{-after-}ao) = f(s)\text{-after-}ao$. Isomorphic FSMs are equivalent, but the converse does not necessarily hold. Note that we do not require equivalent machines to be minimal.

Given a trace $\omega \in (IO)^*$ of length $|\omega|$, let $Pref(\omega)$ be the set of all prefixes of ω. We define a linear FSM $W = (X, x_0, I, D_\omega)$, where D_ω is a transition relation, such that $|X| = |\omega| + 1$, and there exists a bijection $f: X \to Pref(\omega)$, such that $f(x_0) = \varepsilon$, $(x_i, ao, x_{i+1}) \in D_\omega$ iff $f(x_i)ao = f(x_{i+1})$ for all $i = 0, \ldots, |\omega| - 1$, in other words, $Tr_W = Pref(\omega)$. We call it an *ω-machine W*.

While the set of traces of the ω-machine is $Pref(\omega)$, there are many FSMs which have the trace ω among other traces. We restrict our attention to the class of FSMs with at most n states and alphabets I and O, denoted $\mathfrak{I}(n, I, O)$. An FSM $C = (S, s_0, I, O, T)$, $C \in \mathfrak{I}(n, I, O)$ is called an *ω-conjecture*, if $\omega \in Tr_C$. Let $\mathfrak{I}_\omega(n, I, O)$ be the set of all ω-conjectures in the set $\mathfrak{I}(n, I, O)$. Clearly, the ω-machine is also an ω-conjecture, if $|\omega| < n$.

The states of the ω-machine $W = (X, x_0, I, D_\omega)$ and an ω-conjecture $C = (S, s_0, I, O, T)$, $C \in \mathfrak{I}_\omega(n, I, O)$ are closely related to each other. A state of the ω-machine reached after any prefix of the trace ω corresponds to a unique state of the ω-conjecture that is reached after that prefix. Formally, there exists a mapping $\mu: X \to S$, such that $\mu(x) = s_0\text{-after-}f(x)$, the state reached by C when the trace $f(x) \in Pref(\omega)$ is executed. The mapping μ induces a partition π_C on the set X such that x and x' belong to the same block of the partition π_C, denoted $x =_{\pi_C} x'$, iff $\mu(x) = \mu(x')$.

Given an ω-conjecture C with the partition π_C, let D be an ω'-conjecture with the partition π_D, such that $\omega' \in Pref(\omega)$, we say that the partition π_C is an *expansion* of the partition π_D, if its projection to ω' coincides with the partition π_D; viz $\pi_D = \{P \cap X' | P \in \pi_C\}$ where $X' = \{x_i \in X \mid i \leq |\omega'|\}$.

An input sequence $\alpha \in I^*$ is a *checking sequence* for a complete FSM M with n states if for each FSM $N \in \mathfrak{I}(n, I, O)$, such that $N \cong_\alpha M/s$, where $s \in S$, it holds that $N \cong M/s$. The trace $tr_s(\alpha)$, where α is a checking sequence, is called a *checking trace* of M. In this definition, we allow uncertainty in the initial state of M since it may have other states which converge with the initial state on a checking trace (an example of such an FSM can be found in Sect. 5).

Checking sequence is a special type of checking experiments for FSM, it is usually considered for FSM based testing when a reset operation in FSM implementations is unavailable or formidably costly to execute.

3 Problem Statement and Related Work

We consider the following closely related problems, passive and active FSM inference as well as checking sequence construction. Significantly, we restrict our setting to the case where a FSM may not be reset, so that the definitions we give here refer to a single trace. Actually, if a FSM can be reliably reset, the reset sequences can be included in the trace, so the definitions below can cover the general case. We state the problems using the definitions given above.

Passive inference is a classical problem whereby given a trace ω we need to build an ω-conjecture with a minimal number of states [2, 6, 13].

Active inference, aka active automata learning, is another problem addressed in the literature [5]. Restated in our FSM context, given a black box, which behaves as an unknown minimal complete strongly connected FSM with the input alphabet I and the number of states equal to n, infer the FSM, i.e. build an ω-conjecture equivalent to the FSM and its checking trace ω.

The checking sequence problem differs from active inference in assuming that the expected behavior of a black box with at most n states submitted for testing is given as a strongly connected FSM M called a specification machine (which is unknown in active inference) and we need to determine its checking trace ω. The relation to passive inference is direct, once ω is constructed, any ω-conjecture must be equivalent to M.

In this section, we briefly discuss the existing approaches addressing these problems which do not rely on the existence of a reset operation.

3.1 Passive Inference from a Single Trace

Passive FSM inference problem is stated by Kella in 1971 [13] as sequential machine identification and later as system/automaton identification problem by Gold [6]. The problem has been studied ever since. The problem is known to be computationally very hard, nevertheless, numerous proposals have been made, mainly on developing state merging techniques to transform an ω-machine into an ω-conjecture as small as possible, see, e.g., [13, 26] etc. The most recent approaches are based on satisfiability (SAT) solvers [1, 11].

In Sect. 4, we propose an approach to build an ω-conjecture within a bound on the number of states using a SAT solver that avoids obtaining conjectures which were already considered.

3.2 Checking Sequence Problem

The problem of checking sequence generation from an FSM has a long history starting from work of Moore [14] and Hennie [10]. Almost all existing methods require a machine be complete and minimal. Moreover, the vast majority of the proposed methods only apply to FSMs which have distinguishing sequences or distinguishing sets, see, e.g. [4, 7, 12, 21, 22, 25]. Not all FSMs possess these sequences and their construction is a non-trivial problem. Only few methods can generate checking sequence from complete and minimal FSM which has just characterization set and no other distinguishing sets, see [10, 17, 18]. Moreover, they cannot be called efficient, since the size of a checking sequence generated by using characterization set grows exponentially with the length and number of sequences in characterization set [24].

The problem of checking sequence generation without even checking the existence of distinguishing sequences or finding an "optimal" or any other characterization set remains open, to the best our knowledge. In Sect. 5 we propose an approach that does not assume any distinguishing or characterization set computation.

3.3 Active Inference Without Reset

Active inference has most often been addressed in the context of learning from samples and queries [5, 8], so that the problem of dealing with a single trace has not received a lot of attention. An early attempt was proposed by [19], as an adaptation to Angluin's L* algorithm. It assumes that an external oracle can be queried to provide a coun- terexample (hence an input sequence to distinguish the black box and the conjecture), and starts with the knowledge of a homing sequence. More recently an approach was proposed that does not require an external oracle, but still assumes knowledge of a characterization set [9].

However, the assumptions about the existence of an external oracle, knowledge of homing or state characterizing sequences, such as distinguishing sequences and char- acterization sets, are not easy to justify in practice, therefore the problem of active inference of FSMs with neither reset operation nor strong assumptions about a given back box remains open. In Sect. 6 we propose an approach that does not require such assumptions.

4   Passive Inference with SAT Solving

Since an ω-machine is itself an ω-conjecture, the minimization problem boils down to merging states of the ω-machine without introducing traces that would contradict the trace ω. Therefore by encoding a trace into a Boolean formula, and expressing state merging possibilities in that formula, we may use a SAT solver to determine acceptable mergers.

4.1   Problem Encoding

Here we present a procedure for encoding a trace into a Boolean formula, and at the same time express a constraint on the number of states.

Let $W = (X, x_0, I, D_\omega)$ be an ω-machine. To find an ω-conjecture with at most n states amounts to determine a partition π on the set of states X such that the number of blocks does not exceed n. This problem can be casted as a constraint satisfaction problem (CSP) [3]. Let X be $\{x_0, \ldots, x_{|\omega|}\}$, so each integer variable represents a state of the ω-machine. Since the ω-machine is deterministic, the state variables satisfy the following constraint:

$\forall x_i, x_j \in X$:

if $x_i \not\approx x_j$ then $x_i \neq x_j$ and

if $\exists a \in I$ s.t. $out(x_i, a) = out(x_j, a) = o$ then $x_i = x_j \Rightarrow x_i\text{-after-}ao = x_j\text{-after-}ao$ $\qquad$ (1)

If the number of states in an ω-conjecture to be constructed should be at most n then each state variable $x_i \in \{0, \ldots, n-1\}$. Then an assignment of values to variables in $\{x_0, \ldots, x_{|\omega|}\}$ such that the formula (1) is satisfied defines a mapping $\mu\colon X \rightarrow S$, where S is the set of states of an ω-conjecture, i.e., the mapping μ defines a partition of X into n blocks.

These formulas can be translated to SAT using unary coding for each integer variable $x \in X$, such that x is represented by n Boolean variables $v_{x,0}, \ldots, v_{x,n-1}$. For each $x \in X$, we have the clause:

$$v_{x,0} \vee \ldots \vee v_{x,n-1} \qquad (2)$$

These clauses mean that each state of the ω-machine W should be in at least one block.

For each state $x \in X$ and all $i, j \in \{0, \ldots, n-1\}$ such that $i \neq j$, we have the clauses:

$$\neg v_{x,i} \vee \neg v_{x,j} \qquad (3)$$

The clauses mean that each state of the ω-machine W should be in at most one block.

Since a sought-after ω-conjecture must be deterministic, the formula (1) is encoded into the following clauses. First, distinguishable states of W should be in different blocks, so for every $x, y \in X$ such that $x \not\approx y$ and all $i \in \{0, \ldots, n-1\}$

$$\neg v_{x,i} \vee \neg v_{y,i} \qquad (4)$$

Second, states of W equivalent w.r.t. to some input if placed in the same block must have their successors also in one block. Hence for all $x_i, x_j \in X$ such that $out(x_i, a) = out(x_j, a) = o$ and all $i, j \in \{0, \ldots, n-1\}$ we have a formula which can directly be translated into clauses

$$\left(v_{x,i} \wedge v_{x',i}\right) \Rightarrow \left(v_{(x\text{-after-}ao),i} \Rightarrow v_{(x'\text{-after-}ao),i}\right) \qquad (5)$$

To simplify learning that $x = y$ for some $x, y \in X$ we further rewrite the clauses (4) and (5) using auxiliary variables $e_{x,y}$ modeling the fact that $x = y$. For every $x, y \in X$ such that $x \not\approx y$ we have

$$\neg e_{x,y} \qquad (6)$$

For all $x, y \in X$ such that $out(x, a) = out(x, a) = o$, we have

$$e_{x,y} \Rightarrow e_{x\text{-after-}ao, y\text{-after-}ao} \qquad (7)$$

The relation between auxiliary state variables is expressed in the following clauses. For every $x, y \in X$ and all $i \in \{0, \ldots, n - 1\}$

$$e_{x,y} \wedge v_{x,i} \Rightarrow v_{y,i} \tag{8}$$

$$\neg e_{x,y} \wedge v_{x,i} \Rightarrow \neg v_{y,i} \tag{9}$$

The resulting Boolean formula is the conjunction of clauses (2), (3), (6), (7), (8) and (9). To check its satisfiability one can use any of the existing solvers. If a solution exists then we have an ω-conjecture with n or fewer states. The latter is obtained from the determined partition on X. In the context of passive inference, we are usually interested in finding an ω-conjecture as small as possible. This requires several trials with varying values of n.

4.2 Passive Inference of Different (New) Conjectures

In the context of active inference as well as checking sequence construction we aim at obtaining a single ω-conjecture while avoiding constructing isomorphic conjectures. A key building block will be provided by the following procedure to infer a conjecture that differs from already considered conjectures. We identify isomorphic conjectures by their common partition, hence we add as a constraint that we look for an ω-conjecture that does not expand a set of "forbidden" partitions. If such ω-conjectures are found they will be used in Sects. 5 and 6 to augment the trace ω by adding suffixes that eliminate distinguishable conjectures until only one remains.

Algorithm 1. *Infer_conjecture(ω, n, Π)*
Input: A trace ω, an integer n, and a set of partitions Π
Output: An ω-conjecture with at most n states such that its partition does not expand any partition in Π, or False.

1. *formula* = conjunction of the clauses (2), (3), (6), (7), (8) and (9)
2. **for all** $\pi \in \Pi$ **do**
3.   *clause* = False
4.   **for all** x, y such that $x =_\pi y$ **do**
5.   *clause* = *clause* $\vee \neg e_{x,y}$
6.   **end for**
7.   *formula* = *formula* $\wedge$ *clause*
8. **end for**
9. **return** *call-solver(formula)*

5   Checking Sequence Construction

The idea of the proposed method for checking sequence (trace) generation is to find an FSM that reacts as the given specification FSM to a current input sequence using passive inference and eliminate it by extending the sequence with a suffix distinguishing the two machines or forbidding the passive inference from further regeneration if they cannot be distinguished any further. This process iterates until no more conjectures distinguishable from the given FSM can be found. The procedure is implemented in Algorithm 2.

Algorithm 2. Generating checking trace
Input: A complete strongly-connected FSM M with n states
Output: A checking trace ω

1. $\omega := \varepsilon$
2. $\Pi := \varnothing$
3. **while** an ω-conjecture C is returned by *Infer_conjecture*(ω, n, Π) **do**
4.   **if** C-after-$\omega \times M$-after-ω is complete **then**
5. $\Pi := \Pi \cup \{\pi_C\}$
6.   **else**
7.   Determine an input sequence βa such that β is a shortest transfer sequence from the state C-after-ω to a state with the undefined input a in C-after-$\omega \times M$-after-ω
8. $\omega := \omega tr(\beta a)$, where $tr(\beta a)$ is the trace of M-after-ω
9.   **end if**
10. **end while**
11. **return** ω

Algorithm 2 calls *Infer_conjecture*(ω, n, Π), which in turn calls a SAT solver constraining it to avoid solutions of already considered conjectures.

Note that the Boolean formula used by the SAT solver is built incrementally by saving a current formula and adding only new clauses each time a trace ω or a set of partitions Π is augmented.

Theorem 1. Given an FSM M with n states, Algorithm 2 returns a checking trace ω.

Sketch of the proof. When Algorithm 2 terminates the resulting trace ω is indeed a checking one, since by the post-condition of *Infer_conjecture* no conjecture exists that is distinguishable from the given FSM M, after having executed ω. Note that all complete conjectures equivalent to M are excluded because as soon as one if found (including possibly M itself), according to the Lemma, its partition is added to Π. Algorithm 2 always terminates, because the number of all possible conjectures with the fixed input alphabet within a given bound on the number of states n is finite.

Example. Consider the FSM in Fig. 1, it has no distinguishing sequence, its characterization set is $\{a, b\}$.

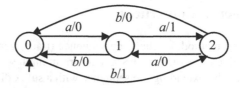

Fig. 1. The FSM M

This example is used in [17], where a method for checking sequence generation from a minimal FSM without distinguishing sequence is proposed. Using this example the authors of [17] compare their method with those of [10, 18] and report that the length of checking sequence obtained by their method is 120, while that of [10] is 171 and 248 of [18].

Algorithm 1 implemented in a prototype tool presented in Sect. 6 returns the checking sequence $\omega = a0a1a0a1b0b1b0a0b0b1a0a1b0a0a1$ of length 15. Figure 2 shows intermediate complete ω-conjectures obtained executing Algorithm 1. Notice that the last but one conjecture is actually the FSM M, though, the same trace is also accepted by another conjecture, which is eliminated using the suffix $b0a0a1$.

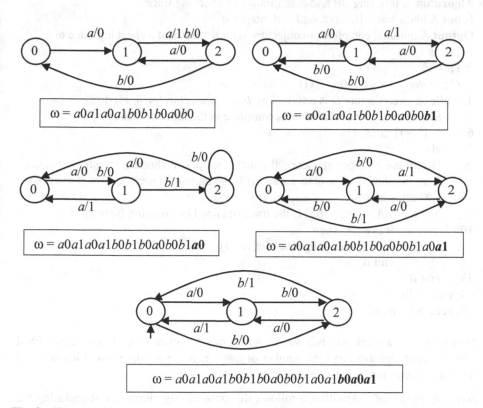

Fig. 2. The ω-conjectures generated by Algorithm 1 along with their versions of ω; suffixes in bold show how ω grows.

Note that the algorithm does not require the FSM to be minimal, moreover, it can be adapted to accept even a partial FSM. We are not aware of any method for checking sequence construction for FSMs which are partially defined and have compatible states, i.e., machines without characterization set. The only existing method which deals with such machines is [16], but it relies on the usage of the reset operation, as opposed to the approach proposed here.

6   Active Inference Approach

The iterative approach of Algorithm 2, which relied on computing a checking experiment for an ω-conjecture that was consistent with the current prefix trace can be adapted to active inference. The trick is to find a checking experiment not between the reference FSM M and the ω-conjecture, but between two possible ω-conjectures and retain the one that is consistent with the observations on the black box.

Given a black box BB, which behaves as an unknown minimal complete strongly connected FSM with the input alphabet I and a number of states equal to n, Algorithm 3 infers the FSM and constructs its checking trace.

Algorithm 3. Inferring BB and determining its checking trace
Input A black box BB, input set I and integer n
Output A minimal complete ω-conjecture with n states and a checking trace ω
1: $\omega := \varepsilon$
2: $\Pi := \varnothing$
3: $C := Infer\_conjecture(\omega, n, \Pi)$
4: **while** an ω-conjecture D is returned by $Infer\_conjecture(\omega, n, \Pi)$ **do**
5:     **if** D/D-after-$\omega \times C/C$-after-ω is complete in the input set I **then**
6:         $\Pi := \Pi \cup \{\pi_D\}$
7:     **else**
8:         Determine an input sequence βa such that β is a shortest transfer sequence from the state C-after-ω to a state with the undefined input a in D/D-after-$\omega \times C/C$-after-ω
9:         $\omega := \omega tr(\beta a)$, where $tr(\beta a)$ is the trace obtained by applying βa to BB
10:             **if** $\omega \notin Tr_C$ **then**
11:                 $C := Infer\_conjecture(\omega, n, \Pi)$
12:             **end if**
13:     **end if**
14: **end while**
15: **return** C and ω

Theorem 2. If a black box behaves as a minimal complete strongly connected FSM with the input alphabet I and the number of states equal to n, Algorithm 3 infers it and constructs a checking sequence and trace for it.

Sketch of the proof. Algorithm 3 follows the steps of Algorithm 2, just replacing the FSM M by a current conjecture. This does not influence its termination since it only occurs when no more distinguishable conjecture can be found. And at some point, because the black box behaves as a FSM with n states, it will be returned by *Infer_conjecture*, so that the remaining conjecture is equivalent to the FSM of the black box initialized in some state. The resulting trace accepted by that state is a checking one, as in Theorem 1.

Example. Consider that the FSM M in Fig. 1 is a BB. Six intermediate complete ω-conjectures shown in Fig. 3 are obtained executing Algorithm 3. The last two conjectures both accept $\omega = a0a1a0b0b1b0b1a0a1b0a0a1a0a1$. Both end up in state 2

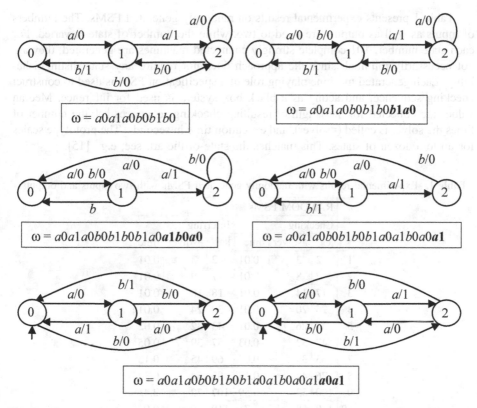

Fig. 3. The ω-conjectures generated by Algorithm 3 along with their versions of ω; suffixes in bold show how ω grows.

from which they cannot be distinguished. The algorithm returns ω as a checking trace and the last but one conjecture which is isomorphic to FSM $M/2$. The last conjecture is isomorphic to FSM $M/0$. Indeed this trace is accepted by M in two states, 0 and 2.

The expected complexity of the proposed approach could be estimated by viewing it as a mutation-based technique which kills mutants. In our approach at each iteration only a mutant surviving a current trace can be generated and then killed, drastically reducing the complexity of mutation-based techniques. A naive worst-case estimation based on number of (potential) mutants would be grossly overestimated. This explains why we provide in the next section experimental results on the observed complexity with random machines.

7 Experiments

The prototype was developed on C++ depending only on a SAT Solver Cryptominisat [23], as a backend. All the experiments were performed on a virtual machine (VirtualBox) with 8 GiB of RAM and one CPU used. The computer has the processor 7-3770 and 16 GiB of RAM.

Table 1 presents experimental results on randomly generated FSMs. The numbers of inputs as well as outputs are fixed to two, while the number of state is varied. For each state number, 101 complete strongly connected machines are generated; they are not necessarily minimal, since the approach does not require any state distinguishability. Each generated machine playing role of a specification FSM is used to construct checking sequence, and acting as a black box system is used for inference. Median values are collected for the length of resulting checking sequences $|\omega|$, the number of times the solver is called (#solver), and execution time in seconds. The prototype scales for up to a dozen of states. This matches the state-of-the-art, see, e.g., [15].

Table 1. Experimental results with randomly generated FSMs with two inputs and outputs.

n	RANDOM FSMs					
	Checking			Inferring		
	$|\omega|$	#solver	time	$|\omega|$	#solver	time
1	2	3	0.01	2	3	0.01
2	7	8	0.01	7	9	0.01
3	17	14	0.01	18	18	0.01
4	26	20	0.01	30	24	0.01
5	37	26	0.01	43	32	0.02
6	47	32	0.03	57	39	0.05
7	63	39	0.07	69	45	0.13
8	76	44	0.17	83	54	0.32
9	100	53	0.59	107	72	2.4
10	118	58	1.7	119	70	9.0
11	146	69	18.5	146	83	161

To assess the performance of the prototype to various numbers of inputs and outputs, another series of experiments reported in Table 2 were performed for machines with five states. Our experiments by varying their numbers separately show, unsurprisingly, that increasing number of inputs or outputs have opposite effects on the effectiveness, the more inputs the more complex the solutions (the search space is larger) but the more outputs the easier the solutions (more outputs increase distinguishability).

In addition, we performed another series of experiments using randomly generated lock machines (Table 3). A lock FSM (aka Moore lock, defined by him) with n states has a unique "unlocking" input sequence of length n which executes the "remotest" transition, the transitions not covered by this sequence all lead to the initial state resetting the lock. We consider lock machines as ultimate test for active inference and checking sequence generation methods. As before for each number of states we generate 101 random locks with two inputs and two outputs and collect the same parameters as above. Clearly, for a fixed number of states, locks differ only in labelling of unlocking sequences, which effects the performance of the prototype, since it chooses inputs completing and distinguishing conjectures following the lexicographical order.

Table 2. Experimental results with randomly generated arbitrary FSMs with five states.

#inputs = #outputs	RANDOM FSMs					
	Checking			Inferring		
	$|\omega|$	#solver	time	$|\omega|$	#solver	time
2	37	26	0.01	43	32	0.02
3	51	40	0.03	57	47	0.05
4	68	53	0.04	70	58	0.09
5	74	62	0.05	81	71	0.12
6	88	73	0.07	95	85	0.2
7	101	83	0.09	109	99	0.3
8	113	95	0.12	121	111	0.38
9	121	102	0.12	127	122	0.5
10	138	114	0.18	145	136	0.72
20	257	212	0.63	276	261	3.2
30	377	312	1.3	425	391	10
40	525	412	2.5	517	571	22

Table 3. Experimental results with randomly generated lock FSMs.

n	RANDOM LOCKs					
	Checking			Inferring		
	$|\omega|$	#solver	time	$|\omega|$	#solver	time
1	2	3	0.01	2	3	0.01
2	7	8	0.01	7	7	0.01
3	22	16	0.01	23	22	0.01
4	57	28	0.04	58	61	0.05
5	110	40	0.41	127	164	0.79
6	255	58	7.8	269	514	21
7	488	456	870	456	2202	970

It is interesting to notice that active inference and checking sequence construction have comparable lengths of the resulting input sequences. After all, in both cases a checking sequence for the same machine is generated.

We observe that the length of resulting sequences grows polynomially, the number of times the solver is called linearly and time exponentially with the number of states.

8 Conclusions

We have presented a method that can infer a model of a non-resettable black box FSM for which we only know an upper bound n on the number of states. It produces the model along with the input sequence that was used for inferring it. The algorithm terminates on a final model that is equivalent to the black-box FSM up to initialization, and since it identifies a unique machine such that the input sequence is a checking sequence for this FSM.

The main benefit of this approach is that it only requires a bound on the number of states, no other assumption is needed, and the system does not have to be reset. This implies that it may have a wide spectrum of applications. The performance of active inference methods is usually assessed through the number of interactions with a system that are needed to infer it. Experiments have shown that the length of the input sequence implied by our approach is quite good. Another issue comes from the internal computations needed by the inference algorithm to build the model of the system. The method relies on a SAT solver to propose conjecture FSMs that are consistent with an observed trace. Unfortunately, this induces an exponential growth in the number of states, and this has been the limiting factor in our experiments. However, being able to infer state machines of up to a dozen states is in itself interesting for a large range of applications (many systems have relatively small state-space for the control part of their computations).

The approach seems promising, and can be improved in several directions. First, we have encoded the constraints for passive inference in a straightforward way, which puts a high burden on the constraint solver. It should be possible to encode the problem with more elements from the trace and FSM-structure to help the solver, with some guidance. Another direction we are investigating is to extract more information from previous conjectures and observations so as to reduce the number of calls to the solver to a minimum. In many cases, the calls to the solver can be avoided because it is possible to derive further checking experiments from the structure of the past conjecture(s). Instead of calling the solver to identify a new conjecture, it could be possible to refine the current conjecture.

Acknowledgements. This work was partially supported by MESI (Ministère de l'Économie, Science et Innovation) of Gouvernement du Québec and NSERC of Canada.

References

1. Abel, A., Reineke, J.: MeMin SAT-based exact minimization of incompletely specified mealy machines. In: IEEE/ACM International Conference on Computer-Aided Design (ICCAD), pp. 94–101 (2015)
2. Biermann, A.W., Feldman, J.A.: On the synthesis of finite-state machines from samples of their behavior. IEEE Trans. Comput. **100**(6), 592–597 (1972)
3. Carbonnel, C., Cooper, M.C.: Tractability in constraint satisfaction problems: a survey. Constraints **21**(2), 115–144 (2016)
4. Boute, R.T.: Distinguishing sets for optimal state identification in checking experiments. IEEE Trans. Comput. **23**, 874–877 (1974)
5. De la Higuera, C.: Grammatical Inference: Learning Automata and Grammars. Cambridge University Press, Cambridge (2010)
6. Gold, E.M.: Complexity of automaton identification from given data. Inf. Control **37**(3), 302–320 (1978)
7. Gonenc, G.: A method for the design of fault detection experiments. IEEE Trans. Comput. **19**, 551–558 (1970)

8. Groz, R., Li, K., Petrenko, A., Shahbaz, M.: Modular system verification by inference, testing and reachability analysis. In: Suzuki, K., Higashino, T., Ulrich, A., Hasegawa, T. (eds.) FATES/TestCom -2008. LNCS, vol. 5047, pp. 216–233. Springer, Heidelberg (2008). doi:10.1007/978-3-540-68524-1_16

9. Groz, R., Simao, A., Petrenko, A., Oriat, C.: Inferring finite state machines without reset using state identification sequences. In: El-Fakih, K., Barlas, G., Yevtushenko, N. (eds.) ICTSS 2015. LNCS, vol. 9447, pp. 161–177. Springer, Cham (2015). doi:10.1007/978-3-319-25945-1_10

10. Hennie, F.C.: Fault-detecting experiments for sequential circuits. In: Proceedings of the Fifth Annual Symposium on Circuit Theory and Logical Design, pp. 95–110 (1965)

11. Heule, M.J.H., Verwer, S.: Exact DFA identification using SAT solvers. In: Sempere, José M., García, P. (eds.) ICGI 2010. LNCS, vol. 6339, pp. 66–79. Springer, Heidelberg (2010). doi:10.1007/978-3-642-15488-1_7

12. Hierons, R.M., Ural, H.: Optimizing the length of checking sequences. IEEE Trans. Comput. **55**, 618–629 (2006)

13. Kella, J.: Sequential machine identification. IEEE Trans. Comput. **100**(3), 332–338 (1971)

14. Moore, E.F.: Gedanken experiments on sequential machines. Autom. Stud. Ann. Math. Stud. **34**, 129–153 (1956)

15. Oliveira, A.L., Silva, J.P.M.: Efficient algorithms for the inference of minimum size DFAS. Mach. Learn. **44**(1), 93–119 (2001)

16. Petrenko, A., Yevtushenko, N.: Testing from partial deterministic FSM specifications. IEEE Trans. Comput. **54**(9), 1154–1165 (2005)

17. Porto, F.R., Endo, A.T., Simao, A.: Generation of checking sequences using identification sets. In: Groves, L., Sun, J. (eds.) ICFEM 2013. LNCS, vol. 8144, pp. 115–130. Springer, Heidelberg (2013). doi:10.1007/978-3-642-41202-8_9

18. Rezaki, A., Ural, H.: Construction of checking sequences based on characterization sets. Comput. Commun. **18**, 911–920 (1995)

19. Rivest, R.L., Schapire, R.E.: Inference of finite automata using homing sequences. In: Hanson, S.J., Remmele, W., Rivest, Ronald L. (eds.) Machine Learning: From Theory to Applications. LNCS, vol. 661, pp. 51–73. Springer, Heidelberg (1993). doi:10.1007/3-540-56483-7_22

20. Sabnani, K., Dahbura, A.: A protocol test generation procedure. Comput. Netw. **15**, 285–297 (1988)

21. Simão, A., Petrenko, A.: Generating checking sequences for partial reduced finite state machines. In: Suzuki, K., Higashino, T., Ulrich, A., Hasegawa, T. (eds.) FATES/TestCom -2008. LNCS, vol. 5047, pp. 153–168. Springer, Heidelberg (2008). doi:10.1007/978-3-540-68524-1_12

22. Simao, A., Petrenko, A.: Checking sequence generation using state distinguishing subsequences. In: The IEEE ICST Workshops, pp. 48–56 (2009)

23. Soos, M.: CryptoMiniSat – a SAT solver for cryptographic problems (2009). http://www.msoos.org/cryptominisat

24. Vasilevski, M.P.: Failure diagnosis of automata. Cybernetics, Plenum Publishing Corporation, New York, No 4, pp. 653–665 (1973)

25. Yannakakis, M., Lee, D.: Testing finite state machines: fault detection. J. Comput. Syst. Sci. **50**, 209–227 (1995)

26. Yao, M., Petrenko, A., Bochmann, G.V.: Conformance testing of protocol machines without reset. In: Proceedings of the IFIP Thirteenth International Symposium on Protocol Specification, Testing and Verification, pp. 241–256. North-Holland Publishing Co. (1993)

Safety and Security Testing

Safety-Complete Test Suites

Wen-ling Huang[2] and Jan Peleska[1,2](✉)

[1] Verified Systems International GmbH, Bremen, Germany
[2] Department of Mathematics and Computer Science,
University of Bremen, Bremen, Germany
{huang,jp}@cs.uni-bremen.de

Abstract. In this paper, a novel safety-related variant of complete test suites for finite state machines is introduced. Under certain hypotheses which are similar to the ones used in the well-known W-Method or the Wp-Method, the new method guarantees to uncover every safety violation, while erroneous outputs without safety-relevance may remain undetected. In well-defined situations that can be precisely pre-determined from the reference model, this leads to a substantial reduction of test cases in comparison to the size of the analogous Wp-test suites. We advocate this new test suite for situations, where exhaustive testing of the complete system is too expensive. In these cases, strong guarantees with respect to fault coverage should only be given for the errors representing safety violations, while it is considered as acceptable if less critical errors remain undetected.

Keywords: Model-based testing · Complete testing theories · Safety

1 Introduction

Motivation. Complete test suites guarantee to uncover all conformance violations of the implementation under test checked against a given reference model, provided that certain hypotheses – typically captured in a fault model – are fulfilled. This ideal test strength has attracted many researchers over the last 50 years, so that a large variety of contributions exists (a comprehensive overview has been given in [4, Sect. 5]). On the other hand, the often infeasible size of the test suites involved has frequently prevented their practical application. As a result, there is a considerable interest in testing strategies allowing to focus the effort on certain critical properties, while requiring lesser fault coverage for non-critical ones; we name [7] as one example among a multitude of publications in this field which is typically denoted as *property-oriented testing*.

Main Contributions. A novel contribution to property-oriented testing for the domain of finite state machines is presented. Our approach modifies the well-known Wp-Method in such a way, that complete coverage for output and

© IFIP International Federation for Information Processing 2017
Published by Springer International Publishing AG 2017. All Rights Reserved
N. Yevtushenko et al. (Eds.): ICTSS 2017, LNCS 10533, pp. 145–161, 2017.
DOI: 10.1007/978-3-319-67549-7_9

transition faults (including addition of new states) is guaranteed, if these lead to erroneous outputs representing safety-violations. To this end, an abstraction concept for outputs is introduced, so that it can be formally captured whether an erroneous replacement of another output for the expected one presents a safety violation or just a non-critical deviation. In contrast to other publications in this field, we formally prove that our strategy is complete with respect to this safety-related fault coverage. We show by means of examples, that applying this *Safety-complete Wp-Method* can lead to significantly reduced test suites in comparison to the Wp-Method, though this is not guaranteed, but depends on the nature of the reference model and its safety-related abstraction.

Overview. In Sect. 2, basic terms and concepts are introduced, so that this paper remains sufficiently self-contained. In Sect. 3, the Safety-complete Wp-Method is introduced, and its completeness properties are proven. In Sect. 4, three small case studies are presented that provide some insight into the situations where the new method leads to a significant test case reduction. Section 5 presents the conclusion.

2   Notation and Technical Background

A *deterministic finite state machine (DFSM)* is a tuple $M = (Q, \underline{q}, \Sigma_I, \Sigma_O, h)$ denoting the finite state space Q, initial state $\underline{q} \in Q$, finite input and output alphabets Σ_I and Σ_O, and the transition relation $h \subseteq Q \times \Sigma_I \times \Sigma_O \times Q$. For deterministic machines, pre-state q and input x uniquely determine the associated output y and the post-state q', such that $h(q, x, y, q')$ holds. We assume that all DFSMs are *completely specified*. This means that for every q and every x, there exists y and q' such that $h(q, x, y, q')$.

The *after operator* q-after-$\overline{x}$ maps a pre-state q and a finite sequence $\overline{x}$ of inputs to the uniquely determined post-state q' resulting from repetitive application of h. The *language* of a DFSM is the set of finite input/output traces $\overline{x}/\overline{y} \in \Sigma_I^* \times \Sigma_O^*$ resulting from applying all $\overline{x} \in \Sigma_I^*$ to the initial state $\underline{q}$ and associating the output trace $\overline{y}$ which is uniquely determined by $\underline{q}$, $\overline{x}$, and h. Two DFSMs are *I/O-equivalent ($M \sim M'$)* if they produce the same language. The language of a state q is the set of $\overline{x}/\overline{y}$ generated by applying all $\overline{x} \in \Sigma_I^*$ to q. The *prime machine* **prime**(M) of a DFSM M is the minimal DFSM producing the same language as M.

A *test suite* is a subset $\mathrm{TS} \subseteq \Sigma_I^*$, each $\overline{x} \in \mathrm{TS}$ is a *test case*. This simplified notation is possible, since only deterministic machines are considered, so that the input trace $\overline{x}$ uniquely determines the output trace to be expected according to the reference DFSM. An implementation *passes* a test case $\overline{x}$ if the application of this input sequence produces an output sequence $\overline{y}$, such that $\overline{x}/\overline{y}$ is in the language of the reference DFSM.

For sets of input traces $A, B \subseteq \Sigma_I^*$, the expression $A.B$ denotes the set of all input traces resulting from concatenating a trace $\overline{x} \in A$ with a trace $\overline{x}' \in B$. Given a collection of sets of input traces indexed over the states of a DFSM M, say, $W_q \subseteq \Sigma_I^*, q \in Q$, the notation $A \oplus \{W_q \mid q \in Q\}$ is used to denote the set of all input traces $\bar{x}.\bar{x}'$ where $\bar{x} \in A$ and $\bar{x}' \in W_{(q\text{-after-}\bar{x})}$. Σ_I^k denotes the set of all input traces of length $k \geq 0$. For input or output traces $\bar{z} = z_1 \ldots z_k$, the following notation is used for trace sections.

$$\bar{z}^{[i,j]} = z_i.z_{i+1} \ldots z_j \text{ where } 1 \leq i \leq j \leq k.$$

Given a reference DFSM M, the *W-Method* defines the test suite

$$\mathcal{W}(M) = V. \bigcup_{i=0}^{m-n+1} \Sigma_I^i.W,$$

where V is a *state cover* and W is a *characterisation set*. A state cover is a set of input traces, such that every state of M can be reached by q-after-$\bar{x}$ for some $\bar{x} \in V$. V contains the empty trace ε which "reaches" the initial state of M. It is assumed that **prime**(M) has n states and that the prime machine representing the true behaviour of the SUT has at most $m \geq n$ states. A characterisation set W contains input traces distinguishing all states of **prime**(M). This means that for each pair of distinct states q, q' of **prime**(M), there exists an $\bar{x} \in W$ such that $\bar{x}$ applied to q produces an output trace which differs from the one resulting from application of $\bar{x}$ to q'. It is shown in [1,10] that test suite $\mathcal{W}(M)$ uncovers every violation of I/O-equivalence, provided that the prime machine representing the true behaviour of the implementation does not have more than m states.

The *Wp-Method* [2,8] is an alternative test strategy which has the same test strength as the W-Method, but requires fewer test cases.

$$\mathcal{W}_p(M) = V.W \cup \left(V. \bigcup_{i=0}^{m-n} \Sigma_I^i.W\right) \cup \left(V.\Sigma_I^{m-n+1} \oplus \{W_q \mid q \in Q(\mathbf{prime}(M))\}\right)$$

Here V, W are defined as above. The *state identification sets* W_q are subsets of W, such that each W_q contains sufficient input traces to distinguish q from every other state in **prime**(M).

3 A Safety-Complete Wp-Method

3.1 Safety-Related Output Abstractions

Let $M = (Q, \underline{q}, \Sigma_I, \Sigma_O, h)$ be a deterministic completely specified FSM. Then any reflexive and transitive relation $\leq_s \subseteq \Sigma_O \times \Sigma_O$ is called a *safety-related output abstraction*. The intuition behind this definition is that $y \leq_s y'$ indicates that an erroneous output of y' instead of an expected output y does not induce a safety violation. Reflexivity just indicates that the occurrence of the output expected according to the reference model M can never be a safety violation. Transitivity implies that output z must also be a safe replacement of w, if $w \leq_s y \wedge y \leq_s z$ holds. Relation $\leq_s$ induces an equivalence relation $\sim_s$ on $\Sigma_O \times \Sigma_O$ by defining

$$y_1 \sim_s y_2 \equiv y_1 \leq_s y_2 \wedge y_2 \leq_s y_1$$

Example 1. Consider a train onboard controller which compares actual train speed against the allowed speed and progressively outputs

$$\Sigma_O = \{\texttt{ok}, \texttt{warning}, \texttt{ServiceBrakeTrigger}, \texttt{EmergencyBrakeTrigger}\},$$

depending on how much the train is overspeeding. The outputs **ok** and **warning** are shown on the display unit of the train engine driver, whereas the outputs `ServiceBrakeTrigger` and `EmergencyBrakeTrigger` directly act on the train's braking system. The service brake slows the train down with lower braking force than the emergency brake, so that the latter is used only as the "last resort", when warnings and service brake interventions do not suffice. These considerations induce a safety-related output abstraction $\leq_s$ as the reflexive and transitive closure of

$$\texttt{ok} \leq_s \texttt{warning} \leq_s \texttt{ServiceBrakeTrigger} \leq_s \texttt{EmergencyBrakeTrigger}$$

The intuition behind this definition is that a warning or even a braking intervention performed by the controller is an acceptable substitute for an expected ok-output from the safety perspective: the substitute output may be a nuisance (a spurious warning when the speed is within range) or even a severe reduction of reliability (triggering the emergency brake without need), but it does not introduce a safety threat. The same holds for situations where the service brake should be triggered but instead, the emergency brakes are activated.

When an intervention by service brakes or emergency brakes is expected, however, an output **ok** or **warning** would certainly be regarded as a safety hazard.

Next, suppose that the outputs to the train engine driver are extended by status messages

$$\Sigma_O' = \{\mathsf{s}_1, \ldots, \mathsf{s}_n\}.$$

Since these informative messages have no safety-relevance at all, we wish to extend the relation $\leq_s$ in a way expressing that each status message can be replaced by any other output of $\Sigma_O \cup \Sigma_O'$ without causing any safety hazard. This is achieved by extending $\leq_s$ according to the rules

$$\mathsf{s} \sim_s \mathsf{s}' \text{ for all } \mathsf{s}, \mathsf{s}' \in \Sigma_O'$$
$$\mathsf{s} \leq_s \mathsf{e} \text{ for all } \mathsf{s} \in \Sigma_O', \mathsf{e} \in \Sigma_O$$

Finally consider a design extension, where the onboard controller operates in a de-centralised distributed train control environment, so that it switches its own points

$$\Sigma_O'' = \{\mathsf{p}_i^+, \ \mathsf{p}_i^- \mid i = 1, \ldots, m\}$$

along the route (such a system has been investigated, for example, in [3]). Notation p_i^+ stands for switching point number i into the straight position, p_i^- for switching the point into the branching position. From the safety-perspective, switching a point into the desired position cannot be replaced by any other event without introducing a safety hazard. Therefore we extend $\leq_s$ this time as follows.

$$p \leq_s p \text{ for all } \mathbf{p} \in \varSigma_O''$$
$$\mathbf{s} \leq_s \mathbf{p} \text{ for all } \mathbf{s} \in \varSigma_O', \mathbf{p} \in \varSigma_O'' \qquad \qquad \Box$$

Given a safety-related output abstraction $\leq_s$ on $\varSigma_O$, this is extended in the natural way to a reflexive and transitive relation (again denoted by $\leq_s$) on output traces $\iota, \pi \in \varSigma_O^*$ by setting

$$\iota \leq_s \pi \equiv \big(\#\iota = \#\pi \wedge \forall i \in \{1, \dots, \#\iota\} : \iota(i) \leq_s \pi(i) \big)$$

for $\iota, \pi \in \varSigma_O^*$.

Now let q, q' be two states of the same state machine or of different state machines over the same input/output alphabet $(\varSigma_I, \varSigma_O)$. In the latter case, it is assumed without loss of generality that their states come from disjoint sets Q, Q'. Then it is possible to specify a joint output function $\omega : (Q \cup Q') \times \varSigma_I \to \varSigma_O$ which is extended in the natural way to operate on sequences of inputs, i.e. $\omega : (Q \cup Q') \times \varSigma_I^* \to \varSigma_O^*$. Let $\overline{x} \in \varSigma_I^*$ be an input trace. We define

$$q' \overset{\overline{x}}{\leq_s} q \equiv \big(\omega(q', \overline{x}) \leq_s \omega(q, \overline{x}) \big).$$

Intuitively speaking, $q' \overset{\overline{x}}{\leq_s} q$ states that applying input trace $\overline{x}$ to state q produces an output sequence $\omega(q, \overline{x})$ which is an admissible substitute to the output sequence $\omega(q', \overline{x})$ expected when applying the same input sequence to q'.

Relation $\overset{\overline{x}}{\leq_s}$ induces an equivalence relation on states by defining

$$q' \overset{\overline{x}}{\sim_s} q \equiv \big(q' \overset{\overline{x}}{\leq_s} q \wedge q \overset{\overline{x}}{\leq_s} q' \big)$$

These relations can be extended to sets of input traces in the natural way by defining

$$q' \overset{W}{\leq_s} q \equiv \big(\forall \overline{x} \in W : q' \overset{\overline{x}}{\leq_s} q \big)$$
$$q' \overset{W}{\sim_s} q \equiv \big(\forall \overline{x} \in W : q' \overset{\overline{x}}{\sim_s} q \big)$$

for arbitrary $W \subseteq \varSigma_I^*$. Finally, the specific case where $W = \varSigma_I^*$ is written in the simplified notation

$$q' \leq_s q \equiv \big(q' \overset{\varSigma_I^*}{\leq_s} q \big)$$
$$q' \sim_s q \equiv \big(q' \overset{\varSigma_I^*}{\sim_s} q \big).$$

If $q' \sim_s q$ holds, any input trace applied to q' will lead to an output trace which – regarded from the safety perspective – is an admissible replacement of the outputs expected when applying the same inputs to q and vice versa. If the initial states $\underline{q}$ and $\underline{q}'$ of two state machines M, M' are s-equivalent ($\underline{q}' \sim_s \underline{q}$), we denote this by $M' \sim_s M$.

We call $W_s \subseteq \varSigma_I^*$ an *s-characterisation set* of DFSM M, if and only if

$$q' \overset{W_s}{\sim_s} q \Leftrightarrow q' \sim_s q$$

holds. For any $q \in Q$, $W_{s_q} \subseteq W_s$ is called an *s-state identification set of q*, if and only if

$$\forall q' \in Q : \left(q' \overset{W_{s_q}}{\sim_s} q \Leftrightarrow q' \sim_s q \right)$$

holds. The sets of input traces in W_s and W_{s_q}, respectively, allow to distinguish states from the perspective of their safety-relevant outputs. Conversely, different states are indistinguishable by W_s and W_{s_q}, if their safety-relevant outputs are equivalent, while the non-relevant outputs may differ for certain input traces.

Note that W_s and W_{s_q} coincide with the conventional characterisation sets and state identification sets introduced in [8], if we choose $\leq_s$ to be the reflexive and transitive relation defined by the *diagonal of* Σ_O, that is,

$$\leq_s = \mathbf{diag}(\Sigma_O) = \{(y, y) \mid y \in \Sigma_O\},$$

where every output is only comparable to itself.

The following lemma states an obvious but useful fact about the $\leq_s$-relation, input prefixes, and input suffixes.

Lemma 1. *Let* $\overline{x} = x_1 \ldots x_k$ *and* $1 \leq i < k$. *Let* $q, q' \in Q \cup Q'$ *satisfying* $q' \overset{\overline{x}}{\leq_s} q$. *Define states*

$$q_i = q\text{-}after\text{-}\overline{x}^{[1,i]}$$
$$q'_i = q'\text{-}after\text{-}\overline{x}^{[1,i]}$$

Then $q'_i \overset{\overline{x}^{[i+1,k]}}{\leq_s} q_i$ *holds.* □

3.2   A Safety-Complete Variant of the Wp-Method

Throughout this section, let $M = (Q, \underline{q}, \Sigma_I, \Sigma_O, h)$, $M' = (Q', \underline{q}', \Sigma_I, \Sigma_O, h')$ be completely specified, deterministic, and minimised FSMs over the same input/output alphabet $\Sigma = \Sigma_I \times \Sigma_O$ with $|Q| = n$, $|Q'| \leq m$ and $m \geq n$.

Definition 1 (Safety-related Fault Model). *Let* $\leq_s \subseteq \Sigma_O \times \Sigma_O$ *be a safety-related output abstraction with associated equivalence relation* $\sim_s$. *A safety-related fault model*

$$\mathcal{F} = (M, \sim_s, \mathcal{D}(m))$$

is composed of

1. *the reference model* M,
2. *the conformance relation* $\sim_s$, *and*
3. *the fault domain* $\mathcal{D}(m)$ *consisting of all finite, completely specified, deterministic, and minimised state machines* M' *over input/output alphabet* Σ, *such that* $|Q'| \leq m$ *and* $m \geq n$. □

Definition 2 (Safety-complete Test Suite). *With the definitions above, let* $TS \subseteq \Sigma^*$ *be a test suite.*

1. *TS is called* sound *w.r.t. fault model* $\mathcal{F}$*, if and only if every member* $M' \in \mathcal{D}(m)$ *which is I/O-equivalent to* M *(*$M' \sim M$*) passes the test suite.*
2. *TS is called* safety-exhaustive *w.r.t. fault model* $\mathcal{F}$*, if and only if every member* $M' \in \mathcal{D}(m)$ *which is not safety-equivalent to* M *(*$M' \not\sim_s M$*) fail at least one test case in TS.*
3. *TS is called* safety-complete *w.r.t. fault model* $\mathcal{F}$*, if it is both sound and safety-exhaustive.* $\quad\square$

Theorem 1. *Let* $M = (Q, \underline{q}, \Sigma_I, \Sigma_O, h)$*,* $M' = (Q', \underline{q}', \Sigma_I, \Sigma_O, h')$ *be two completely specified, deterministic, mimimal FSMs with* $|Q| = n$*,* $|Q'| \leq m$ *and* $m \geq n$*. Let* $\leq_s \subseteq \Sigma_O \times \Sigma_O$ *be a safety-related output abstraction. Suppose that*

1. $\varepsilon \in V \subseteq \Sigma_I^*$ *is a state cover of* M*,*
2. $W \subseteq \Sigma_I^*$ *is a characterisation set of* M*, and*
3. $W_s \subseteq \Sigma_I^*$ *is an s-characterisation set of* M*.*

Define

$$A = V.W \text{ and } B = V.\bigcup_{i=0}^{m-n+1} \Sigma_I^i.W_s$$

Then

$$\underline{q}' \overset{A}{\sim} \underline{q} \wedge \underline{q}' \overset{B}{\sim}_s \underline{q}$$

implies $\underline{q}' \sim_s \underline{q}$ *and therefore* $M' \sim_s M$*.*

Proof. We prove by induction over $|\overline{x}|$ that for any $\overline{x} \in \Sigma_I^*$,

1. $\underline{q}' \overset{\overline{x}}{\sim}_s \underline{q}$.
2. $\underline{q}'\text{-after-}\overline{x} \overset{W_s}{\sim}_s \underline{q}\text{-after-}\overline{x}$

Statement 2 is an auxiliary assertion needed to prove Statement 1. The latter directly implies the statement of the theorem.

Induction Base. Statements 1 and 2 trivially hold for $\overline{x} = \varepsilon$.

Induction Hypothesis. Suppose that Statements 1 and 2 are true for some $k \geq 0$.

Induction Step. Let $\overline{x}.x \in \Sigma_I^*$ be any input trace with $|\overline{x}| = k$ and $x \in \Sigma_I$. Let

$$q = \underline{q}\text{-after-}\overline{x}/\overline{y}, \ q_1 = \underline{q}\text{-after-}(\overline{x}/\overline{y}).(x/y)$$

and

$$q' = \underline{q}'\text{-after-}\overline{x}/\overline{y}', q_1' = \underline{q}'\text{-after-}(\overline{x}/\overline{y}').(x/y').$$

From induction hypothesis we have $q' \overset{W_s}{\sim}_s q$.

Since $q' \overset{V.W}{\sim} q$ and since W is a characterisation set of M, the set

$$\{q'\text{-after-}\overline{x} \mid \overline{x} \in V\}$$

contains $n = |M|$ states of M'. Consequently,

$$V' = V. \bigcup_{i=0}^{m-n} \Sigma_I^i$$

is a state cover of M'. Therefore, there exists some input trace $\pi \in V'$ such that $q'\text{-after-}\pi = q'$ (note that it is not necessarily the case that $\overline{x} \in V'$). Let $q_2 = q\text{-after-}\pi$. We wish to show that $q \overset{W_s}{\sim}_s q_2$ holds.

Assume that $\pi \in V.\Sigma_I^i$ for some $i \in \{0, \ldots, m-n\}$. Now assumption $q' \overset{B}{\sim}_s q$ of the theorem, together with Lemma 1 implies again that $q' \overset{W_s}{\sim}_s q_2$.

This fact is now combined with the induction hypothesis which implies that $q' \overset{W_s}{\sim}_s q$. From these facts we can conclude that $q \overset{W_s}{\sim}_s q_2$. Now W_s is an s-characterisation set of M, so $q \overset{W_s}{\sim}_s q_2$ implies $q \sim_s q_2$.

Let $q_3 = q_2\text{-after-}(x/y_1)$. Then $q \sim_s q_2$, $\omega(q,x) = y$, and $\omega(q_2,x) = y_1$ implies $y \sim_s y_1$. From Lemma 1 we have $q_1 = q\text{-after-}x \sim_s q_3 = q_2\text{-after-}x$. Since $\pi.x \in V.\bigcup_{i=1}^{m-n+1} \Sigma_I^i$ we have $q_1' \overset{W_s}{\sim}_s q_3$ and $y \sim_s y'$. Hence we have $q' \overset{\overline{x}.x}{\sim}_s q$ and $q'\text{-after-}(\overline{x}.x) \overset{W_s}{\sim}_s q\text{-after-}(\overline{x}.x)$, which proves the induction step.   □

Theorem 2. *Let* $M = (Q, q, \Sigma_I, \Sigma_O, h)$, $M' = (Q', q', \Sigma_I, \Sigma_O, h')$ *be two completely specified, deterministic, minimal FSMs with* $|Q| = n$, $|Q'| \leq m$ *and* $m \geq n$. *Let* $\leq_s \subseteq \Sigma_O \times \Sigma_O$ *be a safety-related output abstraction. Suppose that*

1. *$\varepsilon \in V \subseteq \Sigma_I^*$ is a state cover of M,*
2. *$W \subseteq \Sigma_I^*$ is a characterisation set of M,*
3. *$W_s \subseteq \Sigma_I^*$ is an s-characterisation set of M, and*
4. *$W_{s_q} \subseteq W_s$ are s-identification sets of M for all $q \in Q$.*

Define

$$A = V.W, \quad C = V. \bigcup_{i=0}^{m-n} \Sigma_I^i.W_s, \quad and \quad D = V.\Sigma_I^{m-n+1} \oplus \{W_{s_q} \mid q \in Q\}.$$

Then

$$q' \overset{A}{\sim}_s q \wedge q' \overset{C}{\sim}_s q \wedge q' \overset{D}{\sim}_s q$$

implies $q' \sim_s q$, *and therefore* $M' \sim_s M$.

Proof. From Theorem 1 we conclude that it suffices to prove that the assumptions of Theorem 2 imply the validity of $q' \overset{B}{\sim}_s q$, with $B = V.\bigcup_{i=0}^{m-n+1} \Sigma_I^i.W_s$

as specified in Theorem 1. Since Theorem 2 is already based on the assumption $\underline{q}' \overset{C}{\sim}_s \underline{q}$, it suffices to prove that

$$\underline{q}' \overset{V.\Sigma_I^{m-n+1}.W_s}{\sim_s} \underline{q}$$

holds.

Let $\overline{x} \in V.\Sigma_I^{m-n+1}$ and define $q = \underline{q}$-after-$\overline{x}$ and $q' = \underline{q}'$-after-$\overline{x}$. We need to show that $q' \overset{W_s}{\sim}_s q$ follows from the assumptions of the theorem.

From assumption $\underline{q}' \overset{D}{\sim}_s \underline{q}$ and Lemma 1, we already have $q' \overset{W_{s_q}}{\sim}_s q$. Since $V' = V.\bigcup_{i=0}^{m-n} \Sigma_I^i$ is a state cover of M' (this has been established in the proof of Theorem 1), there is some $\overline{x}' \in V'$ such that $\underline{q}'$-after-$\overline{x}' = q'$. Let $q_2 = \underline{q}$-after-$\overline{x}'$. Then $q' \overset{W_s}{\sim}_s q_2$ follows from assumption from $\underline{q}' \overset{C}{\sim}_s \underline{q}$ (this has also been shown in detail in the proof of Theorem 1). Since $W_{s_q} \subseteq W_s$, the fact that $q' \overset{W_s}{\sim}_s q_2$ holds implies that $q' \overset{W_{s_q}}{\sim}_s q_2$ holds as well. In combination with $q' \overset{W_{s_q}}{\sim}_s q$, this implies $q_2 \overset{W_{s_q}}{\sim}_s q$, Therefore, $q_2 \sim_s q$ and $q_2 \overset{W_s}{\sim}_s q$. From $q' \overset{W_s}{\sim}_s q_2$ and $q_2 \overset{W_s}{\sim}_s q$, we conclude that $q' \overset{W_s}{\sim}_s q$. This completes the proof. □

The theorem above induces a safety-complete test suite, this time it is based on the original Wp-Method.

Corollary 1 (Safety-complete Wp-Method). *Let $M = (Q, \underline{q}, \Sigma_I, \Sigma_O, h)$ be a completely specified, deterministic, minimal FSM with $|Q| = n$, and let m be a fixed integer satisfying $m \geq n$. Let $\leq_s \subseteq \Sigma_O \times \Sigma_O$ be a safety-related output abstraction. Using the notation and terms introduced in Definitions 1 and 2, and Theorem 2. Then the test suite*

$$TS = V.W \cup \left(V. \bigcup_{i=0}^{m-n} \Sigma_I^i.W_s\right) \cup \left(V.\Sigma_I^{m-n+1} \oplus \{W_{s_q} \mid q \in Q\}\right)$$

is safety-complete with respect to fault model $\mathcal{F} = (M, \sim_s, \mathcal{D}(m))$. □

3.3   Implementation

For implementing an algorithm calculating the safety-complete test suite according to Corollary 1, we proceed as follows.

FSM Abstraction. Given a completely specified, deterministic, minimal FSM $M = (Q, \underline{q}, \Sigma_I, \Sigma_O, h)$, every safety-related output abstraction $\leq_s \subseteq \Sigma_O \times \Sigma_O$ induces an abstraction α_s of the alphabet by mapping each output $y \in \Sigma_O$ to the set of outputs $y' \in \Sigma_O$ that are greater or equal to y according to $\leq_s$.

$$\alpha_s : \Sigma_O \to \mathbb{P}(\Sigma_O); \quad y \mapsto \{y' \in \Sigma_O \mid y \leq_s y'\}$$

The image $\Sigma_O^s = \alpha_s(\Sigma_O)$ is again finite, therefore it can be used as a new output alphabet of a state machine M_s which is an abstraction of M with respect to $\leq_s$ in the following sense.

$$M_s = \mathbf{prime}(Q, \underline{q}, \Sigma_I, \Sigma_O^s, h_s)$$
$$h_s = \{(q, x, \alpha_s(y), q') \mid (q, x, y, q') \in h\}$$

Though M is assumed to be already minimised, the abstracted machine $(Q, \underline{q}, \Sigma_I, \Sigma_O^s, h_s)$ will not be minimised in general, because the output abstraction may result in fewer states of Q being distinguishable. Therefore M_s is specified as the prime machine of $(Q, \underline{q}, \Sigma_I, \Sigma_O^s, h_s)$.

By construction, two different states (q, q') in M_s produce outputs for certain input traces that differ in Σ_O^s. As a consequence, $q \not\sim_s q'$ holds. Therefore, the characterisation set of M_s equals the s-characterisation set W_s of M, as specified in Sect. 3.1. Analogously, the state identification sets of M_s are exactly the s-state identification sets of M. As a consequence, s-characterisation sets and s-state identification sets can be calculated by using the existing algorithms for characterisation sets and state identification sets, but the calculation needs to be performed on the abstracted FSM M_2.

Algorithm. With the FSM abstraction at hand, the algorithm for calculating the safety-complete test suite works as follows.

1. **Input 1.** Reference model $M = (Q, \underline{q}, \Sigma_I, \Sigma_O, h)$ with $|Q| = n$.
2. **Input 2.** Integer m satisfying $m \geq n$.
3. **Input 3.** Deterministic, completely specified, minimised FSM $M_s = (Q_s, \underline{q}_s, \Sigma_I, \Sigma_O^s, h_s)$ resulting from the abstraction of M with respect to $\leq_s$.
4. **Output.** Test suite TS which is safety-complete with respect to fault model $\mathcal{F} = (M, \sim_s, \mathcal{D}(m))$.
5. Calculate state cover V from M.
6. Calculate characterisation set W from M.
7. Calculate characterisation set W_s from M_s.
8. For all $q \in Q_s$, calculate state identification sets W_{s_q} from M_s.
9. Calculate $V.\Sigma_I^{m-n+1} \oplus \{W_{s_q} \mid q \in Q_s\}$ from M_s.
10. Set

$$\text{TS} = V.W \cup \left(V. \bigcup_{i=0}^{m-n} \Sigma_I^i.W_s\right) \cup \left(V.\Sigma_I^{m-n+1} \oplus \{W_{s_q} \mid q \in Q_s\}\right)$$

11. Remove test cases from TS that are prefixes of longer test cases.
12. Return TS.

FSM Open Source Library. We have published the open source C++ library fsmlib-cpp[1] which contains all algorithms needed for implementing the algorithm above. This library also provides essential methods for minimising DFSMs

---

[1] https://github.com/agbs-uni-bremen/fsmlib-cpp.git.

and for making nondeterministic FSMs observable. Moreover, a generator main program is provided which uses these methods to calculated W-Method, Wp-Method, and Safety-complete Wp-Method test suites. An overview over this library is given in the lecture notes [9, Appendix B].

4   Case Studies and Strategy Evaluation

4.1   Control of Fasten Seat Belt and Return-to-Seat Signs in the Aircraft Cabin

Application. The following example is a (slightly simplified) real-world example concerning safety-related and uncritical indications in an aircraft cabin. A *cabin controller* in a modern aircraft switches the *fasten seat belt (FSB) signs* located above the passenger seats in the cabin and the *return to seat (RTS) signs* located in the lavatories according to the rules modelled in the DFSM shown in Table 1.

As inputs, the cabin controller reads the actual position of the fasten seat belts switch in the cockpit, which has the position **f0** (OFF), **f1** (ON), and **f2** (AUTO). Further inputs come from the cabin pressure control system which indicates "cabin pressure low" by event **d1** and "cabin pressure ok" by **d0**. This controller also indicates "excessive altitude" by **e1** or "altitude in admissible range" by **e0**. Another sub-component of the cabin controller determines whether the so-called AUTO condition is true (event **a1**) or false (**a0**).

The cabin controller switches the fasten seat belt signs and return to seat signs on and off, depending on the actual input change and its current internal state. As long as the cabin pressure and the cruising altitude are ok (after initialisation of the cabin controller or if last events from the cabin pressure controller were **d0, e0**), the status of the FSB and RTS signs is determined by the cockpit switch and the AUTO condition: if the switch is in the ON position, both FSB and RTS signs are switched on (output 11 in Table 1). Turning the switch into the OFF position switches the signs off. If the switch is in the AUTO position, both FSB and RTS signs are switched on if the AUTO condition becomes true with event **a1**, and they are switched off again after event **a0**. The AUTO condition may depend on the status of landing gears, slats, flaps, and oil pressure, these details are abstracted to **a1, a0** in our example.

As soon as there occurs a loss of pressure in the cabin (event **d1**) or an excessive altitude is reached, the FSB signs must be switched on and remain in this state, regardless of the actual state of the cockpit switch and the AUTO condition. The RTS signs, however, need to be switched off, because passengers should not be encouraged to leave the lavatories in a low pressure or excessive altitude situation.

After the cabin pressure and the altitude are back in the admissible range, the FSB and RTS signs shall automatically resume their state as determined by the "normal" inputs from cockpit switch and AUTO condition.

Table 1. State-transition table of DFSM specifying the control of FSB signs and RTS signs in an aircraft cabin.

	f0	f1	f2	d1	d0	e1	e0	a1	a0
s_0	$s_0/00$	$s_1/11$	$s_2/00$	$s_3/10$	$s_0/00$	$s_6/10$	$s_0/00$	$s_{12}/00$	$s_0/00$
s_1	$s_0/00$	$s_1/11$	$s_2/00$	$s_4/10$	$s_1/11$	$s_7/10$	$s_1/11$	$s_{13}/11$	$s_1/11$
s_2	$s_0/00$	$s_1/11$	$s_2/00$	$s_5/10$	$s_2/00$	$s_8/10$	$s_2/00$	$s_{14}/11$	$s_2/00$
s_3	$s_3/10$	$s_4/10$	$s_5/10$	$s_3/10$	$s_0/00$	$s_9/10$	$s_3/10$	$s_{15}/10$	$s_3/10$
s_4	$s_3/10$	$s_4/10$	$s_5/10$	$s_4/10$	$s_1/11$	$s_{11}/10$	$s_4/10$	$s_{16}/10$	$s_4/10$
s_5	$s_3/10$	$s_4/10$	$s_5/10$	$s_5/10$	$s_2/00$	$s_{11}/10$	$s_5/10$	$s_{17}/10$	$s_5/10$
s_6	$s_6/10$	$s_7/10$	$s_8/10$	$s_9/10$	$s_6/10$	$s_6/10$	$s_0/00$	$s_{18}/10$	$s_6/10$
s_7	$s_6/10$	$s_7/10$	$s_8/10$	$s_{10}/10$	$s_7/10$	$s_7/10$	$s_1/11$	$s_{19}/10$	$s_7/10$
s_8	$s_6/10$	$s_7/10$	$s_8/10$	$s_{11}/10$	$s_8/10$	$s_8/10$	$s_2/00$	$s_{20}/10$	$s_8/10$
s_9	$s_9/10$	$s_{10}/10$	$s_{11}/10$	$s_9/10$	$s_6/10$	$s_9/10$	$s_3/10$	$s_{21}/10$	$s_9/10$
s_{10}	$s_9/10$	$s_{10}/10$	$s_{11}/10$	$s_{10}/10$	$s_7/10$	$s_{10}/10$	$s_4/10$	$s_{22}/10$	$s_{10}/10$
s_{11}	$s_9/10$	$s_{10}/10$	$s_{11}/10$	$s_{11}/10$	$s_8/10$	$s_{11}/10$	$s_5/10$	$s_{23}/10$	$s_{11}/10$
s_{12}	$s_{12}/00$	$s_{13}/11$	$s_{14}/11$	$s_{15}/10$	$s_{12}/00$	$s_{18}/10$	$s_{12}/00$	$s_{12}/00$	$s_0/00$
s_{13}	$s_{12}/00$	$s_{13}/11$	$s_{14}/11$	$s_{16}/10$	$s_{13}/11$	$s_{19}/10$	$s_{13}/11$	$s_{13}/11$	$s_1/11$
s_{14}	$s_{12}/00$	$s_{13}/11$	$s_{14}/11$	$s_{17}/10$	$s_{14}/11$	$s_{20}/10$	$s_{14}/11$	$s_{14}/11$	$s_2/00$
s_{15}	$s_{15}/10$	$s_{16}/10$	$s_{17}/10$	$s_{15}/10$	$s_{12}/00$	$s_{21}/10$	$s_{15}/10$	$s_{15}/10$	$s_3/10$
s_{16}	$s_{15}/10$	$s_{16}/10$	$s_{17}/10$	$s_{16}/10$	$s_{13}/11$	$s_{22}/10$	$s_{16}/10$	$s_{16}/10$	$s_4/10$
s_{17}	$s_{15}/10$	$s_{16}/10$	$s_{17}/10$	$s_{17}/10$	$s_{14}/11$	$s_{23}/10$	$s_{17}/10$	$s_{17}/10$	$s_5/10$
s_{18}	$s_{18}/10$	$s_{19}/10$	$s_{20}/10$	$s_{21}/10$	$s_{18}/10$	$s_{18}/10$	$s_{12}/00$	$s_{18}/10$	$s_6/10$
s_{19}	$s_{18}/10$	$s_{19}/10$	$s_{20}/10$	$s_{22}/10$	$s_{19}/10$	$s_{19}/10$	$s_{13}/11$	$s_{19}/10$	$s_7/10$
s_{20}	$s_{18}/10$	$s_{19}/10$	$s_{20}/10$	$s_{23}/10$	$s_{20}/10$	$s_{20}/10$	$s_{14}/11$	$s_{20}/10$	$s_8/10$
s_{21}	$s_{21}/10$	$s_{22}/10$	$s_{23}/10$	$s_{21}/10$	$s_{18}/10$	$s_{21}/10$	$s_{15}/10$	$s_{21}/10$	$s_9/10$
s_{22}	$s_{21}/10$	$s_{22}/10$	$s_{23}/10$	$s_{22}/10$	$s_{19}/10$	$s_{22}/10$	$s_{16}/10$	$s_{22}/10$	$s_{10}/10$
s_{23}	$s_{21}/10$	$s_{22}/10$	$s_{23}/10$	$s_{23}/10$	$s_{20}/10$	$s_{23}/10$	$s_{17}/10$	$s_{23}/10$	$s_{11}/10$

First column defines the states (initial state s_0)
First row defines the inputs
Fields s/y denote 'Post-state/Output'

Inputs:
f0, f1, f2 : FSB switch in position OFF, ON, AUTO
d1, d0 : Cabin decompression true, false
e1, e0 : Excessive altitude true, false
a1, a0 : Auto condition true, false
Outputs:
00 denotes (FSB,RTS)=(0,0)
11 denotes (FSB,RTS)=(1,1)
10 denotes (FSB,RTS)=(1,0)

Safety Considerations. Analysing the outputs

$$(\text{FSB}, \text{RTS}) \in \Sigma_O = \{00, 10, 11, 01\}$$

from the safety-perspective, leads to the identification of one safety-critical output $(\text{FSB}, \text{RTS}) = (1, 0)$, which should be set whenever cabin decompression or excessive altitude occurs. If the other outputs $\{00, 11, 01\}$ are changed due to an application error, this is certainly undesirable, but does not represent a safety hazard. Note that the output combination 01 should never occur at all.

These considerations lead to an abstraction function

$$\alpha_s \ : \ \Sigma_O \to \mathbb{P}(\Sigma_O)$$
$$00 \mapsto \{00, 10, 11, 01\}$$
$$11 \mapsto \{00, 10, 11, 01\}$$
$$01 \mapsto \{00, 10, 11, 01\}$$
$$10 \mapsto \{10\}$$

as introduced in Sect. 3.3, and the abstracted FSM described there is obtained by replacing outputs 00, 11 by $\text{YY} = \{00, 10, 11, 01\}$, while leaving every occurrence of output 10 unchanged.

Comparison Wp-Method Versus Safety-Complete Wp-Method. The reference FSM with 24 states as specified in Table 1 is already minimal, and a characterisation set has 4 elements. The minimised version of the FSM abstraction only has 4 states and a characterisation set with 3 elements.

These figures motivate why the Wp-Method requires 549 test cases if the minimised machine representing the implementation has the same number of states as the reference model ($m = n$). The Safety-complete Wp-Method only requires 468 test cases in this situation; this corresponds to a test case reduction of approx. 15%.

4.2 Synthetic Example

Application. The following example does not come from a practical application, but has been constructed to illustrate that the reduction of test cases in comparison to the original Wp-Method can be quite significant. The reference state machine is shown in Table 2.

Safety Considerations. We assume that outputs 1 and 2 can be considered as non-critical, so that they can be abstracted to a single output Y. Output 0 is considered as critical.

Table 2. Example showing the effectiveness of the safety-complete Wp-Method

	a	b	c	d	e
s0	s1/1	s3/2	s2/0	s4/1	s5/1
s1	s1/1	s3/1	s2/0	s4/2	s5/1
s2	s1/1	s3/1	s2/0	s4/1	s5/1
s3	s1/2	s3/2	s1/0	s4/1	s5/1
s4	s1/2	s3/2	s2/0	s4/1	s5/1
s5	s1/0	s3/1	s0/0	s4/1	s6/1
s6	s1/0	s3/1	s2/0	s4/1	s5/1

First column defines the states (initial state s_0)
First row defines the inputs
Fields s/y denote 'Post-state/Output'

Comparison Wp-Method Versus Safety-Complete Wp-Method. The reference machine in Table 2 with its 7 states is already minimal, but the minimised abstracted FSM only has 2 states. As a consequence, both characterisation set and state identification sets of the abstracted machine are significantly smaller. Therefore, the Wp-Methods with assumption $m = n$ requires 87 test cases, while the Safety-complete Wp-Method only requires 41, this corresponds to a test case reduction of approx. 53%.

While this example is of no practical value, it illustrates effectively that test case reductions to less than half of the cases required for the Wp-Method are possible when using the Safety-complete Wp-Method.

4.3   Garage Door Controller

Application. This example has been originally proposed in [6]. We use it here as a negative example: it is not guaranteed that the Safety-complete Wp-Method will always require fewer test cases than the Wp-Method, though the former has lesser test strength than the latter. Therefore it is important to compare the required test case numbers beforehand – for example, by using the algorithms made available in the FSM Library described in [9, Appendix B] – before deciding which test suites to run against the system under test.

The garage door controller uses inputs from a remote control, two sensors indicating whether the door has reached the up position or the down position, respectively, and a light sensor indicating whether the door area is crossed while the door is closing or opening. The controller commands the motor to go down, up, stop, or to reverse the down direction to the up direction. Its detailed behaviour is specified in Table 3.

Safety Considerations. The only output considered as safety-critical is the command to reverse the down-direction to the up direction. All other outputs can be abstracted to some value Y.

Comparison Wp-Method Versus Safety-Complete Wp-Method. Both the reference model in Table 3 and its abstraction are not minimal. It turns out, however, that the minimised abstracted model still has as many states as the minimised reference model. Moreover, the characterisation set and the state identification sets of the abstracted model are larger than the equivalent sets derived from the minimised reference model.

As a consequence, the Wp-Method requires only 17 test cases for $m = n$, while the Safety-complete Wp-Method requires 33 cases.

Table 3. DFSM modelling the garage door controller.

	e1	e2	e3	e4
DU	DC/a1	DU/a3	DU/a3	DU/a3
DD	DO/a2	DD/a3	DD/a3	DD/a3
DSD	DC/a1	DSD/a3	DSD/a3	DSD/a3
DSU	DO/a2	DSU/a3	DSU/a3	DSU/a3
DC	DSD/a3	DD/a3	DC/a1	DO/a4
DO	DSU/a3	DO/a2	DU/a3	DO/a2

Inputs:
e1 : Remote control has been pressed
e2 : Sensor indicates "door reaches down position"
e3 : Sensor indicates "door reaches up position"
e4 : Sensor indicates "light beam crossed"
Outputs:
a1 : Command "start down movement" to motor
a2 : Command "start up movement" to motor
a3 : Command "stop movement" to motor
a4 : Command "reverse down movement to up" to motor
States:
DU : Door is in up position
DD : Door is in down position
DSD : Door is stopped while going down
DSU : Door is stopped while going up
DC : Door is closing
DO : Door is opening

5   Conclusion

We have presented a testing strategy which guarantees to uncover every safety violation when testing an implementation against a deterministic finite state machine reference model. These guarantees hold under the assumption that the true behaviour of the implementation, when expressed by a minimised state machine, does not exceed a certain maximum of states m, in comparison to the number n of states in the minimised reference model. Safety criticality has been modelled by means of a safety-related output abstraction which allows to express that certain outputs can be exchanged by certain others without introducing a safety violation. The new strategy has been derived from the well-known Wp-Method. A proof has been presented which shows that – while no longer guaranteeing to uncover *every* violation of input/output equivalence – the strategy will uncover every failure which ends in an erroneous output representing a safety violation.

First experiments have shown that this Safety-complete Wp-Method may require significantly fewer test cases than the Wp-Method (reductions between 15% and 50% have been observed). It has been indicated by another example, however, that this reduction is not guaranteed.

The concept described here can be extended to more complex systems whose behaviour can be represented by a certain class of Kripke structures over infinite input domains, but with finite domains for internal states and outputs. It has been shown in [5] that a specific input equivalence class construction technique can be applied, so that any complete testing theory valid for FSMs can be translated to a likewise complete equivalence class partition testing strategy for these systems with Kripke semantics.

References

1. Chow, T.S.: Testing software design modeled by finite-state machines. IEEE Trans. Software Eng. **4**(3), SE-178–186 (1978)
2. Fujiwara, S., Bochmann, G.V., Khendek, F., Amalou, M., Ghedamsi, A.: Test selection based on finite state models. IEEE Trans. Software Eng. **17**(6), 591–603 (1991)
3. Haxthausen, A.E., Peleska, J.: Formal development and verification of a distributed railway control system. IEEE Trans. Softw. Eng. **26**(8), 687–701 (2000)
4. Huang, W., Peleska, J.: Complete model-based equivalence class testing. STTT **18**(3), 265–283 (2016). http://dx.doi.org/10.1007/s10009-014-0356-8
5. Huang, W.I., Peleska, J.: Complete model-based equivalence class testing for nondeterministic systems. Formal Aspects Comput. **29**(2), 335–364 (2017). http://dx.doi.org/10.1007/s00165-016-0402-2
6. Jorgensen, P.C.: The Craft of Model-Based Testing. CRC Press, Boca Raton (2017)
7. Li, S., Qi, Z.: Property-oriented testing: An approach to focusing testing efforts on behaviours of interest. In: SOQUA/TECOS (2004)
8. Luo, G., von Bochmann, G., Petrenko, A.: Test selection based on communicating nondeterministic finite-state machines using a generalized wp-method. IEEE Trans. Software Eng. **20**(2), 149–162 (1994). http://doi.ieeecomputersociety.org/10.1109/32.265636

9. Peleska, J., Huang, W.l.: Test Automation - Foundations and Applications of Model-based Testing. University of Bremen (2017). Lecture notes http://www.informatik.uni-bremen.de/agbs/jp/papers/test-automation-huang-peleska.pdf

10. Vasilevskii, M.P.: Failure diagnosis of automata. Kibernetika (Transl.) **4**, 98–108 (1973)

Testing TLS Using Combinatorial Methods and Execution Framework

Dimitris E. Simos[1], Josip Bozic[2(✉)], Feng Duan[3], Bernhard Garn[1],
Kristoffer Kleine[1], Yu Lei[3], and Franz Wotawa[2]

[1] SBA Research, 1040 Vienna, Austria
{dsimos,bgarn,kkleine}@sba-research.org
[2] Institute for Software Technology, Graz University of Technology,
8010 Graz, Austria
{jbozic,wotawa}@ist.tugraz.at
[3] University of Texas at Arlington, Arlington 76019, USA
feng.duan@mavs.uta.edu, ylei@cse.uta.edu

Abstract. The TLS protocol is the standard for secure Internet communication between two parties. Unfortunately, there have been recently successful attacks like DROWN or BREACH that indicate the necessity for thoroughly testing TLS implementations. In our research work, we focus on automated test case generation and execution for the TLS security protocol, where the aim is to make use of combinatorial methods for providing test cases that ideally also reveal previously unknown attacks. This is made feasible by creating appropriate input parameter models for different messages that can appear in a TLS message sequence. In this paper, we present the resulting test case generation and execution framework together with the corresponding testing oracle. Furthermore, we discuss first empirical results obtained using different TLS implementations and their releases.

Keywords: Combinatorial testing · Security testing · Security protocols · TLS

1 Introduction

Software implementations of the Transport Layer Security (TLS) protocol specification are a critical component for the security of the Internet communications and beyond. Software bugs and attacks, such as Heartbleed, DROWN, BREACH and POODLE, still surface in implementations of the TLS protocol, despite many years of analysis (at least for open-source implementations). This can be attributed to the complexity of the protocol and its very high number of interactions.

In this paper, we describe a security testing technique for the TLS protocol. Since the TLS handshake protocol is one of the most important components of TLS, our approach focuses on this part of the protocol in order to test TLS

© IFIP International Federation for Information Processing 2017
Published by Springer International Publishing AG 2017. All Rights Reserved
N. Yevtushenko et al. (Eds.): ICTSS 2017, LNCS 10533, pp. 162–177, 2017.
DOI: 10.1007/978-3-319-67549-7_10

implementations for potential security leaks. After providing some basic definitions, we describe the input model for combinatorial test case generation. Note that this is the first time where combinatorial testing is applied to the testing of the TLS protocol.

For this approach, three different input models are constructed, each for one client-side TLS event, respectively. Every of these events encompasses a specific set of possible parameters and values. In addition to the modelling part, the practical part deals with the implementation of a test execution framework. This has the possibility to communicate, and thus, to attack TLS implementations in an automated manner. The framework comprehends all TLS events according to the TLS standard and can execute a handshake for this purpose.

In particular, the paper is structured as follows: Sect. 2 describes related work while Sect. 3 defines preliminary concepts for the methodology developed in this paper. In Sect. 4 we depict a combinatorial approach for testing TLS which was made feasible by developing the necessary input models and give examples of the generated test sets. Moreover, Sect. 5 describes the test execution framework we have developed for TLS together with a test oracle. Finally, Sect. 6 presents the results of the executions followed by a detailed evaluation and Sect. 7 concludes the paper.

2   Related Work

New activities in security testing were sparked by [11], in which the authors found several critical vulnerabilities in commonly used TLS implementations. The identified bugs were classified as state machine bugs and this put the internal state machines of TLS implementations into the focus, next to and on the same level of criticality as the implementation of pure cryptographic functionality. The systematic testing of TLS implementations based on the principles of these kind of state machine bugs with a tool was presented in [32] and offers the user the possibility to create custom TLS message flows and arbitrarily modify message contents. The strategy for testing of TLS implementations via the exchange of modified messages or injection attacks was also followed in [28] and [12].

The works [11,30] follow a model-based approach for testing TLS implementations, using [29] to extract the respective state machines.

The certificate validation logic in SSL/TLS implementations was tested in [16], and a cross-protocol attack was presented in [26]. Attacks on authentication were presented in [13] and [14]. A plaintext recovery attack was given in [9]. The usage of invalid curves can lead to practical attacks as shown in [21], and new Bleichenbacher side channels and attacks were presented in [27]. A systematic analysis of the security of TLS can be found in [22].

Testing of the newly proposed TLS 1.3 [7] was discussed in [18]. Finally, care has to be taken to compare in detail the security properties that TLS provides and the requirements of any application using it [10].

3 Preliminaries

In this section we detail some preliminary concepts needed for the work carried out in this paper. In particular, we link expressions from the domain of software testing to expressions from the domain of protocol specification. Regarding terminology for protocol specification, we use and refer to RFC 5246, "The Transport Layer Security (TLS) Protocol, Version 1.2" [4].

In their union collectively simply referred to as the *TLS protocol 1.2*, its specification [4] actually defines multiple protocols, some of which operate on top of each other. In this paper, we focus on the *Handshake Protocol*, a member of the *TLS Handshaking Protocols*. The semantics encapsulated in the *Handshake Protocol* are coded in the exchange of *messages* between a client and a server. If a client initially connects to a server and wants to establish a secure connection, it will follow the *Handshake Protocol* and start by sending a `ClientHello` message. According to the specification, the protocol semantics translate into an ordered sequence of Handshake messages that allow a client and server to establish a *secure connection* and start exchanging application data.

The software testing view on the *Handshake protocol* is that it regards these messages as *abstract* events, which appear as ordered sequences in practice. Handshake messages appear in practice with all of their values instantiated during the execution of the Handshake protocol. We only consider protocol compliant sequences of abstract messages. To be able to execute derived test cases from these abstract events, it is necessary to define an *input model* for these abstract events corresponding to Handshake messages. We aim to develop such input models using combinatorial methods for each of these abstract events (see Sect. 4.2), which will be used to instantiate concrete Handshake messages.

We model each abstract event independently and also want to test them individually, but nevertheless we are interested in always continuing the Handshake protocol as long as possible, trying to do a complete Handshake. To that end, we define a standard instantiated Handshake message for each considered client-side Handshake message. These intentionally "harmless" Handshake messages will be used create as complete as possible concrete sequences of Handshake messages. In other words, during our testing it is necessary to distinguish between Handshake messages populated with values chosen for testing one specific Handshake message (whose purpose is to disrupt the normal execution work flow via their values) and template Handshake messages (whose single purpose is to move the current status of Handshake during protocol execution to a particular state). Please note that in any sequence there appears exactly one message, which is derived from the abstract model, while all other messages are template messages (see also Sect. 6). To sum up, we are only actively sending non-standard client messages, and as a result we are testing the server side of the two communicating parties.

4   Combinatorial Testing

Combinatorial Testing (CT) is a widely applicable methodology and technology for software testing. In a combinatorial test plan, all interactions between parameters up to a certain level are covered. For example, in pairwise testing, for every pair of parameters, every pair of values will appear at least once. Furthermore, a CT strategy, called t-way testing, requires every combination of values of any t parameters to be covered by at least one test, where t is referred to as the strength of coverage and usually takes a small value (1 to 6) [24]. Each combination of values of a set of parameters is considered to represent one possible interaction among these parameters.

4.1   Application to Testing of TLS

Even though combinatorial testing is a proven methodology for security testing [31], this is the first time where such a combinatorial approach is being used to test the TLS protocol.

When applying CT to testing TLS, we focus on the possible interactions among parameters of TLS messages. An interaction may accur among those parameters in the same TLS message, or among parameters in different TLS messages. Given a sequence of TLS messages, to capture these interactions among its parameters, we first considered a naive approach: flat CT. It means all parameters of these messages are listed in one model flatly, and every combination of values of any t parameters will be covered. This approach is simple, however, when TLS event sequence is changed, it requires to modify the whole model of flat CT and redo test case generation.

In order to make CT more flexible for multiple TLS event sequences, here we choose another approach: hierarchical CT. That is to say, there are two levels for CT test case generation: intra-message level (lower level) and inter-message level (upper level). On intra-message level, CT will generate t-way test cases for parameters of a single message (client-side). For each type of message, an intra-message t-way test set will be generated from its model separately. On inter-message level, each type of message is expressed as a parameter, and its intra-message t-way test cases are expressed as parameter values. Given a sequence of TLS messages, its messages as parameters and their intra-message t-way test cases as parameter values will then be used to generate inter-message t'-way test cases. Note that, t' can be different from t, e.g., by now, we use 1-way on inter-message level which means CT only be applied on single message.

4.2   Input Parameter Modeling

Since CT creates test cases by selecting values for input parameters and by combining these values, Input Parameter Modeling (IPM) is required to capture the input test space for real-life applicability of CT. IPM mainly works on identifying the parameters, values, and the relations of parameters. According to [17,20], a list of TLS messages can be cataloged, and IPM based on their data structures can be made. In TLS protocol, each message is constructed from two layers: TLS Record Layer (bottom layer), and Protocol Message Layer (top layer, as shown in Table 1, note that Message Body only exists for Handshake Protocol Messages). Since other attributes in these two layers will be determined by values in Message Body, we only need to do IPM on attributes in Message Body for handshake protocol messages.

Table 1. Protocol message layer (Handshake Protocol)

Handshake protocol message		
Message type (1byte, 0x00-0xFF)	Length of message body (3bytes, uint24)	Message body
hello_request(0)	0	empty
client_hello(1)	the length of message body in bytes	ClientHello
server_hello(2)	the length of message body in bytes	ServerHello
certificate(11)	the length of message body in bytes	Certificate
server_key_exchange(12)	the length of message body in bytes	ServerKeyExchange
certificate_request(13)	the length of message body in bytes	CertificateRequest
server_hello_done(14)	0	empty
certificate_verify(15)	the length of message body in bytes	CertificateVerify
client_key_exchange(16)	the length of message body in bytes	ClientKeyExchange
finished(20)	the length of message body in bytes	Finished
(255)		

In this paper, since we only test TLS implementation from client side, IPM is only applied on client-side handshake messages. For example, we do IPM on `ClientHello` message, but not on `ServerHello` message. Here, we list general TLS messages as Table 2, which are used for handshake procedure in Fig. 1. And among all nine messages, only M1, M5, M6 and M7 are client-side messages. Note that M6 is CCS protocol message, not Handshake. According to that, we only have to do IPM on the parameters of M1, M5 and M7.

Table 2. General TLS messages

M1	ClientHello
M2	ServerHello
M3	ServerCertificate
M4	ServerHelloDone
M5	ClientKeyExchange
M6	ClientChangeCipherSpec
M7	ClientFinished
M8	ServerChangeCipherSpec
M9	ServerFinished

Based on the TLS protocol specification, we can derive parameters and possible values for M1, M5 and M7. In practical terms, parameter values may be abstracted and limited in domain size, while some parameters should be subdivided into meta-parameters. For example, in M1, a ClientUnixTime meta-parameter is extracted from "client random" parameter, and assigned $RealTime \pm x$ as part of its abstract values, for detecting potential vulnerability on time processing mechanism of TLS implementations.

A challange is that TLS involves a lot of cipher/compression/Hash/PRF functions. When a handshake message includes a collection (list) of these options, some parameters cannot enumerate all their possible values but only give some representative values. For example, cipher suites of ClientHello message can be any list of the cryptographic options supported by the client. In order to avoid unnecessarily huge domain size for the *cipher suites* parameter, here we only use single cipher suites as its values, but not non-singular lists of suites. Note that, this shortcut may miss some potential interactions since parameter values are limited.

As mentioned earlier, for any TLS standard sequence containing client-side messages: M1, M5 and M7, we first conduct an IPM on these messages, and then create input model for a system under test into the ACTS tool [33]. ACTS is a widely-used tool for generating CT test cases which supports multi-way coverage [25], constraints [23,34], and is well optimized [19].

The input model of M1 can be listed as follows:

```
Protocol Version: TLS10,TLS11,TLS12,DTLS10,DTLS12
Client Unix Time: RealTime,RealTime-x,RealTime+x
Client Random: 28-byteRand
Session ID: NULL,32-byteID
Supported Cipher Suites: TLS_FALLBACK_SCSV,
    TLS_NULL_WITH_NULL_NULL,TLS_RSA_WITH_NULL_SHA256,
    TLS_RSA_WITH_AES_128_CBC_SHA256,
    TLS_DHE_RSA_WITH_CAMELLIA_128_CBC_SHA
Supported Compression Methods: NULL,DEFLATE,LZS
```

Similarly, the input model of M5 can be listed as follows:

```
KeyExchangeAlgorithm: rsa,dhe_dss,dhe_rsa,dh_dss,
    dh_rsa,dh_anon
ClientProtocolVersion: TLS10,TLS11,TLS12,DTLS10,
    DTLS12
ClientRandom: 46-byteRand
PublicValueEncoding: implicit,explicit
Yc: empty,ClientDiffie-HellmanPublicValue
```

Note that, if KeyExchangeAlgorithm is rsa, an EncryptedPreMasterSecret key will be concreted by ClientProtocolVersion and ClientRandom; otherwise, a ClientDiffieHellmanPublic value will be concreted when PublicValueEncoding is explicit.

Also, the input model of M7 can be listed as follows:

```
master_secret: empty,half,default,changebyte,multiply
finished_label: client finished
Hash: empty,half,default,changebyte,multiply
```

Both master_secret and Hash meta-parameters have the same values. These abstract values represent operations to be performed on already dynamically calculated values (from the previous message flow), which are required for concreting a real value for "verify_data" parameter. More details are mentioned in next section.

4.3   Pairwise Test Suites for TLS Testing

With input models for M1, M5 and M7, ACTS can easily generate intra-message test cases for each message, e.g., pairwise (2-way) test cases of M1 are shown in Table 3. For brevity, we only show 10 tests in table, while there are total

Table 3. Pairwise test cases of M1

Protocol version	Client unix time	Client random	Session ID	Supported cipher suites	Supported compression methods
TLS10	RealTime-x	28-byteRand	32-byteID	TLS_FALLBACK_SCSV	DEFLATE
TLS10	RealTime+x	28-byteRand	NULL	TLS_NULL_WITH_NULL_NULL	LZS
TLS10	RealTime	28-byteRand	32-byteID	TLS_RSA_WITH_NULL_SHA256	NULL
TLS10	RealTime-x	28-byteRand	NULL	TLS_RSA_WITH_AES_128_CBC_SHA256	LZS
TLS10	RealTime+x	28-byteRand	32-byteID	TLS_DHE_RSA_WITH_CAMELLIA_128_CBC_SHA	NULL
TLS11	RealTime	28-byteRand	NULL	TLS_FALLBACK_SCSV	LZS
TLS11	RealTime-x	28-byteRand	32-byteID	TLS_NULL_WITH_NULL_NULL	NULL
TLS11	RealTime+x	28-byteRand	NULL	TLS_RSA_WITH_NULL_SHA256	DEFLATE
TLS11	RealTime	28-byteRand	32-byteID	TLS_RSA_WITH_AES_128_CBC_SHA256	DEFLATE
TLS11	RealTime-x	28-byteRand	NULL	TLS_DHE_RSA_WITH_CAMELLIA_128_CBC_SHA	LZS
...	...	...	...	...	...

25 pairwise tests for input model of M1. By using ACTS, we also generate 30 pairwise tests for M5 and 25 pairwise tests for M7. Note that, pairwise test set may not be able to trigger all possible failures during message processing, but it is a good starting point for applying CT on TLS.

5   Execution Framework

In this section we give an overview about the execution framework for security testing of TLS implementations. In order to execute the test cases, we developed a framework that reads the generated test sets and executes them against any implementation of TLS. The result is an execution method that offers the ability to configure and execute test cases in an automated manner.

The framework itself builds upon TLS-Attacker [6], an implementation for analyzing TLS libraries. The initial implementation encompasses the possibility to establish a TLS handshake and to specify individual parameters for this purpose. However, in our case we adapted the framework in order to test TLS implementations according to concrete values coming from combinatorial testing.

Figure 1 depicts one handshake procedure of the TLS protocol. It encompasses a set of client and server side messages that are exchanged between the peers. Each messages is called a TLS event. During the translation process from abstract to concrete test cases, several values are generated dynamically, whereas other values is prespecified. If no "unexpected" behavior is encountered during the handshake, a hopefully secure connection is established.

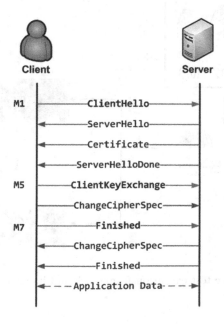

Fig. 1. TLS handshake and tested messages.

However, since the intention in our approach lies on detecting abnormal behavior of TLS implementations, two different approaches can be taken. First, the order of TLS events can be manipulated, thus deviating from the default sequence. This approach was demonstrated in a simple example in [15]. Another option would be to check the default sequence by manipulating the concrete parameter values of some of the individual TLS events. In this way, we might provoke a reaction from the server, which could lead to different behavior of the tested SUTs.

In this paper, parameter values of client-side TLS events are changed dynamically. An abstract overview of the functionality of the implementation is given in Fig. 2. First, the generated concrete values are read by the test execution framework (TEF). Actually, we execute the TLS handshake as one test case. In addition to the message flow, one specific type of client-side message is tested per test case. For example, first we test whether manipulating the ClientHello message, but keeping the default dynamically generated values of the other messages will result on a termination of the handshake procedure. Then, values for ClientKeyExchange are manipulated while all other TLS events are processed via standard messages (see Sect. 3). Finally, client's Finished message reads the generated values from the combinatorial test sets.

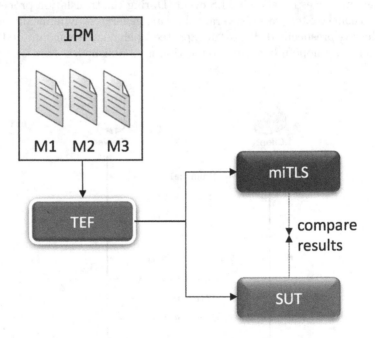

Fig. 2. The test execution framework and its environment.

5.1   Test Oracle

Constructing the test oracle for security testing of protocols has been realized in the following way. Specifying an expected output value on the concrete level is hard to define because of the complexity of the TLS protocol in general. Moreover, every TLS implementation has its own mechanisms and could react in a different way to the same input values. Because of this, our approach defines the oracle on an abstract level. Since the message flow of the TLS handshake is known, we define the oracle based on the flow of TLS events of a reference implementation. For this cause we have selected as reference implementation the **miTLS**, where some security properties have been proven correct. Every test set is executed against miTLS, where all sent and received messages are recorded. Afterwards, the same test set is used on the individual SUTs, thereby recording their corresponding replies. In the aftermath, as depicted in Fig. 2, we compare execution traces from both the reference implementation and the individual SUT.

5.2   Testing Procedure

In order to give a demonstration, let's discuss a test case where we test `ClientHello`. As mentioned, the concrete values can be read in their current form or they represent an operation that needs to be processed on a parameter. The first test case from the pairwise test set for M1 (see Table 3) reads as follows:

`TLS10,RealTime-x,28-byteRand,32-byteID,TLS_FALLBACK_SCSV,DEFLATE`

The values indicate that the client offers TLS 1.0 as its supported protocol, whereas TLS_FALLBACK_SCSV and DEFLATE are picked as the cipher suite and compression method, respectively. On the other hand, the value for Unix time indicates an operation on a value. Here the current real-time is subtracted by the value x, i.e. an amount of 10, which stands for years. Additionally, the values 28-byteRand and 32-byteID instruct not to make any changes but to use the agreed values for the random number and session ID. Finally, the framework generates the following message according to the values:

```
Protocol Version: TLS10
Client Unix Time: Sat Jun 09 04:33:32 CEST 2007
Client Random: 01 4B ...
Session ID:
Supported Cipher Suites: 56 00
Supported Compression Methods: 01
```

In our execution framework, each of the parameters is dealt with individually. This means that the program can distinguish between assigned values and operations. As depicted above, the cipher suite and compression methods are defined in their unique hexadecimal form of their byte representations.

The functionality of `ClientKeyExchange` is different from M1 in the sense that more of their values are generated in run-time. Take an example from the first row in M5:

```
rsa,TLS10,46-byteRand,explicit,ClientDiffie-HellmanPublicValue
```

This IPM differs from the others with regard to the fact that it does not encompass one fixed type of message. According to the chosen key exchange algorithm either a RSA-encrypted premaster secret message or Diffie-Hellman public value. Both message types have specific parameters. Whereas the first covers the client protocol version and random value for the pre-master secret, the second encompasses the public value `Yc`. In case that the client has already sent the public value in the certificate, the public value encoding is **implicit**. Otherwise, **explicit** instructs to send `Yc` inside the new message. A RSA-encrypted message with the previous value for `KeyExchangeAlgorithm` might have the following looks:

```
KeyExchangeAlgorithm: rsa
ClientProtocolVersion: TLS10
ClientRandom: C5 FE ...
```

In contrast to both examples above, `Finished` is fully generated according to run-time values. By reading the values from the M7's IPM we get:

```
half,client finished,changebyte
```

Usually the master secret represents a 48-byte value that is calculated during the handshake. The Hash is calculated on-the-fly as well by taking into consideration previous TLS events, thus producing a 32-byte value. The finished label will always remain the same. In order to give an example, let's assume that the obtained **master_secret** looks the following way:

```
59 7A E7 37 A6 C9 18 90  C9 C7 99 44 57 FE 06 BC
CF 20 A3 DE 12 56 3B DE  12 AE 10 B4 2E CB 06 61
8C DC 96 FE 77 07 37 B7  E9 73 D5 93 32 E6 9E 9D
```

The 32-byte value of **Hash** looks like:

```
C5 11 5E C7 56 7\,A 9A E2  2A 1F 9B F3 38 5D FB 08
38 D0 31 B5 D3 B7 35 42  13 F2 64 58 12 26 92 A9
```

The concrete values indicate that the first byte array has to be cut in half, i.e. using only half of its value further. On the other hand, **changebyte** will perform an operation where the first byte of the calculated hash will be exchanged by the byte 0xFF. Finally, the resulting message will have the following values:

```
master_secret:
   59 7A E7 37 A6 C9 18 90   C9 C7 99 44 57 FE 06 BC
   CF 20 A3 DE 12 56 3B DE
finished_label: client finished
Hash:
   FF 11 5E C7 56 7\,A 9A E2   2A 1F 9B F3 38 5D FB 08
   38 D0 31 B5 D3 B7 35 42   13 F2 64 58 12 26 92 A9
```

By changing these two values we intend to surprise the system by submitting similar but malformed expected values. In such way, the SUT might be tricked into unexpected behaviour.

6 Evaluation

Since the execution framework is meant for testing of TLS implementations, five different programs have been installed for this purpose. As already mentioned, the reference implementation is miTLS ver. 0.9 [2], whereas the other tested SUTs are OpenSSL ver. 1.0.1e [3], wolfSSL ver. 3.10.2 [8], mbed TLS ver 2.4.2 [5] and GnuTLS ver 3.5.9 [1]. As noted before, three client-side messages have been tested with 25, 30 and 25 inputs, respectively. The obtained results are depicted in Table 4. The results show the results from three different SUT, which are categorized according to three types of outputs. The first column depicts how many times a complete handshake (comp) could be established between the framework and the SUT. Additionally, we can see how many times the attempt was fully rejected (reject), i.e. by getting no or only one response (for example an alert message) from the server. Finally, the number of incomplete handshakes (incomp) depicts the situation where no handshake was established but the attempt was not initially rejected either.

Table 4. Evaluation results

SUT	miTLS			OpenSSL			mbed TLS		
	comp	reject	incomp	comp	reject	incomp	comp	reject	incomp
M1	0	25	0	1	24	0	1	17	7
M5	0	30	0	0	0	30	0	0	30
M7	0	25	0	1	0	24	1	0	24

The goal of the framework is to offer an automated linkage between combinatorial testing and protocol testing, i.e. it should be able to test any TLS implementation by requiring only minor tester interaction. Usually only the port is changed in order to access another SUT. As explained before, the default TLS handshake is executed by manipulating values of the emphasized client-side messages. No additional preferences are set. We want to examine whether for the same inputs, different output traces will be achieved.

The testing proceeds in the following way. As mentioned earlier, there are three test scenarios and in each of them we want to execute the entire TLS handshake. When testing M1, the values from its IPM will be used, whereas M5 and M7 will have standard on-the-fly generated values. Also, when testing M5, we use standard messages for M1 and M7. Finally, for M7 the framework does not make use of the IPM for M1 and M5 since it uses similarly standard messages for M1 and M5. This means that we are testing the whole handshake in each scenario but change values only for one TLS event. In such way, we want to see how the manipulation of one single TLS event affects the overall handshake.

When testing M1, OpenSSL does not continue with the handshake procedure for any of the submitted values by throwing a decode error. This may happen because of protocol version or cipher suite negotiation. However, mbed TLS does return more results, even succeeding in establishing a handshake between both peers. In other cases, a BAD_RECORD_MAC is thrown after the client's Finished message. This leads to the conclusion that because of specific concrete values for M1 a different behavior from the recorded one for miTLS is triggered after a few messages. Investigating these values might be of interest for the tester. In other cases, the execution terminates after the ServerHelloDone message. The rest of the results usually indicates cipher suite negotiation failures and terminates the execution. This is as well the case with wolfSSL, where the handshake usually breaks up with a SSL_accept failed error. This is the same case with miTLS and GnuTLS, which fail because of diverse HANDSHAKE_FAILUREs or message MAC verification failures. In general, it seems that miTLS resists handshake attempts by far more than all other applications, as we *expected* it should.

For M5, OpenSSL as well as mbed TLS an error is thrown after server's hello done message. Also, wolfSSL cannot match any cipher suite, whereas GnuTLS throws HANDSHAKE_FAILUREs. The reasons for the results from the first tested SUTs are problems with the specific key exchange messages. In some cases, errors are triggered because the SUT expects a RSA-encrypted message. This usually leads to the termination of the handshake procedure. In summary, testing for M5 seems to produce most difficulties for all SUTs.

Finally, the test results for M7 are as follows. OpenSSL usually reaches a state where client's Finished message is received, after which an alert terminates the execution. The operations done on the dynamically generated values for master_secret and Hash are detected by the SUT, which causes the breakup. However, in one case a handshake was finalized successfully. Similar results are obtained for mbed TLS. On the contrary, miTLS and wolfSSL do not conclude any handshake, which is the case with GnuTLS as well.

In general, some of the obtained results are similar. For example, two different SUTs behave similar when rejecting the same input. Whereas miTLS rejects any further communication with an exception, OpenSSL sends an additional alert message. Although the behavior is not quite the same, it can be concluded that both applications react slightly different when making the same decision.

7 Conclusion

In this paper we generated combinatorial test sets which include dynamically assigned values of individual TLS events. During execution, several abstract messages are generated on-the-fly and populated with concrete data using combinatorial (testing) strategies. During the testing process, the framework tests different SUTs by focusing separately on three of the TLS handshake messages. Every of these events is tested as part of the standard handshake procedure but with manipulated values according to the combinatorial input model. Then, we compared the resulting execution traces to the submitted input and to the results of other SUTs.

The framework was able to test TLS implementations in an automated manner. Also, different test results have been achieved with regards to concrete input values. The analysis of these results and the causes for misbehavior represents an issue for the tester in order to track whether a vulnerability could be detected. In general, we were able to identify test cases that led to non-uniform behavior of TLS implementations. Generating more of such test cases would represent a promising task for the future.

We draw the conclusion that the developed framework and oracle is strong enough to distinguish different behavior among TLS implementations. The obtained results require more investigation in order to track the cause of this behavior and examine whether security leaks have occurred.

However, in order to reach more fine-grained testing results, more effort has to be put in the strengthening the test oracle and generating test cases according to a higher combinatorial strength. In this case, more diverse test cases would be generated that could lead to more thorough testing and make another step towards security testing of TLS. As future work, we plan the framework to be extended further to ease the usability for a tester and provide feedback on the internal processing during execution.

Acknowledgement. The research presented in the paper has been funded in part by the Austrian Research Promotion Agency (FFG) under grant 851205 (Security Protocol Interaction Testing in Practice - SPLIT) and the Austrian COMET Program (FFG).

References

1. The gnutls transport layer security library. http://www.gnutls.org/. Accessed 07 June 2017
2. mitls: A verified reference implementation of tls. https://mitls.org/. Accessed 07 June 2017

3. Openssl. https://www.openssl.org/. Accessed 07 June 2017
4. Rfc 5246. https://tools.ietf.org/rfc/rfc5246.txt. Accessed 31 May 2017
5. Ssl library mbed tls / polarssl. https://tls.mbed.org/. Accessed 07 June 2017
6. Tls-attacker. https://github.com/RUB-NDS/TLS-Attacker. Accessed 04 Dec 2016
7. The transport layer security (tls) protocol version 1.3. https://tools.ietf.org/html/draft-ietf-tls-tls13-07. Accessed 31 May 2017
8. wolfssl. https://www.wolfssl.com/. Accessed 07 June 2017
9. AlFardan, N., Paterson, K.G.: Plaintext-recovery attacks against datagram tls. In: Network and Distributed System Security Symposium (NDSS 2012) (2012)
10. Berbecaru, D., Lioy, A.: On the robustness of applications based on the SSL and TLS security protocols. In: Lopez, J., Samarati, P., Ferrer, J.L. (eds.) EuroPKI 2007. LNCS, vol. 4582, pp. 248–264. Springer, Heidelberg (2007). doi:10.1007/978-3-540-73408-6_18
11. Beurdouche, B., Bhargavan, K., Delignat-Lavaud, A., Fournet, C., Kohlweiss, M., Pironti, A., Strub, P.Y., Zinzindohoue, J.K.: A messy state of the union: taming the composite state machines of tls. In: Proceedings of the 36th IEEE Symposium on Security and Privacy (2015)
12. Beurdouche, B., Delignat-Lavaud, A., Kobeissi, N., Pironti, A., Bhargavan, K.: Flextls: a tool for testing tls implementations. In: 9th USENIX Workshop on Offensive Technologies (WOOT 2015) (2015)
13. Bhargavan, K., Lavaud, A.D., Fournet, C., Pironti, A., Strub, P.Y.: Triple handshakes and cookie cutters: breaking and fixing authentication over tls. In: 2014 IEEE Symposium on Security and Privacy (SP), pp. 98–113. IEEE (2014)
14. Bhargavan, K., Leurent, G.: Transcript collision attacks: Breaking authentication in tls, ike, and ssh. In: Network and Distributed System Security Symposium-NDSS 2016 (2016)
15. Bozic, J., Kleine, K., Simos, D.E., Wotawa, F.: Planning-based security testing of the ssl/tls protocol. In: Proceedings of the IEEE International Conference on Software Testing, Verification and Validation Workshops (ICSTW) (2017)
16. Brubaker, C., Jana, S., Ray, B., Khurshid, S., Shmatikov, V.: Using frankencerts for automated adversarial testing of certificate validation in ssl/tls implementations. In: Proceedings of the 2014 IEEE Symposium on Security and Privacy (2014)
17. Dierks, T., Rescorla, E.: Rfc 5246: The transport layer security (tls) protocol. The Internet Engineering Task Force (2008)
18. Dowling, B., Fischlin, M., Günther, F., Stebila, D.: A cryptographic analysis of the tls 1.3 handshake protocol candidates. In: Proceedings of the 22nd ACM SIGSAC Conference on Computer and Communications Security, pp. 1197–1210. ACM (2015)
19. Duan, F., Lei, Y., Yu, L., Kacker, R.N., Kuhn, D.R.: Optimizing ipog's vertical growth with constraints based on hypergraph coloring. In: 2017 IEEE International Conference on Software Testing, Verification and Validation Workshops (ICSTW), pp. 181–188. IEEE (2017)
20. Hollenbeck, S.: Transport layer security protocol compression methods (2004)
21. Jager, T., Schwenk, J., Somorovsky, J.: Practical invalid curve attacks on TLS-ECDH. In: Pernul, G., Ryan, P.Y.A., Weippl, E. (eds.) ESORICS 2015. LNCS, vol. 9326, pp. 407–425. Springer, Cham (2015). doi:10.1007/978-3-319-24174-6_21
22. Krawczyk, H., Paterson, K.G., Wee, H.: On the security of the TLS protocol: a systematic analysis. In: Canetti, R., Garay, J.A. (eds.) CRYPTO 2013. LNCS, vol. 8042, pp. 429–448. Springer, Heidelberg (2013). doi:10.1007/978-3-642-40041-4_24
23. Kuhn, D.R., Bryce, R., Duan, F., Ghandehari, L.S., Lei, Y., Kacker, R.N.: Chapter one-combinatorial testing: theory and practice. Adv. Comput. **99**, 1–66 (2015)

24. Kuhn, R., Lei, Y., Kacker, R.: Practical combinatorial testing: beyond pairwise. IT Professional **10**(3), 19–23 (2008)
25. Lei, Y., Kacker, R., Kuhn, D.R., Okun, V., Lawrence, J.: Ipog/ipog-d: efficient test generation for multi-way combinatorial testing. Softw. Test. Verification Reliab. **18**(3), 125–148 (2008)
26. Mavrogiannopoulos, N., Vercauteren, F., Velichkov, V., Preneel, B.: A cross-protocol attack on the tls protocol. In: ACM CCS 12: 19th Conference on Computer and Communications Security (2012)
27. Meyer, C., Somorovsky, J., Weiss, E., Schwenk, J., Schinzel, S., Tews, E.: Revisiting ssl/tls implementations: new bleichenbacher side channels and attacks. USENIX Secur. **14**, 733–748 (2014)
28. Morais, A., Martins, E., Cavalli, A., Jimenez, W.: Security protocol testing using attack trees. In: CSE (2), IEEE Computer Society, pp. 690–697 (2009)
29. Raffelt, H., Steffen, B., Berg, T.: Learnlib: A library for automata learning and experimentation. In: Proceedings of the 10th International Workshop on Formal Methods for Industrial Critical Systems (FMICS 2005), pp. 62–71 (2005)
30. de Ruiter, J., Poll, E.: Protocol state fuzzing of tls implementations. In: 24th USENIX Security Symposium (USENIX Security 15), pp. 193–206 (2015)
31. Simos, D.E., Kuhn, R., Voyiatzis, A.G., Kacker, R.: Combinatorial methods in security testing. IEEE Comput. **49**, 40–43 (2016)
32. Somorovsky, J.: Systematic fuzzing and testing of tls libraries. In: Proceedings of the 2016 ACM SIGSAC Conference on Computer and Communications Security (CCS 2016) (2016)
33. Yu, L., Lei, Y., Kacker, R.N., Kuhn, D.R.: Acts: A combinatorial test generation tool. In: 2013 IEEE Sixth International Conference on Software Testing, Verification and Validation (ICST), pp. 370–375. IEEE (2013)
34. Yu, L., Lei, Y., Nourozborazjany, M., Kacker, R.N., Kuhn, D.R.: An efficient algorithm for constraint handling in combinatorial test generation. In: 2013 IEEE Sixth International Conference on Software Testing, Verification and Validation (ICST), pp. 242–251. IEEE (2013)

Using Data Integration for Security Testing

Sébastien Salva[✉] and Loukmen Regainia

LIMOS CNRS UMR 6158, Clermont Auvergne University,
Clermont-ferrand, France
{sebastien.salva,loukmen.regainia}@uca.fr

Abstract. The explosion of digitisation makes a plethora of security data publicly available for developers. These numerous (often complex) documents expose them to the difficulty of choosing the most appropriate solution for securing their applications. We propose in this paper a method based upon data acquisition and integration, which assists developers in the Threat modelling stage and in the security test case execution. The method firstly helps devise Attack Defense Trees by means of a data-store. These trees show attacks, steps and defenses given under the form of security patterns, which are re-usable solutions to design more secure applications. These trees are then used for the test case generation. The data-store integrates test case stubs, which make this generation easier and developers more efficient. We evaluate our approach on 24 participants and show encouraging results on the use of data integration in software engineering.

Keywords: Security · Security patterns · Attack Defense Trees · Test case generation

1 Introduction

Since a decade, it is well admitted that software security is essential and has to be considered through all the software life cycle. Many developers, researchers and organisations have hence made security their hobby-horse and brought several improvements with the proposal of numerous digitised security bases and documents. These take security into consideration at different stages of the software life cycle and are presented with different viewpoints, abstraction levels or contexts. This plethora of diverse documents makes difficult the choices of security solutions and afterwards their validations. Indeed, developers cannot be experts in any field and they clearly lack guidance for conceiving and implementing both secure software and tests.

This work focuses on this issue and studies the possibility of using publicly available security resources for helping developers devise more secure applications. We propose a method, which aims at assisting developers in the Threat modelling stage and in the test case generation and execution. More precisely, the contributions of this paper are highlighted in the following points:

© IFIP International Federation for Information Processing 2017
Published by Springer International Publishing AG 2017. All Rights Reserved
N. Yevtushenko et al. (Eds.): ICTSS 2017, LNCS 10533, pp. 178–194, 2017.
DOI: 10.1007/978-3-319-67549-7_11

- we present a security data acquisition and integration method, which extracts data from various Web and publicly accessible sources to conceive a data-store storing relationships among attacks, security principles, security patterns and test case parts written with the Given When Then (GWT for short) template. *The security pattern intuitively relates countermeasures to threats and attacks in a given context* [8]. These security re-usable solutions often are presented textually or with UML schema and are characterised by a set of structural and behavioural properties;
- from the data-store, our method helps in the generation of Attack Defense Trees (ADTrees [3]) showing the attacker possibilities to compromise an application and the defenses that may be put in place to prevent attacks. We have chosen the ADTree model because it offers the advantage of being easy to understand even for novices in security. These ADTrees are composed of defenses given under the form of security pattern combinations;
- ADTrees serve here to the test case generation. These test cases aim to check whether an application is vulnerable against the attacks exposed in an ADTree and whether security pattern consequences are observed in the application behaviour. Pattern consequences are observable events resulting from the good contextualisation and implementation of the pattern in an application. From an ADTree, our method extracts attack scenarios, GWT test case stubs and related procedures composed of comments or blocks of code, which aim at guiding the developer in the test case completion. As ADTrees can be formalised with formal expressions, called ADTerms, we strictly define the test case generation and execution.

Besides, we concentrated our attention on quality criteria and on education while the design of this method. ADTrees are indeed constructed with concrete data extracted from the CAPEC base[1]. ADTrees also express security pattern combinations with respect to several criteria, i.e., Unambiguity, Navigability and Comprehensibility, which are quality criteria proposed in [1], the last two respectively related to: *the ability to direct a software designer among collaborative and related patterns; the ease to understand patterns by both a novice and expert developer.* Test case stubs are also structured to ease Readability and Re-usability and to try to increase Effectiveness.

We have generated a data-store specialised to the context of Web applications (Web sites), which is composed of 215 CAPEC attacks, 26 security patterns and 669 test case parts. We employed this data-store to evaluate on 24 human subjects the benefits of using the notion of data acquisition and integration in the software life cycle. This evaluation shows encouraging results about Comprehensibility and Effectiveness.

The remainder of the paper is organised as follows: Sect. 2 presents some related work. The data integration step is shortly presented in Sect. 3. The next section shows how ADTrees are generated by means of the data-store. Section 5 addresses the test case generation and execution. We present our evaluation in Sect. 6 and finally conclude in Sect. 7.

---

[1] https://capec.mitre.org/

2   Related Work

A plethora of papers deals with model-based security testing. Due to lack of room, we only present some of them related to our work, which consider models not to describe the implementation behaviour but rather to express the attacker's goals or the vulnerability causes of the system [4–6,9]. Some authors focused on trees (Attack trees, Security Activity Graphs, etc.), which express the treats or attacks or vulnerability causes that should be prevented in systems. From these models, test cases are then written to check whether attacks can be successfully executed. Morais et al. introduced a security testing approach specialised for protocols [6]. Attack scenarios are extracted from an Attack tree and are converted to Attack patterns and UML specifications. From these, attack scripts are manually written and are completed with the injection of (network) faults. In [5], data flow diagrams are converted into Attack trees from which sequences are extracted. These sequences are composed of events combined with parameters related to regular expressions allowing the generation of concrete values. These events are then replaced with blocks of code to produce test cases. In [4], test cases are generated from Threat trees. The latter are completed with parameters associated to regular expressions. Security scenarios are extracted from the Threat trees and are manually converted to executable test scripts. Shahmehri et al. proposed a passive testing approach to detect vulnerabilities [9]. The undesired vulnerabilities are modelled with models called SGMs, which are specialised DAGs showing security goals, vulnerabilities and eventually mitigations. Detection conditions are then semi-automatically extracted and given to a monitoring tool, which returns test verdicts.

These works take Threat models as inputs, which are manually written. If these lack of details (parameters, attack steps, etc.), the final test cases will be too abstract as well. Furthermore, these methods do not give any recommendation on how to write tests and on how to structure them. Hence, developers lack guidance to write tests and to reuse them. This paper proposes a method, which semi-automatically infer Attack Defense Trees, composed of attacks steps, techniques and defenses. To ease the understanding and readability of the generated test case stubs, we associate in our data-store every attack and defense step to some test case sections, which are classified w.r.t. an application context and to an attack step or security pattern.

Few works tackled the testing of security patterns, which is another topic of this paper. Yoshizawa et al. introduced a method for testing whether behavioural and structural properties of patterns can be observed in the traces of instrumented applications [10]. Given a security pattern, two test templates (OCL expressions) are written, one to specify the pattern structure and another to describe its behaviour. Then, developers have to make templates concrete by writing Selenium scripts for experimenting the application. The latter returns traces on which the OCL expressions are verified. In contrast to the previous paper, our inferred ADTrees firstly help developers choose for every attack, the combinations of patterns that can be used as countermeasures. Then, our testing approach aims at testing the security pattern consequences. We do not check the structure of the patterns. Hence, our approach is complementary to the previous one.

We also proposed a semi-automatic data integration method in [7], in order to extract a pattern classification. We took inspiration from this paper to infer pattern combinations. In contrast, the notion of data-store, its architecture, the considered security properties and the test case generation and execution are new contributions.

3   Data Integration

3.1   Data-Store Architecture Presentation

Figure 1(a) exposes the meta-model of the first part of the data-store used to integrate relationships among attacks, attack steps, techniques, security principles and security patterns. The entities of Fig. 1(a) refer to these security properties. To increase the precision of the relations, we chose to decompose attacks into sub-attacks, and into attack steps. These steps are associated to countermeasures, allowing to prevent or counter attack steps. We also decompose security patterns into strong points, which are sub-properties expressing pattern key design features. Relying on a hierarchical organisation of security principles, the method maps countermeasure clusters to principles and strong points to principles. As countermeasures usually are detailed properties, we gather them into clusters (groups) to reach about the same abstraction levels as those of the security principles.

The meta-model of Fig. 1(a) is extended with new entities and relations, which are required for the testing process. This extension is depicted in Fig. 1(b). An attack step is also associated to a Test architecture and to one Application context. The context refers to an application family, e.g., Android applications, or Web sites. The "Test Architecture" entity refers to textual paragraphs explaining the points of observation and control, testers or tools required to execute the

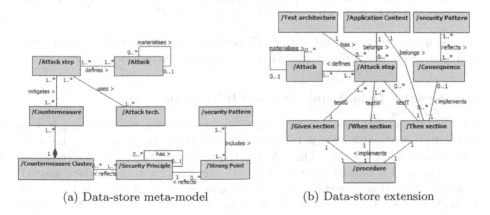

(a) Data-store meta-model   (b) Data-store extension

Fig. 1. Datastore Metamodels

attack step on an application, which belongs to an Application context. Next, we map attack steps onto GWT test case sections. For readability and re-usability purposes, we chose to consider the "Given When Then" pattern to break up test cases into several parts:

- the Given section aims at putting an application under test in a known state;
- the When section triggers some actions;
- the Then section is used to check whether the conditions of success of the test case are meet (assertions). In our context, we suppose that a Then section returns "$Pass_{st}$" if an attack step st has been successfully executed on an implementation and "$Fail_{st}$" otherwise.

Likewise, we map security pattern consequences onto Then sections to check whether the consequences of the pattern can be observed in the application traces. We assume that a Then section returns "$Fail_{sp}$" if a consequence of the security pattern sp is not observed from the implementation. For instance, if an application is conceived with the "Input Guard" pattern, then unexpected inputs should bring the application to a quiescent state (no output) or outputs reflecting errors should be observed.

Each test case section is linked to one procedure stored in the Procedure table of the data-store, which implements the section. A Given, When or Then section can be reused with several attack steps or security patterns. With regard to the meta-model given in Fig. 1(b), a GWT test case section (and procedure) is classified according to one application context and one attack step or pattern consequence.

In some specific application contexts, the procedures can be completed with comments or with blocks of code to ease the test case development. When the procedure content can be reused with any application in a precise context, we call it *Generic procedure*:

Definition 1 (Generic procedure). *Let C be an Application context. A Generic procedure is a block of code, related to a Given, When or Then test case section, that can be used with any application of C;*

The data-store must only contain Generic procedures related to an application context. It worth mentioning that an empty procedure is generic.

3.2   Security Data Acquisition and Integration

This section summarises a data integration example for the Web application (Web sites) context. We chose to focus on the CAPEC base to extract information about security attacks. The CAPEC base offers an open and rich catalogue of attacks in a comprehensive schema. We conceived a tool for data acquisition and extraction, based on text mining and on the ELT (Extraction, Load, Transform) tool Talend[2]. With it, we automatically scanned all the CAPEC

---

[2] https://talend.com/

base (Version 2.8) and collected 215 attacks, 209 steps, 448 techniques and 217 countermeasures, knowing that attacks can share steps, attack techniques and countermeasures. Among these, we gathered 75 attacks and 142 attack steps specialised for the context of Web sites.

As security patterns are described in an abstract manner with texts, we manually collected security patterns, their strong points and consequences from the catalogue given in [12]. We gathered 26 security patterns, 43 consequences and 36 strong points. We also integrated the inter-pattern relations given in [11]. We organised 66 security principles found in the literature into a hierarchy composed of four levels, from the most abstract to the most concrete principles.

The data integration of the GWT test case sections was automatically performed. For a given attack, the CAPEC base provides two text sections called "Attack Prerequisites" and "Resources Required". We automatically scanned these paragraphs and completed 209 procedures including comments composed of the two previous paragraphs. Each procedure is associated to one Given test case section (one section for each attack step). For every step st, we added one When test case section and one procedure composed of comments listing the techniques related to st. Still in the CAPEC documents, the paragraphs "Indicators" and "Outcomes" provide some directives and conditions on an attack step realisation. In the same way as previously, we automatically scanned these paragraphs and, for every attack step, we completed the data-store with one Then section associated to one procedure, itself composed of the two previous paragraphs of the CAPEC base given as comments. In this way, we generated 627 GWT test case sections. For every security pattern consequence found in the data-store, a Then test case section and its related procedure are also automatically inserted. The procedure is composed of comments listing the consequence, which have to be observed from the application traces. In the context of Web applications, we observed that several procedures can be completed with blocks of code calling penetration testing tools. We completed 32 procedures, which cover 43 attack steps. We used the tools Selenium and ZAProxy[3], which is a penetration testing tool covering various Web vulnerabilities.

This data-store is available here[4].

4   Threat Modelling

Before presenting how our method assists developers in threat modelling, we recall some notions about the ADTree model.

4.1   Attack Defense Trees (ADTrees)

ADTrees *are graphical representations of possible measures an attacker might take in order to attack a system and the defenses that a defender can employ*

---

to protect the system [3]. As illustrated in Figs. 3(a) and 3(b), ADTrees have two different kinds of nodes: attack nodes (red circles) and defense nodes (green squares). A node can be *refined* with child nodes and can have one child of the opposite type (linked with a dashed line). Node refinements can be disjunctive (like in Fig. 3(a)) or conjunctive. The former is recognisable by edges going from a node to its children. The latter is graphically distinguishable by connecting these edges with an arc. We extend these two refinements with the sequential conjunctive refinement of attack nodes, defined by the same authors in [2]. This operator expresses the execution order of child attack nodes. Graphically, a sequential conjunctive refinement is depicted by connecting the edges, going from a node to its children, with an arrow. For instance, the node "Attack Step" in Fig. 3(b) is refined with a sequence of others steps. Alternatively, an ADTree T can be formulated with an algebraic expression called ADTerm and denoted $\iota(T)$. In short, the ADTerm syntax is composed of operators having types given as exponents in $\{o, p\}$ with o modelling an opponent and p a proponent. $\vee^s, \wedge^s, \overrightarrow{\wedge}^s$, with $s \in \{o, p\}$ respectively stand for the disjunctive refinement, the conjunctive refinement and the sequential conjunctive refinement of a node. A last operator c expresses counteractions (dashed lines in the graphical tree).

4.2 Attack Defense Tree Generation

The first stage of our method takes place in the Threat modelling phase of the software life cycle, which occurs while the requirement analysis. Threat modelling is a process consisting in identifying and describing the attacker's goals and capabilities, as well as identifying the potential threats of an application. Different methods can be followed, e.g., DREAD, or STRIDE. Our method starts to semi-automatically generate an ADTree by means of the data-store. The ADTree generation is illustrated in the the fourth first steps of Fig. 2. We present them below.

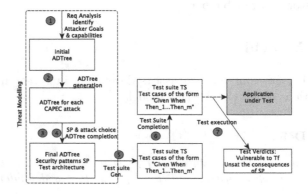

Fig. 2. Threat modelling and security testing steps

Step 1: Initial ADTree design

The developer initially establishes a first ADTree T whose root node represents the attacker's goal, which may be refined with child nodes. The ADTree T describes attack combinations, which can be applied on the application. We here assume that T at least has leaves labelled by attacks kept in the data-store. Otherwise, a semantic alignment may be required to replace some labels by similar attack names.

Figure 3(a) depicts an ADTree example: the goal, given in the root node, is to inject malicious code into an application. This node is disjunctively refined with two children expressing two more concrete attacks, CAPEC-66: SQL Injection and CAPEC-244: Cross-Site Scripting via Encoded URI Schemes.

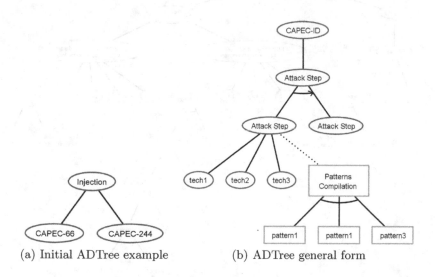

(a) Initial ADTree example   (b) ADTree general form

Fig. 3. ADTrees examples

Step 2: ADTree generation

Usually, yhe ADTree T does not include enough details on how the attack is sequenced and on the defenses expressing how the application can be protected. Implementing a secure application and deriving test cases from this kind of tree remains a tedious task. The data-store can be used to augment T. For every node labelled with an attack Att, we automatically generate an ADTree denoted $T(Att)$. The architecture of the data-store leads to the generation of ADTrees having the general form illustrated in Fig. 3(b). The root of an ADTree $T(Att)$ is labelled by Att. This node may have children expressing more concrete attacks and so forth. The most concrete attacks have step sequences (edges connected with an arrow). These steps are connected to techniques with a disjunctive refinement. The lowest attack steps in the ADTree are also linked to defense nodes, which may be the roots of sub-trees expressing security pattern combinations whose purpose is to counteract the attack step.

We implemented the ADTree generation with a tool, which takes attacks of the data-store and yields XML files. These can be edited with the tool *ADTool* [3]. For instance, Fig. 4 depicts the ADTree of the attack CAPEC-66, which was exported from ADTool. Each lowest attack step has a defense node expressing pattern combinations. Step 2.1, which identifies the possibilities to inject malicious code through the application inputs, requires more patterns than the other steps to filter these inputs. Some of them have relations: for instance "Application Firewall" can be replaced by "Input Guard" with "Output Guard".

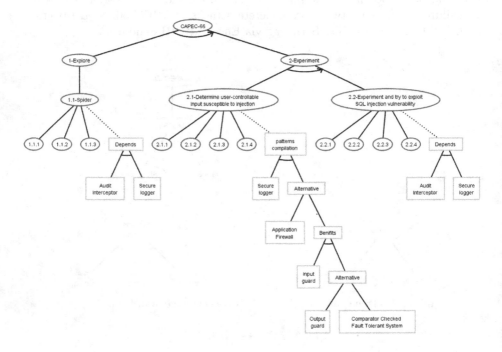

Fig. 4. ADTree of the Attack CAPEC-66

Step 3: Security pattern choice

The developer can now edit the ADTrees $T(Att)$ to keep or remove attack steps w.r.t. the application context. He or she also has to choose the security patterns that have to be contextualised and implemented in the application. After this step, we assume that a defense node either is labelled by a security pattern (it does not have children) or has a conjunctive refinement of nodes labelled by security patterns. The lowest nodes labelled by attack steps, must be linked to a defense node.

As a result of the steps 2 and 3, the generated ADTrees have specific forms and are expressed with specific ADTerms:

Proposition 1. *An ADTree $T(Att)$ achieved by the previous steps has an ADTerm $\iota(T(Att))$ having one of these forms:*

1. $\vee^p(t_1, \ldots, t_n)$ with $t_i (1 \leq i \leq n)$ an ADTerm also having one of these forms:
2. $\overrightarrow{\wedge}^p(t_1, \ldots, t_n)$ with $t_i (1 \leq i \leq n)$ an ADTerm having the form given in (2) or (3);
3. $c^p(st, sp)$, with st an ADTerm expressing an attack step and sp an ADTerm modelling a security pattern combination.

The first ADTerm expresses children nodes labelled by more concrete attacks. The second one represents sequences of attack steps. The last expression is composed of an attack step st refined with techniques, which can be counteracted by a security pattern combination sp. In the remainder of the paper, we call the last expression Basic Attack Defence Step, shortened as BADStep. These shall be particularly useful to build GWT test case stubs:

Definition 2 (Basic Attack Defence Step (BADStep)). A BADStep b is an ADTerm of the form $c^p(st, sp)$, where st is an ADTerm modelling an attack step and sp an ADTerm of the form sp_1 or $\wedge^o(sp_1, \ldots, sp_m)$ modelling a security pattern conjunction.
defense$(b) = \{sp_1 \mid b = c^p(st, sp_1)\} \cup \{sp_1, \ldots, sp_m \mid b = c^p(st, \wedge^o(sp_1, \ldots, sp_m))\}$

Step 4: Final ADTree generation
In the initial ADTree T, each attack node labelled by Att is now automatically replaced with the ADTree $T(Att)$. This can be done by substituting every term Att in the ADTerm $\iota(T)$ by $\iota(T(Att))$. We denote T_f the resulting ADTree. It depicts a logical breakdown of the various options available to an adversary and the defences, materialised with security patterns, which have to be inserted into the application model.

In this step, we also extract from the data-store a description of the test architecture required to run the attacks on the application under test and to observe its reactions.

5   Test Suite Generation

The semantics of an ADTree can be defined in terms of attack-defense scenarios. In general terms, a scenario is a minimal combination of events leading to the root attack, minimal in the sense that, if any event is omitted from the attack scenario, then the root goal will not be achieved. The semantics of an Adtree T_f, i.e. its scenario set, can be extracted from its ADTerm $\iota(T_f)$:

Definition 3 (Attack scenarios). Let T_f be an ADTree and $\iota(T_f)$ be its ADTerm. The set of Attack scenarios of T_f, denoted $SC(T_f)$ is the set of clauses of the disjunctive normal form of $\iota(T_f)$ over $BADStep(T_f)$.

An attack scenario s of $SC(T_f)$ is an ADTerm over BADSteps. $BADStep(s)$ denotes the set of BADSteps of s. We also denote $SP(s)$ the security pattern set found in s: $SP(s) = \{sp \mid \exists b \in BADStep(s) : sp \in \text{defense}(b)\}$. By extension, $BADStep(T_f)$ stands for the set of BADSteps found in $\iota(T_f)$; $SP(T_f)$ is the security pattern set of $\iota(T_f)$, found in all its scenarios.

Step 5: Test suite generation

Let us consider a security scenario $s \in SC(T_f)$. Given a BADStep $b = c^p(st, sp) \in BADStep(s)$, we generate the GWT test case $TC(b)$, which aims at checking whether the application under test I is vulnerable to the attack step st and whether the consequences of the security patterns in defense(b) can be observed from I. $TC(b)$ is assembled from the data-store by means of the following steps:

1. the data-store provides for st, with the relations $testG$, $testW$ and $testT$, one Given section, one When section and one Then section, each related to one procedure. The Then section aims to assert whether the application is vulnerable to the attack step st;
2. the data-store provides from the security pattern set defense(b) a set of other Then sections, each related to procedures. These Then sections aim to check whether the security pattern consequences can be observed from the application behaviours;
3. all these sections are assembled to make up the GWT test case stub $TC(b)$.

By applying these steps on all the scenarios of $SC(T_f)$, we obtain the test suite TS with $TS = \{TC(b) \mid b = c^p(st, sp) \in BADStep(s) \text{ and } s \in SC(T_f)\}$.

We implemented these steps to yield GWT test case stubs compatible with the Cucumber framework[5], which supports a large number of languages. Figure 5 gives a test case stub example obtained with our tool from the first step of the attack CAPEC-66 depicted in Fig. 4. The test case lists the Given When Then sections in a readable manner. Every section is associated to a Generic procedure stored into another file. The procedure related to the When section is given in Fig. 6. The comments comes from the data-store and are extracted from the CAPEC base. This procedure includes a generic block of code; the "getSpider()" method relates to the call of the ZAProxy tool, which crawls a Web application to get its URLs. In this example, it only remains for the developer to complete the initial URL before testing whether the application can be explored.

```
Feature: CAPEC-66: SQL Injection
#1. Explore
Scenario: Step1.1 Survey application
#The attacker first takes an inventory of the functionality exposed by the application.
Given    a new scanning session
When     spider the application
Then     the application is spidered
#assertions for security pattern testing
Then    Output Guard security pattern is present
Then    Input Guard security pattern is present
```

Fig. 5. A GWT test case example

---

[5] https://cucumber.io/

```
@When("^spider the application")
public void theApplicationIsSpidered() {
// Try one of the following techniques :
//   1.  Spider web sites for all available links
//   2.  Sniff network communications with application using a utility such as WireShark.
getSpider().setMaxDepth(10);
url = "URL to be scanned";
try { spider(url);
} catch (InterruptedException e) {e.printStackTrace();}
waitForSpiderToComplete();}
```

Fig. 6. The procedure related to the When section of Fig. 5

Step 6: Test case stub completion

Now, the developer has to complete the previous GWT test case stubs. We believe that the decomposition of the test case and its link to the ADTree T_f (associations among steps, security patterns and procedures) make this step easier. In addition, the Generic procedures, composed of comments or blocks of code should make him or her more effective in the test case writing.

Step 7: Test suite execution

Once the GWT test case stubs are completed, these can be executed on the application under test I. The test architecture allowing the experimentation of I is described in the report provided by Step 4.

After the execution of one test case $TC(b)$ on I, denoted $TC(b)||I$, we obtain sets of verdict messages of the form "$Pass_{st}$", "$Fail_{st}$" or "$Fail_{sp}$", resulting from its assertions (see Sect. 3.1):

Definition 4 (Test verdict sets). *Let I be an application under test, $b = c^p(st, sp) \in BADStep(T_f)$ with* defense$(b) = \{sp_1, \ldots, sp_m\}(m > 0)$ *and $TC(b) \in TS$ be a test case. The execution of $TC(b)$ on I leads to a verdict set, denoted* Verdict$(TC(b)||I)$*, which can be:*

- *$\{Fail_{st}\}$ (resp. $\{Pass_{st}\}$) means I is (resp. does not appear to be) vulnerable to the attack step st and that the consequences of the security patterns are observed;*
- *$\{Pass_{st}, Fail_{sp_1}, \ldots, Fail_{sp_k}\}$ means I does not appear to be vulnerable to the attack step st but some consequences of the security patterns $sp_1, \ldots, sp_k$ are not observed;*
- *$\{Fail_{st}, Fail_{sp1}, \ldots, Fail_{sp_k}\}$ means I is vulnerable to the attack step st and that some consequences of the security patterns $sp_1, \ldots, sp_k$ are not observed.*

From these verdict messages, we define two first relations. The first relation *vulnerable* defines that an application I is vulnerable to a BADStep b if the message $Fail_{st}$ belongs to the verdict set Verdict$(TC(b)||I)$. The relation *unsat^c* defines that I does not satisfies the consequences of the pattern sp if the message $Fail_{sp}$ belongs to Verdict$(TC(b)||I)$:

Definition 5 (Test case verdicts). *Let I be an implementation, T_f be an ADTree, $b = c^p(st, sp) \in BADStep(T_f)$ and $TC(b) \in TS$ be a test case.*

1. I vulnerable $b = true$ if $\{Fail_{st}\} \in \text{Verdict}(TC(b)||I)$, false otherwise;
2. I unsat^c sp if $sp \in$ defense(b) and $Fail_{sp} \in \text{Verdict}(TC(b)||I)$.

We now define the relation *effective* on a scenario $s \in SC(T_f)$, composed of the BADSteps $b_1, \ldots, b_n$ and on I to formally state whether s detects vulnerabilities on I. The relation *effective* is evaluated by substituting every BADStep term b_i with the evaluation of I vulnerable b_i. These relations help define and evaluate the final implementation relations.

Definition 6 (Implementation relations). *Let I be an implementation, T_f be an ADTree, and $s \in SC(T_f)$, with $BADStep(s) = \{b_1, \ldots, b_n\}$.*

1. σ : $BADStep(s) \rightarrow \{true, false\}$ is a substitution $\{b_1 \rightarrow (I$ vulnerable $b_1), \ldots, b_n \rightarrow (I$ vulnerable $b_n)\}$;
2. *s effective I, if the evaluation of the result $s\sigma$ of applying σ to s returns true;*
3. I vulnerable $T_f \Leftrightarrow_{def} \exists s \in SC(T_f)$ s effective I;
4. I unsat^c $SP(T_f) \Leftrightarrow_{def} \exists sp \in SP(T_f), I$ unsat^c sp.

6   Evaluation

We empirically studied two scenarios on 24 participants to assess whether developers can take profit of our approach. The duration of each scenario was set at most to one hour and half. The participants are third to fourth year computer science undergraduate students, having good skills in the development and test of Web applications.

The participants were given the task of choosing security pattern combinations to prevent two attacks, CAPEC 244: Cross-Site Scripting via Encoded URI Schemes, and CAPEC 66: SQL Injection, on two deliberately vulnerable Web sites, *RopeyTasks* and *The Bodgeit Store*. We also asked the participants to write test cases with the tool Selenium in order to: show that both Web sites are vulnerable to the two attacks, show that the application behaviours do not include at least one consequence of the security pattern "Input Guard" and at least one consequence of "Output Guard".

In the first scenario, denoted Part 1, we supplied the CAPEC base, two concrete attack examples, the detailed steps showing how to manually perform them along with the expected outcomes and the security pattern catalogue given in [12]. In the second scenario, denoted Part 2, we also supplied the ADTrees of the two attacks (Fig. 4 is one of them) along with the generated *GWT* test case stubs for each attack step. At the end of each scenario, the students were invited to fill in a form listing ten questions. Due to lack of room, we only present the questions and results concerning the test case generation:

- Q7: Was it easy to write test cases?
- Q8: How long did you take for writing test cases?
- Q9: How confident are you about your test cases?
- Q10: Provide your test cases (or suites).

These questions was asked in order to evaluate the following criteria:

- C1: Comprehensibility: does our method ease the test case development?
- C2: Effectiveness: can the test cases detect defects?
- C3: Efficiency: does our method help reduce the time needed to write tests?

6.1   Experiment Results

We extracted the following results from the forms returned by the participants (available here[6]). We collected the answers of Question Q7, proposing this four-valued scale: *easy, fairly easy, difficult, very difficult.* Figure 7 depicts the distribution of the participant opinions.

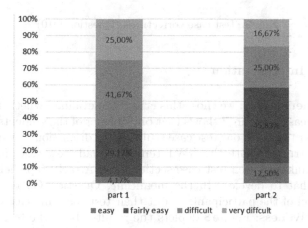

Fig. 7. Response rates for Question Q7

We collected the time spent by the participants for writing test cases. The participants needed between 15 and 70 min in Part 1, while they took between 20 min and 86 min in Part 2. On average, they spent 46 min in Part 1 and 60 min in Part2. The levels of confidence of the participants is estimated with Question Q9. The possible answers were for both scenarios: *very sure, sure, fairly sure, not sure.*

We finally analysed the test cases given by the participants and evaluated their correctness with regard to four aspects: 1&2: detection (with at least one test case) that both applications are vulnerable to the attacks CAPEC 66 and CAPEC 244; 3&4: detection that the application behaviours do not include the consequences of the patterns "Input Guard" and "Output Guard". As we considered this last aspect as difficult for students, we expected at least one Then test case section for every pattern. Figure 8 presents the number of participants who meet these aspects.

---

[6] http://regainia.com/research/companion.html

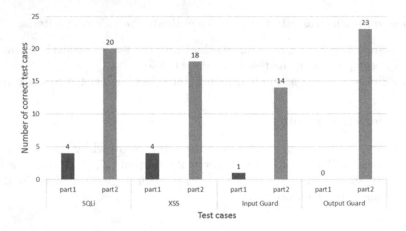

Fig. 8. Test case correctness (Question Q10)

6.2   Result Interpretation

C1 Comprehensibility: we chose this criteria to evaluate whether our method makes testing easier. Figure 7 shows that one quarter of the students found easier the test case writing with our test case stubs. After discussion, it turned out that the test case structure with the GWT template made test cases more readable and that the links between test case sections and Attack steps helped students understand what to develop. In the meantime, Question Q9 reveals that the confidence level of the participants about their test cases increases by 20, 83%.

   C2 Effectiveness: Figure 8 depicts the results about the test case correctness. The columns "SQLi" and "XSS" provide the number of test cases allowing to reveal that the attacks can be successfully executed on the applications. In Part 1, few participants developed complete test cases despite the detailed steps we provided (assertions were missing or incorrect in most of the test cases). The number of correct test cases strongly increases in Part 2 thanks to the comments the participants found in the procedures. The columns "Input Guard" and "Output Guard" give the number of Then sections (and procedures) allowing to show that the consequences of these security patterns are not observed from the application behaviours. This task was much more difficult for the students as they are not yet expert in security patterns. Hence, it is not surprising to see that only one student was able to write at least an assertion showing that the Input Guard consequences are not present. The number of correct Then sections rises to 14 (58, 3%) in Part 2. With the pattern "Output Guard", the number of correct Then sections rises from 0 to 23 in Part 2. We can conclude that the test case correctness strongly increases with our approach.

   C3 Efficiency: on average, the participants took 46 min for writing test cases from scratch and 60 min with the use of our method. The additional time spent in Part 2 can be explained when we alongside focus on Effectiveness and Comprehensibility. Indeed, after discussion with the participants, we deduced that they took more time to follow and analyse the ADTrees, to read the comments in procedures, etc. As a result, almost all the test cases are correct in Part 2 (more assertions, etc.).

7 Conclusion

We have presented a method taking advantage of data integration for guiding developers devise more secure applications from the Threat modelling stage to the testing one. The method generates ADTrees and test case stubs allowing to check whether an application is vulnerable to attacks and whether security pattern consequences are observable from the application behaviour. We conducted an evaluation of the method, which shows it makes the participants more effective on security testing. But, several issues remain open. For instance, our method does not take into consideration the size of the ADTrees in the Threat modelling stage. This is a strong limitation since large trees are usually unreadable, which contradicts the method purposes. The ADTree reduction could be a first solution on this problem. But, the literature does not yet provide a generic method for this kind of reduction. Besides the tree structure, the node meaning must be taken into account in the node aggregating process, which must preserve the semantics of the ADTree.

References

1. Alvi, A.K., Zulkernine, M.: A comparative study of software security pattern classifications. In: 2012 Seventh International Conference on Availability, Reliability and Security, pp. 582–589 (2012)
2. Jhawar, R., Kordy, B., Mauw, S., Radomirović, S., Trujillo-Rasua, R.: Attack trees with sequential conjunction. In: Federrath, H., Gollmann, D. (eds.) SEC 2015. IAICT, vol. 455, pp. 339–353. Springer, Cham (2015). doi:10.1007/978-3-319-18467-8_23
3. Kordy, B., Mauw, S., Radomirović, S., Schweitzer, P.: Attack-defense trees. J. Logic Comput. **24**(1), 55–87 (2014). Oxford Journals
4. Marback, A., Do, H., He, K., Kondamarri, S., Xu, D.: A threat model-based approach to security testing. Softw. Pract. Exp. **43**(2), 241–258 (2013)
5. Marback, A., Do, H., He, K., Kondamarri, S., Xu, D.: Security test generation using threat trees. In: ICSE Workshop on Automation of Software Test, pp. 62–69, May 2009
6. Morais, A., Martins, E., Cavalli, A., Jimenez, W.: Security protocol testing using attack trees. In: International Conference on Computing Science and Engineering, vol. 2, pp. 690–697, August 2009
7. Regainia, L., Salva, S.: A methodology of security pattern classification and of attack-defense tree generation. In: Proceedings of the 3rd International Conference on Information Systems Security and Privacy (ICISSP). SciTePress, Porto, February 2017
8. Schumacher, M.: Security Engineering with Patterns: Origins, Theoretical Models, and New Applications. Springer-Verlag, New York (2003)

9. Shahmehri, N., Mammar, A., Montes De Oca, E., Byers, D., Cavalli, A., Ardi, S., Jimenez, W.: An advanced approach for modeling and detecting software vulnerabilities. Inf. Softw. Technol. **54**(9), 997–1013 (2012)

10. Yoshizawa, M., Kobashi, T., Washizaki, H., Fukazawa, Y., Okubo, T., Kaiya, H., Yoshioka, N.: Verifying implementation of security design patterns using a test template. In: 9th International Conference on Availability, Reliability and Security, pp. 178–183, September 2014

11. Yskout, K., Heyman, T., Scandariato, R., Joosen, W.: A system of security patterns (2006)

12. Yskout, K., Scandariato, R., Joosen, W.: Do security patterns really help designers?. In: Proceedings of the 37th International Conference on Software Engineering ICSE 2015, vol. 1, pp. 292–302. IEEE Press, Piscataway (2015)

Test Selection and Quality Estimation

A "Strength of Decision Tree Equivalence"-Taxonomy and Its Impact on Test Suite Reduction

Hermann Felbinger(✉), Ingo Pill, and Franz Wotawa

Institute for Software Technology,
Graz University of Technology, Graz, Austria
{felbinger,ipill,wotawa}@ist.tugraz.at

Abstract. Being able to reduce test suites without having to execute them for assessing the effects on their fault detection capabilities is quite appealing. In this direction, we proposed recently to characterize test suites via inferred decision trees and use these for comparisons in a reduction process. The equivalence relation underlying the comparisons plays obviously a significant role for the effectiveness achieved and efficiency experienced. In this paper, we explore five such relations that take different aspects into account and investigate their impact on test suite reduction, their effectiveness in fault detection, and computation time. We report corresponding results, and show as well as prove that the equivalence relations build a taxonomy.

Keywords: Test suite reduction · Decision tree equivalence

1 Introduction

Today, our software tends to be improved and extended almost constantly during its life cycle. Correspondingly, also the test suites we use for their validation tend to grow with new product features, the isolation of faults to be avoided in the future, and with the advent of new concepts for generating tests effective at unveiling specific software issues. The impact of software testing on the overall development costs, however, demands keeping test suites as small as possible while preserving their fault detection capabilities. Consequently, we need effective test suite reduction approaches in order to manage resources and costs related to a test suite's execution, validation, and management.

Even when focusing on predefined faults (like for mutation testing [9]) such that we knew exactly which faults some test case t can identify, finding a minimum sized test suite able to identify a maximum of faults, is an instance of the set cover problem that is one of Karp's 21 NP-complete problems [19]. Still, drawing on effective heuristics, researchers faced the challenge and proposed various strategies to tackle the problem, e.g., [4,12,13,15,22,24]. Known strategies rely, e.g., on existing links between requirements and test cases, on analyzing

© IFIP International Federation for Information Processing 2017
Published by Springer International Publishing AG 2017. All Rights Reserved
N. Yevtushenko et al. (Eds.): ICTSS 2017, LNCS 10533, pp. 197–212, 2017.
DOI: 10.1007/978-3-319-67549-7_12

execution traces that can cover others, or on preserving coverage and mutation scores as indicators for a test suite's effectiveness.

An attractive feature of the approach introduced by Felbinger et al. in [10] is that we do not need to execute the program under test for assessing the fault detection capabilities when removing a test case. The underlying idea was that every test suite T should at least partially capture the behavior of the program under test in a sufficient way. The strategy then is to use machine learning for model extraction, in order to derive representative characterizations from T and a reduced test suite T'. We proposed in [10] the following reduction process: Initially, we learn a characterizing decision tree from T, and when successively trying to remove test cases $t \in T$, we infer for each potential removal another decision tree from the updated test suite T'. If the decision tree for T' is *equivalent* to the initial one, we assume that the fault detection capabilities were not affected, and proceed with trying to remove further test cases. Otherwise, we go back one step and re-add t. The reduction terminates after a preconfigured number of unsuccessful, random tries to remove a further test case. With avoiding to execute T, we still could achieve reductions from 60 to 99% in our evaluation. Our approach for decision tree learning is limited to test cases t represented as some vector $t = \langle x_1, .., x_k, out \rangle$ of k input values and an expected output value *out*. The inputs are either numeric of an infinite domain, numeric of a finite domain, or discrete strings or numbers. The output type has to be of a finite domain, whose values then build the labels of the decision trees' leaf nodes.

Since such a test suite reduction depends on an equivalence relation for decision trees, the following questions arise immediately: Which methods are there for determining equivalence? Are there more than structural and misclassification equivalence as discussed and used in [10] (coined syntactic and semantic equivalence there), and is there a relation between them? What is their impact on the efficiency and effectiveness of the reduction process?

Imagining variants, one has to take the characteristics of the derived trees into account. According to [17], optimizing a decision tree to a minimal number of nodes which would allow us to compare minimal or canonical ones, is in NP. Thus, the algorithm used to infer the decision trees in [10] is based on a statistical measure (the information gain of variables) and does not stringently build optimal decision trees. Consequently, trees inferred from different test suites might appear different in respect of their strict structure. Exploring flexibility in this respect, we consider five variants for checking some trees' equivalence. In particular, we consider in Sect. 4 structural ($\equiv$), spine ($=^s$), decision ($=^d$), table ($=^t$), and misclassification ($=^m$) equivalence aiming to cover and explore various decision tree aspects. We show and prove that these variants build a taxonomy as shown in Fig. 1 in respect of their strength. We report in Sect. 5 on our corresponding experiments, considering computation time and the achieved reductions as well as the impact on fault detection capabilities. In Sect. 6 we conclude on our findings and line out future work.

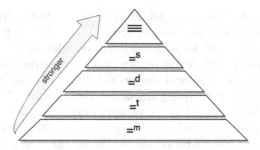

Fig. 1. Taxonomy of equivalence relation in respect of their strength.

2   Related Work

Safavian and Landgrebe provide a survey of decision tree classifiers in [26]. They address the design, search strategies, issues like missing values and robustness, and potential problems of decision trees in their survey. In [21] Moret provides a common framework of definitions and notations for decision trees. In [7] Dattatreya and Kanal introduce the usage of decision trees in pattern recognition. In this context they define pattern recognition as "the assignment of a physical object or an event to one of the prespecified categories". They consolidate the major methodologies for decision tree design, bring out those methodologies' commonalities, provide insight into multistage classification, explode the myth that decision trees are always simple to design and use, mention areas of applications of decision trees, and aid a decision tree designer to select an appropriate technique for the particular problem of interest.

Cockett introduces in [6] different notions of decision tree equivalence. These notions are structural, decision, and transposition equivalence that are similar to some of the notions we use in this work, which are structural, spine, and decision equivalence, but Cockett uses the notion of coalgebras to describe decision trees and the equivalence relations. In [28] Zantema presents a simple efficient algorithm to establish whether two decision trees are equivalent or not. This algorithm is an axiomatization for decision equivalence as we use it in this work. The complexity of this algorithm is bounded by the product of the number of nodes n and m of both decision trees ($O(n * m)$). The algorithm only processes decision trees representing discrete valued variables as decision nodes. In our work we also cover numeric inputs, which are handled by binary splits. The authors in [5] present an algorithm that reduces a decision tree by replacing the decision tree with a smaller equivalent decision tree. To find an irreducible tree using the reduction algorithm they also use decision and transposition equivalence. In [29] the authors address the question, whether for a given decision tree, a decision tree decision equivalent to the given one can be found, for which no decision equivalent decision tree of smaller size exists. Breslow and Aha provide an overview over methods how to simplify a decision tree in [2].

The underlying idea that a model inferred from a test suite can be used to indicate the fault detection effectiveness of the test suite was initially published in [11]. In [11] Felbinger et al. show that a linear correlation between model inference based test suite quality assessment without executing the program under test might depend on the structural properties, the types of inputs, and the number of discrete outputs of the program under test. Some initial results of test suite reduction without executing the program under test are provided in [10]. The promising results in [10], where reductions of 60–99% were possible, while still keeping coverage and mutation score almost the same, led to this work, where we used the same reduction algorithm. In [10] structural and misclassification equivalence were used to obtain the results. Briand et al. [3] describe a test suite refinement approach that relies on the black box testing technique Category-Partition [23] and machine learning. They use categories and choices to define the functional properties of a program under test, where categories are associated with choices. E.g. a category representing an inequality relation has two choices of an inequality relation that are either greater than or less than. Based on these categories they transform test cases into abstract test cases. These abstractions are tuples of choices and an expected output value or an equivalence class of expected output values. Like in our work, they use the C4.5 algorithm [25] to learn a decision tree in [3]. But in contrast to our work, where we learn a decision tree from the raw values in a test suite, they learn decision trees from the abstractions obtained by category-partitioning.

Since test suite reduction has been of interest for decades, there is a tremendous amount of further related work. We refer the interested reader to [1,27] for detailed overviews.

3   Preliminaries

In our work, we infer a decision tree D from a test suite T via the well-known algorithm C4.5 [25]. Such a decision tree is a directed tree $D = (V, E)$ having nodes V and directed edges E connecting nodes. V can be split into decision nodes and leaf nodes, where a decision node has outgoing edges and represents a decision (i.e., a relational equation) like $x > 0$ (see Fig. 2) for some numeric input x, or x equals $\langle discrete\,value\rangle$ for discrete inputs. A leaf node is a terminal one and offers a discrete classification. An edge (v, v') is a pair of nodes $(v, v' \in V)$, where v is parent of v'. For simplicity, we assume a function $\rho\colon DT \to V$ that returns the root node of a decision tree, with the universe of decision trees DT under consideration as input domain. Further we assume a function $\lambda\colon V \to J \cup C$ that returns the content of a node, with the union of the set of decisions J and the set of classifications C as range. The decision trees in this work are binary such that each decision node has exactly two outgoing edges. The answer of a decision, e.g., whether we have $x > 0$, is represented by an edge label that can be accessed via a function $\gamma\colon E \to \{T, F\}$. In our decision trees, paths are sequences containing nodes and connecting edges, starting from the root node, following down the tree, and ending at a leaf node. We define a path Π in a decision tree as follows:

Definition 1 (Path). *A path Π of length $|\Pi| = l$ in a decision tree D is a sequence of nodes $v_0...v_{l-1}$ such that there is an edge from v_i to v_{i+1} for $0 \leq i < l - 1$, starting with $v_0 = \rho(D)$ and ending at a leaf node v_{l-1}.*

With C4.5, decision trees are constructed top down, where decision nodes get selected using a statistical property called *information gain* that measures how well a decision separates the $t \in T$ according to their expected outcome [20]. A test case t is classified in a decision tree by following the decision nodes from the root node, down the tree to some leaf node, according to the values in t. Not necessarily all input variables appear in a decision tree, but numeric variables can occur also multiple times in different decision nodes, even in the same path. We define equivalence for decision trees as follows:

Definition 2 (Equivalence Relation). *Decision Tree Equivalence is a reflexive, symmetrical, and transitive binary relation R between two decision trees D_1 and D_2 from the universe of decision trees DT, such that:*

reflexivity: $\forall D \in DT : D R D$
symmetry: $\forall D_1, D_2 \in DT : D_1 R D_2 \rightarrow D_2 R D_1$
trans.: $\forall D_1, D_2, D_3 \in DT : D_1 R D_2 \wedge D_2 R D_3 \rightarrow D_1 R D_3$

In our work, we consider the equivalence of decision trees when reducing test suites. When trying to remove test cases from a test suite T without effecting changes in the decision tree, the achieved reduction is an indicator of the reduction process' effectivity:

Definition 3 (Reduction). *Given a test suite T and a reduced test suite $T' \subseteq T$, the achieved reduction is defined via the difference in their sizes:*

$$reduction = \frac{|T| - |T'|}{|T|} \tag{1}$$

When we infer a decision tree, we derive a hypothesis h regarding an approximation of a function f that we can use to predict f's outcome for future input values. Strategies for estimating the accuracy of such a hypothesis include k-folds cross validation [16], or assessment with additional input and output values [20]. In principle, for evaluating a hypothesis h, we can use the function $error(h, S)$ as given in Eq. 2 in order to obtain a result in the range 0..1:

$$error(h, S) = \frac{1}{|S|} \sum_{t \in S} \delta(f(t), h(t)) \tag{2}$$

Equation 2 requires three parts: First, some set S that should be different to T (from which the hypothesis was learned) containing vectors t of input values and an expected output. Second, the target function $f : I^k \rightarrow O$, where I is the type of the k inputs and O represents the set of all possible outputs. Third, a function δ that detects deviating outcomes of f and h–returning 1 if $f(t) \neq h(t)$ for some $t \in S$ and 0 otherwise.

4   Equivalence Taxa

For our investigation, we considered five decision tree equivalence relations, ranging from structural equivalence to misclassification equivalence. Before showing at the end of this section that they form a taxonomy in respect of their strength, let us formally introduce them for the decision trees $D_1 = (V_1, E_1)$ and $D_2 = (V_2, E_2)$ first.

Structural Equivalence ($\equiv$): Two decision trees D_1 and D_2 are structurally equivalent, if and only if each node $v_1 \in V_1$ has a corresponding node $v_2 \in V_2$ and each edge $e_1 \in E_1$ has a corresponding edge $e_2 \in E_2$ connecting an equivalent pair of nodes. Structural equivalence can be represented using a function EQUAL: $V \times V \rightarrow \{\textit{True}, \textit{False}\}$, which we define recursively as follows: For two decision trees D_1, D_2, and nodes $v_1 \in V_1$, $v_2 \in V_2$, EQUAL returns $\textit{True}$, if and only if:

1. $\lambda(v_1) = \lambda(v_2)$
2. $\forall (v_1, v_i) \in E_1, \exists (v_2, v_j) \in E_2, 0 \leq i, j < 2|$
   $\gamma(v_1, v_i) = \gamma(v_2, v_j) \wedge \text{EQUAL}(v_i, v_j)$ *(and vice versa)*

Using this function, we define structural equivalence of two decision trees as follows:

Definition 4 (Structural equivalence). *Two given decision trees D_1, D_2 are structurally equivalent if and only if the function* EQUAL$(\rho(D_1), \rho(D_2))$ *returns* True.

EQUAL terminates if it detects different node contents or different edge labels, or if all nodes have been visited.

Example 1 (Structural equivalence). Figure 2 shows two structurally equivalent decision trees where decision nodes, leaf nodes, and edges are equivalent and on the same position in both decision trees.

Spine Equivalence ($=^s$): A decision tree consists of a set of spines SP. A spine $(\Pi, c) \in SP$ is described by a path Π to a leaf node v, such that $c = \lambda(v)$. Spine equivalence requires bag equivalence to hold, which is defined as:

Definition 5 (Bag equivalence). *Two paths Π_1 and Π_2 are equivalent as bags, if except for the ordering they contain nodes with precisely the same content and with equivalently labelled outgoing edges, such that for all $v_1 \in \Pi_1$ there exists an equivalent node $v_2 \in \Pi_2$ and vice versa, where $\lambda(v_1) = \lambda(v_2)$ and $\gamma(v_1, v_i) = \gamma(v_2, v_j)$.*

From the definitions of a path and bag equivalence, we define spine equivalence as:

Definition 6 (Spine equivalence). *Two decision trees D_1 and D_2 are spine equivalent if for the respective sets of spines SP_1 and SP_2, for every spine $(\Pi_1, c_1) \in SP_1$ there exists a spine $(\Pi_2, c_2) \in SP_2$ and vice versa, such that Π_1 and Π_2 are bag equivalent and $c_1 = c_2$.*

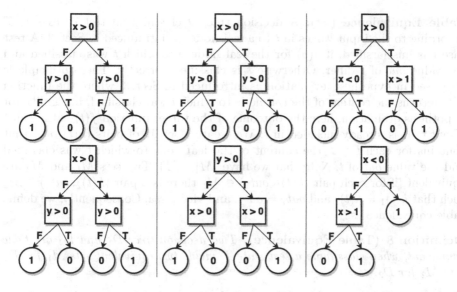

Fig. 2. Structurally (left), spine- (middle), and decision-equivalent (right) trees.

Example 2 (Spine equivalence). Figure 2 shows two spine equivalent decision trees where the order of decision nodes in the paths differ, but the spines are equivalent. However, these decision trees are not structurally equivalent.

Decision Equivalence ($=^d$): A constraint built from a spine's path is a conjunction of equivalence relations that contain a decision node's content and its outgoing edge's label for all decision nodes in the path. Satisfying a constraint classifies the inputs to that spine's c. In a decision tree, there may be multiple spines for some c. For decision equivalence, we thus build a summarizing constraint for each c as a disjunction of the corresponding conjunctions of the individual spines for c. E.g., from the top right decision tree in Fig. 2, a constraint ψ of paths from spines with $c = 1$ is $(x > 0 = F \wedge x < 0 = T) \vee (x > 0 = T \wedge x > 1 = T)$. More formally, we define decision equivalence as:

Definition 7 (Decision equivalence). *Two decision trees D_1 and D_2 are decision equivalent, if for all leaf nodes $v_1 \in V_1$ an equivalent leaf node $v_2 \in V_2$ exists, and for each constraint ψ_1 of D_1 there exists a constraint ψ_2 in D_2 where the following equation holds:*

$$\psi_1 \text{ equals } \psi_2 \tag{3}$$

Equation 3 is true, if no valuation exists for which ψ_1 is satisfiable and ψ_2 is unsatisfiable, and vice versa.

Example 3 (Decision equivalence). Figure 2 shows two decision equivalent decision trees that do not contain the same decision nodes and are therefore not spine equivalent.

Table Equivalence ($=^t$): A decision tree D classifies all test cases $t \in T$ according to the input values in t to a leaf node, as introduced in Sect. 3. A test case t is misclassified, if $\lambda(v)$ for the leaf node v to which t was classified and the value *out* of t differ. Otherwise t is classified correctly. These principle is also used in hypothesis evaluation as introduced in Sect. 3, where the function $h(t)$ returns the content of the leaf node to which t was classified, but unlike for hypothesis evaluation, here the outcome of the target function $f(t)$ is the value of *out* that is already included in t. We create a set M of pairs $(h(t), out)$ that contains for each $t \in T$ the content of the leaf node to which t was classified and the value *out* of t. Note that we have $|M| = |T|$. Two sets M_1 and M_2 are equivalent, if for each pair $(h(t)_1, out_1) \in M_1$ there is a pair $(h(t)_2, out_2) \in M_2$ such that $h(t)_1 = h(t)_2$ and $out_1 = out_2$, and vice versa. Consequently, we define table equivalence as:

Definition 8 (Table Equivalence). *Two decision trees D_1 and D_2 are table equivalent, when classifying a test suite T yields two equivalent sets M_1 for D_1 and M_2 for D_2.*

Example 4 (Table equivalence). Figure 3 shows two decision trees that are table equivalent if T does not contain a test case $t = \langle 1, 1, 1 \rangle$, because then $h(t) \neq out$ only for the lower decision tree. These decision trees are not decision equivalent.

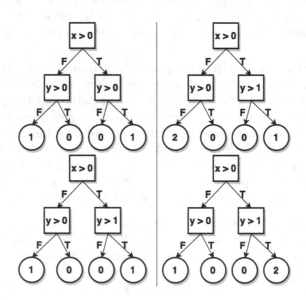

Fig. 3. Table (left) and misclassification-equivalent (right) trees.

Misclassification Equivalence ($=^m$): Two decision trees D_1 and D_2 are equivalent regarding their misclassification rate $error(D, T)$, if the following two conditions hold:

1. $error(D_2, T) = error(D_1, T)$.
2. For all distinct contents in the leaf nodes $C_1 \subset V_1$ an equivalent classification exists in the leaf nodes $C_2 \subset V_2$ and vice versa.

Definition 9 (Misclassification equivalence). *A decision tree D_2 is misclassification equivalent to a reference decision tree D_1, when classifying T, if the following equation holds:*

$$error(D_2, T) = error(D_1, T) \wedge$$
$$\forall v_1 \in C_1, \exists v_2 \in C_2 | v_1 = v_2 \text{ (and vice versa)} \tag{4}$$

Example 5 (Misclassification equivalence). Figure 3 shows two decision trees where the same classifications exist in both decision trees as visualized by the leaf nodes. If T contains two test cases $t_1 = \langle 0, 0, 2 \rangle$ and $t_2 = \langle 1, 2, 2 \rangle$, the decision trees are misclassification equivalent, but not table equivalent.

Theorem 1. *The five defined methods to determine equivalence of decision trees can be presented in a subset order, where for a decision tree D inferred from a test suite T, subsets $DT_{\equiv} \subset DT$, $DT_{=^s} \subset DT$, $DT_{=^d} \subset DT$, $DT_{=^t} \subset DT$, and $DT_{=^m} \subset DT$ from the universe of decision trees DT exist, which contain decision trees that were inferred from a test suite $T' \subseteq T$, and are equivalent to D. These subsets are ordered as*

$DT_{\equiv} \subseteq DT_{=^s} \subseteq DT_{=^d} \subseteq DT_{=^t} \subseteq DT_{=^m}$, *for subsets,*
$DT_{\equiv} \subset DT$ *representing structural equivalent decision trees,*
$DT_{=^s} \subset DT$ *representing spine equivalent decision trees,*
$DT_{=^d} \subset DT$ *representing decision equivalent decision trees,*
$DT_{=^t} \subset DT$ *representing table equivalent decision trees, and*
$DT_{=^m} \subset DT$ *representing misclassification equivalent decision trees.*

Proof (sketch). Structural equivalence implies that all paths are equivalent. If all paths are equivalent, spine equivalence is ensured. If paths in two decision trees only have different orders of nodes, the decision trees are spine equivalent, but not structurally equivalent. Spine equivalence implies that all nodes contain the same content. Building constraints from the paths in spines ensures that the constraints are equivalent, because they contain the same contents of nodes and the same outgoing edges of the decision nodes. If a node is missing or redundant in a path of two decision equivalent decision trees, this contradicts spine equivalence. Decision equivalence implies that each possible input valuation leads to an equivalent classification or misclassification. Equivalent classifications for all possible input values ensure table equivalence, because table equivalence depends only on the classification of a test suite T, which contains only a subset of all possible input values. If a pair of decision trees is table equivalent, but test cases are missing for boundary values of the decisions, different decision nodes in a path lead to equivalent classifications for a test suite T, but not for each possible input valuation. This fact contradicts decision equivalence. Table equivalence implies that two decision trees provide equivalent classifications for a test suite T, independently of whether a test case was correctly classified or misclassified. If all test cases in T are equally classified or misclassified, misclassification equivalence is given. A misclassification equivalent pair of decision trees where classifying a test suite T yields the same misclassification rate, but different test cases from T are misclassified, violates table equivalence.   ■

As stated in Theorem 1, structural equivalence is the strongest method to determine equivalence of two decision trees, meaning that even if the four other equivalence check methods evaluate to true, structural equivalence can be false. Decision equivalence is the costliest method due to the NP-completeness of determining inequality of two constraints. Misclassification equivalence is the weakest method to determine equivalence of two decision trees, because it neither considers the structure of the decision tree nor the relation of inputs to outputs.

5   Experimental Evaluation

We used three different Java programs for our proof-of-concept experiments, generated combinatorial test suites using the tool ACTS[1], and evaluated the reduced test suites' fault detection effectiveness via their mutation score. For generating mutants, we used the Major mutation framework [18].

5.1   Results

The three examples are Triangle, TCAS, and UTF8, as introduced in [10]. For test suite reduction, we implemented the *REDUCE* algorithm from [10] in Java and instantiated the *equals* method in *REDUCE* at line 12 by all 5 equivalence methods introduced in Sect. 4. The input values for *iterations* and *retries* of *REDUCE* were set to 2 and $\frac{|T|}{10}$ respectively, since the results in [10] show that these values allow high reductions. To infer decision trees from a test suite, we used the Java library Weka [14] and its implementation J48 of the algorithm C4.5. In the configuration options of Weka, we disabled pruning and set the minimum number of leaf nodes to 1. The expected outcome for a test case was derived with the original program. We obtained test suites of size 343 (Triangle), 1840 (UTF8), and 11021 (TCAS), and generated 35 (Triangle) and 147 (UTF8) mutants. For the TCAS example, we used the 41 existing mutants[2]. In order to determine decision equivalence, we applied the SMT-solver Z3 [8] that provides a Java-API. For calculating the misclassification rate, we used the decision tree evaluation method integrated in the Weka library. Since the *REDUCE* algorithm selects potentially redundant test cases randomly, we executed the algorithm for each example 10 times per equivalence method and plot the execution time and the resulting reduction for each execution. All experiments ran on a MacBook Pro with an Intel Core i5 2.7 GHz CPU, 16 GB RAM, an SSD, and OS X 10.11.6. The resulting reductions and the runtime to obtain these reductions for the

---

[1] http://csrc.nist.gov/groups/SNS/acts.
[2] http://sir.unl.edu/portal/bios/tcas.php.

Triangle example are shown in Fig. 4. The results in Fig. 4 show that decision equivalence is multiple times slower than other equivalence methods. Structural equivalence is fastest, misclassification and table equivalence allow the highest reductions. Reductions of structural equivalence are lowest. The results in Fig. 5 for the UTF8 example show that structural and spine equivalence are fastest, but the reductions are around 30% lower than for the other equivalence methods. Also for the UTF8 example decision equivalence was slowest. For the TCAS example the results in Fig. 6 show that all reductions only vary in a range of around 10%. Also for TCAS, structural and spine equivalence are fastest and decision equivalence is slowest on average. The highest reductions were obtained by table and misclassification equivalence.

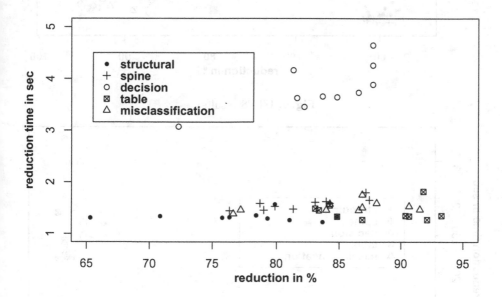

Fig. 4. Triangle results.

5.2   Discussion

Our results suggest that structural equivalence, whose complexity is linear in the number of nodes in a decision tree, is the fastest and decision equivalence is the slowest equivalence method. Deciding decision equivalence is an NP-complete problem and each pair of equivalent constraints in two decision trees gives the worst case. When using misclassification equivalence, which allows the highest reductions, the time to reduce T was slightly higher than for structural equivalence. For evaluating a potential loss of the test suite's fault detection effectiveness, we derived the mutation score for all reduced test suites as reported in Fig. 7. The mutation score of the initial test suites was 1 for each example. For each example in Fig. 7, the equivalence methods are ordered according to

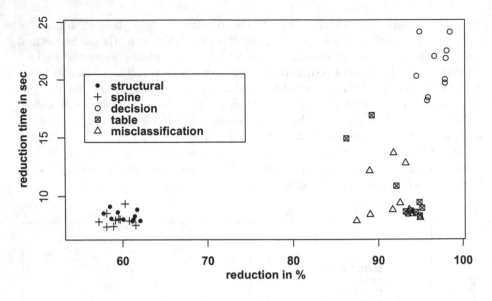

Fig. 5. UTF8 results.

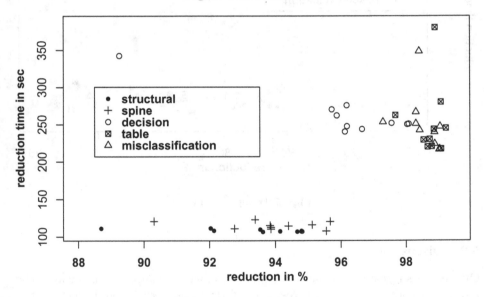

Fig. 6. TCAS results.

their strength from left to right, starting on the left with the strongest one. The results show that for the strongest equivalence method there was almost no decline of mutation score, but for weaker methods the mutation score decreased. In particular for the UTF8 example, the median mutation score dropped to values in the range 0.6 to 0.7 for decision, table, and misclassification equivalence.

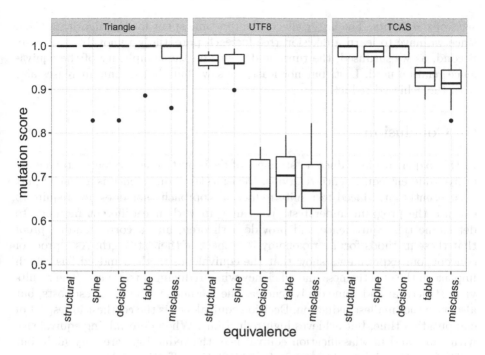

Fig. 7. Mutation score of reduced test suites.

These weak mutation scores origin in the fact that the initial test suite contained test cases with unknown values, which were approximated automatically while inferring a tree by the C4.5 algorithm. These approximations increased potential uncertainties of the tree to predict future outputs for additional input values. The dots in the plots for Triangle, UTF8, and TCAS represent outliers from the obtained results.

Using structural or spine equivalence provided similar reductions at similar costs. Although decision equivalence allowed high reductions, the computation time was highest from all equivalence methods. Table and misclassification equivalence provided the highest reduction results for our examples, consuming more time than structural and spine equivalence (but in most cases less time than decision equivalence). The mutation score results suggest the highest loss of fault detection effectiveness to occur when using table or misclassification equivalence. Therefore, if the execution time of the tests in the finally reduced test suite is low, structural equivalence should be chosen. If keeping the fault detection capabilities as high as possible for a reduced test suite, also structural equivalence should be chosen. In all other cases the results suggest that misclassification equivalence is an educated choice. Promising results of an empirical evaluation of structural and misclassification equivalence were provided in [10]. With our results, we clarify that the runtime of the reduction approach depends on three parts. First, the runtime depends on the size of the test suite and the domain sizes of the inputs. The latter affects the run-time spent for the algorithm C4.5, since we have to learn a decision tree for each potentially removable test case. Second, as we surmised, the runtime depends on the complexity of the equivalence relation used. Last, but not least, we saw that the runtime increases also with the achieved reduction.

6   Conclusion

In this paper, we introduce a "strength of decision tree equivalence"-taxonomy of five different equivalence relations. Decision tree equivalence is a crucial part of a recently introduced test suite reduction approach that does not require to execute the program under test. We came up with five different methods to determine this equivalence and provide a theorem and a corresponding proof that these methods form a taxonomy in respect of their strength. As a proof of concept, our experiments show that the equivalence method indeed has a high impact on the effectiveness and efficiency when reducing a test suite. The results yield structural and spine equivalence as the methods with the lowest costs, but also with the smallest reduction. Decision equivalence is the costliest in respect of computation time, but achieves high reductions. When determining equivalence with table and misclassification equivalence, the reductions are very high, but suffer from the highest decrease in fault detection effectiveness.

Underpinning the reduction approach itself and the selection of the most appropriate equivalence relation will require an evaluation with additional, realistic scenarios. If some T does not contain redundancies, no reduction is possible. For detecting that T does not contain redundancies structural equivalence should be chosen, because it is the least time consuming relation to determine. Since the structure (control flow, data flow, lines of code, etc.) of the program under test affects the reduction, with more examples possibly a classification can be created such that we could derive from the program structure in combination with background information on how T was generated which equivalence method would be best suited.

For our current experiments, we used first order mutants for evaluating the effectiveness in fault detection, but towards applicability of the reduction approach in practice, an examination with higher order mutants shall be part of future work. In future work we will extend also our empirical evaluation, considering more examples from application domains like automotive control software. Here an open research question is also how such a program's structure affects the test suite reduction approach of [10] in general.

Acknowledgment. We thank the ECSEL Joint Undertaking (supported by the EU Horizon 2020 programme and the ECSEL member states) for funding this work under grant agreement 662192 (3Ccar). This Joint Undertaking receives support from the European Union's Horizon 2020 research and innovation programme and the ECSEL member states.

References

1. Biswas, S., Mall, R., Satpathy, M., Sukumaran, S.: Regression test selection techniques: a survey. Informatica **35**(3), 289–321 (2011)
2. Breslow, L.A., Aha, D.W.: Simplifying decision trees: a survey. Knowl. Eng. Rev. **12**(1), 1–40 (1997)
3. Briand, L.C., Labiche, Y., Bawar, Z.: Using machine learning to refine black-box test specifications and test suites. In: 8th International Conference on Quality Software, pp. 135–144 (2008)
4. Chen, T.Y., Lau, M.F.: Dividing strategies for the optimization of a test suite. Inf. Process. Lett. **60**(3), 135–141 (1996)
5. Cockett, J.R.B., Herrera, J.A.: Decision tree reduction. J. ACM **37**(4), 815–842 (1990)
6. Cockett, J.: Discrete decision theory: manipulations. Theor. Comput. Sci. **54**(2), 215–236 (1987)
7. Dattatreya, G., Kanal, L.: Decision trees in pattern recognition. In: Progress in Pattern Recognition 2, pp. 189–240. Elsevier Science Publishers B.V. (1985)
8. De Moura, L., Bjørner, N.: Z3: an efficient SMT solver. In: Ramakrishnan, C.R., Rehof, J. (eds.) TACAS 2008. LNCS, vol. 4963, pp. 337–340. Springer, Heidelberg (2008). doi:10.1007/978-3-540-78800-3_24
9. DeMillo, R.A., Lipton, R.J., Sayward, F.G.: Hints on test data selection: help for the practicing programmer. Computer **11**(4), 34–41 (1978)
10. Felbinger, H., Wotawa, F., Nica, M.: Test-suite reduction does not necessarily require executing the program under test. In: International Conference on Software Quality, Reliability and Security Companion, pp. 23–30 (2016)
11. Felbinger, H., Wotawa, F., Nica, M.: Empirical study of correlation between mutation score and model inference based test suite adequacy assessment. In: 11th International Workshop on Automation of Software Test, pp. 43–49 (2016)
12. Fraser, G., Wotawa, F.: Redundancy based test-suite reduction. In: Dwyer, M.B., Lopes, A. (eds.) FASE 2007. LNCS, vol. 4422, pp. 291–305. Springer, Heidelberg (2007). doi:10.1007/978-3-540-71289-3_23
13. Gotlieb, A., Marijan, D.: Flower: Optimal test suite reduction as a network maximum flow. In: 2014 International Symposium on Software Testing and Analysis (ISSTA), pp. 171–180 (2014)
14. Hall, M., Frank, E., Holmes, G., Pfahringer, B., Reutemann, P., Witten, I.H.: The weka data mining software: an update. SIGKDD Explor. Newsl. **11**(1), 10–18 (2009)
15. Harrold, M.J., Gupta, R., Soffa, M.L.: A methodology for controlling the size of a test suite. ACM Trans. Softw. Eng. Methodol. (TOSEM) **2**(3), 270–285 (1993)
16. Hastie, T., Tibshirani, R., Friedman, J.: The Elements of Statistical Learning. Springer Series in Statistics. Springer, New York (2009). doi:10.1007/978-0-387-84858-7
17. Hyafil, L., Rivest, R.: Constructing optimal binary decision trees is NP-complete. Inf. Process. Lett. **5**(1), 15–17 (1976)
18. Just, R.: The major mutation framework: efficient and scalable mutation analysis for Java. In: Proceedings of the 2014 International Symposium on Software Testing and Analysis, pp. 433–436. ACM (2014)
19. Karp, R.M.: Reducibility among combinatorial problems. In: Miller, R.E., Thatcher, J.W., Bohlinger, J.D. (eds.) Complexity of Computer Computations. The IBM Research Symposia Series, pp. 85–103. Springer, Boston (1972). doi:10.1007/978-1-4684-2001-2_9

20. Mitchell, T.M.: Machine Learning, vol. 8. McGraw-Hill, Boston (1997)
21. Moret, B.M.: Decision trees and diagrams. ACM Comput. Surv. (CSUR) **14**(4), 593–623 (1982)
22. Offutt, A.J., Pan, J., Voas, J.M.: Procedures for reducing the size of coverage-based test sets. In: Proceedings of the 12th International Conference on Testing Computer Software, pp. 111–123. ACM (1995)
23. Ostrand, T.J., Balcer, M.J.: The category-partition method for specifying and generating fuctional tests. Commun. ACM **31**(6), 676–686 (1988)
24. Polo Usaola, M., Reales Mateo, P., Pérez Lamancha, B.: Reduction of test suites using mutation. In: de Lara, J., Zisman, A. (eds.) FASE 2012. LNCS, vol. 7212, pp. 425–438. Springer, Heidelberg (2012). doi:10.1007/978-3-642-28872-2_29
25. Quinlan, J.R.: C4.5: Programs for Machine Learning. Morgan Kaufmann Publishers Inc., San Francisco (1993)
26. Safavian, S.R., Landgrebe, D.: A survey of decision tree classifier methodology. IEEE Trans. Syst. Man Cybern. **21**(3), 660–674 (1991)
27. Yoo, S., Harman, M.: Regression testing minimization, selection and prioritization: a survey. Softw. Test. Verif. Reliab. **22**(2), 67–120 (2012)
28. Zantema, H.: Decision trees: equivalence and propositional operations. In: 10th Netherlands/Belgium Conference on AI (NAIC), pp. 157–166 (1998)
29. Zantema, H., Bodlaender, H.L.: Finding small equivalent decision trees is hard. Int. J. Found. Comput. Sci. **11**(2), 343–354 (2000)

Quality Estimation of Virtual Machine Placement in Cloud Infrastructures

Jorge López(⊠), Natalia Kushik, and Djamal Zeghlache

SAMOVAR, CNRS, Télécom SudParis/Université Paris-Saclay,
9 Rue Charles Fourier, 91000 Évry, France
{jorge.lopez,natalia.kushik,djamal.zeghlache}@telecom-sudparis.eu

Abstract. A virtual machine (VM) placement module is a component/part of a cloud (computing) infrastructure, which chooses the *best* host(s) to allocate the requested VMs. In the literature, skewed or biased criteria are often used to determine the correctness of a placement module. Therefore, the quality of existing placement solutions is not always assessed adequately. In this paper, we propose a distance function that estimates the quality of the placement by comparing it with an optimal solution. We show how this distance function is utilized for testing and monitoring the behavior of VM placement implementations. To validate our approach a simulator has been developed and used for estimating the quality of different placement modules running under various scenarios. Preliminary experimental results on VM placement algorithms implemented in widely used platforms, such as OpenStack show that very often VMs are placed very far from the optimal solutions.

Keywords: Quality estimation · Distance functions · Integer linear programming · Virtual machine placement · Testing · Monitoring

1 Introduction

Cloud computing is a computer paradigm, which is based on sharing physical resources. Physical resource sharing enables flexibility, robustness, fast provisioning, fast resource (re-)allocation, etc. Corresponding applications have grown in usage and in demand in recent years; state-of-the-art applications must guarantee fast provisioning (see, for example [17]), and cloud computing aids to achieve such goals. Essentially all *planning* concerning the resource distribution and virtualization is performed by a corresponding *cloud manager*, which needs to be thoroughly tested and verified. One of the principal tasks of a cloud manager is the proper placement of VMs, i.e., choosing *the best* host for a given VM. In the literature, many placement algorithms have been proposed (see, for example [11]); in particular, Masdari et al. presented a comprehensive survey on these algorithms [15].

As VM placement is one of the main tasks of cloud managers, it is critical to properly test the implementations of the corresponding placement algorithms.

© IFIP International Federation for Information Processing 2017
Published by Springer International Publishing AG 2017. All Rights Reserved
N. Yevtushenko et al. (Eds.): ICTSS 2017, LNCS 10533, pp. 213–229, 2017.
DOI: 10.1007/978-3-319-67549-7_13

Currently, researchers mainly focus on evaluating the placement algorithms with respect to specific criteria rather than testing/monitoring their implementations. Some algorithms are shown to have better performance than others, i.e., they are known to find a corresponding list of hosts for a given set of virtual machines faster. However, such evaluations can be subjective, and moreover optimization criteria can contradict each other. It is arguable if the allocation speed can be considered as a good way to assess the overall correctness of a given placement algorithm. Therefore, the question arises: what is the correct way to assess a virtual machine placement algorithm and corresponding implementation? As mentioned above, in the literature, little attention is paid to this problem. The latter motivates us to propose novel techniques for the placement algorithm assessment as well as for testing its implementation under the assumptions that (i) placement requests are sequentially applied, (ii) the total number of VMs remains unknown, and (iii) limits of the physical resources are finite and known in advance. Assuming a good assessment technique can be found, yet another important question that arises is the following: How to properly verify and monitor the implementation correctness and how to generate *good* test suites for checking the behavior of a given virtual machine placement module?

Therefore, the problem statement is as follows: Given a VM environment, i.e., physical resource limits and VM configurations, and a VM initial placement algorithm to manage the VM placement on this VM environment together with its implementation, one has to (i) assess the correctness/efficiency of the algorithm, (ii) provide methods for the run-time monitoring of the placement implementation, and (iii) derive test suites for the effective assessment of the optimality of the placement implementation. Note that the scope of this work focuses on the initial placement problem, and not in re-allocation/migration or other placement-related problems, such as the selection of the correct overcommit ratio.

To tackle the stated problems, we present a distance function in order to assess the quality of the virtual machine placement algorithm by calculating the distance of the algorithm's *solution* to the optimal one. The introduced distance or metric is further utilized for effective test generation. In fact, we propose to generate the input data for placing so that the VM environment's resource utilization is maximal. To obtain this configuration a proper Integer Linear Programming (ILP) [20] problem is formally stated and solved. Namely, the VM environment information is used to describe an Integer Linear Program that maximizes the VM resource utilization given the cloud infrastructure and VM configuration setup; this can be considered a boundary testing approach [16]. We discuss the use of the distance function to statically verify that a given placement algorithm always returns a result close enough to the optimal one. Likewise, we analyze the use of this function to monitor placement implementations with limited controllability. Finally, in order to show the validity of our approach, we present experimental results that follow a simulation process for different VM environments and placement algorithms.

The paper is structured as follows. Section 2 introduces the required background and the addressed problem. Section 3 contains the related work. Section 4 presents the assessment of a placement module quality by introducing a distance function, while Sect. 5 is devoted to testing and monitoring placement implementations. Section 6 contains the experimental evaluation, and finally Sect. 7 concludes the paper.

2 Background

In this section, we briefly describe the necessary concepts used throughout the paper.

2.1 Virtual Machine Placement in Cloud Infrastructures

In the context of cloud computing, a host machine or simply a *host* is a physical computing device that provides its resources to isolated computing components, i.e., *virtual machines*. A cloud infrastructure is composed of a *set* of heterogeneous interconnected hosts with different resource capacities; usually, such hosts are commodity hardware. When hosts have a shared and common storage, a virtual machine (VM) can be executed in any of such hosts or migrated from one to another. A cloud infrastructure typically contains a cloud manager or orchestrator; the cloud manager is composed of distinct management modules, including, the placement module, which assigns the VMs to the appropriate hosts. A simplified cloud infrastructure is depicted in Fig. 1.

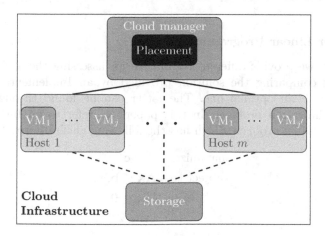

Fig. 1. Cloud computing infrastructure

Hosts and VMs have different limits on physical/virtual resources (or resource parameters). We assume that each VM has the same set of resource parameters as the physical resource parameters of the host executing that VM. For instance, a given host might have 64 CPUs, 96 GB of RAM, and 1 Gbps of available (network) bandwidth. Note that we consider a coupled architecture, i.e., the VM resources cannot be taken from diverse hosts, such as taking RAM from one host, and CPU from another.

In Fig. 2 we depict an example of a cloud infrastructure, which is occupied by different types of virtual machines. This cloud infrastructure is later used as our running example. Consider the arrangement of VMs in the depicted cloud infrastructure, performed by a placement module. If a new request to allocate a VM with 2 CPUs and 2 GB of RAM comes, there is no possibility to complete the request without performing a rearrangement of the VMs in the cloud infrastructure. In fact, VM migrations are considered to be very expensive. Consequently, we consider that a placement algorithm rejects the placement of the VM if migrations are necessary. Further, we consider placement and migrations as different tasks. A placement module is in charge of finding the *best* host(s) in the cloud infrastructure to allocate the requested VMs (without migration).

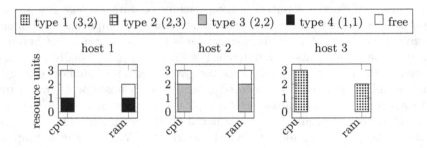

Fig. 2. Cloud computing infrastructure placement/usage

2.2   Integer Linear Programming

In this paper, we provide different techniques for assessing the VM placement algorithm by comparing the solution provided by an Implementation Under Test (IUT) with an optimal one. The latter can be found through a corresponding optimization problem. In this paper, we refer to an Integer Linear Programming (ILP) problem which has the following general form [20]:

$$
\begin{aligned}
\text{maximize} \quad & \mathbf{c}^T \mathbf{x} \\
\text{subject to} \quad & \mathbf{A}\mathbf{x} \leq \mathbf{b}, \\
& \mathbf{x} \geq \mathbf{0}, \\
& \mathbf{x} \in \mathbb{Z}^n
\end{aligned}
$$

Where $\mathbf{x}$ is a vector of n non-negative integers, $\mathbf{c}$ and $\mathbf{b}$ are integer vectors, and $\mathbf{A}$ is an integer matrix. The function to maximize is the *cost function* representing the objective (or goal) of the optimization problem. The remainder of the problem formulation presents the *constraints* of the problem, i.e., what the maximization of the cost function is subject to. Finally, the ILP problem represents in most cases a typical combinatorial optimization problem; the latter means that there exists a finite number of possible solutions, and the solutions must be integer-valued. A given instance of the optimization problem is the tuple (F, c), where F is a domain of feasible points, and c is a cost function such that $c : F \mapsto \mathbb{Z}_+$. The solution of the optimization problem is to find $f \in F$ such that $c(f) \geq c(y); \forall y \in F$; in this case, the point f is a globally optimal solution.

In the literature, algorithms to solve linear programming problems have been studied since the 1940s. One of most popular ones is the Dantzig's Simplex algorithm [7]. Correspondingly, to solve ILP problems, the cutting plane methods based on Gomory's algorithm [10] can be applied. Modern tools for solving instances of ILP problems as Gurobi [19], use such cutting plane methods and others. It is important to mention that even if the ILP problem is NP-hard, in practice, problems with hundreds or thousands of variables can be easily solved in a few seconds.

3 Related Work

In this section, we briefly discuss the existing criteria and methodologies to determine the quality of a virtual machine placement module, i.e., IUT. To some extent, all VM placement schemes found in the literature try to assess the quality of the proposed algorithm with respect to a number of criteria, commonly favoring their implementation. A large number of research papers proposing novel algorithms tend to focus on the execution time. The approaches typically model the VM placement problem as the known bin-packing problem (or similar) [1,3,8], which is NP-hard. The objective of bin packing is to minimize the number of containers of size V necessary to *pack* a fixed number of objects of different sizes. However, in a cloud infrastructure, VM (allocation) requests come at different time instances and the requested VM types are not known in advance. Therefore, solving the bin packing problem for a batch of requested machines guarantees optimality in resource utilization for the allocated batch, not guaranteeing the overall optimality in the resource utilization. For that reason, many researchers have devoted their efforts to propose approximation algorithms [22] and they estimate the quality of their algorithms with respect to their time complexity. The latter overlooks any other quality measures, including the optimality of the resource utilization.

Nonetheless, works devoted to categorizing the algorithms with respect to their optimization goals have also been published. Such works are mostly surveys, an interested reader can refer to some comprehensive works in [15,21]. The categories used to classify the papers, i.e., the optimization goals provide a good notion of the important aspects to evaluate a VM placement IUT. Resource utilization and energy consumption are among the most common criteria used to evaluate a placement implementation, aside from the time/performance discussed above. Nonetheless, due to the nature of such works the quality estimation is not the target of their research. Therefore, little attention is paid to the quality estimation and comparison of different placement algorithms. As a consequence, such works do not consider how to effectively test any VM placement implementation.

In [9], the authors describe in detail what are the relevant criteria to do a comparative analysis of VM placement algorithms, their classification, and conclude about their advantages. The discussion (Sect. 8 of their work) entitled "Comparison of VMP techniques" is interesting as the authors make conclusions based on the characteristics and properties of the proposed solutions. However, even if the conclusions are convincing, there is no formal proof nor experimental evaluation to support the statements. Furthermore, the discussion focuses only on a small number of VM placement schemes.

Finally, there exist some works, which aim to evaluate the quality of the placement algorithms using a set of metrics over the resulting configurations of a given set of inputs, similar to our proposal. In [5,14], the authors employ CloudSim [2,4], a toolkit for the simulation of cloud computing environments. Both of the previously mentioned works use a similar set of metrics: (i) SLA violation, the average percentage of time which a host CPU utilization was over 100%; (ii) Performance degradation due to VM migrations, and finally (iii) Energy consumption (proposed only in [14]). Another common characteristic of both works is the fact that they employ existing data sets and do not focus on test generation.

To the best of our knowledge, there exists no work in the literature that presents different methods for the quality estimation of a VM placement module based on measuring the distance from an optimal solution. Furthermore, we are not aware of the methods for effective test suite generation which can be used in conjunction to the metrics/distance functions; similarly, no methods to derive properties for monitoring and verification of the IUT at run-time are known to the authors. Finally, when evaluating the quality of placement IUT, the approaches assume a fixed number (usually 2 or 3) of virtual machine parameters, e.g., they consider only CPU and RAM, differently from our approach, which generalizes the notion to multidimensional vectors.

4   Virtual Machine Placement Quality Estimation

In this section, we present an approach to evaluate the quality of a virtual machine placement module in a given cloud infrastructure. The approach is based on *distance functions*. The introduced distances or metrics can be further used for checking functional properties of the VM placement modules.

4.1   Definitions and Notations

Let h be a host in a cloud infrastructure. We represent h as a tuple referring to its physical resource limits, i.e., $h \in \mathbb{Z}_+^p$, where p is the total number of physical resource parameters. We assume each physical resource parameter of a host is expressed as a multiple of an elementary resource unit (CPU, RAM, storage, etc., are multiples of their respective elementary resource unit), i.e., the elements are normalized by their respective reference unit. As an example, a host with 3

CPUs and 1GB of RAM whose minimal unit values are $1\ CPU^1$ and $512MB$ of RAM, can be represented as the pair $(3, 2)$. In practice, virtual infrastructure managers overuse the available physical resources under the assumption that not all virtual machines use all available resources at all time [18]. We assume that the overcommit factor is taken into consideration for all values of all hosts' physical resource parameters. Consider the previous host $(3, 2)$, virtual infrastructure managers might consider overusing the RAM of this host by a factor of two, in this case, the host's physical limits are $(3, 4)$.

As previously stated, a VM is assumed to have the same virtual resource parameters as the physical resource parameters of the cloud infrastructure. Therefore, we define a VM in the same manner as a host. Let vm be a virtual machine represented as a tuple of its virtual resource limits, i.e., $vm \in \mathbb{Z}_+^p$, where p is the total number of physical resource parameters.

A cloud infrastructure CI being a collection of hosts is represented as a tuple $CI = \langle h_1, h_2, \ldots, h_m \rangle$, where $h_i = (h_{i_1}, h_{i_2}, \ldots, h_{i_p}) \in \mathbb{Z}_+^p$ and m represents the total number of hosts in the cloud infrastructure. As an example, consider the cloud infrastructure with CPU and RAM parameters depicted in Fig. 2. The cloud infrastructure can be represented as the following object: $CI = \langle (3, 2), (3, 3), (3, 2) \rangle$.

Each cloud infrastructure has an associated and finite number of possible VM configurations, i.e., a fixed amount of possible VMs with *different* virtual resource requirements. We denote the VM configuration setup (VC) of n different configuration types, similarly to a cloud infrastructure: let VC be a virtual machine configuration setup referred to as a tuple of n elements, where each element is a VM, i.e., $VC = \langle vm_1, vm_2, \ldots, vm_n \rangle$, where $vm_j = (vm_{j_1}, vm_{j_2}, \ldots, vm_{j_p}) \in \mathbb{Z}_+^p$, and $\forall j, j', vm_j \neq vm_{j'}$ if $j \neq j'$, n is the number of distinct possible VM configurations (often also seen as VM types). As an example, consider the VM configuration setup depicted in Fig. 2, this configuration is represented by the following object: $VC = \langle (3, 2), (2, 3), (2, 2), (1, 1) \rangle$.

Given a virtual machine configuration, and a cloud infrastructure, a *placement configuration* represents which type of virtual machines are allocated at each given host. Formally, we denote a Placement Configuration PC in the following manner: PC can be represented by the matrix $PC_{m \times n}$, $pc_{ij} \in \mathbb{N} \cup \{0\}$, where pc_{ij} represents the number of VMs with a vm_j configuration placed on the h_i host.

As an example, consider the cloud infrastructure and virtual machine configuration setup depicted in Fig. 2, the matrix $PC_{m \times n} = \left(\begin{smallmatrix} 0 & 0 & 0 & 1 \\ 0 & 0 & 1 & 0 \\ 1 & 0 & 0 & 0 \end{smallmatrix} \right)$ can be interpreted as: in the first host $h_1 = (3, 2)$ one VM of the fourth configuration type, i.e., $vm_4 = (1, 1)$ is allocated; in the second host $h_2 = (3, 3)$ one VM of the third configuration type, i.e. $vm_3 = (2, 2)$ is placed (or allocated), and finally, on the third host $h_3 = (3, 2)$ a VM of the first configuration type $vm_1 = (3, 2)$ is placed.

A virtual machine placement request is a *batch* or *list* of VMs of different configuration types. Formally a request r can be denoted as follows. Let VC be

---

[1] Number of cores in compute-centric applications.

a virtual machine configuration setup. A virtual machine placement request r is a tuple of n elements, in which each element represents the requested number of VMs of the corresponding type in VC. Particularly, $r = \langle q_1, q_2, \ldots, q_n \rangle$, where $q_j \in \mathbb{N} \cup \{0\}$; r represents a request for a collection of VMs, where q_j is the number of VMs of the type vm_j, for $j = 1, 2, \ldots, n$. In a straightforward manner, a request can be extended to a request sequence $\alpha = r_1 r_2 \ldots r_l$. Given a request sequence α, α_{i_j} denotes the requested quantity of VMs of the type j in the i-th request. As an example, a virtual machine placement request $\langle 0, 0, 0, 2 \rangle$ for the VM configuration setup $VC = \langle (3, 2), (2, 3), (2, 2), (1, 1) \rangle$ as depicted in Fig. 2, is a request for two VMs of the fourth type, i.e. $vm_4 = (1, 1)$.

A placement algorithm $\mathcal{A}$ takes as inputs a cloud infrastructure CI, a virtual machine configuration setup VC, an initial placement configuration PC, a request r, and produces as an output a new placement configuration PC'. The behavior of $\mathcal{A}$ can be extended to request sequences by considering the output of $\mathcal{A}$ as the initial configuration PC for the next request in the sequence α.

4.2   Placement Quality Evaluation

As mentioned in Sect. 3, there exist some works [5,9,14], which propose different criteria to evaluate the quality of placement implementations. To some extent, we question some of the criteria, for instance, SLA violation reflects not an incorrect placement, but an incorrect definition of the limits of the hosts. Then, what is a good criterion to determine the quality of a placement algorithm? From the functional point of view *an efficient resource-aware placement scheme tries to optimally place VMs on the PMs (Physical Machines i.e., hosts) such that the overall resource utilization is maximized* [15]. From the previous statement three important conclusions can be made: (i) the optimal placement maximizes the resource utilization, (ii) the quality of the placement implementation decreases as it moves away from the *optimal placement*, and (iii) the correctness of an algorithm can be measured with respect to its optimality.

To define a proper distance function, we first introduce the concept of overall resource utilization. For the lack of a proper definition, we define it as follows: the overall resource utilization measures the total number of resource units taken by the allocated virtual machines in the cloud infrastructure.

Definition 1. *Given a cloud infrastructure, a virtual machine configuration and a placement configuration, the overall resource utilization f is a function defined as:* $f(CI, VC, PC) = \sum_{i=1}^{m} \sum_{j=1}^{n} (pc_{ij} * \sum_{k=1}^{p} vm_{j_k})$. *Note that the image of f is the set of natural numbers (including zero)* $\mathbb{N} \cup \{0\}$.

An intuitive explanation of the construction of f is the following. The overall resource utilization is the sum of all resources utilized in all hosts of the infrastructure CI, i.e. $f(CI, VC, PC) = \sum_{i=1}^{m} f'(h_i, VC, PC)$, where $f'(h_i, VC, PC)$ is the resource utilization on the host i. The resource utilization on the host i is the sum of all resources taken by all VMs of all different types allocated in the host, i.e., $f'(h_i, VC, PC) = \sum_{j=1}^{n} f''(h_i, vm_j, PC)$.

The sum of all resources taken by a VM is $\sum_{k=1}^{p} vm_{j_k}$ and correspondingly the quantity of VMs of a type vm_j allocated in a host h_i is pc_{ij}. Therefore, $f''(h_i, vm_j, PC) = pc_{ij} * \sum_{k=1}^{p} vm_{j_k}$.

An important remark is that a placement configuration can be obtained from the simulation of an implementation of $\mathcal{A}$ and a request sequence α. Given α, we denote the placement configuration obtained from the simulation of $\mathcal{A}$ as $PC = sim(\mathcal{A}, \alpha)$.

As mentioned above, the distance for the algorithm assessment depends on an optimal placement. We define an optimal solution with respect to the maximal resource utilization in the following manner:

Definition 2. *The algorithm $\mathcal{O}$ is optimal with respect to the overall resource allocation, if it holds that $f(CI, VC, sim(\mathcal{O}, \alpha)) \geq f(CI, VC, sim(\mathcal{A}, \alpha))$, $\forall \mathcal{A} \in \mathcal{P}$, where $\mathcal{P}$ is the set of all possible placement algorithms.*

To measure the distance between the overall resource utilization of a given algorithm or its implementation and an optimal resource utilization, we define the distance as a simple Euclidean distance[2], namely:

Definition 3. *A resource utilization distance d is defined as the metric $d : \mathcal{N} \cup \{0\} \times \mathcal{N} \cup \{0\} \mapsto \mathcal{N} \cup \{0\}, d(x, y) = |x - y|$, where x is the resource utilization of a given implementation and y is the resource utilization of an optimal algorithm $\mathcal{O}$.*

Intuitively, this distance expresses how far the overall resource utilization is from an optimal solution. In the following sections, we highlight the usefulness of this definition.

5 Testing, Monitoring, and Validating Placement Modules

In this section, we discuss how the proposed VM placement quality evaluation approach can be used when testing placement modules in cloud infrastructures. In this case, the corresponding placement module represents the implementation under test (IUT) and the conclusion about its quality is made based on the value of the distance d from an optimal solution.

5.1 Boundary Test Case Generation for Placement Modules

Given an IUT (a placement module), we propose deriving a series of requests that produce the maximum possible resource utilization for the given cloud infrastructure (and VM configuration). To achieve this, an appropriate ILP problem can be formulated and solved to find the corresponding values bringing the value of the function f to its maximum. In this case, the ILP formulation is somewhat

---

[2] The obtained overall resource utilization is a natural number, therefore Euclidean or other metrics can be considered.

straightforward. The cost function to optimize is the resource utilization function f, and the goal is the maximization of that function. The constraints are the limits of the hosts in the cloud infrastructure. The unknowns are the number of VMs of different types on each host, representing the placement configuration matrix. The general form of the problem is the following:

$$\text{maximize} \qquad f = \sum_{i=1}^{m} \sum_{j=1}^{n} \left(pc_{ij} * \sum_{k=1}^{p} vm_{j_k} \right)$$

$$\text{subject to} \quad \sum_{j=1}^{n} vm_{j_k} * pc_{ij} \leq h_{i_k}; \forall i = 1, \ldots, m; k = 1, \ldots, p,$$

$$\mathbf{PC} \geq \mathbf{0},$$

$$pc_{ij} \in \mathbb{Z}, \forall i = 1, \ldots, m; j = 1, \ldots, n$$

For the cloud infrastructure and VM configuration setup of the running example, the solution of the following ILP problem provides maximal resource utilization:

$$\text{maximize} \quad f = 5pc_{11} + 5pc_{12} + 4pc_{13} + 2pc_{14} + 5pc_{21} + 5pc_{22} + 4pc_{23} + 2pc_{24} +$$
$$5pc_{31} + 5pc_{32} + 4pc_{33} + 2pc_{34}$$

subject to

$$3pc_{11} + 2pc_{12} + 2pc_{13} + 1pc_{14} \leq 3 \text{ (Max CPU host 1)},$$
$$2pc_{11} + 3pc_{12} + 2pc_{13} + 1pc_{14} \leq 2 \text{ (Max RAM host 1)},$$
$$3pc_{21} + 2pc_{22} + 2pc_{23} + 1pc_{24} \leq 3 \text{ (Max CPU host 2)},$$
$$2pc_{21} + 3pc_{22} + 2pc_{23} + 1pc_{24} \leq 3 \text{ (Max RAM host 2)},$$
$$3pc_{31} + 2pc_{32} + 2pc_{33} + 1pc_{34} \leq 3 \text{ (Max CPU host 3)},$$
$$2pc_{31} + 3pc_{32} + 2pc_{33} + 1pc_{34} \leq 2 \text{ (Max RAM host 3)},$$
$$pc_{11}, pc_{12}, pc_{13}, pc_{14}, pc_{21}, pc_{22}, pc_{23}, pc_{24}, pc_{31}, pc_{32}, pc_{33}, pc_{34} \geq 0,$$
$$pc_{11}, pc_{12}, pc_{13}, pc_{14}, pc_{21}, pc_{22}, pc_{23}, pc_{24}, pc_{31}, pc_{32}, pc_{33}, pc_{34} \in \mathbb{Z}$$

A solution to the ILP problem (arranged as a matrix) is: $\left(\begin{smallmatrix} 1 & 0 & 0 & 0 \\ 0 & 0 & 0 & 3 \\ 1 & 0 & 0 & 0 \end{smallmatrix} \right)$.

As mentioned above, we are interested in maximizing the resource utilization for the given CI and VC. For this reason, we provide a test sequence (or a test suite) that leads to the maximal resource utilization of a particular cloud infrastructure, i.e., when no more VMs can fit. We furthermore assume that such test generation technique can be treated as a boundary [16] one, by assigning the boundary values on the maximal resource utilization.

Once *the fullest* placement configuration is obtained, a test suite needs to be derived from this placement configuration. A test sequence, in this case, is a request sequence α. To determine the order and the grouping of VMs on each request, we introduce the in-order conjecture.

In-order conjecture: Given a sequential list of individual elements (or VMs) with different resource utilization to allocate into the containers (or hosts), sequentially allocating the elements in the list sorted in ascending order by their overall resource utilization is the most difficult arrangement to allocate.

The reasoning behind the in-order conjecture is that as the containers fill up available resources, independently from the allocation strategy. As a consequence, allocating the largest elements at the end is only possible if the allocation chooses the *best* configuration. As a support to this claim, it can be seen that heuristic methods for greedy allocation algorithms obtain their best results when allocating in reverse order [6, 12].

Due to the in-order conjecture, to thoroughly test the placement modules under stressful conditions, each request contains a single VM and the requests are arranged in ascending order with respect to their overall resource utilization, namely $u(vm_j) = \sum_{k=1}^{p} vm_{j_k}$.

In the running example, $\alpha = \langle 0,0,0,1\rangle\langle 0,0,0,1\rangle\langle 0,0,0,1\rangle\langle 1,0,0,0\rangle\langle 1,0,0,0\rangle$ is a test suite of one sequence. This is a request for three VMs of type 4, and two VMs of type 1. This test suite can be further applied to an IUT of an algorithm $\mathcal{A}$, and the verdict about its quality can be made based on the distance function d. As the optimal algorithm/implementation $\mathcal{O}$ we consider an idealized algorithm (*oracle*) that provides the solution PC to the ILP problem.

The set of constraints for the ILP problem can differ. In particular, two cases are possible: (i) all the hosts are empty when the test sequence represented by a set of VM placement requests, is applied; (ii) the IUT has an initial placement configuration which corresponds to already executed sequences of requests. In case (i), we in fact assume that the VM placement implementation is initialized, i.e., before any test sequence we are allowed to apply a corresponding reliable RESET. If that is the case, then the test sequence that brings the IUT to *full* hosts' resource utilization should be applied. In case (ii), the VM placement module works with an initial placement configuration PCI. In other words, the hosts or containers are currently executing (hosting) VMs. This fact can be interpreted by an absence of the corresponding RESET input. In other words, the IUT is not *switched off* nor tested in a complete isolation. In fact, it receives the boundary test suite given its current configuration (PCI). The latter means that the user requests that have been previously implemented, are not lost. In order to derive the proper test sequence one can adapt the set of constraints listed above. We still maximize the function f, however we now assume that some of the unknowns of the ILP are bounded by a positive integer. This fact can be expressed by the following system of linear constraints:

$$pc_{ij} \geq pci_{ij}; \forall i = 1, \ldots, m; j = 1, \ldots, n$$

In order to obtain a test suite, the placement configuration to be considered is the matrix $PC - PCI$, where PC is the matrix obtained from the solution of the ILP problem. Consider the placement in the running example, assume that the initial configuration is exactly as shown. $PC - PCI = \begin{pmatrix} 0&0&0&2 \\ 0&0&1&1 \\ 1&0&0&0 \end{pmatrix} - \begin{pmatrix} 0&0&0&1 \\ 0&0&1&0 \\ 1&0&0&0 \end{pmatrix} = \begin{pmatrix} 0&0&0&1 \\ 0&0&0&1 \\ 0&0&0&0 \end{pmatrix}$. The obtained test sequence is the following: $\alpha_I = \langle 0,0,0,1\rangle\langle 0,0,0,1\rangle$.

5.2   Static Code/algorithm Analysis

Given the resource utilization function f together with the distance d measuring the optimality of a given solution, one can use various static code/algorithm analysis techniques in order to estimate their quality. Such analysis can, on one hand include a random simulation of the placement algorithm $\mathcal{A}$, and on the other hand can allow to perform the backtracking to discover if a given value v of a distance can eventually be reached. In particular, given the algorithm $\mathcal{A}$ that is implemented in the VM placement module under test, the value v of the distance d between the computed resource utilization for the output of algorithm $\mathcal{A}$ and the optimal algorithm $\mathcal{O}$ that corresponds to the proper ILP solution, the question arises: does there exist an input α to the algorithms $\mathcal{A}$ and $\mathcal{O}$, such that $d(f(CI, VC, sim(\mathcal{A}, \alpha)), f(CI, VC, sim(\mathcal{O}, \alpha)) \geq v$. This problem can be represented as a formal verification or model checking issue and the possibility and complexity of solving such issue essentially depend on the definition of the functions d and f. In our case, the way that the distance from an optimal solution as well as the resource utilization function are defined, allows to reduce the problem to a simpler one, using the following system of linear inequalities over the natural numbers:

$$\sum_{i=1}^{m}\sum_{j=1}^{n}\left((pc_{ij} - pco_{ij}) * \sum_{k=1}^{p} vm_{j_k}\right) \geq v \text{ Or } \sum_{i=1}^{m}\sum_{j=1}^{n}\left((pc_{ij} - pco_{ij}) * \sum_{k=1}^{p} vm_{j_k}\right) \leq -v$$

Here, $sim(\mathcal{O}, \alpha) = PCO$ and $sim(\mathcal{A}, \alpha) = PC$.

If this problem has a solution then there exists a set of requests taking the cloud infrastructure from the initial configuration to that one where the distance between the current solution and an optimal one is greater or equal to v.

5.3   Dynamic VM Placement Execution

We assume that dynamic VM placement quality estimation involves the execution of the system under test, i.e., the placement module itself. In this case, the distance function d can serve as an *oracle* that allows either to take the decision about the optimality of the system under test, or can help to provide an appropriate alarm during the system monitoring.

The distance function d can also be used when the IUT, i.e., the VM placement module, has a limited controllability. Consider the case when no inputs can be applied to the IUT and the tester can only observe the user VM placement requests as well as the resulting configurations. Whenever an input sequence $\alpha = r_1 \ldots r_l$ is observed, one can compute the value of the f function for the current resource utilization, after the last request r_l was processed. In this case, for the given input $\alpha = r_1 \ldots r_l$ the optimal solution of $\mathcal{O}$ can be calculated. Together with that, the distance between the resource utilization of the provided solution $f(VI, VC, sim(\mathcal{A}, \alpha))$ that is observed by the tester and the optimal solution $f(VI, VC, sim(\mathcal{O}, \alpha))$ can be computed via the application of the function d. Similar to the first case (Sect. 5.2), given the constant v representing the largest allowed distance, whenever the computed distance is greater or equal to v an alarm signaling this fact can be produced.

We note that for optimization and scalability reasons some additional calculations can be performed in advance, before the monitoring itself. For example, one can collect specific critical input sequences for which the resulting value of the d function must be computed at run-time. For the set of such user requests, a tester can pre-calculate the optimal solutions and the corresponding values of the function f. Whenever such request sequence is observed, the tester only compares the value v with the given distance and signals when the VM placement produces the solution farther than required. If the value v remains constant, one can use a combination between the approaches from Sects. 5.2 and 5.3. If the verification analysis can return all possible user requests that lead to the result which is *very far* from the optimal solution, w.r.t. the defined f and d functions, these sequences of requests can be stored additionally. Whenever a preamble of any of such sequence is observed during the monitoring, a proper warning can be produced regarding the distance to the optimal resource utilization. Consider the running example for $v = 4$, where the request sequence $\alpha = \langle 0, 0, 0, 1 \rangle \langle 0, 0, 1, 0 \rangle \langle 1, 0, 0, 0 \rangle$ has been observed. If a new request $\langle 1, 0, 0, 0 \rangle$ is observed, $f(VI, VC, sim(\mathcal{A}, \alpha)) = 11$. However, $f(VI, VC, sim(\mathcal{O}, \alpha)) = 16$ and thus, a monitoring alert is produced.

Finally, a heuristic to compute the optimal resource utilization can be used in order to provide verdicts at run-time. Adding constraints similar to the non-initialized resource utilization, but over the sum of all different requested types of VMs makes the maximal resource utilization equals the sum of all requested resources. Thus, the usage of this heuristic can essentially improve the monitoring by reducing the complexity of the corresponding ILP problem.

6   Experimental Evaluation

In order to validate our approach experimental evaluation is presented. We propose a methodology, which is based on three stages, namely: (i) The generation of test suites for different cloud infrastructures and VM configuration setups using the boundary testing approach; (ii) The simulation of the obtained test suite as a request sequence for different placement algorithm implementations (IUTs); and finally (iii) Evaluating the quality of the IUTs using the defined distance function d.

Experimental Setup. To generate the test suites, the Gurobi [19] tool was employed for solving the ILP problems. After obtaining the proper values for the placement configuration semi-manual processes were involved, namely translating the solutions into the test suites and executing the simulator against them.

In this work, the simulator has been developed in order to perform the experimental evaluation. It is an ad-hoc simulator written in Java. More information about the tool, including its source code can be found in [13]. Currently, the simulator implements two algorithms. The first algorithm is a greedy *first fit* (FF) algorithm. The FF algorithm places the requested VM into the first host that is able to fit it. The second algorithm is an *available random* (AR) algorithm. The AR algorithm pre-filters the hosts in the cloud infrastructure. The resulting list of hosts from the AR algorithm contains the hosts that can fit the requested VM. Later on, the selection of the host is done with a uniformly distributed random choice. An interesting note on the AR algorithm is that AR with additional filters is the algorithm used in the placement module of the well-known OpenStack virtualization platform [18]. Due to the fact that random algorithms might generate different placement configurations, thus different distances can be obtained, our simulator runs each simulation 100 times and computes the average distance. Since we focus on the initial placement problem and not on re-allocation/migration, when an unfulfillable request comes the algorithms reject the request, and continue accepting the following requests (if any).

Experimental Results. To present our obtained results, we first summarize the test cases generated using the Gurobi software (Table 1). As it can be seen, the test suite generation is quite fast. All the test cases have been introduced into the simulator. All simulations and test generation were run on a MacBook Pro with a 2.3 GHz Intel Core i5 CPU, and 16 GB of RAM @ 1333 MHz DDR3.

Table 1. Test cases

TC	Environment	ILP details	Sol. time	Comments
1	$m = 2$, $n = 4$, $p = 2$	8 unknowns, 4 constraints	0 m 0.018 s	A very small example
2	$m = 3$, $n = 4$, $p = 2$	12 unknowns, 6 constraints	0 m 0.017 s	The paper's running example. Gurobi input and solution files available in [13]
3	$m = 3$, $n = 4$, $p = 2$	12 unknowns, 6 constraints	0 m 0.020 s	Increased hosts' capacity, considering real server capacity
4	$m = 9$, $n = 4$, $p = 2$	36 unknowns, 18 constraints	0 m 0.048 s	Real hosts' capacity, bigger cloud infrastructure

In Table 2, we summarize the simulation results. It can be clearly seen that the distances (from an optimal) of the FF algorithm are smaller than the distances of the AR algorithm for all test cases. Further, the simulation is also performed faster. These results are in fact expected since the FF algorithm does not perform any pre-selection of hosts. As a conclusion, the quality of the algorithm used in the widespread OpenStack placement module is lower than a very simple first fit algorithm.

Table 2. Simulation results

TC	$|\alpha|$	FF Avg. d	AR Avg. d	FF Sim. time	AR Sim. time
1	4	0	4.45	0 m 0.005 s	0 m 0.025 s
2	5	5	5.5	0 m 0.007 s	0 m 0.018 s
3	78	35	79.25	0 m 0.07 s	0 m 0.087 s
4	270	210	230.95	0 m 0.219 s	0 m 0.443 s

7   Conclusions

In this paper, we have proposed a distance function, which allows to effectively assess the quality of a placement module implementation. The metric being introduced measures the distance between the IUT resource utilization and an optimal resource utilization. Furthermore, different approaches for testing, monitoring, and verification of the IUT, represented by a VM placement module in a cloud infrastructure, have been proposed; these approaches are coherent with the proposed distance. In order to validate our approach, a simulator of such infrastructures has been developed. Interesting results have been obtained, including the assessment of the placement algorithm used in the widespread OpenStack platform, which is very far from the optimal with respect to resource utilization.

This paper presents an initial approach to effectively assess the quality of placement modules. Different aspects of our approach can be improved and extended. First, we plan to generate test suites for real case studies to further validate our approach. Also, our simulator can be expanded to (i) parse the cloud infrastructure and VM configuration setup from a defined file format, and (ii) based on the configurations, automatically generate the test suites and simulate the results by integrating the ILP solution into our tool. Furthermore, we intend to study other criteria for the placement optimality, for example, energy consumption, performance, etc., and propose and calculate the distances for them. One of the interesting questions is in fact the study of multi-criteria evaluation of the optimality using the listed parameters. The previously mentioned extensions and enhancements represent the future work for the short term.

Acknowledgments. The authors would like to thank Professor Nina Yevtushenko for fruitful discussions. The results obtained in this work were partially funded by the Celtic-Plus European project SENDATE, ID C2015/3-1; French National project CARP (FUI 19); Bilateral contracts with Orange Labs.

References

1. Babu, K.R.R., Samuel, P.: Virtual machine placement for improved quality in IAAS cloud. In: 2014 Fourth International Conference on Advances in Computing and Communications, pp. 190–194, August 2014
2. Beloglazov, A., Buyya, R.: Optimal online deterministic algorithms and adaptive heuristics for energy and performance efficient dynamic consolidation of virtual machines in cloud data centers. Concurrency Comput. Pract. Exp. **24**(13), 1397–1420 (2012). http://dx.doi.org/10.1002/cpe.1867
3. Bonde, D.: Techniques for Virtual Machine Placement in Clouds. Master's thesis, Indian Institute of Computer Science and Engineering (2010)
4. Calheiros, R.N., Ranjan, R., Beloglazov, A., De-Rose, C.A.F., Buyya, R.: Cloudsim: a toolkit for modeling and simulation of cloud computing environments and evaluation of resource provisioning algorithms. Softw. Pract. Exp. **41**(1), 23–50 (2011). http://dx.doi.org/10.1186/s13677-015-0045-5
5. Chowdhury, M.R., Mahmud, M.R., Rahman, R.M.: Implementation and performance analysis of various VM placement strategies in cloudsim. J. Cloud Comput. **4**(1), 20 (2015). http://dx.doi.org/10.1186/s13677-015-0045-5
6. Culberson, J.C., Luo, F.: Exploring the k-colorable landscape with iterated greedy. Cliques, coloring, and satisfiability: second DIMACS implementation challenge, pp. 245–284 (1996)
7. Dantzig, G.: Linear Programming and Extensions. Princeton University Press, Princeton (1963)
8. Fei, M., Feng, L., Zhen, L.: Multi-objective optimization for initial virtual machine placement in cloud data center. J. Inf. Comput. Sci. **9**(16), 5029–5038 (2012)
9. Gohil, B., Shah, S., Golechha, Y., Patel, D.: A comparative analysis of virtual machine placement techniques in the cloud environment. Int. J. Comput. Appl. **156**(14), 12–18 (2016)
10. Gomory, R.E.: Outline of an algorithm for integer solutions to linear programs. Bull. Am. Math. Soc. **64**(5), 275–278 (1958)
11. Khebbache, S., Hadji, M., Zeghlache, D.: Scalable and cost-efficient algorithms for VNF chaining and placement problem. In: 2017 20th Conference on Innovations in Clouds, Internet and Networks (ICIN), pp. 92–99, March 2017
12. Lewis, R.: A general-purpose hill-climbing method for order independent minimum grouping problems: a case study in graph colouring and bin packing. Comput. Oper. Res. **36**(7), 2295–2310 (2009)
13. López, J.: Vmplacementsim. Web Resource. https://github.com/jorgelopezcoronado/VMPlacementSim
14. Mann, Z.A., Szabó, M.: Which is the best algorithm for virtual machine placement optimization? Concurrency Comput. Pract. Exp. **29**(10), e4083-n/a (2017). e4083 cpe.4083
15. Masdari, M., Nabavi, S.S., Ahmadi, V.: An overview of virtual machine placement schemes in cloud computing. J. Netw. Comput. Appl. **66**, 106–127 (2016)
16. Mathur, A.P.: Foundations of Software Testing, 1st edn. Addison-Wesley Professional, Indianapolis (2008)
17. Mechtri, M., Benyahia, I.G., Zeghlache, D.: Agile service manager for 5G. In: NOMS 2016–2016 IEEE/IFIP Network Operations and Management Symposium, pp. 1285–1290, April 2016
18. OpenStack: Deep dive: virtual machine placement in openstack: web resource. https://platform9.com/blog/virtual-machine-placement-openstack/

19. Optimization, G., et al.: Gurobi optimizer reference manual. 2, 1–3 (2012). http://www.gurobi.com
20. Papadimitriou, C.H., Steiglitz, K.: Combinatorial Optimization: Algorithms and Complexity. Prentice-Hall Inc., Upper Saddle River (1982)
21. Pires, F.L., Barán, B.: Virtual machine placement literature review. CoRR abs/1506.01509 (2015). http://arxiv.org/abs/1506.01509
22. Vazirani, V.V.: Approximation Algorithms. Springer-Verlag New York Inc., New York (2001)

Homing Sequence Derivation with Quantified Boolean Satisfiability

Hung-En Wang[1], Kuan-Hua Tu[1], Jie-Hong R. Jiang[1,2(✉)],
and Natalia Kushik[3,4]

[1] Graduate Institute of Electronics Engineering,
National Taiwan University, Taipei, Taiwan
jhjiang@ntu.edu.tw
[2] Department of Electrical Engineering,
National Taiwan University, Taipei, Taiwan
[3] SAMOVAR, CNRS, Télécom SudParis, Université Paris-Saclay, Évry, France
[4] Tomsk State University, Tomsk, Russia

Abstract. Homing sequence derivation for nondeterministic finite state
machines (NFSMs) has important applications in system testing and
verification. Unlike prior methods based on explicit tree based search,
in this work we formulate the derivation of a preset homing sequence in
terms of a quantified Boolean formula (QBF). The formulation allows
implicit NFSM representation and compact QBF encoding for effective
computation. Different encoding schemes and QBF solvers are evaluated
for their suitability to homing sequence derivation. Experimental results
show the generality and feasibility of the proposed method.

1 Introduction

Model based testing techniques rely on formal specifications of the system under
test. Whenever such systems are reactive, i.e., are working in a request-response
mode, one of the appropriate formal models to describe the system behaviour
is the finite state machine (FSM). Therefore, a significant branch of research in
model based testing is devoted to FSM based testing.

Classical FSM based testing techniques, which are known to start with the
W-method [4,18] are mostly based on three main assumptions/steps: (1) to reach
a given state from the initial one, (2) to traverse the transitions under each input,
and (3) to distinguish the state that was reached from all other FSM states. The
derivation of the corresponding test sequences in this case is based on solving
state identification problems for the specification FSM [11].

FSM state identification is performed via an application of either distinguishing (for the initial state) or homing/synchronizing (for the current or final FSM
state) sequences. The length of these sequences as well as the complexity of
their derivation significantly depend on the type of the specification FSM. For
distinguishing sequences (DSs), even for complete and deterministic machines
the decision problem of DS existence is PSPACE-complete. However, for homing

© IFIP International Federation for Information Processing 2017
Published by Springer International Publishing AG 2017. All Rights Reserved
N. Yevtushenko et al. (Eds.): ICTSS 2017, LNCS 10533, pp. 230–242, 2017.
DOI: 10.1007/978-3-319-67549-7_14

and synchronizing sequences (HSs and SSs) for deterministic complete machines the upper bounds on the corresponding length are known to be polynomial [14].

For nondeterministic FSMs, the complexity upper bounds rise higher. The existence check becomes PSPACE-complete while the length of the shortest HS or SS for the machine is exponential with respect to the number of states. Development of complex (embedded) systems that can have nondeterministic behaviour due to various reasons, such as limited controllability and observability, therefore motivates studying the possibilities for reducing the complexity, at least for specific FSM classes [19].

In this paper, we consider non-initialized complete nondeterministic FSMs and we propose to improve the performance of HS existence checking and derivation using scalable FSM representation. We note that existing solutions for this problem mostly rely on the derivation of the homing tree which is built based on the successor tree [8] with the proper usage of truncating/termination rules [14]. For nondeterministic machines, not only the width but the height of this tree can grow exponentially before the nodes are truncated and thus, any search of the shortest HS in the homing tree is either length-bounded or requires exponential number of steps. Note that in this case, one of the most costly operations is shown to be the computation of the set of successors of a subset of FSM states [5]. In this paper, we circumvent deriving the homing tree and computing successor state sets.

The enabling technology of our computation is quantified Boolean formula solving, which has been advanced in recent years [6,12,17]. Quantified Boolean formulas (QBFs) are an extension to propositional formulas for their allowance of universal and existential quantification over variables. The additional quantifiers make QBFs exponentially more succinct than quantifier-free formulas in encoding many decision problems. Essentially, quantified Boolean satisfiability (QSAT) is PSPACE-complete in contrast to the NP-completeness of its Boolean satisfiability (SAT) counterpart. The generality of QBF and advancement of QSAT motivate our study of HS existence checking and derivation with QBF solving.

We implicitly represent the specification FSM as a Boolean circuit/formula. The HS existence checking and derivation can thereby be reduced to the corresponding QBF solving. In addition, we propose several techniques to enhance the scalability for QBF solving of homing sequences. Experimental results show promising applicability of our method.

The rest of this paper is organized as follows. After introducing backgrounds of homing sequence and QBF in Sect. 2, we present the QBF encoding of homing sequence computation in Sect. 3. We discuss some crucial implementation issues in Sect. 4. Experimental evaluation is then given in Sect. 5. Finally, we conclude this paper and outline future work in Sect. 6.

2   Preliminaries

2.1   Finite State Machine and Homing Sequence

A *finite state machine* (FSM) is a five tuple $M = (Q, Q_{init}, I, O, T)$, where Q is a finite set of states, $Q_{init} \subseteq Q$ is the set of initial states, I is the input alphabet,

O is the output alphabet, and $T \subseteq Q \times I \times O \times Q$ is the transition relation. In the sequel, we assume an FSM is uninitialized, that is, $Q_{init} = Q$. Since the initial state set is assumed to be all possible states, we omit specifying Q_{init} in the sequel. We write $|Q|$ to denote the cardinality of the state set Q; we write $|I|$ and $|O|$ to denote the sizes of the input and output alphabets, respectively; we write $|T|$ to denote the number of transitions in T. A *trace* is a sequence of the form $q_0, i_1, o_1, q_1, i_2, o_2, \ldots, q_n$, such that $(q_{k-1}, i_k, o_k, q_k) \in T$ for all $1 \leq k \leq n$.

A *deterministic* FSM (DFSM) is an FSM, where for each current-state input pair $(q, i) \in Q \times I$, there exists at most one output next-state pair $(o, q') \in O \times Q$ such that $(q, i, o, q') \in T$. Otherwise, the machine is a *nondeterministic* FSM (NFSM). A finite state machine is *complete* if for each current-state input pair (q, i), there exists at least one output next-state pair (o, q') such that $(q, i, o, q') \in T$. A finite state machine is called *(fully) observable* if for each current-state input output triple (q, i, o), there exists at most one next-state q' such that $(q, i, o, q') \in T$.

Given an FSM, a *homing sequence* (HS) is an input sequence such that after running the machine under this input sequence, by observing the corresponding output response, the final state after the execution can be uniquely determined. A homing sequence can be either *nonadaptive* (or called *preset*), which is a fixed input strategy regardless of the output response, or *adaptive*, which is an input strategy that determines the next input symbol based on the so-far observed output response. In this work, we consider the problem of finding a preset homing sequence for a complete NFSM.

An uninitialized complete NFSM has the following property.

Proposition 1. *Given an uninitialized complete NFSM, if there exists a homing sequence of length n, then there exists a homing sequence of length $n + 1$.*

It is because given an uninitialized complete NFSM, with a homing sequence of length n, we can easily extend it to a length $n+1$ homing sequence by adding an arbitrary input symbol to the head of the sequence. After taking the first state transition, the possible current states are a subset of all states. Hence, applying the original homing sequence of length n, the final state can be determined by observing the output sequence.

Note that Proposition 1 is especially interesting for non-observable FSMs for which a prolongation of a homing sequence is not necessarily a homing sequence itself. However, it shows that any prefix can be added to a given homing sequence without ruining the property of the final state identification via the observation of an output response.

2.2   Quantified Boolean Formula

A Boolean variable takes a value in the Boolean domain $\mathbb{B} = \{\bot, \top\}$, with $\bot$ and $\top$ representing FALSE and TRUE, respectively. A *Boolean formula* ϕ consists of Boolean variables and Boolean connectives, which we denote negation, conjunction, disjunction, implication, and equivalence by symbols $\neg$, $\wedge$, $\vee$, $\rightarrow$, and $\leftrightarrow$, respectively. A vector of Boolean variables is denoted by a letter in bold, such as $\boldsymbol{x}$ of variables $(x_1, x_2, \ldots, x_n)$. Given two vectors of Boolean variables $\boldsymbol{x} = (x_1, x_2, \ldots, x_n)$ and $\boldsymbol{y} = (y_1, y_2, \ldots, y_n)$, we use "$\boldsymbol{x} = \boldsymbol{y}$" to denote $\bigwedge_{i=1}^{n} x_i \leftrightarrow y_i$, the bit-wise equivalence between $\boldsymbol{x}$ and $\boldsymbol{y}$.

For a Boolean formula ϕ and a Boolean variable x, we use $\phi|_x$ to denote the induced formula obtained from ϕ by assigning variable x to $\top$. Similarly, $\phi|_{\neg x}$ denotes the formula obtained from ϕ by assigning variable x to $\bot$. A *satisfying assignment* is a complete assignment of truth values to each variable that makes the formula evaluate to $\top$. The *on-set* of a Boolean formula ϕ is the collection of its satisfying assignments to ϕ.

A *literal* ℓ is either a Boolean variable x or its negation $\neg x$. A *clause* is a disjunction of literals. A Boolean formula is in the *conjunctive normal form* (CNF) if it is a conjunction of clauses.

A *quantified Boolean formula* (QBF) Φ can be expressed in a *prenex form* as follows.

$$Q_1 x_1, \ldots, Q_k x_k . \phi, \tag{1}$$

where $Q_i \in \{\exists, \forall\}$ is the quantifier over variable x_i, and ϕ is a quantifier-free Boolean formula over variables $x_1, \ldots, x_k$. A variable x_i with $Q_i = \exists$ (respectively $Q_i = \forall$) is referred to as an *existential variable* (respectively a *universal variable*). We call $Q_1 x_1, \ldots, Q_k x_k$ the *prefix* of Φ, denoted Φ.pfx, and call the quantifier-free formula ϕ the *matrix* of Φ, denoted Φ.mtx. A prenex-form QBF is called in the *prenex conjunctive normal form* (PCNF) if the matrix is expressed as a CNF formula. In the sequel, unless otherwise said, we assume a QBF is expressed in PCNF.

Given the QBF Φ of (1), the *quantification level* of variable x_i is defined to be the number of quantifier alternations between the quantifiers $\exists$ and $\forall$ from left (outer) to right (inner) plus one. A QBF is of l *quantification levels* if the number of quantifier alternations between $\exists$ and $\forall$ from Q_1 to Q_k is $l - 1$. In this work, our considered QBFs are of quantification levels 2 or 3.

The QBF $\exists x_1, Q_2 x_2, \ldots, Q_k x_k . \phi$ is true if one of $Q_2 x_2, \ldots, Q_k x_k . \phi|_{x_1}$ and $Q_2 x_2, \ldots, Q_k x_k . \phi|_{\neg x_1}$ is true. On the other hand, the QBF $\forall x_1, Q_2 x_2, \ldots, Q_k x_k . \phi$ is true if both $Q_2 x_2, \ldots, Q_k v_k . \phi|_{x_1}$ and $Q_2 x_2, \ldots, Q_k v_k . \phi|_{\neg x_1}$ are true. A QBF Φ is true if there exist *Skolem functions* for the existential variables of Φ such that substituting the existential variables with their corresponding Skolem functions in Φ.mtx makes the resultant formula a tautology. By duality, a QBF Φ is false if there exist *Herbrand functions* for the universal variables of Φ such that substituting the universal variables with their corresponding Herbrand functions in Φ.mtx makes the resultant formula unsatisfiable. A detailed exposition of Skolem and Herbrand functions can be found in [1].

3   QBF for Bounded-Length Homing Sequence Existence Checking and Derivation

Given a uninitialized complete NFSM $M = (Q, I, O, T)$, we aim at finding a shortest homing sequence. We search from length 1 to the theoretical upper bound $2^{\binom{|Q|}{2}} - 1$ of a shortest homing sequence [10]. We present the QBF formulation of the bounded homing sequence checking as follows.

Since Q, I, O are all finite, we perform Boolean encoding on the states, input symbols, and output symbols with current-state variables s, next-state variables s', input variables x, and output variables y. Then the transition relation T of the machine can be represented by the characteristic function $T(s, x, y, s')$ in terms of the encoding Boolean variables. In our QBF formulation, we rely on time-frame expansion and denote the variables at the tth time-frame with a superscript index t.

Then the QBF corresponding to the existence of homing sequence of length n can be expressed as follows.

$$\exists X, \forall Y, \forall S, \forall S^*.[\Delta^{(n)}(X, Y, S) \wedge \Delta^{(n)}(X, Y, S^*) \rightarrow (s^n = s^{*n})], \quad (2)$$

where variables $S = (s^0, \ldots, s^n)$, $X = (x^1, \ldots, x^n)$, $Y = (y^1, \ldots, y^n)$, $S^* = (s^{*0}, \ldots, s^{*n})$, and $\Delta^{(n)}$ is the conjunction of the transition relation of n time-frames, i.e., $\Delta^{(n)}(X, Y, S) = \bigwedge_{k=1}^{n} T(s^{k-1}, x^k, y^k, s^k)$ and $\Delta^{(n)}(X, Y, S^*) = \bigwedge_{k=1}^{n} T(s^{*k-1}, x^k, y^k, s^{*k})$. In the expression, the variables s^* are fresh variables as the instantiated versions of their counterparts s.

The formula asks whether there exists an input sequence of length n, such that for any two traces with same output response, we can always conclude that the final states of the two traces are the same. Clearly, an input sequence satisfies such a constraint if and only if it is a homing sequence.

Proposition 2. *Formula (2) is true if and only if the underlying NFSM has a homing sequence of length n.*

Proposition 3. *If Formula (2) is true, then the Skolem functions for variables X correspond to a homing sequence of the underlying NFSM.*

4   Implementation

In this section, we discuss some implementation details in generating Formula (2) for QBF solving.

4.1   Input Symbol Encoding

The size of input alphabet may not necessarily be in the form of 2^j for some j. If some binary code is unused in representing any input symbol, the QBF solver may assign the unused code for the existential variables. In this case, the solver can falsify the transition relation and make Formula (2) true. However, the unused code does not correspond to any input symbol and cannot form a 'legal' homing sequence. Hence unused codes for input symbol encoding should be avoided.

There are two methods to eliminate unused input codes. The first one is to modify the matrix of Formula (2) by restricting x^t, for $t = 1, \ldots, n$, in Formula (2) to only used codes. Essentially, the characteristic functions expressing the used codes of $x^1, \ldots, x^n$ are conjuncted with Formula (2). The second one is to assign two or more codes to the same input symbol to make all codes used, which can avoid adding more clauses to Formula (2), and gain flexibility in circuit minimization.

In our implementation, we used $\lceil \log_2 |I| \rceil$ bits to encode the input symbols. Consider the input alphabet I with j symbols. It requires $\lceil \log_2 j \rceil$ bits for the encoding. We let each of the first $2^{\lceil \log_2 j \rceil} - j$ symbols be associated with two consecutive codes, and let each of the rest be associated with one of the remaining codes. For instance, if the input alphabet is $\{a, b, c\}$, both codes "00" and "01" are associated with 'a', and "10" and "11" are associated with 'b' and 'c', respectively.

4.2   Minimization of Transition Relation

To improve the efficiency of QBF solving, it is desirable to simplify the matrix of a QBF. Therefore, minimizing the transition relation of the NFSM under homing sequence derivation helps to simplify Formula (2) and improve QBF solving efficiency.

The characteristic function of the transition relation can be naively built by the on-set of T, i.e., by disjoining the characteristic function of each transition, which corresponds to a conjunction of literals of state, input, and output variables. It can be represented as a Boolean formula or a logic circuit. Two-level or multi-level logic minimization algorithms can be applied to reduce the size of the formula/circuit.

To simplify the QBF matrix, one may also exploit different state encoding methods. In our implementation, we study the effects of binary encoding and onehot encoding[1]. The empirical results on our generated benchmark instances are shown in Table 1, where Column "$|T|$" shows the number of transitions in T of each NFSM, Columns "#gates (bin)" and "#gates (1hot)" show the numbers of gates in the final simplified circuits under binary state encoding and onehot encoding, respectively, and Column "ratio (bin/1hot)" shows the ratio of the gate count of binary encoding to the gate count of onehot encoding. In the experiments, the input encoding method described at the end of Sect. 4.1 is applied, with the same encoding strategy applied on output symbols. Also, circuit minimization is applied on each case. Note that unlike input encoding, unused state codes do not affect the correctness of QBF analysis. We do not assign multiple codes for one state; otherwise, this encoding may introduce state equivalence in our formula and complicate the homing sequence derivation. Encoding for output symbols has no such an unused code problem, too. In the experiment, however, output is encoded in the same way as the input. As can be seen, binary encoding yields gate counts about 70% to 90% of those yielded by onehot encoding.

---

[1] By onehot encoding, n states $q_1, q_2, \ldots, q_n$ are encoded with n bits $b_1, b_2, \ldots, b_n$, one for each state, such that state q_i, $i \in \{1, \ldots, n\}$, is coded with $b_i = 1$ and $b_j = 0$ for $j \neq i$.

Table 1. Gate count comparison under different state encodings

Case	$|Q|/|I|/|O|$	$|T|$	#gates (bin)	#gates (1hot)	Ratio (bin/1hot)
0	5/2/2	13	43	64	0.67
1	5/2/2	17	39	60	0.65
2	5/2/2	18	50	76	0.66
3	5/2/2	17	38	54	0.70
4	5/2/2	14	37	58	0.64
5	10/5/5	153	480	531	0.90
6	10/5/5	139	466	566	0.82
7	10/5/5	147	451	527	0.86
8	10/5/5	154	475	591	0.80
9	10/5/5	142	459	536	0.86
10	13/7/7	371	1071	1169	0.92
11	13/7/7	385	1092	1214	0.90
12	13/7/7	384	1067	1197	0.89
13	13/7/7	381	1046	1172	0.89
14	13/7/7	394	1073	1200	0.89
15	15/8/8	517	1435	1758	0.82
16	15/8/8	567	1507	1760	0.86
17	15/8/8	528	1463	1677	0.87
18	15/8/8	539	1421	1723	0.82
19	15/8/8	523	1451	1700	0.85
20	20/10/10	1087	3211	3563	0.90
21	20/10/10	1147	3243	3539	0.92
22	20/10/10	1071	3130	3692	0.85
23	20/10/10	1094	3101	3482	0.89
24	20/10/10	1116	3234	3637	0.89

4.3   QBF Negation for Quantification Level Minimization

Simplifying transition relation is in general desirable. It is unclear, however, whether to represent the transition relation in two-level or multi-level circuits, especially when Tseitin transformation [16] is applied to convert a circuit into a CNF formula for PCNF-based QBF solvers. Tseitin transformation[2] uses inter-

---

[2] In Tseitin transformation, an intermediate variable is introduced for each internal gate output, and a number of clauses are generated to characterize the relation of consistent valuations between input and output variables of each gate. For example, the circuit in Fig. 1(a) can be converted into the CNF formula $(x \vee \neg u) \wedge (y \vee \neg u) \wedge (\neg x \vee \neg y \vee u) \wedge (\neg u \vee w) \wedge (\neg z \vee w) \wedge (u \vee z \vee \neg w)$, in which two intermediate variables u and w are used and the first (resp. last) three clauses describe $u \leftrightarrow (x \wedge y)$ (resp. $w \leftrightarrow (u \vee z)$).

mediate variables in circuit-to-CNF conversion. It makes the final QBF having an extra innermost layer of existential quantification over these intermediate variables. That is, Formula (2), which is of two quantification levels, will become a QBF with three quantification levels of the following form

$$\exists X, \forall Y, \forall S, \forall S^*, \exists Z.\phi, \tag{3}$$

where ϕ is a CNF formula converted from a circuit representing $[\Delta^{(n)}(X, Y, S) \wedge \Delta^{(n)}(X, Y, S^*) \rightarrow (s^n = s^{*n})]$ and variables Z are the intermediate variables introduced in the CNF conversion. Having many such intermediate variables introduced by Tseitin transformation for each internal gate output of the logic circuit may degrade QBF solving performance.

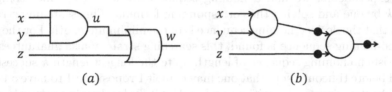

(a)   (b)

Fig. 1. (a) A logic circuit implementing function $(x \wedge y) \vee z$. (b) An AIG representing the circuit in (a), with each circle representing an AND gate, and a bubble on an edge representing an inverter.

The minimization procedure represents the transition relation in terms of an and-inverter graph (AIG) [13], which consists of 2-input AND gates and inverters. Figure 1(b) shows an example of AIG of the circuit in Fig. 1(a), where a circle represents a 2-input AND gate and a bubble on an edge represents an inverter. AIGs allow compact representation of Boolean circuits and are widely used in logic synthesis and verification [7]. As shown in Table 1, since the number of gates in the minimized circuit (AIG) is about three times the number $|T|$ of transitions, the introduced extra variables will be more than those of the on-set approach. To be seen in the experiments in Sect. 5, the naive on-set representation of the transition relation, which corresponds to a circuit consisting of $|T|$ multi-input AND gates and 1 multi-input OR gate, has only $|T|$ intermediate variables and sometimes makes QBF solving more efficient.

It has been observed that a QBF and its negation often exhibit different solving characteristics [1]. Negating Formula (2) through Tseintin transformation yields

$$\forall X, \exists Y, \exists S, \exists S^*, \exists Z.\psi, \tag{4}$$

where ψ is a CNF formula converting from the circuit representing $\neg[\Delta^{(n)}(X, Y, S) \wedge \Delta^{(n)}(X, Y, S^*) \rightarrow (s^n = s^{*n})]$ and variables Z are the intermediate variables by the Tseitin conversion. Observe that Formula (4) has only two quantification levels, in contrast to the three quantification levels of Formula (3). The experimental comparison will be shown in Sect. 5.

5   Experimental Results

The proposed QBF method is tested on a Linux machine with Intel Xeon E5-2630 CPU (2.3 GHz) and 200 GB RAM. Several state-of-the-art QBF solvers are tested and compared, including DepQBF [12], RAReQS [6], QELL [17], and the 2QBF solver in Berkeley ABC [2,3]. We randomly generated 25 test cases by the tool FSMTest-1.0 [15] for performance evaluation.[3] Binary encoding is applied, and for input encoding, all the codes are used as discussed in Sect. 4.1. Circuit minimization is also applied to minimize the transition relation of each case. Then Tseitin transformation is applied to convert the formulas into PCNF for DepQBF, RAReQS, and QELL. For each case, its potential homing sequences of length k, for $k = 1, \ldots, 1023$, are tested under a timeout limit of 7200 s. In the experiments, we find a homing sequence by iteratively increasing the length k by one and solving the corresponding formula. This searching strategy ensures that the derived homing sequence is of the minimum length. For the cases where no-homing sequence is found, this searching strategy also guarantees that there exists no homing sequence of length up to the longest length k successfully checked before timeout. Note that one may exploit Proposition 1 to have a binary search-like strategy starting with some $k > 1$. If it finds a homing sequence under k, one can decrease k to look for a shorter homing sequence. Otherwise, one can increase k by some number to look for a longer homing sequence.

Table 2 shows the statistics of different QBF solvers on solving the 25 test cases. The number of states, and the sizes of input and output alphabets of each case are listed in Column "$|Q|/|I|/|O|$". For each solver, Columns "result" show the final answer, which is one of the three outcomes: "SAT" indicating homing sequence found, "UNSAT" indicating no homing sequence exists, and "TO" indicating timeout on testing homing sequence existence under a length greater than the number reported in Columns "len". Columns "time" show the total solving time (in seconds) of each solver up to the length reported in Columns "len". Columns "len" show the longest sequence length successfully checked before termination, which is the length of the found homing sequence for the SAT case, the length upper bound for the UNSAT case, and the last verified length for the TO case.

---

[3] We note that the process of FSM generation can be seen as a simple task. However, deriving an FSM with the corresponding properties such as observability, degree of non-determinism, etc., makes this task more complex. In the FSM generation process in [15], a machine that is not observable was automatically dropped to generate another machine with the same cardinality of input/output alphabet and the same number of states, which is observable. Note that our QBF formulation is not limited to observable NFSMs. We experimented with observable FSMs only as even in the observable case the exponential upper bound on the length of homing sequence is known to be attainable. On the other hand, for simplicity, the number of outputs was chosen to be equal to the number of FSM inputs. In total, we generated 25 machines for which the number of inputs varied from 2 to 10 and the number of states was in the range from 5 to 20, correspondingly. Note that, in most of the cases, neither the number of states nor the number of inputs can be represented by an appropriate power of two. The latter allows to better experiment with our heuristics proposed for input/state encoding.

Table 2. Performance comparison of different QBF solvers

Case	$|Q|/|I|/|O|$	DepQBF			RAReQS			QELL			ABC		
		Result	Time	Len	Result	Time	Len	Result	Time	Len	Result	Time	Len
0	5/2/2	SAT	0.07	3	TO	7200	2	SAT	0.04	3	SAT	0.28	3
1	5/2/2	TO	7200	560	TO	7200	2	TO	7200	70	TO	7200	53
2	/2/2	SAT	11.32	5	TO	7200	2	SAT	0.15	5	SAT	0.41	5
3	5/2/2	TO	7200	9	TO	7200	2	TO	7200	133	UNSAT	5503	1023
4	5/2/2	TO	7200	7	TO	7200	2	TO	7200	13	TO	7200	13
5	10/5/5	TO	7200	4	TO	7200	1	TO	7200	5	TO	7200	6
6	10/5/5	TO	7200	4	TO	7200	1	TO	7200	5	SAT	818	6
7	10/5/5	TO	7200	4	TO	7200	1	TO	7200	5	TO	7200	6
8	10/5/5	TO	7200	4	TO	7200	1	TO	7200	5	SAT	5293	7
9	10/5/5	TO	7200	4	TO	7200	1	SAT	1122	5	SAT	30.18	5
10	13/7/7	TO	7200	3	TO	7200	1	TO	7200	4	TO	7200	5
11	13/7/7	TO	7200	3	TO	7200	1	TO	7200	4	TO	7200	5
12	13/7/7	TO	7200	3	TO	7200	1	TO	7200	4	TO	7200	5
13	13/7/7	TO	7200	3	TO	7200	1	TO	7200	4	TO	7200	5
14	13/7/7	TO	7200	3	TO	7200	1	TO	7200	4	TO	7200	5
15	15/8/8	TO	7200	3	TO	7200	1	TO	7200	3	TO	7200	4
16	15/8/8	TO	7200	3	TO	7200	1	TO	7200	3	TO	7200	4
17	15/8/8	TO	7200	3	TO	7200	1	TO	7200	3	TO	7200	4
18	15/8/8	TO	7200	3	TO	7200	1	TO	7200	3	TO	7200	4
19	15/8/8	TO	7200	3	TO	7200	1	TO	7200	3	TO	7200	4
20	20/10/10	TO	7200	2	TO	7200	1	TO	7200	3	TO	7200	4
21	20/10/10	TO	7200	2	TO	7200	1	TO	7200	3	TO	7200	4
22	20/10/10	TO	7200	2	TO	7200	1	TO	7200	3	TO	7200	4
23	20/10/10	TO	7200	2	TO	7200	1	TO	7200	3	TO	7200	4
24	20/10/10	TO	7200	2	TO	7200	1	TO	7200	3	TO	7200	4

As can be seen from Table 2, most cases are reported timeout for each solver, with no homing sequence found within length 6 for the 10-state cases to length 4 for the 20-state cases. We observed that for the cases with 5 states, each solver seems to show its own strength. DepQBF performs very well on case 1; ABC performs well on case 3; QELL yields a more balanced result compared to the other solvers. In overall performance, ABC outperforms other solvers, with at least one more length verified in each of the larger cases. The only one UNSAT case, reported by ABC, has no homing sequence within length upper bound 1023, and this is in fact the theoretical upper bound of shortest homing sequence [10] for a 5-state NFSM. The outstanding performance of ABC is not surprising as the homing sequence QBFs favor a circuit-based solver due to its natural circuit representation of transition relation.

Note that although all solvers timed out on all the cases with 13 and more states, the scalability of the proposed method can still be seen through the longest lengths that successfully verified before timeout in these cases from Table 2. For most of the cases, the successfully checked lengths seem to be small. It suggests that computing homing sequence for NFSM is challenging. In fact, there are exponentially many input sequences of a given length, and for a NFSM the problem of checking whether an input sequence is homing is known to belong to the PSPACE complexity class [9]. The complexity of checking if a given sequence is homing for nondeterministic machine is "hidden" in the costly operation of an i-successor [9] of a given state subset. Moreover, the higher is the nondeterminism degree of the machine, the slower is the check that for each state pair and each common output response at these states, the final state is unique. The latter makes it unpromising to directly apply any brute force search or even truncated successor tree approach in a large scale. In this paper, we discuss possible heuristics how this complexity can be reduced via the usage of FSM scalable representations and corresponding QBF solvers.

Table 3. Performance comparison under different formula construction methods

Case	$|Q|$	DepQBF					RAReQS					QELL				
		m	o	m+c	o+c	o+b	m	o	m+c	o+c	o+b	m	o	m+c	o+c	o+b
1	5	560	14	1023	22	14	2	5	20	20	5	70	25	19	19	25
3	5	9	14	21	22	14	2	6	20	20	6	133	38	19	19	39
11	13	3	2	6	6	2	1	2	6	6	2	4	5	5	6	5
13	13	3	2	6	6	2	1	2	6	6	2	4	5	5	6	5
21	20	2	2	4	4	2	1	2	4	5	2	3	4	4	4	4
23	20	2	2	4	4	2	1	2	4	5	2	3	4	4	4	4

As discussed in Sect. 4, there can be different options in formula generation. Solver performance may also be affected by the chosen options, especially the PCNF-based solvers, DepQBF, RAReQS, and QELL. In Table 3, we compare solver performance in five different options of formula generation. Six test cases in the above experiment are selected, including two small ones with 5 states, two medium ones with 13 states, and two large ones with 20 states. The three PCNF-based solvers, DepQBF, RAReQS and QELL are compared. Since the 2QBF solver in ABC takes an AIG as its input, it does not need Tseitin transformation and the methods mentioned in Sect. 4 seem not affecting much the ABC performance. So ABC is excluded in this comparison.

In Table 3, each entry shows the verified length before the timeout, Columns "m" show the result of applying circuit minimization on transition relation without complementing the formula. They are also the results shown in the above experiment. Columns "o" show the results using the on-set of transition relation without minimization and having no formula negation. Columns "m+c" show the results using minimized circuits and applying formula negation. Columns "o+c" show the results using the on-set of transition relation without minimization, but with formula negation. Each of "m", "o", "m+c", "o+c" uses all codes for input and output encodings. On the other hand, Columns "o+b" do not use all codes for encoding, and clauses are added to constrain inputs to legal code assignments. Both circuit minimization and formula negation are not applied in Columns "o+b".

It can be seen that for DepQBF, transition relation minimization is beneficial in most cases. Also, formula negation substantially improves the performance, with the verified lengths doubled within timeout, and even case 1 reached the pre-specified upper bound 1023 before timeout (about 1542 s for solving case (1). On the other hand, for RAReQS, using the onset of transition relation without circuit minimization is better in most of the cases. Moreover, solving the negated formula is also much faster than solving the original formula, with the verified lengths increased to at least 2.5 times. As for QELL, transition relation minimization or solving negated formula significantly improves the solving of the 5-state cases, but the verified lengths slightly drops in the larger cases. Comparing Column "o" and Column "o+b" in any of the three solvers, we see that the ways of handling unused codes in input encoding seem not having notable effects on the solver performance.

6   Conclusions

We have formulated the problem of finding preset homing sequence of an uninitialized NFSM as QBF solving. Different implementation issues in formula construction have been discussed. Experiments have been done comparing different QBF solvers on existence checking and derivation of homing sequences for NFSMs. The effects of circuit minimization and formula negation have been studied. The results have suggested that circuit-based QBF solver ABC is the most powerful one in our applications, while other solvers may not be as effective due to the Tseitin transformation overhead. On the other hand, for PCNF-based solvers, complementing Formula (2), which reduces the number of quantification levels, tends to improve solving efficiency. Moreover, different PCNF-based solvers may have their preferred encoding methods. We believe that the approach proposed in the paper should outperform the classical ones, based on the derivation of the truncated successor tree, but the comparison remains to be done.

For future work, we plan to conduct experiments comparing our approach against the classical methods. We will extend our formulation to finding adaptive homing sequences and to consider initialized NFSMs under partial observability. Moreover, it would be interesting to study how our proposed approach performs on 'hard' FSMs that are known to have the homing sequence but of an exponential length, i.e., to stress-test the QBF solvers over the machines for which the exponential upper bound is reachable. We therefore plan to implement the derivation of such machines, using for example an algorithm given in [10].

Acknowledgements. The authors are grateful to Prof. Nina Yevtushenko for initiating this work and for valuable discussions. This work was supported in part by the joint project between the Ministry of Science and Technology (MOST) of Taiwan and Russian Science Foundation (RSF) of Russia under grants MOST 105-2923-E-002-016-MY3 and RSF 16-49-03012.

References

1. Balabanov, V., Jiang, J.H.R.: Unified QBF certification and its applications. Formal Methods Syst. Des. **41**(1), 45–65 (2012)
2. Balabanov, V., Jiang, J.-H.R., Scholl, C., Mishchenko, A., Brayton, R.K.: 2QBF: challenges and solutions. In: Creignou, N., Le Berre, D. (eds.) SAT 2016. LNCS, vol. 9710, pp. 453–469. Springer, Cham (2016). doi:10.1007/978-3-319-40970-2_28
3. Brayton, R., Mishchenko, A.: ABC: an academic industrial-strength verification tool. In: Touili, T., Cook, B., Jackson, P. (eds.) CAV 2010. LNCS, vol. 6174, pp. 24–40. Springer, Heidelberg (2010). doi:10.1007/978-3-642-14295-6_5
4. Chow, T.S.: Testing software design modeled by finite-state machines. IEEE Trans. Softw. Eng. **4**(3), 178–187 (1978)
5. Haddad, A.R.: Efficient Algorithms for Constructing Preset Distinguishing Sequences for Nondeterministic Finite State Machines. Master's thesis, American University of Sharjah (2016)
6. Janota, M., Klieber, W., Marques-Silva, J., Clarke, E.: Solving QBF with counterexample guided refinement. In: Cimatti, A., Sebastiani, R. (eds.) SAT 2012. LNCS, vol. 7317, pp. 114–128. Springer, Heidelberg (2012). doi:10.1007/978-3-642-31612-8_10
7. Jiang, J.H.R., Devadas, S.: Logic synthesis in a nutshell. In: Wang, L.T., Chang, Y.W., Cheng, K.T. (eds.) Electronic Design Automation: Synthesis, Verification, and Test. Elsevier (2009)
8. Kohavi, Z.: Switching and Finite Automata Theory. McGraw-Hill, New York (1978)
9. Kushik, N.G., Kulyamin, V.V., Evtushenko, N.V.: On the complexity of existence of homing sequences for nondeterministic finite state machines. Program. Comput. Softw. **40**(6), 333–336 (2014)
10. Kushik, N., Yevtushenko, N.: On the length of homing sequences for nondeterministic finite state machines. In: Konstantinidis, S. (ed.) CIAA 2013. LNCS, vol. 7982, pp. 220–231. Springer, Heidelberg (2013). doi:10.1007/978-3-642-39274-0_20
11. Lee, D., Yannakakis, M.: Principles and methods of testing finite state machines - a survey. Proc. IEEE **84**(8), 1090–1123 (1996)
12. Lonsing, F., Biere, A.: DepQBF: a dependency-aware QBF solver. J. Satisfiability, Boolean Model. Comput. **7**(2–3), 71–76 (2010)
13. Mishchenko, A., Chatterjee, S., Jiang, J.H.R., Brayton, R.K.: FRAIGs: a unifying representation for logic synthesis and verification. In: ERL Technical report. UC Berkeley (2005)
14. Sandberg, S.: 1 homing and synchronizing sequences. In: Broy, M., Jonsson, B., Katoen, J.-P., Leucker, M., Pretschner, A. (eds.) Model-Based Testing of Reactive Systems. LNCS, vol. 3472, pp. 5–33. Springer, Heidelberg (2005). doi:10.1007/11498490_2
15. Shabaldina, N., Gromov, M.: FSMTest-1.0: a manual for researches. In: EWDTS. pp. 1–4 (2015)
16. Tseitin, G.: On the complexity of derivation in propositional calculus. In: Studies in Constructive Mathematics and Mathematical Logic, pp. 466–483 (1970)
17. Tu, K.-H., Hsu, T.-C., Jiang, J.-H.R.: QELL: QBF reasoning with extended clause learning and levelized SAT solving. In: Heule, M., Weaver, S. (eds.) SAT 2015. LNCS, vol. 9340, pp. 343–359. Springer, Cham (2015). doi:10.1007/978-3-319-24318-4_25
18. Vasilevskii, M.: Failure diagnosis of automata. Kibernetika **4**, 98–108 (1973)
19. Yenigün, H., Yevtushenko, N., Kushik, N.: Some classes of finite state machines with polynomial length of distinguishing test cases. In: SAC, pp. 1680–1685 (2016)

Synchronizing Heuristics: Speeding up the Slowest

Ömer Faruk Altun[1], Kamil Tolga Atam[1], Sertaç Karahoda[1(✉)], and Kamer Kaya[1,2]

[1] Computer Science and Engineering, Faculty of Engineering and Natural Sciences, Sabanci University, Tuzla, Istanbul, Turkey
{ofarukaltun,atam,skarahoda,kaya}@sabanciuniv.edu
[2] Department Biomedical Informatics, The Ohio State University, Columbus, OH, USA

Abstract. Computing a shortest synchronizing word of an automaton is an NP–hard problem. Therefore, heuristics are used to compute short synchronizing words. SYNCHROP is among the best heuristics in the literature in terms of word lengths. The heuristic and its variants such as SYNCHROPL have been frequently used as a baseline to judge the quality of the words generated by the new heuristics. Although, its quality is good, the heuristics are significantly slow especially compared to much cheaper heuristics such as GREEDY and CYCLE. This makes them infeasible for large-scale automatons. In this paper, we show how one can improve the time performance of SYNCHROP and its variants by avoiding unnecessary computations which makes these heuristics more competitive than they already are. Our experimental results show that for 2500 states, SYNCHROP can be made 70–160× faster, via the proposed optimizations. In particular, for 2500 states and 32 letters, the SYNCHROP execution reduces to 66 s from 4745 s. Furthermore, the suggested optimizations become more effective as the number of states in the automata increase.

Keywords: Finite state automata · Synchronizing words · Synchronizing heuristics

1 Introduction

A *synchronizing word* w for an automaton A is a sequence of inputs such that no matter at which state A currently is, if w is applied, A is brought to a particular state. Such words do not necessarily exist for every automaton. An automaton with a synchronizing word is called *synchronizing automaton.*

Synchronizing automata have practical applications in many areas. For example in model based testing [1] and in particular for finite state machine based testing [2], test sequences are designed to be applied at a particular state. Note

N. Yevtushenko et al. (Eds.): ICTSS 2017, LNCS 10533, pp. 243–256, 2017.
DOI: 10.1007/978-3-319-67549-7_15

that a finite state machine given as the specification can be viewed as an automaton by omitting the output symbols labeling the transitions of the finite state machine. The implementation under test can be brought to the desired state by using a synchronizing word. Similarly, synchronizing words are used the generate test cases for synchronous circuits with no reset feature [3]. Even when a reset feature is available, there are cases where reset operations are too costly to be applied. In these cases, a synchronizing word can be used as a compound reset operation [4]. Natarajan puts forward another surprising application area, part orienters, where a part moving on conveyor belt is oriented into a particular orientation by the obstacles placed along the conveyor belt [5]. The part is in some unknown orientation initially, and the obstacles should be placed in such a way that, regardless of the initial orientation of the part, the sequence of pushes performed by the obstacles along the way makes sure that the part is in a unique orientation at the end. Volkov presents more examples for the applications of synchronizing words together with a survey of theoretical results related to synchronizing automata [6].

As noted above, not every automaton is synchronizing. As shown by [7], checking if an automaton with n states and p letters is synchronizing can be performed in time $O(pn^2)$. For a synchronizing automaton, finding a shortest synchronizing word (which is not necessarily unique) is of interest from a practical point of view for obvious reasons (e.g., shorter test sequences in testing applications, or less number of obstacles for parts orienters, etc.).

The problem of finding the length of a shortest synchronizing word for a synchronizing automaton has been a very interesting problem from a theoretical point of view as well. This problem is known to be NP-hard [7], and coNP-hard [8]. Another interesting aspect of the problem is the following. It is conjectured that for a synchronizing automaton with n states, the length of the shortest synchronizing sequence is at most $(n-1)^2$, which is known as the Černý Conjecture in the literature [9,10]. Posed half a century ago, the conjecture is still open and claimed to be one of the longest standing open problem in automata theory. The best upper bound known for the length of a synchronizing word is $(n^3 - n)/6$ as provided by [11].

Due to the hardness results given above for finding shortest synchronizing words, there exist heuristics in the literature, known as *synchronizing heuristics*, to compute short synchronizing words. Among such heuristics are GREEDY [7], CYCLE [12], SYNCHROP [13], SYNCHROPL [13], and FASTSYNCHRO [14]. In terms of complexity, these heuristics are ordered as follows: GREEDY/CYCLE with time complexity $O(n^3 + pn^2)$, FASTSYNCHRO with time complexity $O(pn^4)$, and finally SYNCHROP/SYNCHROPL with time complexity $O(n^5 + pn^2)$ [13,14], where n is the number of states and p is the size of the alphabet. This ordering with respect to the worst case time complexity is the same if the actual performance of the algorithms are considered (see for example [14,15] for experimental comparison of the performance of these algorithms).

The SYNCHROP heuristic and its variants such as SYNCHROPL have been commonly used as a baseline to evaluate the performance of new heuristics in terms of synchronizing word length. However, since these heuristics are slow, a limited experimental setting with small-scale automata is usually employed for comparison purposes. For this reason, there exist attempts to improve the performance; for instance, a faster variant FASTSYNCHRO of SYNCHROP has been proposed in the literature. FASTSYNCHRO proposes a cheaper way to choose path to follow while generating the synchronizing words. However, the performance improvement comes with an increase on the average length of the synchronizing words [13,14].

In this work, we propose a set of techniques to make SYNCHROP much faster without changing its nature. Hence, the synchronizing words generated by the heuristic will be the same. The impact of the proposed techniques is two-fold: first, the SYNCHROP heuristic becomes more competitive to be used as a stronger benchmark for the new heuristics; our experimental results show that for 2500 states, SYNCHROP can be made 70–160× faster with our optimizations. Second, the heuristic becomes feasible to be used in practice; for instance, with 2500 states and 32 letters in the automaton, the execution time of the heuristic reduces to 66 s from 4745 s. Furthermore, the experiments reveal that suggested optimizations become more effective as the size of the automaton increases. As we will discuss later, it is straightforward to apply some of the proposed techniques to SYNCHROPL.

The rest of the paper is organized as follows: In Sect. 2, we introduce the notation used in the paper and explain SYNCHROP in detail. The proposed optimizations are introduced at Sect. 3 and experimental results are given in Sect. 4. Section 5 discusses threats to validity and Sect. 6 concludes the paper.

2   Background and Notation

A (complete and deterministic) *automaton* is defined by a triple $A = (S, \Sigma, \delta)$ where $S = \{1, 2, \ldots, n\}$ is a finite set of n states, Σ is a finite alphabet consisting of p input letters (or simply *letters*). $\delta : S \times \Sigma \to S$ is a transition function.

An element of the set Σ^* is called a *word*. For a word $w \in \Sigma^*$, we use $|w|$ to denote the length of w, and ε is the empty word. We extend the transition function δ to a set of states and to a word in the usual way. We have $\delta(i, \varepsilon) = i$, and for a word $w \in \Sigma^*$ and a letter $x \in \Sigma$, we have $\delta(i, xw) = \delta(\delta(i, x), w)$. For a set of states $C \subseteq S$, we have $\delta(C, w) = \{\delta(i, w) | i \in C\}$.

For a set of states $C \subseteq S$, let $C^2 = \{\langle i, j \rangle | i, j \in C\}$ be the set of all *multisets* with cardinality 2 with elements from C, i.e. C^2 is the set of all subsets of C with cardinality 2, where repetition is allowed. An element $\langle i, j \rangle \in C^2$ is called a *pair*. Furthermore, it is called *a singleton pair* (or *an s–pair*) if $i = j$, otherwise it is called *a different pair* (or *a d–pair*). The set of s–pairs and d–pairs in C^2 are denoted by C_s^2 and C_d^2 respectively.

A word w is said to be a *merging word for a pair* $\langle i, j \rangle \in S^2$ if $\delta(\{i, j\}, w)$ is singleton. Note that, for an s-pair $\langle i, i \rangle$, every word (including ε) is a merging word. A word w is called a *synchronizing word for an automaton* $A = (S, \Sigma, \delta)$ if $\delta(S, w)$ is singleton. An automaton A is called *synchronizing* if there exists a synchronizing word for A. In this paper, we only consider synchronizing automata.

As shown by [7], deciding if an automaton is synchronizing can be performed in time $O(pn^2)$ by checking if there exists a merging word for $\langle i, j \rangle$, for all $\langle i, j \rangle \in S^2$.

We use the notation $\delta^{-1}(i, x)$ to denote the set of those states with a transition to state i with letter x. Formally, $\delta^{-1}(i, x) = \{j \in S | \delta(j, x) = i\}$. We also define $\delta^{-1}(\langle i, j \rangle, x) = \{\langle k, \ell \rangle \mid k \in \delta^{-1}(i, x) \land \ell \in \delta^{-1}(j, x)\}$.

2.1   The SYNCHROP heuristic

SYNCHROP is composed of two phases. In the first phase, which is common to almost all existing heuristics, a shortest merging word $\tau_{\langle i,j \rangle}$ for each $\langle i, j \rangle \in S^2$ is computed by using a breadth first search such as the one given in Algorithm 1.

Algorithm 1. Computing shortest merging words for state pairs (Phase 1)

---

    input : An automaton $A = (S, \Sigma, \delta)$
    output: A shortest merging word $\tau_{\langle i,j \rangle}$ for all $\langle i, j \rangle \in S^2$
1 let Q be an initially empty queue; // Q: BFS frontier
2 $P = \emptyset$; // P: the set of nodes in the BFS forest constructed so far
3 **foreach** $\langle i, i \rangle \in S_s^2$ **do** push $\langle i, i \rangle$ onto Q, insert $\langle i, i \rangle$ into P, and set $\tau_{\langle i,i \rangle} = \varepsilon$;
4 **while** $P \neq S^2$ **do** // we still have some more pairs to discover
5      $\langle i, j \rangle$ = pop the next item from Q;
6   **foreach** $x \in \Sigma$ **do**
7   **foreach** $\langle k, \ell \rangle \in \delta^{-1}(\langle i, j \rangle, x)$ **do**
8   **if** $\langle k, \ell \rangle \notin P$ **then**
9                  $\tau_{\langle k,\ell \rangle} = x\tau_{\langle i,j \rangle}$;
10   push $\langle k, \ell \rangle$ onto Q;
11                  $P = P \cup \{\langle k, \ell \rangle\}$;

Algorithm 1 performs a breadth first search (BFS), and therefore constructs a BFS forest, rooted at s–pairs $\langle i, i \rangle \in S_s^2$, where these s–pair nodes are the nodes at level 0 of the BFS forest. A d–pair $\langle i, j \rangle$ appears at level k of the BFS forest if $|\tau_{\langle i,j \rangle}| = k$.

In almost all synchronizing heuristics, a second phase generates a synchronizing word in a constructive, step-by-step fashion. The heuristics keep track of the current set C of states, which is initially the entire set of states S. At each iteration, the cardinality of C is reduced at least by one. This is accomplished by picking a d-pair $\langle i, j \rangle \in C_d^2$, and considering $\delta(C, \tau_{\langle i,j \rangle})$ as the next active set in the next iteration. Since $\tau_{\langle i,j \rangle}$ is a merging sequence for (at least) the states i and j, the cardinality of $\delta(C, \tau_{\langle i,j \rangle})$ is guaranteed to be smaller than that of C. The synchronizing heuristics differ from each other in the way they pick the d-pair $\langle i, j \rangle \in C_d^2$ to be used at each iteration.

For a set of states $C \subseteq S$, let the cost $\phi(C)$ of C be defined as

$$\phi(C) = \sum_{i,j \in C} |\tau_{\langle i,j \rangle}|$$

$\phi(C)$ is a heuristic indication of how hard it is to bring the set C to a singleton. The intuition here is that, the larger the cost $\phi(C)$ is, the longer a synchronizing word would be required to bring C to a singleton set.

During the iterations of SYNCHROP, the selection of $\langle i,j \rangle \in C_d^2$ that will be used is performed by favoring the pair with the minimum possible cost $\delta(C, \tau_{\langle i,j \rangle})$. Based on this cost function, the second phase of SYNCHROP is given in Algorithm 2.

Algorithm 2. Computing a synchronizing word (Phase 2 of SYNCHROP)

---

    input : An automaton $A = (S, \Sigma, \delta)$ and $\tau_{\langle i,j \rangle}$ for all $\langle i,j \rangle \in S^2$
    output: A synchronizing word Γ for A
1 $C = S$; // C: current state set
2 $\Gamma = \varepsilon$; // Γ: synchronizing word to be constructed, initially empty
3 **while** $|C| > 1$ **do** // still not a singleton
4     $minCost = \infty$
5   **foreach** *d–pair* $\langle i,j \rangle \in C_d^2$ **do**
6        $thisPairCost = \phi(\delta(C, \tau_{\langle i,j \rangle}))$
7   **if** $thisPairCost < minCost$ **then**
8           $minCost = thisPairCost$
9           $\tau' = \tau_{\langle i,j \rangle}$
10    $\Gamma = \Gamma\, \tau'$; // append τ' to the synchronizing word
11    $C = \delta(C, \tau')$; // update current state set with τ'

---

3 Speeding up SYNCHROP and its Variants

In this section, we will introduce three improvements for increasing the performance of SYNCHROP. The first improvement explained in Sect. 3.1 precomputes the cost of $\delta(C, \tau_{\langle i,j \rangle})$ under certain conditions to eliminate some redundant cost computations. The improvement explained in Sect. 3.2 is in fact an improvement over the approach given in Sect. 3.1 where the precomputations are delayed until they are necessary. Finally in Sect. 3.3, we explain a particular improvement that can accelerate the first iteration of SYNCHROP, which in practice is the most expensive iteration of SYNCHROP.

3.1 Eliminating Redundant Cost Computations

The first improvement is based on the following observation. For each d–pair $\langle i,j \rangle \in C_d^2$, the cost $\phi(\delta(C, \tau_{\langle i,j \rangle}))$ is calculated at line 6 of Algorithm 2. Suppose that for two different d–pairs $\langle i,j \rangle, \langle i',j' \rangle \in C_d^2$, we have $\tau_{\langle i,j \rangle} = \tau_{\langle i',j' \rangle}$. In this case, we surely have $\delta(C, \tau_{\langle i,j \rangle}) = \delta(C, \tau_{\langle i',j' \rangle})$. Therefore, computing the cost $\phi(\delta(C, \tau_{\langle i,j \rangle}))$ and $\phi(\delta(C, \tau_{\langle i',j' \rangle}))$ separately is a redundant work.

One approach to eliminate these redundant cost computations can be the following. For an integer $k \geq 1$, consider the set of non–empty words $\Sigma^{\leq k}$ of length at most k. Formally, $\Sigma^{\leq k} = \{\sigma \mid \sigma \in \Sigma^*, 1 \leq |\sigma| \leq k\}$. In each iteration of SYNCHROP, one can precompute the cost $\phi(\delta(C, \sigma))$ for all $\sigma \in \Sigma^{\leq k}$. For any d–pair $\langle i,j \rangle \in C_d^2$, one can then simply look up the precomputed cost $\phi(\delta(C, \tau_{\langle i,j \rangle}))$ when $|\tau_{\langle i,j \rangle}| \leq k$. For a word $\sigma \in \Sigma^{\leq k}$, let $\Phi(\sigma)$ be this precomputed cost of $\phi(\delta(C, \sigma))$ for the current iteration with the active state set C. Although, the values of $\phi(\delta(C,\sigma))$ and $\Phi(\sigma)$ are the same, the main difference is that ϕ is an expensive function and Φ is a data structure that stores a set of precomputed values of ϕ. Using the precomputed cost $\Phi(\sigma)$ for all $\sigma \in \Sigma^{\leq k}$, the second phase of SYNCHROP can be modified as shown in Algorithm 3.

Algorithm 3. Computing a synchronizing word (modified Phase 2 of SYNCHROP)

---

    input : An automaton $A = (S, \Sigma, \delta)$ and $\tau_{\langle i,j \rangle}$ for all $\langle i,j \rangle \in S^2$, an integer
        $k \geq 1$
    output: A synchronizing word Γ for A

1 $C = S$; // C: current state set
2 $\Gamma = \varepsilon$; // Γ: synchronizing word to be constructed, initially empty
3 **while** $|C| > 1$ **do** // still not a singleton
4   **foreach** $\sigma \in \Sigma^{\leq k}$ **do** $\Phi(\sigma) = \phi(\delta(C,\sigma))$; // precompute $\Phi(\sigma)$
5      $minCost = \infty$
6   **foreach** d–*pair* $\langle i,j \rangle \in C_d^2$ **do**
7   **if** $|\tau_{\langle i,j \rangle}| \leq k$ **then**
8              $thisPairCost = \Phi(\tau_{\langle i,j \rangle})$
9   **else**
10             $thisPairCost = \phi(\delta(C,\tau_{\langle i,j \rangle}))$
11   **if** $thisPairCost < minCost$ **then**
12             $minCost = thisPairCost$
13             $\tau' = \tau_{\langle i,j \rangle}$
14      $\Gamma = \Gamma\,\tau'$; // append τ' to the synchronizing word
15      $C = \delta(C,\tau')$; // update current state set with τ'

Although the improvement is always useful for eliminating duplicate computations in theory, one needs to be careful in practice. Indeed, the larger the value of k is, the more benefit one can obtain by eliminating such computations. However, the number of precomputed costs, and hence, the amount of memory to store the results of these computations also increase exponentially with k. Formally, for a given k, the number of different sequences whose costs are precomputed is equal to

$$K = \sum_{\ell=1}^{k} p^\ell = \frac{p^{k+1} - 1}{p - 1} - 1$$

where p is the alphabet size. We need to use $\Theta(K)$ space to store the precomputed costs. Let C be the active state set for the current iteration; each sequence τ can be applied with $\Theta(|C| \times |\tau|)$ automata accesses and the cost of the new state set $\delta(C,\tau)$ can be computed in $O(|C|^2)$ time and $O(|C|)$ extra memory to store the next active state set. Since there are K possible sequences in total, the overall cost of the precomputation phase for a single iteration is

$$O\left(|C|\sum_{\ell=1}^{k} \ell p^\ell + |C|^2 K\right) = O\left(|C|\frac{p - (k+1)p^{k+1} + kp^{k+2}}{(p-1)^2} + |C|^2 K\right).$$

To avoid the first part, we interleaved the automata accesses and cost computations; since $\Phi(\sigma)$ is computed for all $\sigma \in \Sigma^{\leq k}$, the state set $\delta(C, \sigma)$ can be stored and used to compute $\delta(C, \sigma x)$ with only $O(|C|)$ automata accesses for all $x \in \Sigma$ and $\sigma \in \Sigma^{<k}$. Overall, this yields $O(|C|K)$ automata accesses and $O(|C|^2 K)$ time complexity for a single iteration. This implementation requires $O(|C|k)$ extra space to store the intermediate active state sets.

3.2   Lazy Computation of Sequence Costs

The approach explained in Sect. 3.1 precomputes $\Phi(\sigma)$ for all $\sigma \in \Sigma^{\leq k}$. However in an iteration of Algorithm 3, the only $\Phi(\sigma)$ values that we benefit from are the ones for which $\sigma = \tau_{\langle i,j \rangle}$ for some $\langle i, j \rangle \in C_d^2$. Therefore, rather than precomputing $\Phi(\sigma)$ for all $\sigma \in \Sigma^{\leq k}$, it is better if we could precompute $\Phi(\sigma)$ for only those $\sigma \in \Sigma^{\leq k}$ such that $\sigma = \tau_{\langle i,j \rangle}$ for some $\langle i, j \rangle \in C_d^2$.

One way of accomplishing this is to use a lazy computation approach to construct the data structure Φ. More explicitly, one can compute $\Phi(\sigma)$ for a $\sigma = \tau_{\langle i,j \rangle}$ the first time it is used in the iteration, and then store it for further uses in the same iteration. Algorithm 4 given below implements this approach.

Algorithm 4. Computing a synchronizing word (modified Phase 2 of SYN-CHROP with lazy $\Phi(\sigma)$ computation

---

    input : An automaton $A = (S, \Sigma, \delta)$ and $\tau_{\langle i,j \rangle}$ for all $\langle i, j \rangle \in S^2$, an integer
          $k \geq 1$
    output: A synchronizing word Γ for A

1   $C = S$; // C: current state set
2   $\Gamma = \varepsilon$; // Γ: synchronizing word to be constructed, initially empty
3   **while** $|C| > 1$ **do** // still not a singleton
4   **foreach** $\sigma \in \Sigma^{\leq k}$ **do** $\Phi(\sigma) = \infty$;
5      $minCost = \infty$;
6   **foreach** d-$pair$ $\langle i, j \rangle \in C_d^2$ **do**
7   **if** $|\tau_{\langle i,j \rangle}| \leq k$ **then**
8   **if** $\Phi(\tau_{\langle i,j \rangle}) = \infty$ **then**
9                  $\Phi(\tau_{\langle i,j \rangle}) = \phi(\delta(C, \tau_{\langle i,j \rangle}))$
10              $thisPairCost = \Phi(\tau_{\langle i,j \rangle})$
11   **else**
12              $thisPairCost = \phi(\delta(C, \tau_{\langle i,j \rangle}))$
13   **if** $thisPairCost < minCost$ **then**
14              $minCost = thisPairCost$
15              $\tau' = \tau_{\langle i,j \rangle}$
16      $\Gamma = \Gamma \tau'$; // append τ' to the synchronizing word
17      $C = \delta(C, \tau')$; // update current state set with τ'

Similar to the improvement described above, the space complexity for this improvement is also $\Theta(K)$ when a simple vector/array is used for Φ and the sequences are indexed and queried based on their ordered letters. Let C be the active state set in the current iteration. With lazy computation, the number of different sequences, and hence, the number of cost computations, is bounded by the number of state pairs $\langle i, j \rangle \in C_d^2$. Considering $C = O(n)$, this yields a space complexity of $O(\min(K, n^2))$. This complexity can be easily obtained with a set or better with a hash table. Obviously, using such data structures will increase the query costs to the precomputed values. In our implementation, we use a simple vector for Φ that implies a $\Theta(K)$ complexity. However, we also select k in a way that makes $K = O(n^2)$ as described below.

Lazy computation does not have an impact on theoretical time complexity since all the cost computations are already meant to be done by the original SYNCHROP. That is there is no redundant cost computation incurred by the improvement. However, the k value still needs to be set to have a better memory utilization. To restrict the memory usage in a judicious way, we use the largest integer that satisfies

$$\left| \{ \langle i, j \rangle \in S_d^2 : \tau_{\langle i,j \rangle} \in \Sigma^{\leq k} \} \right| \geq \sum_{\ell=1}^{k} p^\ell.$$

The right-hand of the inequality is the amount of memory that will be used and the left-hand side is the number of pairs in S_d^2 that can benefit from the improvement with maximum sequence length k. Since the left-hand side is $O(n^2)$, the memory complexity follows.

3.3   Accelerating the First Iteration

The final improvement that will be suggested in this paper is based on the following observation.

Lemma 1. *Let $C \subseteq S$ be a subset of states and $\langle i, j \rangle, \langle i', j' \rangle \in C_d^2$ be two d–pairs such that $\tau_{\langle i,j \rangle} = \sigma \tau_{\langle i',j' \rangle}$ for some $\sigma \in \Sigma^*$. If $\delta(C, \sigma) \subseteq C$ then $\phi(\delta(C, \tau_{\langle i,j \rangle})) \leq \phi(\delta(C, \tau_{\langle i',j' \rangle}))$.*

Proof. We have $\delta(C, \tau_{\langle i,j \rangle}) = \delta(\delta(C, \sigma), \tau_{\langle i',j' \rangle}) \subseteq \delta(C, \tau_{\langle i',j' \rangle})$, where the last step is due to the fact that $\delta(C, \sigma) \subseteq C$. Since $\delta(C, \tau_{\langle i,j \rangle}) \subseteq \delta(C, \tau_{\langle i',j' \rangle})$, we have $\phi(\delta(C, \tau_{\langle i,j \rangle})) \leq \phi(\delta(C, \tau_{\langle i',j' \rangle}))$.

Lemma 1 suggests that in an iteration of SYNCHROP if we have a set C, d–pairs $\langle i, j \rangle, \langle i', j' \rangle \in C_d^2$ satisfying the preconditions stated in Lemma 1, then we can eliminate the consideration of the d–pair $\langle i', j' \rangle$ in that iteration, since we will always have $\phi(\delta(C, \tau_{\langle i,j \rangle})) \leq \phi(\delta(C, \tau_{\langle i',j' \rangle}))$. Although it may feel highly unlikely to fulfill the preconditions of Lemma 1, Corollary 1 given below explains how Lemma 1 can easily be used in the first iteration of SYNCHROP.

Corollary 1. *For two d–pairs $\langle i, j \rangle, \langle i', j' \rangle \in S_d^2$ if $\tau_{\langle i,j \rangle} = \sigma \tau_{\langle i',j' \rangle}$ for some $\sigma \in \Sigma^*$, then $\phi(\delta(S, \tau_{\langle i,j \rangle})) \leq \phi(\delta(S, \tau_{\langle i',j' \rangle}))$.*

Proof. Consider Lemma 1 when $C = S$.

Corollary 1 gives us the following improvement opportunity. In the first iteration of SYNCHROP, it is sufficient to consider only those d–pairs $\langle i, j \rangle \in S_d^2$ such that $\tau_{\langle i,j \rangle}$ is not a suffix of $\tau_{\langle i',j' \rangle}$ for any other d–pair $\langle i', j' \rangle \in S_d^2$. Notice how Algorithm 1 constructs the shortest merging sequences by using other shortest merging sequences as suffix at line 9.

3.4   Speeding up SYNCHROPL

The proposed techniques can be exploited also for SYNCHROP variants such as SYNCHROPL and FASTSYNCHRO. Let $C \subseteq S$ be the current active state set. For a sequence $\sigma \in \Sigma^*$, SYNCHROPL uses the cost function

$$\phi_{PL}(\delta(C,\sigma)) = \phi(\delta(C,\sigma)) + f(\sigma) = \sum_{i,j \in C} |\tau_{\langle i,j \rangle}| + f(\sigma)$$

where $f(.)$ is a function used to make the shorter sequences more preferable. It is suggested to use $f(\sigma) = |\sigma|$ where $|\sigma|$ denotes the length of the sequence σ [13]. The improvements based on precomputation and lazy computation can be easily adapted for this cost function. However, applying the last improvement is not straightforward since we omit the suffix sequences which are shorter than the sequences the improvement takes into account.

Using the proposed techniques with other cost functions such as the cardinality of active state sets, i.e., $\phi'(\delta(C,\sigma)) = |\delta(C,\sigma)|$, is also possible. However, the speedups for cheaper heuristics may not be as much as the ones that we obtain for SYNCHROP which we will show in the next section.

4   Experimental Results

All the experiments in the paper are performed on a single machine running on 64 bit CentOS 6.5 equipped with 64 GB RAM and a dual-socket Intel Xeon E5-2620 v4 clocked at 2.10 GHz where each socket has 8 cores (16 in total) and 20 MB cache. We only used a single core and all the speedups are obtained with no parallelization. The codes are compiled with gcc 4.9.2 with the -O3 optimization flag enabled.

To measure the impact of the proposed techniques, we used randomly generated automatons[1] with $n \in \{500, 1000, 1500, 2000, 2500\}$ states and $p \in \{2, 8, 32\}$ inputs. For each (n, p) pair, we randomly generated 5 different automata and executed each algorithm on them. The values in the figures and the tables are the averages of these 5 executions for each configuration.

4.1   Selecting the Target to Optimize

As described above, SYNCHROP has two phases where the first is common to many other synchronizing heuristics. In a previous study, we proposed algorithms

---

[1] For each state s and input x, $\delta(s, x)$ is randomly assigned to a state $s' \in S$.

to parallellize the first phase on a shared-memory multicore system [16]. The second phase is the one which makes SYNCHROP recognized as one of the slowest heuristics in the literature. This is why we, in this study, targeted this phase. We measured the execution times of the phases individually to observe the impact of the second phase's execution time to the overall execution time. As Table 1 shows, the second phase is responsible for almost all the execution time of the heuristic.

Table 1. The ratio of the execution time of Phase 2 (Algorithm 2) to the overall execution time of SYNCHROP, i.e., Phase 1 (Algorithm 1) + Phase 2.

		n: number of states				
		500	1000	1500	2000	2500
p	2	0.991	0.997	0.999	0.999	0.999
	8	0.991	0.998	0.999	0.999	1.000
	32	0.982	0.995	0.998	0.999	0.999

4.2 Impact of the Proposed Techniques

To measure the impact of the proposed techniques, we run them on the random automata we generated as explained above. Table 2 shows the results of these experiments. The timings in the table are for the whole heuristic, Phase 1 and Phase 2, for each variant. As the results show, the proposed improvements, especially lazy cost computation, reduce the runtime of SYNCHROP significantly and more than 100 speedups are obtained for some automata type. For each n and p, the exact speedups for each variant are given in Fig. 1. As the trend of each subfigure shows, the impact of the proposed techniques increase with n. Although, the speedups seem to decrease with increasing p, the absolute difference between the naive SYNCHROP's execution time and those of the proposed variants increase.

As expected, each of the proposed techniques increases the performance, but with different amounts; the lazy cost computation is proven to be the most useful one. We later target the first iteration and added the third one described in Sect. 3.3 on top of lazy computation. Although its impact is not significant in practice, we were expecting more. Because, when the execution times of the Phase 2 iterations for the proposed lazy computation variant are measured, as Fig. 2 shows, the first one dominates the overall execution time. Here the figure shows only the case for $n = 2500$. However, the same trend can be obtained for other automata sizes. We show the trend here for completeness and point out the bottleneck of our implementation for future studies. To overcome this bottleneck, other suffix or subset-based improvements can be applied. A promising one is representing an active state set with an unknown cost as a union/difference of other active sets whose costs are precomputed. This representation, with an efficient implementation, can be a great tool to reduce the number of cost computations.

Table 2. The execution times of the SYNCHROP variants (in seconds) for $n \in \{500, 1000, 1500, 2000, 2500\}$ and $p \in \{2, 8, 32\}$. The first row for each p value is the baseline implementation from [15] and the second one is our baseline implementation. The next two rows are the variants with precomputation and lazy cost computation, respectively. The fifth and the last row is the one with additional first iteration optimization on top of lazy computation. Each value is average of five executions.

	Algorithm	n: number of states				
		500	1000	1500	2000	2500
$p = 2$	Baseline [15]	6.2	72.0	324.5	969.1	2309.3
	Naive	2.6	30.4	133.3	382.5	881.7
	Precompute	1.3	10.0	67.5	108.6	308.7
	Lazy	0.2	0.9	2.1	4.3	7.7
	First Iter.	0.1	0.6	1.6	3.2	5.4
$p = 8$	Baseline [15]	9.5	123.1	682.8	2179.7	5440.8
	Naive	6.3	90.4	418.5	1247.3	2946.0
	Precompute	1.8	42.4	93.1	164.4	1687.2
	Lazy	0.3	1.7	8.6	19.9	33.1
	First Iter.	0.3	1.6	7.9	18.6	31.2
$p = 32$	Baseline [15]	12.9	162.5	785.3	2438.3	6085.4
	Naive	9.7	140.4	658.2	2008.7	4745.6
	Precompute	3.0	11.8	625.0	1113.9	1691.9
	Lazy	0.9	8.4	22.4	43.4	68.3
	First Iter.	0.9	8.2	22.0	42.1	66.7

5   Threats to Validity

We consider several threats to validity of the methods suggested in this paper. First of all, to eliminate any implementation errors we may have in the new algorithms, we always check if a word w found by our implementations is a synchronizing word or not, by checking if $\delta(S, w)$ is singleton or not.

At each iteration, SYNCHROP selects a pair with minimum cost. Therefore the computed synchronizing sequence may change by picking a different pair with same cost. Algorithms 3 and 4 search the pair as in Algorithm 2, i.e. they pick the same pair by avoiding redundant computation. We also carefully implemented the variants in such a way that even the tie-breaking mechanisms become the same for all variants. In this way, we are able to check if the synchronizing words are the same for each variant which was the case in our experiments. On the other hand, the use of Corollary 1 can possibly eliminate some pairs with a minimum cost. Hence the algorithm may pick different pair with same cost. However we observed the same synchronizing sequences in our experiments (Table 3).

Since we consider the speed ups over our naive SYNCHROP implementation, we need to be sure that our baseline implementation is competitive in

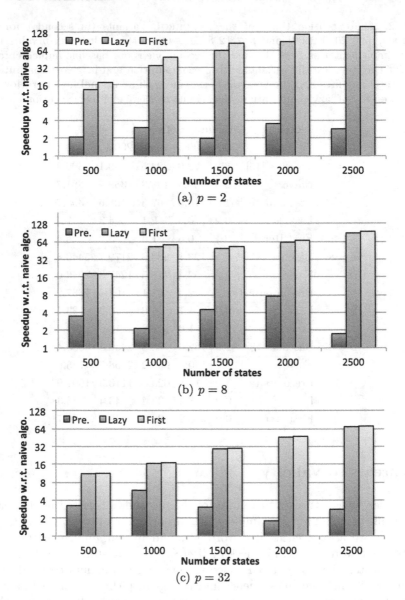

Fig. 1. The speedup values normalized w.r.t. the naive SYNCHROP baseline for $n \in \{500, 1000, 1500, 2000, 2500\}$ and $p \in \{2, 8, 32\}$.

terms of performance and word lengths. In this respect, we compared the synchronizing word lengths of our naive implementation and those of [15] for 75 automata used in our experiments; the average ratio of the former to the latter is 1.01 for SYNCHROP, with a standard deviation of 0.02. In order to judge the time performance of our naive variant objectively, we also compared our naive

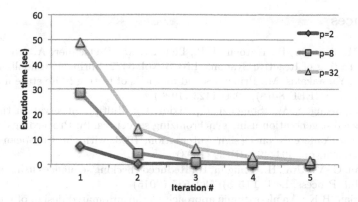

Fig. 2. The execution times of the iterations of the Lazy variant for $n = 2500$.

Table 3. The length of the synchronizing sequences for $n \in \{500, 1000, 1500, 2000, 2500\}$ and $p \in \{2, 8, 32\}$.

p	n: # automata states				
	500	1000	1500	2000	2500
2	78.6	111.2	147.4	160.6	192.8
8	45.4	70.2	85.6	98.6	111.2
32	37.8	54.8	66.6	78.2	88.0

implementation to the one in [15] as shown in Table 2. The comparison shows that our naive implementation is comparable to the state-of-the-art used in the literature.

6   Conclusion and Future Work

In this work, we proposed techniques to speedup SYNCHROP which is shown to produce shorter synchronizing words compared to cheaper heuristics such as GREEDY and CYCLE. Using various optimizations, we obtained order(s) of magnitude speed up for SYNCHROP. The techniques suggested in this paper become more effective as the size, i.e., the number of states, of the automata increases. With these improvements, SYNCHROP is more scalable and is highly practical even for automata with thousands of states.

Acknowledgments. This work was supported by The Scientific and Technological Research Council of Turkey (TÜBİTAK) [grant number 114E569].

    We would like to thank the authors of [15] for providing their heuristics implementations, which we used to compare our naive baseline implementation as given in Table 2.

References

1. Broy, M., Jonsson, B., Katoen, J.-P., Leucker, M., Pretschner, A. (eds.): Model-Based Testing of Reactive Systems. LNCS, vol. 3472. Springer, Heidelberg (2005)
2. Lee, D., Yannakakis, M.: Principles and methods of testing finite state machines-a survey. Proc. IEEE **84**(8), 1090–1123 (1996)
3. Cho, H., Jeong, S.-W., Somenzi, F., Pixley, C.: Multiple observation time single reference test generation using synchronizing sequences. In: Proceedings of the 4th European Conference on Design Automation, 1993, with the European Event in ASIC Design, pp. 494–498. IEEE (1993)
4. Jourdan, G.-V., Ural, H., Yenigün, H.: Reduced checking sequences using unreliable reset. Inf. Process. Lett. **115**(5), 532–535 (2015)
5. Natarajan, B.K.: An algorithmic approach to the automated design of parts orienters. In: 27th Annual Symposium on Foundations of Computer Science, Toronto, Canada, 27–29 October 1986, pp. 132–142. IEEE Computer Society (1986)
6. Volkov, M.V.: Synchronizing automata and the Černý conjecture. In: Martín-Vide, C., Otto, F., Fernau, H. (eds.) LATA 2008. LNCS, vol. 5196, pp. 11–27. Springer, Heidelberg (2008). doi:10.1007/978-3-540-88282-4_4
7. Eppstein, D.: Reset sequences for monotonic automata. SIAM J. Comput. **19**(3), 500–510 (1990)
8. Olschewski, J., Ummels, M.: The complexity of finding reset words in finite automata. In: Hliněný, P., Kučera, A. (eds.) MFCS 2010. LNCS, vol. 6281, pp. 568–579. Springer, Heidelberg (2010). doi:10.1007/978-3-642-15155-2_50
9. Černý, J.: Poznámka k homogénnym experimentom s konečnými automatmi. Matematicko-fyzikálny časopis **14**(3), 208–216 (1964)
10. Černý, J., Pirická, A., Rosenauerová, B.: On directable automata. Kybernetika **7**(4), 289–298 (1971)
11. Pin, J.-E.: On two combinatorial problems arising from automata theory. North-Holland Math. Stud. **75**, 535–548 (1983)
12. Trahtman, A.N.: Some results of implemented algorithms of synchronization. In: 10th Journees Montoises d'Inform (2004)
13. Roman, A.: Synchronizing finite automata with short reset words. Appl. Math. Comput. **209**(1), 125–136 (2009)
14. Kudlacik, R., Roman, A., Wagner, H.: Effective synchronizing algorithms. Expert Syst. Appl. **39**(14), 11746–11757 (2012)
15. Roman, A., Szykula, M.: Forward and backward synchronizing algorithms. Expert Syst. Appl. **42**(24), 9512–9527 (2015)
16. Karahoda, S., Erenay, O.T., Kaya, K., Türker, U.C., Yenigün, H.: Parallelizing heuristics for generating synchronizing sequences. In: Wotawa, F., Nica, M., Kushik, N. (eds.) ICTSS 2016. LNCS, vol. 9976, pp. 106–122. Springer, Cham (2016). doi:10.1007/978-3-319-47443-4_7

Testing Timed and Distributed Systems

GREP: Games for the Runtime Enforcement of Properties

Matthieu Renard[1], Antoine Rollet[1(✉)], and Yliès Falcone[2]

[1] LaBRI, Bordeaux INP, University of Bordeaux, Bordeaux, France
{matthieu.renard,antoine.rollet}@labri.fr
[2] Univ. Grenoble Alpes, CNRS, Inria, Grenoble INP, LIG, 38000 Grenoble, France
ylies.falcone@univ-grenoble-alpes.fr

Abstract. We present GREP, a tool for the runtime enforcement of (timed) properties. GREP takes an execution sequence as input (*stdin*), and modifies it (*stdout*) as necessary to enforce the desired property, when possible. GREP can enforce any regular timed property described by a deterministic and complete Timed Automaton. The main novelties of GREP are twofold: it uses game theory to improve the synthesis of enforcement mechanisms, and it accounts for *uncontrollable* events, i.e. events that cannot be controlled by the enforcement mechanisms and thus have to be released immediately. We present an overview of GREP and validate its usability with a performance evaluation.

1 Runtime Enforcement of Timed Properties with Uncontrollable Events

Runtime Verification (RV, [5,10,12]), also referred to as passive testing [2,8], consists in checking if the execution of a running system satisfies some given specification. Unlike static verification, RV studies a real execution of a system, possibly after deployment. This paper deals with *runtime enforcement* (RE, [6,11,13,19]), an extension of runtime verification where executions are corrected when they violate the desired property (see [9] for an overview). An enforcement mechanism (EM) modifies the execution of a running system: it takes an execution as input and outputs a possibly-different execution. One of the advantages of RE is that the whole specification of the system under scrutiny is not necessary to generate an EM, only a property that should be satisfied by its output is needed. The general scheme is given in Fig. 1.

We distinguish two categories of actions: *controllable* actions which can be modified by an enforcement mechanism, and *uncontrollable* actions which can only be observed by the enforcement mechanism. Enforcement mechanisms should be *sound*, *compliant* and *optimal*, meaning that the output should satisfy the specification when possible, the output should be as close to the input as possible, and the output should be maximal, respectively. In [16,17], we introduce runtime enforcement for timed properties with uncontrollable events, and we propose a game approach for generating the EM in [18]. A comparison of this

© IFIP International Federation for Information Processing 2017
Published by Springer International Publishing AG 2017. All Rights Reserved
N. Yevtushenko et al. (Eds.): ICTSS 2017, LNCS 10533, pp. 259–275, 2017.
DOI: 10.1007/978-3-319-67549-7_16

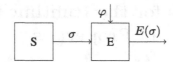

Fig. 1. Schematic description of an enforcement mechanism E, modifying the execution σ of the system S to $E(\sigma)$, so that it satisfies the property φ.

approach with related work may also be found in [16]. GREP implements the game approach of [18] extended to timed properties.

1.1 Timed Properties and Automata

In this paper, properties are modelled with regular timed properties described by Timed Automata (TA) [4]. Consider the following property on a simple shared storage device: after authentication, a user can write a value only if the storage has been unlocked for at least 2 time units. (Un)locking the device is decided by another party, meaning that it is not controllable by the user. This property is formalised by the TA φ_t given in Fig. 2, with the alphabet of uncontrollable actions $\{\texttt{LockOn}, \texttt{LockOff}, \texttt{Auth}\}$. In φ_t, the set of locations is $L = \{l_0, l_1, l_2, l_3\}$; the initial location is l_0; the set $X = \{x\}$ made of a single clock x is used to model time; the alphabet of all actions is $\Sigma = \{\texttt{Auth}, \texttt{LockOn}, \texttt{LockOff}, \texttt{Write}\}$; the set of accepting locations is $G = \{l_1, l_2\}$; and the set of transitions Δ contains, for example, $(l_1, x \geq 2, \texttt{Write}, \emptyset, l_1)$. A transition is composed of an initial location, a guard, an action, a set of clocks to reset, and a target location. For instance, the transition $(l_1, x \geq 2, \texttt{Write}, \emptyset, l_1)$ means that location l_1 is reached from location l_1 if the $\texttt{Write}$ action occurs when clock x is greater than or equal to 2, with no clock to reset; and $(l_2, \top, \texttt{LockOff}, \{x\}, l_1)$, means that l_1 is reached from l_2 when the $\texttt{LockOff}$ action occurs, resetting clock x while taking the transition.

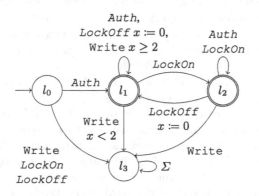

Fig. 2. Property φ_t modelling writes on a shared storage device [17]

1.2   Description of the Approach

The strategy of GREP is based on the enforcement approach proposed in [16,18]. As shown in Fig. 1, an EM may be seen as a function from timed words to timed words, with the ability to delay some controllable actions using a memory, but with no possibility to act on uncontrollable actions. This mechanism should ensure the correctness of the output sequence (*soundness*), that the order of controllable actions is preserved and that uncontrollable actions are immediately released (*compliance*), and that the output is maximal (*optimality*). All these definitions, as well as the proofs of correctness and details of the EM generation, at two levels of abstraction (functional and operational), are provided in [16]. Notice that unlike the approach in [15], there could be some situations where the property may not be enforceable, since uncontrollable actions cannot be retained.

Let us provide the intuition on the approach using an example. Consider property φ_t given in Fig. 2, and the input sequence $(1, Auth)$ $(1, LockOn)$ $(2, Write)$ $(1, LockOff)$ $(1, LockOn)$ $(1, Write)$ $(1, LockOff)$. Table 1 gives the evolution of the system at different time instants, providing the output of the EM at a given date, its complete expected output if no other event is received (the output at an infinite date), and the state of the memory (the stored controllable actions) at an infinite date. At $t = 1$ and $t = 2$ respectively, $Auth$ and $LockOn$ actions are received. Since they are uncontrollable actions, they are released immediately. At $t = 4$, action $Write$ is received. Since it is controllable and to prevent reaching a bad state a bad state, it is stored in the memory. At $t = 5$, the uncontrollable action $LockOff$ is received and immediately released. Now it is possible to emit the stored $Write$ action, but only after 2 time units. For this reason, $(2, Write)$ is added at the end of σ_s meaning that $Write$ should be emitted in 2 time units, and it is removed from σ_c. At $t = 6$, another uncontrollable $LockOn$ action is received and immediately released. At this step, it is not possible to emit $Write$ anymore, then it is removed from the end of σ_s and put back at the beginning of σ_c. At $t = 7$, another controllable $Write$ action is received and stored (added at the end of σ_c). At $t = 8$, the last uncontrollable $LockOff$ action is received, allowing to emit the two $Write$ actions after 2 time units. Thus, they are placed at the end of σ_s and removed from σ_c. Since no other action is received afterwards, the two $Write$ actions are released at $t = 10$.

1.3   Games

In order to improve the computation time of the EM at runtime, it is possible to pre-compute the behaviour of the EM ahead of the execution and storing it. For this purpose, we use game theory. GREP builds a two-player game graph representing the possible actions of the EM and the system under scrutiny (that acts as the environment). Each vertex of the graph belongs to one of these two players, and each edge represents a possible action of the player that owns the source vertex. GREP then solves a Büchi game by computing a set of nodes

Table 1. Table showing the evolution of the enforcement mechanism with input $(1, Auth) (1, LockOn) (2, Write) (1, LockOff) (1, LockOn) (1, Write) (1, LockOff)$ over time.

t	Output	Complete expected output	Buffer
1	$(1, Auth)$	$(1, Auth)$	ϵ
2	$(1, Auth) (1, LockOn)$	$(1, Auth) (1, LockOn)$	ϵ
4	$(1, Auth) (1, LockOn)$	$(1, Auth) (1, LockOn)$	Write
5	$(1, Auth) (1, LockOn) (3, LockOff)$	$(1, Auth)$ $(1, LockOn)$ $(3, LockOff)$ $(2, Write)$	ϵ
6	$(1, Auth)$ $(1, LockOn)$ $(3, LockOff)$ $(1, LockOn)$	$(1, Auth)$ $(1, LockOn)$ $(3, LockOff)$ $(1, LockOn)$	Write
7	$(1, Auth)$ $(1, LockOn)$ $(3, LockOff)$ $(1, LockOn)$	$(1, Auth)$ $(1, LockOn)$ $(3, LockOff)$ $(1, LockOn)$	Write Write
8	$(1, Auth)$ $(1, LockOn)$ $(3, LockOff)$ $(1, LockOn) (2, LockOff)$	$(1, Auth)$ $(1, LockOn)$ $(3, LockOff)$ $(1, LockOn)$ $(2, LockOff)$ $(2, Write)$ $(0, Write)$	ϵ
10	$(1, Auth)$ $(1, LockOn)$ $(3, LockOff)$ $(1, LockOn)$ $(2, LockOff)$ $(2, Write)$ $(0, Write)$	$(1, Auth)$ $(1, LockOn)$ $(3, LockOff)$ $(1, LockOn)$ $(2, LockOff)$ $(2, Write)$ $(0, Write)$	ϵ

of the graph from which there exists a winning strategy. More details may be found in [18]. Using this approach allows us to avoid the exploration of the whole execution tree at runtime.

More precisely, GREP proceeds in three steps: first, it computes a symbolic graph, which is a finite abstraction of the (infinite) semantics of the TA; then it computes the game graph and the winning strategy for the EM; finally the EM follows the strategy to enforce the property.

The symbolic graph abstracting the semantics of the TA is similar to the usual zone graph used to compute reachability on TAs (see for example [7]), except that the successor relation is more constraining. In the usual zone graph, it is only required that a state in a vertex (vertices can be seen as sets of states of the semantics of the TA that share the same location) can reach a state in the successor vertex, whereas for our purpose it is required that all the states in a vertex can reach a state in the successor vertex. This holds for delay transitions (transitions representing elapse of time) and action transitions (representing a transition in the TA) which are built in the same way. We also require that each vertex has at most only one time successor (i.e. a node reached by letting time elapse, as opposed to nodes reached by outputting events (action successors)). An algorithm to compute such a graph is given in [3], for example.

The game graph is then built upon this symbolic abstraction graph. Each vertex of the symbolic abstraction graph is duplicated, one of the resulting vertices belongs to player 0 (the EM), and the other to player 1 (the environment). Each of these vertices is then associated with words taken from a finite, prefix-closed set of controllable words, each vertex being duplicated again for every word from this set. This set of controllable words is computed to ensure that the strategy is always the best one (the one outputting the maximal word) using only these vertices. For a formal description of this set in case of untimed properties, see [18]. The edges of the game graph represent the actions of the player: an edge leaving a node belonging to player 0 represents either the emission of the first event of the associated word (which represents the stored controllable actions), leading to a vertex belonging to player 0 again, since an EM can output multiple events at the same time, or to the same node which belongs to player 1, meaning that the EM decides not to emit for the moment and lets the environment play. An edge leaving a vertex belonging to player 1 leads to a vertex belonging to player 0, and represents either the reception of an uncontrollable event (changing the symbolic state to an action successor), the reception of a controllable event (changing the associated word), or the elapse of time (changing the symbolic state to the time successor). Nodes that are their own time successor (i.e. that contain all the valuations reached by letting time elapse) have their corresponding edge replaced by an edge leading to the same vertex which belongs to player 0. This corresponds to receiving no more event, thus allowing us to consider finite inputs, but with infinite plays over the graph (since there will be a loop between a node belonging to player 0 where the EM will decide not to emit anything, and the environment not receiving any event and being stable by elapse of time). A formal definition of the game graph for untimed properties can be found in [18] too. GREP builds a game graph which is similar, except that some nodes have time successors.

After having constructed the game graph, GREP computes the winning set of nodes of the Büchi game with Büchi nodes (the nodes to be always reachable) defined as all the vertices of the game graph whose symbolic location of a vertex is an accepting location of the TA for player 0.

Then, GREP can follow a real execution on the game graph, by watching the node that has been reached so far by its output, and the nodes that can be reached by emitting stored controllable actions (i.e. following the corresponding edges in the game graph). Whenever a winning node is reached by player 0, the strategy is to emit as many events as possible, remaining in a winning node all the time. Since the winning nodes are winning a Büchi game, it is always possible for player 0 to stay in a winning node whenever one is reached. Whenever a winning node is reached, the output of the EM is then guaranteed to satisfy the property.

An example of game graph associated with property φ_t given in Fig. 2 is provided in Fig. 3. In this graph, nodes are labelled with a tuple (l, z, w, p), where l is the location of the TA associated with the node, z is the zone (set of clock constraints), w is the word of controllable actions as described previously, and p is the player: 0 for the enforcement mechanism, and 1 for the environment. The square node is the initial node, the blue (rectangular) ones are the winning nodes, and the nodes that are double-circled are the nodes whose locations are accepting. Note that in our example, all the accepting nodes (double-circled) are winning (blue, rectangular). The edges have different colours and heads, depending on their role: green edges (filled triangular heads) correspond to the EM emitting its first stored controllable action, blue ones (empty triangular heads) to the EM not emitting (thus letting the environment play), red (filled diamond heads) and orange (empty diamond heads) edges correspond to the reception of an uncontrollable event and a controllable one, respectively, and purple ("vee" heads) edges represent the elapse of time (they lead to the time successor).

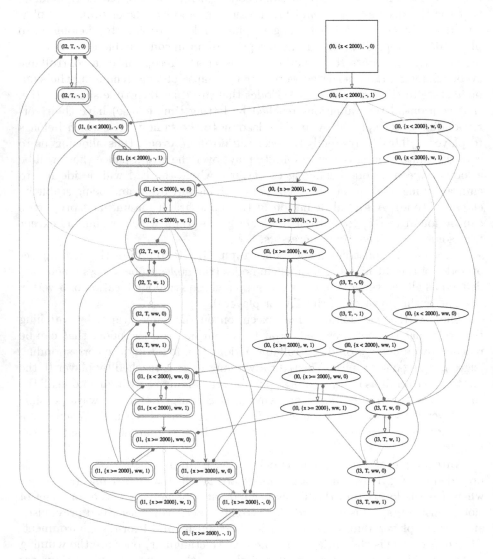

Fig. 3. Game graph associated with property φ_t (Color figure online)

2   General Description of GREP

GREP is a tool of about 6,000 lines of code[1] developed using the C language, available at https://github.com/matthieurenard/GREP. GREP is essentially composed of 2 modules (cf Fig. 4): Symbolic Computing Module (SCM) and Enforcement Monitor Module (EMM). It loads a TA file describing the desired property, and reads the inputs directly from *stdin*. The output of the EM is sent to *stdout*. This approach allows one to use GREP with off-the-shelf applications.

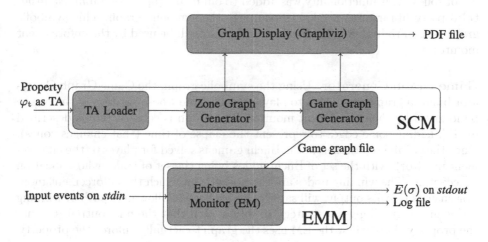

Fig. 4. General architecture of GREP

2.1   Symbolic Computing Module (SCM)

The Symbolic Computing Module is composed of three main components: a TA loader, the zone graph generator, and the game graph generator.

TA Loader. The TA loader is the component that parses a file containing the description of a timed automaton and loads it into a C structure. The file of the automaton is a textual description following a grammar designed for this purpose. The automaton must be also deterministic and complete (see [4]). If the automaton is not deterministic, the behaviour is undefined. Once the timed automaton is loaded, a symbolic graph is computed by the Zone Graph Generator to abstract its infinite semantics into a finite graph.

Zone Graph Generator. From the timed automaton, a symbolic graph is constructed using zones. Compared to a classical zone graph (used to compute reachability), this symbolic graph satisfies additional constraints. (A zone graph usually requires that, between a node and its successor, there exists a state of

---

[1] Calculated with cloc (https://github.com/AlDanial/cloc).

the semantics of the timed automaton in the first node that leads to a state in its successor). In this symbolic graph, all states in a node must lead to the successor. An algorithm to compute this symbolic graph satisfying these constraints is given in [3]. This algorithm has been implemented to compute the symbolic graph in this module. In GREP, zones are represented by Difference Bound Matrices (DBMs), using the UPPAAL DBM library (udbm, [1]), and its C API. The algorithm requires some functionality that is not provided by this C API (some of them exist in some higher-level wrappers), such as complementing zones into a list of zones. This functionality was added to our own wrapper of udbm. No other third-party library was needed to compute the symbolic graph. This symbolic graph is used to build the final game graph, that will be used by the enforcement monitor.

Game Graph Generator. Using the symbolic graph, the Game Graph Generator builds a graph over which to play a Büchi game whose strategy is the one to be followed by the enforcement monitor. The graph is constructed as described in [18], adding some edges to represent the elapse of time (that changes zones). Once the graph is constructed, the Büchi game is solved for player 0 (the enforcement monitor), with the set of Büchi nodes being the set of nodes whose location is accepting. The winning nodes are the nodes from which the enforcement monitor ensures that its output will satisfy the property. Following a path of winning nodes in the graph gives a strategy to follow such that the final output satisfies the property. This is how the EM uses the graph to actually enforce the property.

2.2   Enforcement Monitor Module (EMM)

The EMM module uses the SCM module to compute the output for a given input. It has five main public functions: $init(G)$, $getStrat()$, $delay(t)$, $eventRcvd(e)$, and $emit()$. Function $init(G)$ initialises the EMM following the strategy from graph G. Function $getStrat()$ gives the strategy to follow, i.e. whether the first action of the buffer should be output or not. Since time is abstracted by the zone graph for SCM, SCM needs to be notified that some time has passed, which is done by using function $delay(t)$, where t is the number of time units that have elapsed since the last call to delay, or the creation of the enforcement mechanism for the first call. Time units only need to be consistent with the ones used in the property. Function $eventRcvd(e)$ is used to inform the EMM that an event e has been read from the input. In this case, the EMM acts differently depending on the controllability of the event. Function $emit()$ is used to output the first action of the buffer (uncontrollable events are output by function $eventRcvd()$, as required by compliance).

Note that these functions allow one to use the EMM in both the online (real-time) and offline (with a trace as input) settings. All these functions, except function $getStrat()$, return the number of time units required to reach the time successor of the current node (∞ if there is no time successor). It is the number of time units given to function $delay()$ if no event is received before and the strategy is not to emit.

```
   input  : The game graph G, the input sequence of events, through function
            read ()
   output: The output of the enforcer mechanism, through function emit()
 1 init(G);
 2 del ← ∞;
 3 while The input sequence has not been read entirely do
 4 |   (δ, a) ← read ();
 5 |   while del ≤ δ do
 6 |   |   δ ← δ − del;
 7 |   |   del ← delay(del);
 8 |   |   while getStrat() = EMIT do
 9 |   |   |   emit();
10 |   |   end
11 |   end
12 |   delay(δ);
13 |   del ← eventRcvd(a);
14 end
15 while del < ∞ or getStrat() = EMIT do
16 |   while getStrat() = EMIT do
17 |   |   emit();
18 |   end
19 |   if del < ∞ then
20 |   |   del ← delay(del);
21 |   end
22 end
```

Algorithm 1. Main algorithm to enforce a property in offline mode

Thus, the general algorithm to use EMM in the offline setting is given in Algorithm 1. Basically, EMM follows a path in the game graph. Thus, it considers the current node as the node reached by its output, and explores the strategy tree from this node. EMM also stores the controllable actions that have not been output yet, and uses them to compute the possible output. Since the output should be the longest possible, with minimal possible delays, computing the strategy requires to explore the tree of all possible strategies. This is done by exploring the game graph, simulating the emission of the controllable actions of the buffer at all possible time instants. In each node belonging to player 0, if the successor by emitting (green, empty triangular head arrow in the game graph) is winning, then it is explored, and if the time successor is also winning, it is explored as well, since waiting before emitting could allow the EMM to output more events. Each node is then associated with a score, corresponding to the number of actions that have been emitted to reach the node. Then, EMM stores the node that has the biggest score, and the strategy to follow to reach it. If two nodes have the same score, then the lowest common ancestor is computed, and the one node that can be reached by emitting from this ancestor (the other node can be reached from this ancestor by waiting) is kept as the node to reach (this corresponds to computing the lexicographical order). This process is repeated for each node with the same score, with the previous stored node, such that in the end the stored node is the minimal node (for the lexicographic order) of all the nodes with the highest score.

Note that computing an output such that all actions are emitted whenever it is possible to emit them does not require to explore the strategy tree. Depending on the property, the two outputs could be the same (i.e. if the property is such that letting time elapse never enables a transition that eventually allows the EMM to output more events), thus the EMM can work faster by using an optimisation that does not compute any tree, but outputs actions whenever possible (i.e. when the successor node by emitting is winning) if it is specified to do so.

2.3   User Interface

GREP is shipped with two executables: one to use the enforcement mechanism in offline mode, and the other in the online mode. Both of them take their input on the standard input. In the offline mode, the input is composed of events in the form (t, a), where t is a date and a is an action, controllable or uncontrollable. In the online mode, only the action is given, the date is computed from the real time through a call to gettimeofday(). Note that these executables may build only on UNIX-like systems because of some system calls such as gettimeofday() and clock_gettime(). Excepting this, the tool is not system-dependent. The output (events with their dates) is printed on the standard output. Several options may be used:

- One of the two options -a <automatonFile> or -g <graphFile> must be passed to specify the property. The file <automatonFile> should be in the same format as the file shown in appendix A. The file <graphFile> should be a file saved by this executable (see option -s), loading this kind of file should be faster than loading an automaton file since it contains the graph, which does not need to be computed again.
- -s <graphFile> saves the game graph in <graphFile>, to be loaded in another execution (see option -g).
- -z <zoneGraphFile> draws the zone graph using graphviz and store it (as PDF) in <zoneGraphFile>.
- -d <gameGraphFile> draws the game graph using graphviz and store it (as PDF) in <gameGraphFile>.
- -t <timeFile> logs times between the reception of two events in the file <timeFile>. This option is used to benchmark the program.
- -l <logFile> prints all the logs in <logFile>.
- -f (fast) use the optimised version, where actions are output whenever they can be instead of outputting the longest word possible with minimal dates.

If options -s, -z, -d, or -t are not given, then the corresponding action will just not happen. For example, without -z, the zone graph will not be saved. If

none of the options among -a and -g is given, the program will print an error
and abort. If both are given, then the automaton file is used. If option -1 is
not given, then the standard error is used as log file, which is not recommended
(we recommend always using the option -1). If the option -f is not given, then
the enforcement mechanism will output as many events as possible, with the
lowest possible dates; enabling the option will make it output actions if it is
possible (i.e. if the node of the game graph reached by outputting is winning).
Using option -f is usually faster, but the outputs might differ depending on the
property. Example usage:
```
game_enf_offline -a phiext.tmtn -l log \
    -d gameGraph.pdf < input
```
will enforce the property described in the file phiext.tmtn, logging in the file
log, reading its events from the file input. It will also draw the game graph in
the file gameGraph.pdf.

The enforcement mechanism logs the mode in which it runs (default or fast)
at the beginning, and when it stops, it logs the input, its output, the controllable
actions that have not been output (what remains in its buffer), and a verdict that
is WIN if its output satisfies the property, or LOSS otherwise (some properties
might not be enforced as explained in [17]).

```
Enforcer initialized in default mode.
Shutting down the enforcement mechanism...
Summary of the execution:
Input: (0, Write) (1, Auth) (2, Write) (3, LockOn)
            (4, Write) (5, LockOff) (6, LockOn) (7, LockOff)
Output: (1, Auth) (2, Write) (2, Write) (3, LockOn)
            (5, LockOff) (6, LockOn) (7, LockOff) (9, Write)
Remaining events in the buffer:
VERDICT: WIN
enforcement mechanism shutdown.
```

Listing 1.1. Example log file produced by GREP

For example, considering that phiext.tmtn is the file given in appendix
A, the previous command with the input file containing the sequence:
$(0, Write)$ $(1, Auth)$ $(2, Write)$ $(3, LockOn)$ $(4, Write)$ $(5, LockOff)$
$(6, LockOn)$ $(7, LockOff)$, produces the output:
$(1, Auth)$ $(2, Write)$ $(2, Write)$ $(3, LockOn)$
$(5, LockOff)$ $(6, LockOn)(7, LockOff)$ $(9, Write)$. The produced log file is
given in Listing 1.1.

3   Performance Evaluation

The performance of GREP has been evaluated on three properties that come
along with TiPEX, the tool to which we compare. TiPEX (see [14]) is, to our
knowledge, the only other tool that acts as an enforcement mechanism for timed
regular properties. These properties are described in Fig. 5. The safety property

states that there should always be 5 time units between two r actions. The co-safety property states that the first r action should be followed by a g action, with a delay of at least 6 time units. The response property states that every grant (g) action should be followed by a release (r) action within 15 to 20 time units, without any grant action occurring between them.

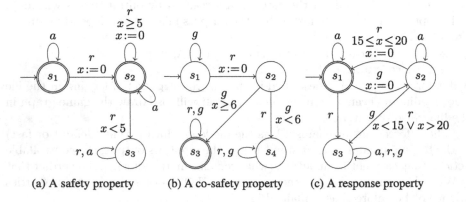

(a) A safety property   (b) A co-safety property   (c) A response property

Fig. 5. Properties used to benchmark GREP

For each of these properties, GREP has been run 100 times on every input among 100 inputs of 1000 events randomly generated. The time between the reception of two events has been saved for all of these executions. The same times have been computed for TiPEX[2], reducing the number of inputs and iterations to have the benchmarks run in a reasonable amount of time. Figures 6 and 7 give a graphical visualisation of the performances of GREP and TiPEX.

Figures 6 and 7 are obtained as follows: each input is iterated several times (100 for GREP, less for TiPEX), and the computation times of the tool between the reads of two consecutive events of the input are stored. Then, the median time is computed for each of these times between all the iterations. We then plot the logarithm (in base 10) of these times against the reads of the events. We use a logarithmic scale in nanoseconds because many values are low, and they would be merged in a line when using a linear scale. The results for GREP with option − f are given only for the safety property because they are similar to the results without the option for the two other properties. We can see that GREP is faster than TiPEX by several orders of magnitude. GREP outputs many events in less than $10\,\mu s$ (4 on the graphs), whereas TiPEX takes at least 1 ms (6 on the graph) to output them. For the safety property, we can see that for some inputs, GREP takes an increasing amount of time to compute the strategy. This is due to the exploration of the strategy tree, which grows with the number of stored

---

[2] We patched TiPEX to retrieve the times as we do in our tool, only modifying it to get times properly, and did not change the behaviour inside the part that is being measured.

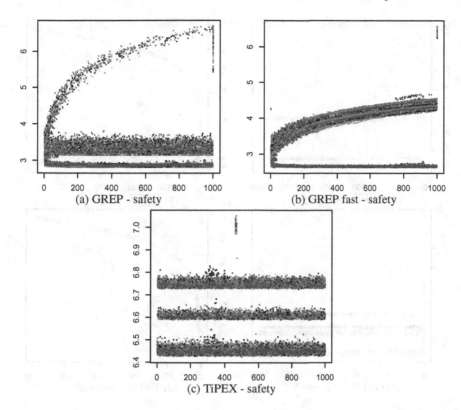

Fig. 6. Comparison of timings of GREP and TiPEX on the safety property. "GREP fast" means that option -f is used. The x axis corresponds to the events of the input (from 1 to 1000), and the y axis corresponds to the logarithm of the timings (in nanoseconds) between the reads of the events.

controllable actions. Using the optimised setting (-f) allows GREP to compute its output faster, as shown in Fig. 6b. The last vertical line has also many high values, because it represents the time to emit all the remaining actions after the last event from the input was read. For the co-safety and response properties, GREP is less variable than for the safety property, mainly because its strategy is simpler: it consists in either emitting everything in the co-safety (once state s_3 is reached) or emitting nothing for the response property, if the first stored controllable is an r while in state s_1. TiPEX, on the other hand, takes a linearly-increasing amount of time to emit some events.

4   Discussion and Concluding Remarks

As shown in Sect. 3, GREP provides better computing times than TiPEX. There are several factors that can explain this. The implementation language is one of these factors: GREP is implemented in C, which produces assembly code that

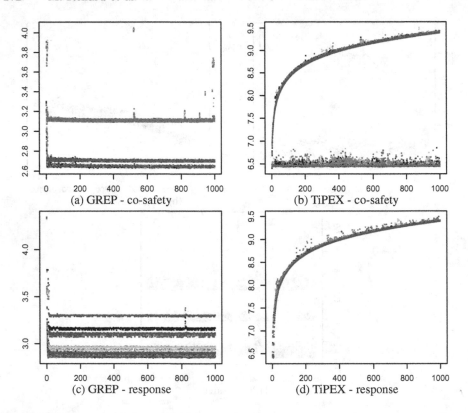

(a) GREP - co-safety   (b) TiPEX - co-safety

(c) GREP - response   (d) TiPEX - response

Fig. 7. Timings of GREP and TiPEX on the response and co-safety properties. The x axis corresponds to the events of the input (from 1 to 1000), and the y axis corresponds to the logarithm of the timings (in nanoseconds) between the reads of the events.

is fast to execute, whereas TiPEX is implemented in Python, which is a higher-level language that can introduce some overhead in the execution time. Another factor is the use of games to enforce the properties, that allows the EMM to compute the output faster. Indeed, the game graph allows us to know if a node is winning in very little time, where the same computation not using graph needs to consider all the reachable states with the buffer.

Note that our tool was designed primarily to handle uncontrollable events. The properties used in our evaluation/comparison do not feature uncontrollable events because TiPEX only supports controllable events. To our knowledge, there is no other tool that acts as an enforcement mechanism for timed properties with uncontrollable events. We initially used games to precompute (with the game graph) the behaviour of the enforcement mechanism upon the reception of uncontrollable events, but it has also improved the computation time of the output even without any uncontrollable event.

Depending on the property, there could be an exponential blow-up in the number of nodes that have to be visited. The -f option allows the enforcement mechanism to use a strategy (where each event is output as soon as possible) that prevents this blow-up. To further improve the performance of GREP and avoid the blow-up when using the strategy outputting the longest words, we aim at i) computing a better set of controllable words to be associated with nodes, and having a better representation of controllable words. A (more theoretical) possible extension to this work is to determine under which conditions the two strategies (using the optimised version or not) are equivalent.

A   Automaton File

The automaton file describing φ_t (see Fig. 2) follows:

```
automaton {
    cont {Write}
    uncont {Auth, LockOn, LockOff}
    nodes {
        10 [initial];
        11 [accepting];
        12 [accepting];
        13 ;
    }
    clocks {x}
    edges {
        10 ->{Auth}{}{} 11 ;
        10 ->{Write}{}{} 13 ;
        10 ->{LockOn}{}{} 13 ;
        10 ->{LockOff}{}{} 13 ;
        11 ->{LockOn}{}{} 12 ;
        11 ->{Write}{}{x >= 2} 11 ;
        11 ->{LockOff}{x}{} 11 ;
        11 ->{Auth}{}{} 11 ;
        11 ->{Write}{}{x < 2} 13 ;
        12 ->{Auth}{}{} 12 ;
        12 ->{LockOn}{}{} 12 ;
        12 ->{LockOff}{x}{} 11 ;
        12 ->{Write}{}{} 13 ;
        13 ->{Write}{}{} 13 ;
        13 ->{Auth}{}{} 13 ;
        13 ->{LockOn}{}{} 13 ;
        13 ->{LockOff}{}{} 13 ;
    }
}
```

References

1. Uppaal DBM Library. http://people.cs.aau.dk/~adavid/UDBM/. Accessed 27 Apr 2017
2. Alcalde, B., Cavalli, A., Chen, D., Khuu, D., Lee, D.: Network protocol system passive testing for fault management: a backward checking approach. In: de Frutos-Escrig, D., Núñez, M. (eds.) FORTE 2004. LNCS, vol. 3235, pp. 150–166. Springer, Heidelberg (2004). doi:10.1007/978-3-540-30232-2_10
3. Alur, R., Courcoubetis, C., Halbwachs, N., Dill, D., Wong-Toi, H.: Minimization of timed transition systems. In: Cleaveland, W.R. (ed.) CONCUR 1992. LNCS, vol. 630, pp. 340–354. Springer, Heidelberg (1992). doi:10.1007/BFb0084802
4. Alur, R., Dill, D.: The theory of timed automata. In: Bakker, J.W., Huizing, C., Roever, W.P., Rozenberg, G. (eds.) REX 1991. LNCS, vol. 600, pp. 45–73. Springer, Heidelberg (1992). doi:10.1007/BFb0031987
5. Bartocci, E., Falcone, Y., Bonakdarpour, B., Colombo, C., Decker, N., Havelund, K., Joshi, Y., Klaedtke, F., Milewicz, R., Reger, G., Rosu, G., Signoles, J., Thoma, D., Zalinescu, E., Zhang, Y.: First international competition on runtime verification: rules, benchmarks, tools, and final results of CRV 2014. Int. J. Softw. Tools Technol. Transf., 1–40 (2017)
6. Basin, D., Jugé, V., Klaedtke, F., Zălinescu, E.: Enforceable security policies revisited. ACM Trans. Inf. Syst. Secur. **16**(1), 3:1–3:26 (2013)
7. Bengtsson, J., Yi, W.: Timed automata: semantics, algorithms and tools. In: Desel, J., Reisig, W., Rozenberg, G. (eds.) ACPN 2003. LNCS, vol. 3098, pp. 87–124. Springer, Heidelberg (2004). doi:10.1007/978-3-540-27755-2_3
8. Cavalli, A., Gervy, C., Prokopenko, S.: New approaches for passive testing using an extended finite state machine specification. Inf. Softw. Technol. **45**(12), 837–852 (2003)
9. Falcone, Y.: You should better enforce than verify. In: Barringer, H., Falcone, Y., Finkbeiner, B., Havelund, K., Lee, I., Pace, G., Roşu, G., Sokolsky, O., Tillmann, N. (eds.) RV 2010. LNCS, vol. 6418, pp. 89–105. Springer, Heidelberg (2010). doi:10.1007/978-3-642-16612-9_9
10. Falcone, Y., Havelund, K., Reger, G.: A tutorial on runtime verification. In: Engineering Dependable Software Systems, pp. 141–175 (2013)
11. Falcone, Y., Mounier, L., Fernandez, J., Richier, J.: Runtime enforcement monitors: composition, synthesis, and enforcement abilities. Formal Methods Syst. Des. **38**(3), 223–262 (2011)
12. Leucker, M., Schallhart, C.: A brief account of runtime verification. J. Log. Algebr. Program. **78**(5), 293–303 (2009)
13. Ligatti, J., Bauer, L., Walker, D.: Run-time enforcement of nonsafety policies. ACM Trans. Inf. Syst. Secur. **12**(3), 19:1–19:41 (2009)
14. Pinisetty, S., Falcone, Y., Jéron, T., Marchand, H.: TiPEX: a tool chain for timed property enforcement during eXecution. In: Bartocci, E., Majumdar, R. (eds.) RV 2015. LNCS, vol. 9333, pp. 306–320. Springer, Cham (2015). doi:10.1007/978-3-319-23820-3_22
15. Pinisetty, S., Falcone, Y., Jéron, T., Marchand, H., Rollet, A., Nguena Timo, O.L.: Runtime enforcement of timed properties. In: Qadeer, S., Tasiran, S. (eds.) RV 2012. LNCS, vol. 7687, pp. 229–244. Springer, Heidelberg (2013). doi:10.1007/978-3-642-35632-2_23
16. Renard, M., Falcone, Y., Rollet, A., Jéron, T., Marchand, H.: Optimal enforcement of (timed) properties with uncontrollable events. Mathematical Structures in Computer Science, pp. 1–46 (2017)

17. Renard, M., Falcone, Y., Rollet, A., Pinisetty, S., Jéron, T., Marchand, H.: Enforcement of (Timed) properties with uncontrollable events. In: Leucker, M., Rueda, C., Valencia, F.D. (eds.) ICTAC 2015. LNCS, vol. 9399, pp. 542–560. Springer, Cham (2015). doi:10.1007/978-3-319-25150-9_31

18. Renard, M., Rollet, A., Falcone, Y.: Runtime enforcement using Büchi games. In: Proceedings of Model Checking Software - 24th International Symposium, SPIN 2017, Co-located with ISSTA 2017, Santa Barbara, USA, pp. 70–79. ACM Press, July 2017

19. Schneider, F.B.: Enforceable security policies. ACM Trans. Inf. Syst. Secur. 3(1), 30–50 (2000)

Constraint-Based Oracles
for Timed Distributed Systems

Nassim Benharrat[1,3]([✉]), Christophe Gaston[1], Robert M. Hierons[2],
Arnault Lapitre[1], and Pascale Le Gall[3]

[1] CEA, LIST, Laboratory of Model Driven Engineering for Embedded Systems,
P.C. 174, Gif-sur-Yvette 91191, France
{nassim.benharrat,christophe.gaston,arnault.lapitre}@cea.fr
[2] Brunel University London, Uxbridge, Middlesex UB8 3PH, UK
rob.hierons@brunel.ac.uk
[3] Laboratoire MICS, CentraleSupélec, Université Paris-Saclay,
92295 Châtenay-Malabry, France
{nassim.benharrat,pascale.gall}@centralesupelec.fr

Abstract. This paper studies the situation in which the system under
test and the system model are distributed and have the same structure;
they have corresponding remote components that communicate asyn-
chronously. In testing, a component with interface C_i has its own local
tester that interacts with C_i and this local tester observes a local trace
consisting of inputs, outputs and durations as perceived by C_i. An observation made in testing is thus a *multi-trace*: a tuple of (timed) local
traces, one for each C_i. The conformance relation for such distributed
systems combines a classical unitary conformance relation for localised
components and the requirement that the communication policy was satisfied. By expressing the communication policy as a constraint satisfaction problem, we were able to implement the computation of test verdicts
by orchestrating localised off-line testing algorithms and the verification
of constraints defined by message passing between components. Lastly,
we illustrate our approach on a telecommunications system.

Keywords: Model-based testing · Distributed testing · Timed input
output transition systems · Off-line testing · Constraint-based testing

1 Introduction

Distributed systems can be seen as collections of physically remote reactive systems communicating through communication media. The classical approach to
testing such systems involves placing a local tester at each localised interface,
with each local tester only observing the events at its interface. If testers do not
exchange synchronisation messages and there is no global clock, this corresponds
to the ISO standardised distributed test architecture [11]. The result of test execution can be modelled as a collection of logs (local traces); each is a sequence
of messages involving a given localised system.

© IFIP International Federation for Information Processing 2017
Published by Springer International Publishing AG 2017. All Rights Reserved
N. Yevtushenko et al. (Eds.): ICTSS 2017, LNCS 10533, pp. 276–292, 2017.
DOI: 10.1007/978-3-319-67549-7_17

Model-Based Testing (MBT) [8,17,21] aims to automate three central processes in testing, namely: the *test generation* process whose purpose is to extract test cases from a behavioural model of the System Under Test (SUT), the *test execution* process whose purpose is to orchestrate the stimulation of the SUT with input test data and the collection of the SUT's reactions and finally, the *verdict (oracle) computation* phase whose purpose is to analyse the results of test case executions, given as execution traces, in order to identify faults by checking traces against the model[1]. This comparison is based on a conformance relation that relates traces of SUTs and traces of their associated models.

MBT was first explored in a centralised context but extensions to distributed SUTs have been defined, initially motivated by protocol conformance testing [19]. This includes work that uses Input Output Transition System (IOTS) as the modelling formalism [3,9,10]. In the context of distributed testing from Timed IOTS (TIOTS), in [6], we extended the *tioco* conformance relation [14,15,20] to define a conformance relation *dtioco* for timed distributed testing. The model of a distributed SUT is given as a tuple of TIOTSs, each modelling one of the localised subsystems of the SUT. The result of test case execution is a tuple of timed traces (a timed trace is a trace in which delays between consecutive interactions of the tester with the localised SUT are recorded). Under the hypothesis that localised systems communicate in a multi-cast mode, we have shown that the verdict computation process can be conducted by combining centralised MBT techniques for each localised system, using the *tioco* conformance relation, and a step-by-step algorithm whose purpose is to check that the tuple of timed traces is consistent with the underlying communication hypothesis [6].

The goal of this paper is twofold. First, we propose an improvement of the algorithm presented in [6] by formulating the oracle problem as a constraint solving problem. While the previous algorithm analyses a multi-trace by mimicking step by step emissions and receptions of messages, as well as the passage of time, in this article, we reformulate the verification of message passing as a set of inequality constraints that can be supported by a constraint solver. Compared to the one introduced in [6], the new algorithm treats durations between communication actions as real numbers. In [6] those durations had to be representable as multiples of a basic time unit, which only allowed us to consider durations in a set isomorphic to the set of natural numbers. The previous approach also included backtracking. In the new algorithm, durations may be any real number that falls in the theory addressed by the considered solver. Second, we present the tool that solves the oracle problem using both a localised verdict computation approach for *tioco* (presented in [1]) and the verification of constraints to check internal communications between localised systems. We consider a case study modelling a telecommunication system, named *PhoneX* [18] specified as a collection of Timed Input Output Symbolic Transition Systems (TIOSTS), which are symbolic representations of TIOTS.

Section 2 introduces the types of models used and Sect. 3 presents the PhoneX case study. Section 4 recalls the testing framework and introduces the verification

---

[1] When the processes are intertwined testing is on-line; otherwise it is off-line.

of message passing using constraints. Section 5 describes a scalability study, based on the PhoneX example, that applied mutation techniques to generate correct and faulty trace tuples. Section 6 discusses related works and Sect. 7 gives concluding remarks.

2   Modelling Framework

2.1   TIOSTS

Timed Input Output Symbolic Transition Systems (TIOSTS) are symbolic automata built over a signature $\Sigma = (\Omega, A, T, C)$ where $\Omega = (S, F)$ is an equational logic signature with S a set of types and F a set of functions provided with an arity. The functions are interpreted in a model M as usual. A is a set of data variables used to store input values, to denote system state evolutions and to define guards. T is a set of clocks, which are variables whose values are elements of a set D isomorphic to non-negative real numbers and that are used to denote durations. D^+ will denote $D \setminus \{0\}$. M is supposed to contain D. Variables in $A \cup T$ are assigned values by interpretations of the form $\nu : A \cup T \to M$; $M^{A \cup T}$ is the set of all interpretations. Finally, C is a set of channels partitioned as $C^{in} \coprod C^{out}$ where elements of C^{in} (resp. C^{out}) are *input* (resp. *output*) channels. The set of terms $T_\Omega(A)$ over Ω and A is inductively defined as usual and variable interpretations are canonically extended to terms. The set of symbolic actions $Act(\Sigma)$ is $I(\Sigma) \cup O(\Sigma)$ with $I(\Sigma) = \{c?x \mid x \in A, c \in C^{in}\}$ and $O(\Sigma) = \{c!t \mid t \in T_\Omega(A), c \in C^{out}\}$. In order to simplify the exposition, at the level of our modelling framework, we consider messages that contain only a single piece of data. However, at the tooling level, without adding any particular difficulties, messages contain 0 (signals $c!$ or $c?$), 1 or n data ($c!(t_1, \ldots, t_n)$ or $c?(x_1, \ldots, x_n)$, the x_i being different variables of A).

A TIOSTS is a triple $\mathbb{G} = (Q, q_0, Tr)$ where Q is a set of states, q_0 is a distinguished element of Q called the initial state, and Tr is a set of labeled transitions. A transition is defined by a tuple $(q, \phi, \psi, \mathbb{T}, act, \rho, q')$ where q (resp. q') is the source (resp. target) state of the transition, ϕ is a formula, called time guard, of the form $z \leq Cst$ or $z \geq Cst$ where $z \in T$ and Cst is a constant interpreted in D (ϕ constrains the delay at which the action act occurs), ψ is an equational logic formula, called data guard (ψ is a firing condition on attribute variables), $\mathbb{T} \subseteq T$ is a set of time variables (to be reset to 0 when the transition is executed), act is a communication action and ρ assigns terms of $T_\Omega(A)$ to variables in A in order to represent state evolutions. In the sequel, we use $M \models_\nu \varphi$ to say that φ holds for interpretation ν. The set of paths of $\mathbb{G}$ contains the empty sequence ε and all sequences $tr_1. \cdots . tr_n$ of transitions of Tr such that $source(tr_1) = q_0$ and for all $i < n$, $target(tr_i) = source(tr_{i+1})$.

Concrete actions are values exchanged through channels. The set of concrete actions over C is thus $Act(C) = I(C) \cup O(C)$ where $I(C) = \{c?v \mid c \in C^{in}, v \in M\}$ are inputs and $O(C) = \{c!v \mid c \in C^{out}, v \in M\}$ are outputs. Given $act \in Act(C)$ of the form $c\Delta v$ with $\Delta \in \{!, ?\}$, $chan(act)$ refers to c, $\overline{act}$ refers to its mirror action, $c\overline{\Delta}v$ with $\bar{!} =?$ and $\bar{?} =!$. Variable interpretations are canonically extended to symbolic actions $(\nu(c?x) = c?(\nu(x))$ and $\nu(c!t) = c!\nu(t))$.

A concrete action is generally observed after a delay has occurred since the previous occurrence of a concrete action. This is captured by the notion of *events*.

Definition 1 (Events). *The set of (resp. initialised) events over C is defined as $Evt(C) = (D^+ \cup \{\_\}) \times (Act(C) \cup \{\delta\})$ (resp. $IEvt(C) = D^+ \times (Act(C) \cup \{\delta\}))$.*

Pair (d, a) represents the observation of concrete action a after delay d. Following [21], symbol 'δ' is used to denote the absence of observation of a concrete action (*i.e.* quiescence). Let us point out that usually, in a pure timed framework, δ may be useless (e.g. [6,13,14]). Here, the use of δ is a side effect of considering atomic actions as events. Indeed, expressing that a system is quiescent after a duration d has to be representable as an event, and thus, we need a symbol to represent these quiescent situations as a couple (d, δ). Symbol '$\_$' is introduced to denote the absence of the observation of a delay (i.e. $(\_, a)$). We require this so that the first action of a localised trace need not be stamped with a duration. In addition, between two consecutive concrete actions on one location, we require that the delay is greater than zero so that two events do not occur simultaneously. Given $ev \in Evt(C)$, we let $act(ev) = a$ and $delay(ev) = d$ if $ev = (d, a)$ with $d \in D^+$, else $delay(ev) = 0$ $(ev = (\_, a))$. In the sequel $\delta Evt(C)$ denotes $\{ev \in Evt(C) \backslash act(ev) = \delta\}$.

Definition 2 (Timed traces). *The set $ITraces(C)$ of initialised traces over C is[2] $(IEvt(C) \setminus \delta Evt(C))^*.(\varepsilon + \delta Evt(C))$.*
The set $UTraces(C)$ of uninitialised traces over C is $\{u(\sigma) \mid \sigma \in ITraces(C)\}$ where $u(\sigma)$ denotes ε if $\sigma = \varepsilon$ and $(\_, a).\sigma'$ if $\sigma = (d, a).\sigma'$.
The set $TTraces(C)$ of timed traces over C is $UTraces(C) \cup ITraces(C)$.

Any event of an initialised trace contains a duration and a concrete action. For the first event, this duration represents a delay between some distinguished moment (e.g. since the time at which a tester started to measure the duration) and the first observed action. Uninitialised traces are timed traces for which no initial instant is identified. Finally, note that quiescence is only observed at the end of traces, when no communication action follows it. Indeed when a communication action a occurs after a period of time where an implementation remains silent, this period of time is captured by the delay of the event introducing a.

For $\sigma \in TTraces(C)$, $dur(\sigma)$ denotes the *duration of σ*, which is 0 if σ is ε, and otherwise is the sum of all delays of events in σ. $Pref(\sigma)$ denotes the set of *prefixes of σ* defined as $\{\varepsilon\}$ if σ is ε and $Pref(\sigma') \cup \{\sigma\}$ if σ is of the form $\sigma'.ev$. Moreover, for an action a in $Act(C)$, $|\sigma|_a$ denotes the number of occurrences of a in σ. $pref(\sigma, a, n)$ stands for the smallest prefix of σ that contains n occurrences of a when this prefix exists. Finally, using the $pref$ operation, we introduce an operation that measures the elapsed time at the nth occurrence of an event a

---

[2] E^* is the set of finite sequences of elements in E with ε as neutral element for sequence concatenation.

from the beginning of the trace. By convention, if a trace contains strictly fewer than n occurrences of a, then the associated duration is that of the entire trace.

$$dur\_occ(\sigma, a, n) = \begin{cases} dur(pref(\sigma, a, n)) & \text{if } pref(\sigma, a, n) \text{ exists} \\ dur(\sigma) & \text{else} \end{cases}$$

We now define *runs* of transitions of TIOSTS:

Definition 3 (Runs of transitions). *Let* $\mathbb{G} = (Q, q_0, Tr)$ *be a TIOSTS over* Σ. *The set* $Snp_M(\mathbb{G})$ *of snapshots of* $\mathbb{G}$ *is the set* $Q \times M^{A \cup T}$. *For* $tr = (q, \phi, \psi, \mathbb{T}, act, \rho, q') \in Tr$, *the set of runs of* tr *is the set* $Run(tr) \subseteq Snp_M(\mathbb{G}) \times Evt(C) \times Snp_M(\mathbb{G})$ *s.t.* $((q, \nu), ev, (q', \nu')) \in Run(tr)$ *iff there exist* $d \in D$ *and* $\xi : A \cup T \to M$ *satisfying:*

- *for all* $w \in T$, $\xi(w) = \nu(w) + d$,
- *if* $act = c!t$ *then for all* $x \in A$, $\xi(x) = \nu(x)$, *else* $(act = c?x)$ *for all* $y \in A \backslash \{x\}$, $\xi(y) = \nu(y)$,

and such that we have either $ev = (d, \xi(act))$ *or* $ev = (\_, \xi(act))$, $\forall x \in A, \nu'(x) = \xi(\rho(x))$, $\forall w \in \mathbb{T}, \nu'(w) = 0$, $\forall w \in (T \backslash \mathbb{T}), \nu'(w) = \xi(w)$, $M \models_\xi \phi$ *and* $M \models_\xi \psi$.

In Definition 3, ξ is an intermediate interpretation whose purpose is to let time pass from ν for all clocks ($\xi(w) = \nu(w) + d$) and take into account a potential input value (denoted by $\xi(x)$ if $act = c?x$). Guards of the transition should be satisfied by ξ and if it is the case then the transition can be fired resulting on a new interpretation ν' updating data variables according to ρ and resetting clocks occurring in $\mathbb{T}$.

For a path p of $\mathbb{G}$, the *set of timed traces of* p, denoted $TTraces(p)$ is $\{\varepsilon\}$ if $p = \varepsilon$ and if p is of the form $tr_1 \cdots .tr_n$, $TTrace(p)$ contains all sequences of events $ev_1 \cdots ev_n$ such that there exists a sequence of runs $r_1 \cdots r_n$ satisfying: for all $i \leq n$, r_i is a run of tr_i of the form $(snp_i, ev_i, snp'_{i+1})$ and for all $j < n$ we have $snp'_j = snp_{j+1}$ and such that all events are initialised except for $i = 1$, i.e. ev_1 is of form $(\_, a_1)$ and for all $i > 1$, ev_i is of form (d_i, a_i).

By taking into account the particular action δ, the set of timed traces of $\mathbb{G}$, denoted $TTraces(\mathbb{G})$, is defined as:

- For all $p \in Path(\mathbb{G})$ we have $TTraces(p) \subseteq TTraces(\mathbb{G})$,
- For all $\sigma \in TTraces(\mathbb{G})$ such that there exists no path p and no event ev with $act(ev) \in O(C)$ satisfying $\sigma.ev \in TTraces(p)$, we have $\sigma.(d, \delta) \in TTraces(\mathbb{G})$ if $\sigma \neq \varepsilon$ and $(\_, \delta) \in TTraces(\mathbb{G})$ if $\sigma = \varepsilon$.

2.2   Communication and Systems

We now define a *distributed interface* as a collection of localised interfaces.

Definition 4 (Distributed interface). *A distributed interface is a tuple* $\Lambda = (C_1, \cdots, C_n)$, *with* $n \geq 1$, *where for all* $i \leq n$, C_i *is a set of channels such that for any* $i \neq j$ *we have* $C_i^{out} \cap C_j^{out} = \emptyset$. $C(\Lambda)$, *which is equal to* $\bigcup_{i \leq n} C_i$, *is the set of channels of* Λ *with* $C(\Lambda)^{in} = \bigcup_{i \leq n} C_i^{in}$ *and* $C(\Lambda)^{out} = \bigcup_{i \leq n} C_i^{out}$.

$C_i^{out} \cap C_j^{out} = \emptyset$ ensures that for a channel c, messages emitted through c can only be emitted from one sender. This is a simplification hypothesis that makes the later formalisation lighter. In a distributed architecture, for a given localised interface C_i of $\Lambda = (C_1, \cdots, C_n)$, C_i^{int} (resp. C_i^{ext}), defined as $\bigcup \{C_i \cap C_j \mid j \le n \wedge j \ne i\}$ (resp. $C_i \backslash C_i^{int}$), denotes the set of internal channels (resp. external channels) that can be used to exchange messages with other localised subsystems (resp. exchange messages with the system environment). We let $C^{int}(\Lambda)$ denote $\bigcup_{i \le n} C_i^{int}$, $C^{ext}(\Lambda)$ denote $\bigcup_{i \le n} C_i^{ext}$, and $Act(\Lambda)$ denote $I(\Lambda) \cup O(\Lambda)$ with $I(\Lambda) = \bigcup_{i \le n} I(C_i)$ and $O(\Lambda) = \bigcup_{i \le n} O(C_i)$. $I^{int}(\Lambda)$ (resp. $O^{int}(\Lambda)$) is the subset of $I(\Lambda)$ (resp. $O(\Lambda)$) whose elements are inputs (resp. outputs) through internal channels. For any $c!v \in O(\Lambda)$, $Sender(\Lambda, c!v)$ stands for the index j such that $c \in C_j^{out}$. We let $Act^{int}(\Lambda) = I^{int}(\Lambda) \cup O^{int}(\Lambda)$, $Evt(\Lambda) = Evt(C(\Lambda))$, and $Evt_{in}^{int}(\Lambda)$ be the set of events whose action is an internal input. We define $Tup(\Lambda)$ to be $TTraces(C_1) \times \cdots \times TTraces(C_n)$. In the sequel, a distributed interface $\Lambda = (C_1, \cdots, C_n)$ is given. An observation made in a system will be a tuple of timed traces where each timed trace represents a local observation. We first introduce the notion of a *multi-trace*, which is a tuple of timed traces characterising compatible communications between a collection of localised subsystems.

Definition 5 (Multi-traces).   *The set of* multi-traces *of Λ with initial instants, denoted $IMTraces(\Lambda)$, is the subset of $ITraces(C_1) \times \cdots \times ITraces(C_n)$ defined as follows:*

- **Empty multi-trace:** $(\varepsilon, \cdots, \varepsilon) \in IMTraces(\Lambda)$,
- **multi-trace Extension:** *for any* $\mu = (\sigma_1, \ldots, \sigma_n) \in IMTraces(\Lambda)$, *for* $ev \in IEvt(C_i)$ *for* $i \le n$, $(\sigma_1, \ldots, \sigma_i.ev, \ldots, \sigma_n) \in IMTraces(\Lambda)$ *provided that: if* $act(ev) \in I(C_i) \cap I^{int}(\Lambda)$, *we have* $|\sigma_j|_{\overline{ev}} \ge |\sigma_i|_{act(ev)} + 1$ *and* $dur\_occ(\sigma_j, \overline{ev}, |\sigma_i|_{act(ev)} + 1) < dur(\sigma_i.ev)$ *with* $j = Sender(\Lambda, \overline{act(ev)})$.

The set $UMTraces(\Lambda)$ (resp. $MTraces(\Lambda)$) of uninitialised multi-traces *(resp. of* multi-traces*) of Λ is $\{(u(\sigma_1), \cdots, u(\sigma_n)) \mid (\sigma_1, \cdots, \sigma_n) \in IMTraces(\Lambda)\}$ (resp. $UMTraces(\Lambda) \cup IMTraces(\Lambda)$).*

Initialised multi-traces denote tuples of traces, each trace of the tuple being a partial centralised vision of a common distributed execution. The nature of communication considered is multicast, as captured by the property that an internal message can be received at some C_i only if C_i has consumed fewer occurrences of this message than the number of the corresponding output occurrences. Each trace occurring in an initialised multi-trace starts with an event introducing a duration. All those durations are supposed to start at a common initial instant. Of course, in the context of distributed executions it is generally not possible to observe such a common initial instant. Therefore, we defined uninitialised multi-traces in which the initial durations are not observable. Similar rules have been proposed in [16] to express component composition in a distributed setting.

In distributed testing, we assume that there is a separate tester at each localised interface and there is no global clock for globally ordering distributed events. Hence, we cannot make any assumption on the different moments at which the different local testers stop observing their associated interfaces. To capture this, we accept as valid observations, tuples made of multi-trace prefixes.

Definition 6 (Observable multi-traces). *The* set of initialised observable multi-traces of Λ, *denoted* $IOTraces(\Lambda)$, *is the smallest set containing* $IMTraces(\Lambda)$ *and such that for any* $(\sigma_1, \cdots, \sigma_i.ev, \cdots, \sigma_n) \in IOTraces(\Lambda)$ *we have* $(\sigma_1, \cdots, \sigma_n) \in IOTraces(\Lambda)$.
  The set of uninitialised observable multi-traces of Λ, *denoted* $UOTraces(\Lambda)$, *is the set* $\{(u(\sigma_1), \cdots, u(\sigma_n)) \mid (\sigma_1, \cdots, \sigma_n) \in IOTraces(\Lambda)\}$.

Initialised observable multi-traces characterise observations starting at a common initial instant but ending at different instants depending on the considered component of the interface. Of course, since there is a common initial instant it is possible to order the moments at which the observations of the different traces of the tuple occur (σ_i ends before σ_j if $dur(\sigma_i) < dur(\sigma_j)$). However, in general such an initial instant cannot be identified in testing. Therefore, real observations of system executions should be defined by tuples containing only uninitialised traces, which is captured by uninitialised observable multi-traces.

Definition 7. *Let* $\Lambda = (C_1, \cdots, C_n)$ *be a distributed interface. A system over* Λ *is a tuple* $Sys = (\mathbb{G}_1, \cdots \mathbb{G}_n)$ *such that for all* $i \leq n$ *we have* $\mathbb{G}_i$ *is a TIOSTS over a signature of the form* $(\Omega_i, A_i, T_i, C_i)$. *The semantics of* Sys, *denoted* $TTraces(Sys)$ *is defined as* $(TTraces(\mathbb{G}_1) \times \cdots \times TTraces(\mathbb{G}_n)) \cap UOTraces(\Lambda)$.

3   The PhoneX Case Study

PhoneX [18] is a central telecommunication system model describing a protocol to establish sessions between phones. It was initially used as a reference to investigate the test case generation capacities of the platform Diversity[3] by the Ericsson company. In our context, PhoneX is interesting since it allows the number of communicating actors to be parameterised, even though there is only one time constraint in the subsystem models. Figure 1 depicts a scenario of a successful session setup and call establishment between 2 phones. A caller with $Phone_{112}$ initiates a call ($doCall(113)$) to the user of $Phone_{113}$. The PhoneX server, after receiving $Calling(112, 113)$, checks if $Phone_{113}$ is registered, available, and then starts $StartSession(112, 113)$ for communication management and remains available. $Session_{112}^{113}$ informs $Phone_{113}$ that $Phone_{112}$ tried to get in contact ($CalledBy(112)$). The user of $Phone_{113}$ can accept the call ($doAcceptCall$) and informs $Session_{112}^{113}$ using $AcceptingCall$ which can establish communication (multicasting $InitCall$). Each user can end the call (the user of $Phone_{112}$ hangs up, $doEndCall$) and report it ($EndingCall$) to $Session_{112}^{113}$ that closes the connection by multicasting $TermCall$ and becomes available ($EndSession(112, 113)$) again. Figure 2 depicts the architecture. Components

---

[3] https://projects.eclipse.org/proposals/eclipse-formal-modeling-project.

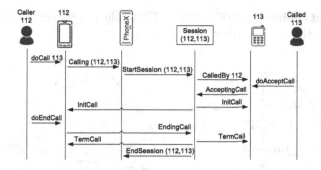

Fig. 1. Interaction scenario of a successful call operation

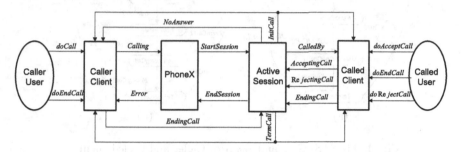

Fig. 2. The PhoneX architecture

Caller Client and *Called Client* define two roles that registered phones can have. *PhoneX* is the component that plays the role of the telecommunication centre. *Active Session* is a generic representation of sessions created by the centre to manage communications between phones. Communication channels model the media used by components in Fig. 2.

Caller client behaviour (Fig. 3(a)). At the *Idle* state, caller *src* receives a call from the environment (a caller) to make a call operation with called *dest*. Then it joins PhoneX central by sending to it *src* and *dest* (caller reaches *Initiating* state). Caller returns to *Idle* state when it receives an error code from PhoneX (PhoneX cannot establish a call due to violated condition of call establishment) or a signal to terminate the call from the active session (due to a call rejection by called client). At *Initiating*, *src* may reach *Established* if a call is established by active session or state *Terminating* if a no-answer (from called client) is observed during a waiting delay. When a call is established (at *Established*), *src* may return to *Idle* by receiving a terminating signal from the active session (due to an ending call by called client) or receive a signal from the environment (a caller) to end the call in progress (caller reaches *UserEndingCall*). At *UserEndingCall*, the caller notifies the active session for terminating the call (caller reaches *Terminating*). At *Terminating*, *src* returns to *Idle* by receiving a terminating signal from the active session.

Called client behaviour (Fig. 3(b)). This role is symmetric (on the called client side) to the one described in Fig. 3(a)).

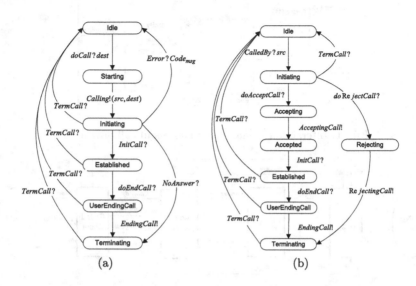

Fig. 3. TIOSTSs $\mathbb{G}_{src}$ and $\mathbb{G}_{dest}$ of Caller and Called clients

PhoneX central behaviour (Fig. 4(a)). At the *Idle* state, PhoneX may receive a call and reach *Calling* or get notified of the ending of an already active session and return to *Idle*. At *Calling*, PhoneX may start a new session (*src, dest*) and return to *Idle* provided that *dest* is a registered and allowed-to-call number in the Client database and there is no active session with called client *dest*. Otherwise, PhoneX may also return to *Idle* when *dest* is not registered in Client database, or calling *dest* is not allowed, or called client *dest* is busy.

Session behaviour (depicted in Fig. 4(b)). When a new session is started, a Session TIOSTS is instantiated. At the *Idle* state, Session receives *src* and *dest* numbers, it then reaches *Starting*. It notifies *dest* with a call operation emitted by *src* and reaches *Initiating*. At *Initiating*, it may reach either *Accepted* when called client accepts the call during a waiting delay or *Terminating* if a no-answer is observed during a waiting delay or the call get rejected. At *Accepted*, active session initiates a call between *src* and *dest* and reaches state *Established*. Then, either caller or called client may end the call (session reaches *Terminating* state). At *Terminating* state session sends a terminating signal to both caller and called clients and reaches *Ending*. Finally, it returns to *Idle* by notifying PhoneX central of ending the active session.

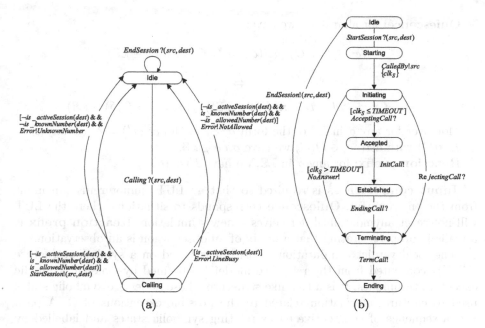

Fig. 4. TIOSTSs $\mathbb{G}_X$ and $\mathbb{G}_S$ of PhoneX Central and Active Session

4   Testing

In [6], we modelled timed distributed systems as tuples $(\mathbb{LS}_1, \ldots, \mathbb{LS}_n)$ where each $\mathbb{LS}_i$ denotes a black box localised system under test. Then we defined a conformance relation *dtioco* to test such a distributed system with respect to a system model $(\mathbb{G}_1, \ldots, \mathbb{G}_n)$. We showed that solving the oracle problem for an observable multi-trace $(\sigma_1, \cdots, \sigma_n)$ reduces to: (a) solve the oracle problem of each σ_i with respect to *tioco* [15] and with $\mathbb{G}_i$ as reference model (unitary testing, see Sect. 4.1) and, (b) check whether $(\sigma_1, \cdots, \sigma_n)$ is an observable (uninitialised) multi-trace. In Sect. 4.1 we briefly recall the principles of a simplified[4] version of the unitary testing algorithm defined in [1]. Then in Sect. 4.2, we introduce the new algorithm based on constraint solving to decide if a tuple is an observational multi-trace. As compared to [1,6], we have slightly adapted our definitions of timed traces in order to deal with events instead of atomic observations such as inputs, outputs or durations; this adaptation has no impact on the results in [1,6].

4.1   Unitary Testing

A Localised subsystem Under Test (LUT) is defined over a set of channels C as a non-empty subset $\mathbb{LS}$ of $UOTraces(C)$ such that:

– **Input completeness:** for any σ in $\mathbb{LS}$ of the form $\sigma'.ev'$, for any $ev \in Evt(C)$ such that $act(ev) \in I(C)$ and $delay(ev) \leq delay(ev')$, we have $\sigma'.ev \in \mathbb{LS}$.

---

[4] Due to the lack of space.

- **Quiescence:** for all $\sigma \in \mathbb{LS}$ we have:

$$\forall ev \in Evt(C).(act(ev) \in O(C) \Rightarrow \sigma.ev \notin \mathbb{LS})$$

$$\Leftrightarrow$$

$$(\sigma \neq \varepsilon \Rightarrow (\forall d \in D^+, \sigma.(d, \delta) \in \mathbb{LS})) \wedge (\sigma = \varepsilon \Rightarrow (\_, \delta) \in \mathbb{LS})$$

Moreover for any σ in $\mathbb{LS}$ of the form $\sigma'.ev'$ with $act(ev') = \delta$, for any $ev \in Evt(C)$ with $act(ev) \in O(C)$ we have $\sigma.ev \notin \mathbb{LS}$.
- **Reaction prefix:** for any σ in $\mathbb{LS}$, we have $Pref(\sigma) \subseteq \mathbb{LS}$.

Input completeness is required so that an LUT cannot refuse an input from the environment. **Quiescence** corresponds to situations where the LUT will not react anymore until it receives a new stimulation. **Reaction prefix** is a realistic property stating that a prefix of an observation is an observation.

The local verdict computation algorithm is based on a symbolic structure $SE(\mathbb{G})_\delta$ computed from the reference model $\mathbb{G}$ obtained by classical symbolic execution techniques. It is a tree-like structure whose nodes are symbolic states used to capture information related to the possible executions of $\mathbb{G}$. A path p is a sequence of consecutive edges relating symbolic states and labelled by symbolic events. The set of executions (uninitialised timed traces) associated to p is characterised by the sequence $ev_1 \cdots ev_n$ of symbolic events labelling the consecutive edges and by the final symbolic state η. Each symbolic event of the sequence is of the form (d_i, act_i) (except ev_1 which is of the form $(\_, act_1)$). Each d_i is a new fresh variable (*i.e.* not used in the definition of $\mathbb{G}$) used to represent durations (they are typed as clocks) and each act_i is of the form $c?z_i$ or $c!t_i$ where z_i is a new fresh variable and t_i is a term built over the same equational logic signature Ω as terms in $\mathbb{G}$ but on a set of new fresh variables. η is of the form $(q, \pi_d, \pi_t, \varrho)$ where q is the state reached in $\mathbb{G}$, π_d is a constraint on new fresh data variables (let F_d be the set of those variables), π_t is a constraint on the set of variables of the form d_i and $\varrho : A \rightarrow T_\Omega(F_d)$ associates symbolic values to variables of $\mathbb{G}$. An uninitialised timed trace $ev'_1 \cdots ev'_n$ belongs to p iff for all $i \leq n$:

- ev'_i is of the form $(\_, act'_i)$ (resp. (d'_i, act'_i)) if ev_i is of the form $(\_, act_i)$ (resp. (d_i, act_i)) and act'_i is of the form $c?z'_i$ (resp. $c!t'_i$) if act_i is of the form $c?z_i$ (resp. $c!t_i$).
- Let x_i (resp. x'_i) stand for the variable z_i (resp. z'_i) if act_i (resp. act'_i) is an input and for the term t_i (resp. t'_i) if act_i (resp. act'_i) is an output. The formula $(\bigwedge_{i \leq n} x_i = x'_i) \wedge \pi_d \wedge \pi_t$ is satisfiable.

The verdict computation algorithm analyses successively all events of $\sigma = ev'_1 \cdots ev'_n$ and at each steps it computes the set of paths to which the already analysed prefix of σ belongs. As soon as possible a verdict is emitted[5]:

---

[5] In accordance with the *tioco* conformance relation.

- *Fail* if $act(ev'_i)$ is an output or δ and the set of path becomes empty, or else $act(ev'_i)$ is an input (d'_i, act'_i) and there exists an event $ev''_i = (d'''_i, act''_i)$ where act''_i is an output (not δ) satisfying $d'''_i < d'_i$ and $ev'_1 \cdots ev'_{i-1}.ev''_i$ belongs to some path of $SE(\mathbb{G})_\delta$.
- *Inconc* if $act(ev'_i)$ is an input (d'_i, act'_i), the set of path becomes empty, and for all events $ev''_i = (d'''_i, act''_i)$ where act''_i is an output (not δ), $d'''_i < d'_i$ we have $ev'_1 \cdots ev'_{i-1}.ev''_i$ does not belong to any path of $SE(\mathbb{G})_\delta$.
- *Pass* if σ is fully analysed without generating any of the previous verdicts.

4.2   Communication Testing

An SUT over Λ is a tuple $\mathbb{S} = (\mathbb{LS}_1, \ldots, \mathbb{LS}_n)$ where $\mathbb{LS}_i$ is an LUT defined over C_i (all $i \leq n$). The semantics of $\mathbb{S}$, denoted $Obs(\mathbb{S}) \subseteq \mathbb{LS}_1 \times \cdots \times \mathbb{LS}_n$, contains all observations that can be made when executing $\mathbb{S}$. The goal of Algorithm 1 is to check whether those observations reveal communication errors by checking whether they are in $UOTraces(\Lambda)$. It is based on the property that an uninitialised observable multi-trace $\mu = (\sigma_1, \cdots, \sigma_n)$ is such that each σ_i is either empty or of the form $(\_, a_i).\sigma'_i$, but in the latter case μ has been obtained from an initialised observable multi-trace of the form $\mu' = (\sigma''_1, \cdots, \sigma''_n)$ where σ''_i is ε for $\sigma_i = \varepsilon$ and of the form $(d_i, a_i).\sigma'_i$ for σ_i of the form $(\_, a_i).\sigma'_i$. Thus, $(\sigma_1, \cdots, \sigma_i.ev, \cdots \sigma_n) \in UOTraces(\Lambda)$ iff there exist durations $d_1, \cdots, d_n$ where $\mu'' = (\sigma''_1, \cdots, \sigma''_i, \cdots \sigma''_n) \in IOTraces(\Lambda)$. We check whether such durations exist by considering them as n variables $d_1, \cdots, d_n$ (of type D); we construct constraints on these variables characterising the properties of observable traces. By definition, only the occurrence of an internal input might break the property. There are two reasons for allowing an initialised observable multi-trace to be extended by an internal input. The first is that a sufficient number of corresponding internal outputs have previously been emitted. The second is that at the time when the extension is performed, the trace emitting the corresponding internal output is no longer observed. If σ_i is the trace extended by internal input a, $\rho = \sigma_i.a$ and σ_j is the trace at the interface that sends $\bar{a}$, the first case correspond to situation in which $pref(\sigma_j, \bar{a}, |\rho|_a)$ exists and C: $d_i + dur(\rho) > d_j + dur\_occ(\sigma_j, \bar{a}, |\rho|_a)$ holds. The latter case corresponds to situations in which $pref(\sigma_j, \bar{a}, |\rho|_a)$ does not exist and C': $d_i + dur(\rho) > d_j + dur(\sigma_j)$ holds. However, by definition of dur_occ, when $pref(\sigma_j, \bar{a}, |\rho|_a)$ does not exist we have that $dur\_occ(\sigma_j, \bar{a}, |\rho|_a) = dur(\sigma_j)$, which means that the constraints C and C' are equivalent. Therefore both cases can be treated in the same way by requiring that C holds, as is done in Algorithm 1. Every new constraint to be considered is added to the set E (line 10). Sat is a function on sets of constraints such that $Sat(E)$ returns $True$ if all constraints in E are simultaneously satisfiable and $False$ otherwise.

Algorithm 1. $ObsMult(\mu, d, \Lambda)$

Data: $\mu = (\sigma_1, \cdots, \sigma_n)$ tuple of traces, $d = (d_1, \cdots, d_n)$ n variables, Λ system signature
Result: a verdict stating whether or not μ is an observable multi-trace

```
1 begin
2       E ← ∅;
3       for i ∈ [1···n] do
4             ρ ← ε ;
5             foreach ev ∈ σi do
6                   ρ ← ρ.ev ;
7                   if act(ev) ∈ I(Cint(Λ)) then
8                         a ← act(ev);
9                         j ← Sender(Λ, act(ev));
10                        E ← E ∪ {(di + dur(ρ) > dj + dur_occ(σj, ā, |ρ|a)};
11                        if ¬Sat(E) then
12                              return Failcom          /* It's not an observable multi-trace */;

13 return Passcom;
```

---

5   Experiments

We implemented the approach by separating the verification of local traces (Sect. 4.1) and the verification of the tuple of traces against the definition of observable multi-traces (Definition 6 and Sect. 4.2). If there are n subsystems, the global verdict $Verdict_g$ has $n+1$ verdicts $(Verdict_1, \ldots, Verdict_n, Verdict_{com})$ where for l in $[1\ldots n]$, $Verdict_l$ is the local verdict in $\{Pass_l, Fail_l, Inconc_l\}$ associated to the lth component and where $Verdict_{com} \in \{Pass_{com}, Fail_{com}\}$ is the verdict relating to the verification of the communication policy.

In order to assess the scalability of the framework, we adopted a mutation-based approach. We first generated multi-traces that are correct by construction with respect to local analyses and communication rules. For this purpose, a global model of the system is built by simulating internal communications using one timed queue per component. Since the reception of a message can be delayed, the model specifies asynchronous communications. Then, we use the symbolic execution platform Diversity[6] to build long traces, focusing on the behaviours that complete communication scenarios as much as possible. Finally, the resulting multi-traces are directly constructed by considering a tuple made of all projections for each component. Generated multi-traces are then modified by applying some simple mutation schemas. Table 1 summaries mutation schemas we applied on a multi-trace μ to produce a set of mutated tuples of traces.

Mutation schemas #1 and #3 require that added or modified events respect syntactic requirements from the system signature and concerning channels and data types. Mutation schema #5 is designed to break the key property of multi-traces, that is that time is necessarily elapsing when messages are transmitted. Let us illustrate with the observable multi-trace $\mu = (\sigma_1, \sigma_2)$ where $\sigma_1 = (\_, c_1?v_1).(1, c_2!v_2).(3, c_3?v_3)$ and $\sigma_2 = (\_, c_2?v_2).(1, c_3!v_3)$. Applying mutation schema #5 consists of breaking the so-called round-trip communication,

---

[6] https://projects.eclipse.org/proposals/eclipse-formal-modeling-project.

Table 1. Mutation schemas on multi-traces

Mut. schema	Description
#1	Choose (randomly) a position in μ and insert an event ev
#2	Choose randomly an event ev in μ and delete it
#3	Choose randomly an event ev in μ and modify its data
#4	Choose randomly an event ev in μ and modify its duration
#5	Choose randomly a round-trip-commnunication (RTC) in μ and break it

abbreviated as the acronym RTC, $c_2!v_2 \rightarrow c_2?v_2 \rightarrow c_3!v_3 \rightarrow c_3?v_3$, for which by construction, the delay between the emission and the reception on the first component has to be strictly greater than the delay between the reception and the emission on the second component. Mutation schema #5 modifies delays between these actions so that there is an internal reception occurring before its corresponding emission is sent. A possible mutation of μ using mutation schema #5 could be $\mu' = (\sigma_1', \sigma_2')$ with $\sigma_1' = (\_, c_1?v_1).(1, c_2!v_2).(1, c_3?v_3)$ and $\sigma_2' = (\_, c_2?v_2).(2, c_3!v_3)$. While the first 4 mutation schemas do not necessarily create faulty multi-traces, mutation schema #5 creates by construction at least a communication fault.

The size of the PhoneX system depends on the number of clients. We consider a system with 3 caller clients, 3 called clients, 3 active sessions and a PhoneX central. In Table 2, the third column (com. checking) give the time[7] needed to solve the constraint associated to the verification of communications described in a multi-trace whose number of events is given in the first column and number of internal communications is given in the second column. The fourth column provides the time[8] needed to analyse all local traces. For each multi-trace, we generate 1000 mutated tuples of traces and we count the ratio of multi-traces that are faulty with regards to communication policy (before last column). Finally, in the last column, we give the average time to check the communication constraint of the mutated tuples. Experiments have been performed on a 3.10 Ghz Intel Xeon E5-2687W working station with 64 GB of RAM on Linux Ubuntu 14.04.

Among classical solvers, we get best results with the Yices SMT solver [5]. The efficiency of Yices for solving constraints of the form $d_i + x > d_j + y$ where x and y are concrete durations together with the fact that constructing the set of constraints from a tuple is linear explains that communication checking is more efficient than unit testing. Unit testing of subsystems is performed by the extension to unitary testing of the symbolic execution platform Diversity which is coupled with several solvers such as Yices, CVC4 or Z3. Regarding symbolic models without timed issues, functionalities (test case generation driven by test purposes, verdict computation) offered by the Diversity test extension are similar to those provided by the tool STG [4].

---

[7] using the Yices SMT solver [5].
[8] using the CVC4 solver [2] embedded in the Diversity platform.

Table 2. Experimental data for correct multitraces and their mutants

Correct multi-traces generated by Diversity				1000 Mutated tuples of traces	
#events	#internal. com	Com. checking	Local. testing (for all traces)	#com. errors	Average of com. checking
759	340	17 ms	6 s 519 ms	713	17.371 ms
1587	700	28 ms	21 s 761 ms	729	27.648 ms
3633	1589	49 ms	1 m 34 s 178 ms	800	40.934 ms
6486	2830	59 ms	7 m 5 s 797 ms	737	60.140 ms
7797	3400	69 ms	10 m 52 s 378 ms	722	66.315 ms
9999	4357	88 ms	24 m 14 s 860 ms	738	80.825 ms

6   Related Work

Testing timed distributed systems from models gives rise to several recent works. In [16], hypotheses are broadly the same as those adopted in this paper, namely a model for each local component, and a testing architecture constituted of independent local testers. [16] mainly focuses on the generation of test cases from a global model built by composing local models and queues, similar to the one that we used in Sect. 5. The main difference is that the correction of the system can boil down to the local correction of each component, without any verification of internal communications. In [13], testing of distributed real-time systems is based on the conformance relation tioco and considers timed automata as models. Testers can be local or global so that the testing architecture does not necessarily reflect the one of the system. The authors focus on the construction of analogue-clock and digital-clock test cases. The question of communications is supported by a compositionality result saying that correctness up to tioco is preserved by parallel composition of timed automata provided that they are input-enabled. Similarly, in [22], local testers that can exchange synchronisation messages are derived from a global timed automaton. Thus, all these works are rather interested in the issue of test case generation, assuming testing hypotheses on communications between components, while we leave aside this question to focus on the analysis of traces with almost no hypotheses on internal communications. Lastly, the use of constraint solvers is often advocated when dealing with software and system testing issues [7]. As an example of usage for the verdict computation in MBT, [12] uses SAT solvers for generating checking sequences from finite state machines.

7   Conclusion

We focus on the oracle problem for testing distributed systems against specifications. A system execution is a tuple of timed local traces, one for each location. An observation is correct iff each local trace is allowed by the corresponding specification component and the tuple of local traces defines a valid communication scenario. The oracle problem is reduced to several instances of the standard oracle problem for centralised testing plus a constraint satisfaction problem for communication. This is implemented as an orchestration coordinating several centralised verdict computations using the Diversity tool and calls to classical constraint solvers. We have carried out experiments with a central telecommunication system which have shown low computation time. Our algorithm is designed for active testing in which we run a test and then check the observation made. It would be interesting to extend it to deal with passive testing.

References

1. Bannour, B., Escobedo, J.P., Gaston, C., Gall, L.P.: Off-line test case generation for timed symbolic model-based conformance testing. In: Nielsen, B., Weise, C. (eds.) ICTSS 2012. LNCS, vol. 7641, pp. 119–135. Springer, Heidelberg (2012). doi:10.1007/978-3-642-34691-0_10

2. Barrett, C., Conway, C.L., Deters, M., Hadarean, L., Jovanović, D., King, T., Reynolds, A., Tinelli, C.: CVC4. In: Gopalakrishnan, G., Qadeer, S. (eds.) CAV 2011. LNCS, vol. 6806, pp. 171–177. Springer, Heidelberg (2011). doi:10.1007/978-3-642-22110-1_14

3. Brinksma, E., Heerink, L., Tretmans, J.: Factorized test generation for multi-input/output transition systems. In: FIP TC6 11th International Workshop on Testing Communicating Systems (IWTCS), vol. 131 of IFIP Conference Proceedings, pp. 67–82. Kluwer (1998)

4. Clarke, D., Jéron, T., Rusu, V., Zinovieva, E.: STG: a symbolic test generation tool. In: Katoen, J.-P., Stevens, P. (eds.) TACAS 2002. LNCS, vol. 2280, pp. 470–475. Springer, Heidelberg (2002). doi:10.1007/3-540-46002-0_34

5. Dutertre, B.: Yices 2.2. In: Biere, A., Bloem, R. (eds.) CAV 2014. LNCS, vol. 8559, pp. 737–744. Springer, Cham (2014). doi:10.1007/978-3-319-08867-9_49

6. Gaston, C., Hierons, R.M., Gall, L.P.: An implementation relation and test framework for timed distributed systems. In: Yenigün, H., Yilmaz, C., Ulrich, A. (eds.) ICTSS 2013. LNCS, vol. 8254, pp. 82–97. Springer, Heidelberg (2013). doi:10.1007/978-3-642-41707-8_6

7. Gotlieb, A.: Constraint-based testing: an emerging trend in software testing. Adv. Comput. 99, 67–101 (2015)

8. Grieskamp, W., Kicillof, N., Stobie, K., Braberman, V.: Model-based quality assurance of protocol documentation: tools and methodology. J. Softw. Testing Verification Reliab. 21(1), 55–71 (2011)

9. Hierons, R.M., Merayo, M.G., Núñez, M.: Implementation relations for the distributed test architecture. In: Suzuki, K., Higashino, T., Ulrich, A., Hasegawa, T. (eds.) FATES/TestCom -2008. LNCS, vol. 5047, pp. 200–215. Springer, Heidelberg (2008). doi:10.1007/978-3-540-68524-1_15

10. Hierons, R.M., Merayo, M.G., Núñez, M.: Using time to add order to distributed testing. In: Giannakopoulou, D., Méry, D. (eds.) FM 2012. LNCS, vol. 7436, pp. 232–246. Springer, Heidelberg (2012). doi:10.1007/978-3-642-32759-9_20

11. Joint Technical Committee ISO/IEC JTC 1. International Standard ISO/IEC 9646–1. Information Technology - Open Systems Interconnection - Conformance testing methodology, framework - Part 1: General concepts. ISO/IEC (1994)

12. Jourdan, G.-V., Ural, H., Yenigün, H., Zhu, D.: Using a SAT solver to generate checking sequences. In: The 24th International Symposium on Computer and Information Sciences, ISCIS 2009, pp. 549–554. IEEE (2009)

13. Krichen, M.: A formal framework for black-box conformance testing of distributed real-time systems. Int. J. Crit. Comput. Based Syst. **3**(1/2), 26–43 (2012)

14. Krichen, M., Tripakis, S.: Black-box conformance testing for real-time systems. In: Graf, S., Mounier, L. (eds.) SPIN 2004. LNCS, vol. 2989, pp. 109–126. Springer, Heidelberg (2004). doi:10.1007/978-3-540-24732-6_8

15. Krichen, M., Tripakis, S.: Conformance testing for real-time systems. Form. Methods Syst. Des. **34**(3), 238–304 (2009)

16. Nguyen, H.N., Zaïdi, F., Cavalli, A.R.: A framework for distributed testing of timed composite systems. In: 21st Asia-Pacific Software Engineering Conference, APSEC, pp. 47–54. IEEE (2014)

17. Petrenko, A., Yevtushenko, N.: Testing from partial deterministic FSM specifications. IEEE Trans. Comput. **54**(9), 1154–1165 (2005)

18. Ericsson International report. Investigation on how to integrate Diversity (MBT tool) and Titan (TTCN-3 executor) to provide an open source MBT tool chain (2016)

19. Sarikaya, B., von Bochmann, G.: Synchronization and specification issues in protocol testing. IEEE Trans. Commun. **32**, 389–395 (1984)

20. Schmaltz, J., Tretmans, J.: On conformance testing for timed systems. In: Cassez, F., Jard, C. (eds.) FORMATS 2008. LNCS, vol. 5215, pp. 250–264. Springer, Heidelberg (2008). doi:10.1007/978-3-540-85778-5_18

21. Tretmans, J.: Model based testing with labelled transition systems. In: Hierons, R.M., Bowen, J.P., Harman, M. (eds.) Formal Methods and Testing. LNCS, vol. 4949, pp. 1–38. Springer, Heidelberg (2008). doi:10.1007/978-3-540-78917-8_1

22. Vain, J., Halling, E., Kanter, G., Anier, A., Pal, D.: Automatic distribution of local testers for testing distributed systems. In: 12th International Baltic Conference on Databases and Information Systems IX, vol. 291, pp. 297–310. IOS Press (2016)

Checking Response-Time Properties of Web-Service Applications Under Stochastic User Profiles

Richard Schumi[1(✉)], Priska Lang[2], Bernhard K. Aichernig[1],
Willibald Krenn[2], and Rupert Schlick[2]

[1] Institute of Software Technology, Graz University of Technology, Graz, Austria
{rschumi,aichernig}@ist.tugraz.at
[2] Austrian Institute of Technology, Vienna, Austria
{Priska.Lang,Willibald.Krenn,Rupert.Schlick}@ait.ac.at

Abstract. Performance evaluation of critical software is important but also computationally expensive. It usually involves sophisticated load-testing tools and demands a large amount of computing resources. Analysing different user populations requires even more effort, becoming infeasible in most realistic cases. Therefore, we propose a model-based approach. We apply model-based test-case generation to generate log-data and learn the associated distributions of response times. These distributions are added to the behavioural models on which we perform statistical model checking (SMC) in order to assess the probabilities of the required response times. Then, we apply classical hypothesis testing to evaluate if an implementation of the behavioural model conforms to these timing requirements. This is the first model-based approach for performance evaluation combining automated test-case generation, cost learning and SMC for real applications. We realised this method with a property-based testing tool, extended with SMC functionality, and evaluate it on an industrial web-service application.

Keywords: Statistical model checking · Property-based testing · Model-based testing · FsCheck · User profiles · Response time · Cost learning

1 Introduction

Statistical model checking (SMC) is a simulation method that can answer both quantitative and qualitative questions. The questions are expressed as properties of a stochastic model which are checked by analysing simulations of this model. Depending on the SMC algorithm, either a fixed number of samples or a stopping criterion is needed. Property-based testing (PBT) is a random testing technique that tries to falsify a given property, which describes the expected behaviour of a function-under-test. In order to test such a property, a PBT tool generates inputs for the function and checks if the expected behaviour is observed.

© IFIP International Federation for Information Processing 2017
Published by Springer International Publishing AG 2017. All Rights Reserved
N. Yevtushenko et al. (Eds.): ICTSS 2017, LNCS 10533, pp. 293–310, 2017.
DOI: 10.1007/978-3-319-67549-7_18

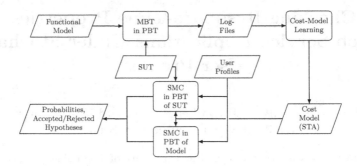

Fig. 1. Overview of the steps for cost-model learning and response-time checking.

In previous work [2,3], we have demonstrated how SMC can be integrated into a PBT tool in order to evaluate properties of stochastic models as well as stochastic implementations. Based on this previous work, we present a simulation method for stochastic user profiles of a web-service application in order to answer questions about the expected response time of a system-under-test (SUT). Figure 1 illustrates this process.

First, we apply a PBT tool to run model-based testing (MBT) with a functional model concurrently in several threads in order to obtain log-files that include the response times of the tested web-service requests. Since the model serves as an oracle, we also test for conformance violations in this phase. This functional aspect was discussed in earlier work [1], here the focus is on timing.

In the next step, we derive response-time distributions per type of service request via linear regression, which was a suitable learning method for our logs. Since the response time is influenced by the parallel activity on the server, the distributions are parametrised by the number of active users. These cost distributions are added to the transitions in the functional model resulting in, so called, cost models. These models have the semantics of stochastic timed automata (STA) [6]. The name *cost model* shall emphasize that our method may be generalized to other type of cost indicators, e.g., energy consumption.

Next, we combine these models with user profiles, containing probabilities for transitions and waiting times, in order to simulate realistic user behaviour and the expected response time. With this simulation we can evaluate response-time properties, like "What is the probability that the response time of each user within a user population is under a certain threshold?" or "Is this probability above or below a specific limit?".

Additionally, we can check such properties directly on the SUT, e.g., to verify the simulation on the model. It is also possible to skip the model simulation and test response-time properties directly on the SUT. However, running a realistic user population on the SUT is time-consuming and might not be feasible due to realistic waiting times. A simulation on the model is much faster. Therefore, also properties that require a larger number of samples can be checked, e.g., Monte Carlo simulation. Our aim is to run the SUT only with a limited number of samples in order to check, if the property results of the model are satisfied by the SUT. Therefore, we test the SUT with the sequential probability ratio test [34], a form of hypothesis testing, as this allows us to stop testing as soon as we have sufficient evidence.

Related Work. A number of related approaches in the area of PBT are concerned with testing concurrent software. For example, Claessen et al. [13] presented a testing method that can find race conditions in Erlang with QuickCheck and a user-level scheduler called PULSE. A similar approach was shown by Norell et al. [28]. They demonstrated an automated way to test blocking operations, i.e. operations that have to wait until a certain condition is met. Another concurrent PBT approach was demonstrated by Hughes et al. [20]. They showed how PBT can be applied to test distributed file-synchronisation services, like Dropbox. The closest related work we found in the PBT community was from Arts [5]. It shows a load-testing approach with QuickCheck that can run user scenarios on an SUT in order to determine the maximum supported number of users. In contrast to our approach, Arts does not consider stochastic user profiles and the user scenarios are only tested on an SUT, but not simulated at model-level.

Related work can also be found in the area of load testing. For example, Draheim et al. [14] demonstrated a load-testing approach that simulates realistic user behaviour with stochastic models. Moreover, a number of related tools, like Neoload perform load testing with user populations [31]. In contrast to our work, load testing is mostly performed directly on the SUT. With our approach, we want to simulate user populations on the model-level as well. There are also many approaches that focus only on a simulation on the model-level [7,9,11,26], but with our method we can also directly test an SUT within the same tool.

The most related tool is UPPAAL SMC [10]. Similar to our approach, it provides SMC of priced timed automata, which can simulate user populations. It also supports testing real implementations, but for this a test adapter needs to be implemented, which, e.g., handles form-data creation. With our method, we can use PBT features, like generators in order to automatically generate form data and we can model in a programming language. This helps testers, who are already familiar with this language, as they do not have to learn new notations.

To the best of our knowledge our work is novel: (1) no other work applies PBT for evaluating stochastic properties about the response time of both real systems and stochastic models, (2) no other work performs cost learning on behaviour models using linear regression. Grinchtein learns time-deterministic event-recording automata via active automata learning [16]. Verwer et al. passively learn probabilistic real-time automata [33]. In contrast, we learn cost distributions and add them to existing automata models for SMC.

Contribution. We present a cost-model learning approach that works with log-files of tests of a PBT tool and derives cost distributions for varying numbers of users. Building upon our previous work, where we integrated SMC into a PBT tool [3], we show how the learned cost models can be applied to simulate the response time of user profiles. With this simulation we can evaluate response-time properties with SMC based on the model. Moreover, we can also check such properties on the real system by applying hypothesis testing and by measuring the real response times instead of the simulated ones. Another contribution is the evaluation of our method by applying it to an industrial web-service application.

Structure. First, Sect. 2 introduces the background of SMC and PBT based on our previous work [3] and it explains cost-model learning. Next, in Sect. 3 we present an example and demonstrate our method. In Sect. 4, we give more details about the process and implementations. Section 5 presents an evaluation with an industrial web-service application. Finally, we conclude in Sect. 6.

2   Background

2.1   Statistical Model Checking (SMC)

SMC is a verification method that evaluates certain properties of a stochastic model. These properties are usually defined with (temporal) logics, and they can describe quantitative and qualitative questions. For example, questions, like *what is the probability that the model satisfies a property* or *is the probability that the model satisfies a property above or below a certain threshold?* In order to answer such questions, a statistical model checker produces samples, i.e. random walks on the stochastic model and checks whether the property holds for these samples. Various SMC algorithms are applied in order to compute the total number of samples needed to find an answer for a specific question or to compute a stopping criterion. This criterion determines when we can stop sampling because we have found an answer with a required certainty. In this work, we focus on the following algorithms, which are commonly used in the SMC literature [24,25].

Monte Carlo Simulation with Chernoff-Hoeffding Bound. The algorithm computes the required number of simulations n in order to estimate the probability γ that a stochastic model satisfies a Boolean property. The procedure is based on the Chernoff-Hoeffding bound [18] that provides a lower limit for the probability that the estimation error is below a value ϵ. Assuming a confidence $1 - \delta$ the required number of simulations can be calculated as follows:

$$n \geq \frac{1}{2\epsilon^2} \ln\left(\frac{2}{\delta}\right)$$

The n simulations represent Bernoulli random variables $X_1, \ldots, X_n$ with outcome $x_i = 1$ if the property holds for the i-th simulation run and $x_i = 0$ otherwise. Let the estimated probability be $\bar{\gamma}_n = (\sum_{i=1}^{n} x_i)/n$, then the probability that the estimation error is below ϵ is greater than our required confidence. Formally we have: $Pr(|\bar{\gamma}_n - \gamma| \leq \epsilon) \geq 1 - \delta$. After the calculation of the number of samples n, a simple Monte Carlo simulation is performed [25].

Sequential Probability Ratio Test (SPRT). This sequential method [34] is a form of hypothesis testing, which can answer qualitative questions. Given a random variable X with a probability density function $f(x, \theta)$, we want to decide, whether a null hypothesis $H_0 : \theta = \theta_0$ or an alternative hypothesis $H_1 : \theta = \theta_1$ is true for desired type I and II errors (α, β). In order to make the decision, we start sampling and calculate the log-likelihood ratio after each observation of x_i:

$$\log \Lambda_m = \log \frac{p_1^m}{p_0^m} = \log \frac{\prod\limits_{i=1}^{m} f(x_i, \theta_1)}{\prod\limits_{i=1}^{m} f(x_i, \theta_0)} = \sum_{i=1}^{m} \log \frac{f(x_i, \theta_1)}{f(x_i, \theta_0)}$$

We continue sampling as long as $\log \frac{\beta}{1-\alpha} < \log \Lambda_m < \log \frac{1-\beta}{\alpha}$. H_1 is accepted when $\log \Lambda_m \geq \log \frac{1-\beta}{\alpha}$, and H_0 when $\log \Lambda_m \leq \log \frac{\beta}{1-\alpha}$ [15].

In this work, we form a hypothesis about the expected response time with the Monte Carlo method on the model. Then, we check with SPRT if this hypothesis holds on the SUT. This is faster than running Monte Carlo directly on the SUT.

2.2 Property-Based Testing (PBT)

PBT is a random-testing technique that aims to check the correctness of properties. A property is a high-level specification of the expected behaviour of a function-under-test that should always hold. For example, the length of a concatenated list is always equal to the sum of lengths of its sub-lists:

$$\forall \, l_1, l_2 \in Lists[T] : length(concatenate(l_1, l_2)) = length(l_1) + length(l_2)$$

With PBT, we automatically generate inputs for such a property by applying data generators, e.g., the random list generator. The inputs are fed to the function-under-test and the property is evaluated. If it holds, then this indicates that the function works as expected, otherwise a counterexample is produced.

PBT also supports MBT. Models encoded as extended finite state machines (EFSMs) [22] can serve as source for state-machine properties. An EFSM is a 6-tuple (S, s_0, V, I, O, T). S is a finite set of states, $s_0 \in S$ is the initial state, V is a finite set of variables, I is a finite set of inputs, O is a finite set of outputs, T is a finite set of transitions. A transition $t \in T$ can be described as a 5-tuple (s_s, i, g, op, s_t), s_s is the source state, i is an input, g is a guard, op is a sequence of output and assignment operations, s_t is the target state [22]. In order to derive a state-machine property from an EFSM, we have to write a specification comprising the initial state, commands and a generator for the next transition given the current state of the model. Commands encapsulate (1) preconditions that define the permitted transition sequences, (2) postconditions that specify the expected behaviour and (3) execution semantics of transitions for the model and the SUT. A state-machine property states that for all permitted transition sequences, the postcondition must hold after the execution of each transition, respectively command [19,29]. Formally we define such a property as follows:

$$cmd.runModel, cmd.runActual : S \times I \to S \times O$$
$$cmd.pre : I \times S \to Boolean, cmd.post : S \times O \times S \times O \to Boolean$$
$$\forall s \in S, i \in I, cmd \in Cmds :$$
$$cmd.pre(i, s) \implies cmd.post(cmd.runModel(i, s), cmd.runActual(i, s))$$

We have two functions to execute a command on the model and on the SUT: $cmd.runModel$ and $cmd.runActual$. The precondition $cmd.pre$ defines the valid inputs for a command. The postcondition $cmd.post$ compares the outputs and states of the model and the SUT after the execution of a command.

PBT is a powerful testing technique that allows a flexible definition of generators and properties via inheritance or composition. The first implementation of PBT was QuickCheck for Haskell [12]. Numerous reimplementations followed for other programming languages, like Hypothesis[1] for Python or ScalaCheck [27]. We demonstrate our approach with FsCheck [1]. FsCheck is a .NET port of QuickCheck with influences of ScalaCheck. It supports a property definition in both, a functional programming style with F# and an object-oriented style with C#. We work with C# as it is the programming language of our SUT.

2.3   Stochastic Timed Automata

Timed automata (TA) were originally introduced by Alur and Dill [4]. Several extensions of TA have been proposed, including stochastically enhanced TA [8] and continuous probabilistic TA [23]. We follow the definition of Stochastic Timed Automata (STA) by Ballarini et al. [6]: An STA can be expressed as a tuple $(L, l_0, A, C, I, E, F, W)$, where the first part is a normal TA (L, l_0, A, C, I, E) and additionally it contains probability density functions (PDFs) $F = (f_l)_{l \in L}$ for the sojourn time and natural weights $W = (w_e)_{e \in E}$ for the transitions. L is a finite set of locations, $l_0 \in L$ is the initial location, A is a finite set of actions, C is a finite set of clocks with real-valued valuations $u(c) \in \mathbb{R}_{>0}$, $I : L \mapsto \mathcal{B}(C)$ is a finite set of invariants for the locations and $E \subseteq L \times A \times \mathcal{B}(C) \times 2^C \times L$ is a finite set of transitions between locations, with an action, a guard and a set of clock resets. The transition relation can be described as follows. For a location l and a clock valuation u the PDF f_l is used to choose the sojourn time d, which changes the state to $(l, u + d)$, where $u + d$ means that the clock valuation is changed $(u + d)(c) = u(c) + d$ for all $c \in C$. After this change, an edge e is selected out of the set of enabled edges $E(l, u+d)$ with the probability $w_e / \sum_{h \in E(l,u+d)} w_h$. Then, a transition to the target location l' of e and $u' = u+d$ is performed. For our models the underlying stochastic process is a semi-Markov process as the clocks are reset at every transition, but we do not assume exponential waiting times and therefore the process is not a standard continuous-time Markov chain.

---

[1] https://pypi.python.org/pypi/hypothesis.

2.4   Integration of SMC into PBT

We have demonstrated that SMC can be integrated into a PBT tool in order to perform SMC of PBT-properties [2,3], which were explained in Sect. 2.2. These PBT-properties can be evaluated on stochastic models, like in classical SMC, as well as on stochastic implementations. For the integration we introduced our own new SMC properties, which take a PBT property, configurations for the PBT execution, and parameters for the specific SMC algorithm as input. Then, our properties perform an SMC algorithm by utilizing the PBT tool as simulation environment and they return either a quantitative or qualitative result, depending on the algorithm. Figure 2 shows how we can evaluate a state-machine property within an SMC property. Such a state-machine property can, e.g., be applied for a statistical conformance analysis by comparing an ideal model to a stochastic faulty implementation or it can also simulate a stochastic model. We evaluated our SMC properties by repeating case studies from the SMC literature and we were able to reproduce the results.

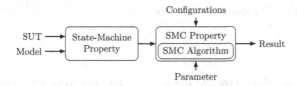

Fig. 2. Data flow diagram of an SMC property.

2.5   Cost-Model Learning

We aim at learning response times or other costs from log-files in order to associate them to behavioural models. This problem can be seen as a classical regression problem. (Note that other types of costs or systems can require different learning methods, like Splines or tree-based models [17,35].) The simplest regression method is the linear least squares regression, which minimizes the difference between the observed and estimated values (called residuals). An advantage of this method is that it may also help in detecting confounding variables, e.g., when the full model does not predict well. For removing these noisy or highly correlated variables, different feature selection algorithms are available [32].

Multiple Regression. The general linear regression model is known as

$$y = X\beta + \epsilon$$

where y is the dependent variable (regressand), X is the design matrix of the independent variables (regressors), β contains the partial derivatives and ϵ is the error term. In more detail, in case of i regressors the cost function for the nth observation is

$$y_n = \beta_0 + x_{n1}\beta_1 + \ldots + x_{ni}\beta_i + \epsilon_n$$

with β_0 as the constant term.

Discrete values are handled via categorical variables that can take on one of a limited number of possible values, called levels. In case of categorical independent variables, to transfer the factors into a linear regression model different coding techniques are available. (If they are not independent, interaction terms can be added [21].) The simplest is dummy coding, where each level of a factor has its own binary dummy variable (indicator variable), set to 1 if the observation has factor level i, 0 otherwise. By definition, these variables are linearly dependent, because the sum of all columns related to the same factor leads to a column of ones, which is the constant intercept term. Therefore, to avoid singularity problems, for each factor it is necessary to have one dummy variable less than the number of factor levels. The factor level that has no dummy variable is the so called reference group of the model. It has zeros in all dummy variables. In case of numerical and categorical regressors, we have a combination that yields $y = X\beta + Z\gamma + \epsilon$, where X is the design matrix for the categorical variables and Z contains the measured values (covariables). γ contains analogous to β the partial derivatives. For more details, see [30].

3 Method

In this section, we show how we derive cost models from logs and how we can apply these models to simulate stochastic user profiles. This approach is demonstrated by an example of an industrial incident manager [1].

This SUT is a web-based tool that supports tasks, like creating, editing or closing incident objects, which are elements of the application domain, e.g., bug reports. These objects include attributes (form data) that are stored in a database and have to be set by the users. The state machine in Fig. 3 on the left represents the tasks of an incident object. To keep it simple, this state machine only represents the tasks of a currently opened incident without attributes. In reality, we also have transitions to switch between objects and a variety of attributes. Hence, this functional model is an EFSM. In our previous work, we have demonstrated how such functional models can be derived from business-rule models of the server implementation [1]. For this paper, we assume existing functional models, although they are created in the same way as before. Each task consists of subtasks, e.g., for setting attributes or for opening a screen. The subtasks of one task can be seen in the middle of Fig. 3. Many subtasks require server interaction. Therefore, they can also be seen as requests.

Based on these functional models, we can perform conventional PBT, which generates random sequences of commands with form data (attributes). While the properties are tested on the SUT, a log is created that captures the response times (costs) of individual requests. The properties are checked concurrently on the SUT in order to obtain response times of multiple simultaneous requests, which represents the behaviour of multiple active users. An example log from a non-productive test system with low computing resources (virtual machine) is

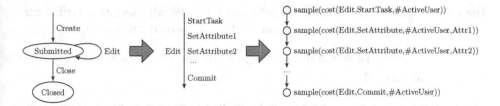

Fig. 3. Cost model of the incident manger.

Table 1. Example log-data of the incident manager.

Task	From	To	Subtask	#ActiveUsers	Attribute	ResponseTime [ms]
Create	Global	Submitted	StartTask	7	–	334
Create	Global	Submitted	SetAttribute	8	Assignee	77
Edit	Submitted	Submitted	StartTask	5	–	286
Create	Global	Submitted	Commit	6	–	918
Edit	Submitted	Submitted	SetAttribute	4	TestOrder	347

represented in Table 1. We record response times of tasks, subtasks, attributes, states (From, To) and simultaneous requests (#ActiveUsers). For this initial logging phase the transitions are chosen with uniform distribution. For learning the cost models, we first did some descriptive statistics and feature selection by applying common wrapper models to the logs, e.g., stepwise regression. Selecting the most important variables yields the linear multiple regression (LMR) model:

$$ResponseTime \sim \#ActiveUsers + Task + Subtask + Attribute$$

For categorical variables (tasks, subtasks and attributes), the dummy coding, as explained in Sect. 2.5, was applied. Listing 1.1 shows the results of the LMR. For this system, the log-file contains 293.361 observations (subtasks). The calculations are done in R version 3.3.2 with the lm function from the stats package.[2] In the left column are the intercept and the regressor variables. The second column shows the estimates of means with empirical standard errors in the third. The fourth column contains the t values that are the ratio of estimate and standard error. The p values in the last column describe the statistical significance of the estimates: low p values, indicate high significance. They are marked with $*$ if $0.01 < p \leqslant 0.05$ and $***$ if $p \leqslant 0.001$. In our LMR model, nearly all variables are significant and are, therefore, used to obtain different probability distributions for costs. These costs can be expressed as functions that take a task, subtask, the number of active users (i.e. a natural number without zero $\mathbb{N}_{>0}$) and an attribute as input and return empirical parameters for probability distributions. For our observed response times, we selected the normal distribution and since the real parameters are unknown, the cost function gives us the parameter μ for

---

[2] https://www.r-project.org/.

the mean (estimate of the LMR output) and σ for the std. deviation (std. error of the LMR output). Both of these parameters are positive real numbers $\mathbb{R}_{>0}$.

$$cost : Task \times Subtask \times \mathbb{N}_{>0} \times Attribute \rightarrow \mathbb{R}_{>0} \times \mathbb{R}_{>0}$$

$$sample : \mathbb{R}_{>0} \times \mathbb{R}_{>0} \rightarrow \mathbb{R}_{>0}$$

We use these parameters for a sample function returning a response-time value, which is chosen according to this normal distribution. The right-hand side of Fig. 3 shows the application of these functions for a task. For each subtask, we introduced a state with the *sampled* sojourn time.

		Estimate	Std. Error	t value	Pr(>|t|)	
1						
2	(Intercept)	405.4160	52.9412	7.658	1.90e-14	***
3	X.ActiveUsers	33.7867	0.3094	109.187	< 2e-16	***
4	Task_IncidentCloseTask	44.7672	52.9505	0.845	0.3979	
5	Task_IncidentCreateTask	365.8872	52.9359	6.912	4.79e-12	***
6	Task_IncidentEditTask	135.8733	52.9421	2.566	0.0103	*
7	Task_Select	−220.7655	52.9422	−4.170	3.05e-05	***
8	Action_SetAttribute	−133.2684	2.3094	−57.706	< 2e-16	***
9	Action_StartTask	−341.9593	1.4774	−231.460	< 2e-16	***
10	Attribute_Assignee	−486.6695	2.8706	−169.539	< 2e-16	***

Listing 1.1. Excerpt of the linear multiple regression output.

In addition to the cost models, also user profiles are needed for the simulation. For our use case they are represented by weights for tasks, by waiting intervals between tasks/subtasks and additionally by waiting factors for the input time, e.g., a delay per character for the time to enter a text. The transition probabilities resulting from the task weights are shown on the left-hand side of Fig. 4. Note, we also included the probability for *select* transitions, which allow a switch between active incident objects. On the right-hand side, a representation of this user profile is shown in the JavaScript Object Notation (JSON) format, which was used for storage. It also includes the mentioned waiting intervals and factors.

This user profile is joined with the cost model in order to obtain a combined model that can be applied to simulate a user. A user population is simulated by executing this model concurrently within one of our SMC properties, which were explained in Sect. 2.4. The combined model has the semantics of a stochastic timed automaton, as explained in Sect. 2.3. The weights of the tasks can be expressed with the transition weights W. The probability density functions F for the sojourn time can be defined with parameters μ and σ of the normal distribution or with intervals for the uniform distribution, which we used for the waiting times of user profiles. Note, for these waiting times, we also introduce states in a similar way as for the subtasks, as illustrated in Fig. 3.

In order to estimate the probability of response-time properties, we perform a Monte Carlo simulation with Chernoff-Hoeffding bound. However, this simulation requires too many samples to be efficiently executed on the SUT and so we only run it on the model. For example, checking the probability that the response time of a *Commit* subtask is under a threshold of one second for each user of a population of 10 users with parameters $\epsilon = 0.05$ and $\delta = 0.01$, requires 1060 samples and returns a probability of 0.593, when a test-case length of three tasks is considered. Fortunately, hypothesis testing requires fewer samples and is, therefore, better suited for the evaluation of the SUT. The probability that

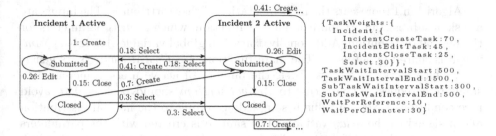

Fig. 4. User profile of the incident manager.

was computed on the model serves as a hypothesis to check, if the SUT is at least as good. We apply it as alternative hypothesis and select a probability of 0.493 as null hypothesis, which is 0.1 smaller, because we want to be able to reject the hypothesis that the SUT has a smaller probability. By running SPRT (with 0.01 as type I and II error parameters) for each user of the population, we can check these hypotheses. The alternative hypothesis was accepted for all users and on average 76.8 samples were needed for the decision.

Algorithm 1. Pseudo code of a CostAttribute class.

Local Variables and Inputs: Task t, Subtask st, Attribute a, function $cost : (\dots) \rightarrow (\mu, \sigma)$
Global Variable: $ActiveUserNum \in \mathbb{N}$ ▷ number of users that have an open request
1: **function** GENERATOR
2:    $ActiveUserNum \leftarrow ActiveUserNum + 1$ ▷ should be locked (Mutex)
3:    $delay \leftarrow sample(cost(t, st, ActiveUserNum, a))$ ▷ sample normal distribution
4:    $sleep(delay)$ ▷ thread should sleep
5:    $ActiveUserNum \leftarrow ActiveUserNum - 1$ ▷ should be locked (Mutex)
6:    **return** $Gen.Constant(delay)$

---

4   Model-Simulation Architecture and Implementations

Here, we detail the integration of the cost models and user profiles into a collective model and we illustrate how such models can be simulated with PBT.

We already presented an existing implementation of MBT with FsCheck [1], which supports automatic form-data generation and EFSMs. Based on this work, we implemented the following extensions in order to support our method. The first extension is a parser that reads the cost distributions and integrates them into the model. In the previous implementation, we had command instances, which represent the tasks and attributes which include generators for different data types (for the generation of form data). Now, we introduce new *CostAttributes* for costs or response times, which can be applied in the same way as normal form-data attributes. The generators of attributes are called during the test-case generation and the generated values can be evaluated within the commands. This helps to check response-time properties.

Algorithm 1 represents the implementation of these attributes. The inputs are a task, a subtask, an attribute and a cost function, which returns parameters for the normal distribution. Additionally, there is a global variable *ActiveUserNum*, which is shared by all users. The main function of a *CostAttribute* is its generator, which works as follows. First, the number of active users is increased to simulate a request. (The access to *ActiveUserNum* should be locked to avoid race conditions.) Next, a value is sampled according to the normal distribution and assigned to the *delay* variable. The sample is created with the parameters μ and σ from the cost function. The next step is a sleep for the time that was sampled. Then, the number of users is decreased. Finally, the generated delay is returned within a constant generator so that it can be checked outside the generator. A constant generator is applied, because the default generators do not support normal distributions, but the *Attribute* has to return an object of type *Gen* for this method. Note, this generator function also applies the generated delay. This is done, because we need to know the number of active users for the generation of a sample and in order to know which user is active it is necessary to directly execute this behaviour, so that we have active users during the generation step. Multiple users are executed concurrently in different threads in an independent way. However, their shared variable *ActiveUserNum* causes a certain dependency between the user threads, because when one user increases this variable, then this affects the response-time distributions of the other users.

Fig. 5. Attribute sequence of a task.

For the user profiles there is a parser as well and the user behaviour is also included in the combined model. The waiting times of a user can be integrated in a similar way as the costs by introducing *WaitAttributes*. Their implementation details are omitted, as they work in the same way as *CostAttributes* except that they do not change the number of active users and they use a uniform distribution instead of a normal distribution. With both these attributes, we are able to implement the sequence of subtasks of tasks as represented in Fig. 5. *WaitAttributes* represent the time that a user needs for the input and *CostAttributes* simulate the response time. Note, the simulation of the model can be done with a virtual time, i.e. a fraction of the actual time.

The selection of the tasks according to the given weights was implemented with a frequency generator. A frequency generator takes a set of weights and generator *Gen* pairs and selects one of the generators according to the weights.

$$Gen.Frequency : \mathcal{P}(\mathbb{R}_{>0} \times Gen) \to Gen$$

This generator was applied in order to choose commands, which handle the execution of tasks. The generator for commands does not only generate commands,

---

Algorithm 2. Pseudo code of the test-case generation.

Input: *spec*: state-machine specification of a PBT tool, *size*: parameter for test-case length
```
1: for i ∈ {1, ..., size} do
2:     gen ← spec.Next(model)                                    ▷ Next returns a command generator
3:     cmd ← gen.Sample()                                        ▷ command is generated
4:     model ← cmd.runModel(model)                               ▷ command is executed
5: function SPEC.NEXT(model)
6:     set ← model.getEnabledTasksWithWeights()                  ▷ set of (weight, Gen[Task])
7:     return Gen.Frequency(set).selectMany(task →
8:         task.Attributes.Generator().selectMany(data →         ▷ generate attribute data
9:             CmdGenerator(task, data)))                        ▷ generator for a command
```

---

but also their required attributes. Algorithm 2 outlines the process of the test-case generation. The algorithm requires a state-machine specification *spec*, which includes a generator for the next state and the initial state of the model. First, there is an iteration over the size parameter and in each iteration the *Next* function of the *spec* is called to obtain a command generator for the current model state. A command *cmd* is sampled according to this generator (Line 3) and executed on the model *cmd.runModel* in order to retrieve a new model, which incorporates the applied state change. This new model is needed in the next iteration for the *Next* function, which works as follows. First, a set of pairs of weights and task generators is retrieved from the *getEnabledTasksWithWeights* function of the model. Based on this set, a frequency generator is build (Line 7). The function *selectMany* of this generator is called to further process the selected value. This function can be applied to a generator in order to build a new generator. It needs an anonymous function as argument, which takes a value of the generator as input and has to return a new generator.

$$Gen[A].selectMany : (A → Gen[B]) → Gen[B]$$

Within this function, a generator is called that generates the attribute data of the task. The *selectMany* function is applied again on this generator and within this function a command generator is created for the given task and data.

5   Evaluation

We evaluated our method by applying it to a web-service application from the automotive domain, which was provided by our industrial partner AVL.[3] We focus on the response times and the number of samples needed, but omit the run-times of the simulation and testing process. The application is called Testfactory Management Suite (TFMS) version 1.7 and it enables various management activities of test fields, like test definition, planning, preparation, execution and data management/analysis for testing engines. Note that there already is a new version of TFMS with better performance, but it was not available for this work.

For our evaluation we focused on one module of the application, the Test Order Manager (TOM). This module enables the configuration and execution of

---

[3] https://www.avl.com.

test orders, which are basically a composition of steps that are necessary for a test sequence at a test field [1]. Figure 6 shows the tasks of an example test order. Each task represents the invocation of a page, entering data for form fields and saving the page. The TOM module contains further sub-models for the creation of test orders, but they are similar to this model, and are therefore omitted.

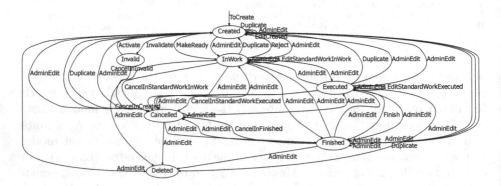

Fig. 6. Example test order model.

We applied our method in order to compute the probability that the response time of a *Commit* subtask is under a threshold of 1.65 s. Hence, we check the probability that all the response times of these subtasks within a sequence of tasks with fixed lengths are under this threshold. Note that we focus on this subtask as it is the most computationally expensive one. For this evaluation a user profile was created in cooperation with domain experts from AVL. This profile was similar to the one shown in Sect. 3, and is therefore omitted. The LMR model was similar as well and also omitted, the only difference was that due to the increased complexity of this module, we had more log-data (929.584 observations). We applied the profile to form user populations of different sizes and we checked the proposed property for test cases with increasing lengths via a Monte Carlo simulation with Chernoff-Hoeffding bound with parameters $\epsilon = 0.05$ and $\delta = 0.01$. This requires 1060 samples per data point. Figure 7 shows the results. Note that test cases of length one have always probability one as the initial task for sub-model selection has no requests and, hence, zero response time. As expected, a decrease in the probability of the property can be observed, when the test-case length or the population size increases. The advantage of the simulation on the model-level is that it runs much faster than on the SUT. With a virtual time of 1/100 of the actual time, we can perform simulations that would take weeks on the SUT within hours.

It is also important to check the probabilities that we received through model simulation on the SUT. This was done as explained in Sect. 3 by applying the SPRT with the same parameters. Table 2 shows the results. Due to the high computation effort, we did not check all data points of Fig. 7. Our focus was on test cases with length three as this was a common length of user scenarios.

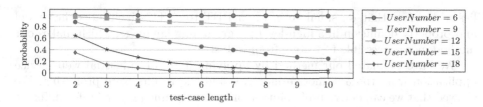

Fig. 7. Simul. result: how likely is it that the response time is under a threshold?

The table shows the hypotheses and evaluation results for different numbers of users. Note that in order to obtain an average number of needed samples, we run the SPRT concurrently for each user of the population and calculate the average of these runs. Multiple independent SPRT runs would produce a better average, but the computation time was too high. Compared to the execution on the model, a smaller number of samples is needed, as the SPRT stops, when it has sufficient evidence. The result column shows that the alternative hypothesis was always accepted. This means that the probabilities of response-time properties on the SUT were at least as good as on the model. The smaller required number of samples of the SPRT (max. 66) compared to Monte Carlo simulation (1060 samples) allowed us to analyse the SUT within a feasible time.

Table 2. Results of the evaluation on the SUT by applying the SPRT.

#Users	H_0	H_1	Result	#Samples needed
6	0.897	0.997	H_1	66.6
9	0.846	0.946	H_1	42.0
12	0.641	0.741	H_1	60.8
15	0.305	0.405	H_1	17.3
18	0.042	0.142	H_1	7.6

6   Conclusion

We have demonstrated that we can exploit PBT features in order to check response-time properties under different user populations both on a model-level and on an SUT. With SMC, we can evaluate stochastic cost models and check properties like, *what is the probability that the response time of a user within a population is under a certain threshold?* We also showed that such probabilities can be tested directly on the SUT without the need for an extra tool. A big advantage of our method is that we can perform simulations, which require a high number of samples on the model in a fraction of the time that would be required on the SUT. Moreover, we can check the results of such simulations on the SUT by applying the SPRT, which needs fewer samples. Another benefit lies in the fact that we simulate inside a PBT tool. This facilitates the model and property definition in a high-level programming language, which makes our method more accessible to testers from industry.

We have evaluated our method by applying it to an industrial web-service application from the automotive industry and the results were promising. We showed that we can derive probabilities for response-time properties for different population sizes and that we can evaluate these probabilities on the real system with a smaller number of samples. In principle, our method can be applied outside the web domain, e.g., to evaluate run-time requirements of real-time or embedded systems. However, for other applications and other types of costs alternative cost-learning techniques [17,35] may be better suited.

In the future, we plan to apply our cost models for stress testing as they help to find subtasks or attributes that are more computationally expensive than others. Additionally, we want to apply our method to compare the performance of different versions of the SUT, i.e. non-functional regression testing.

Acknowledgments. This work was funded by the Austrian Research Promotion Agency (FFG), project TRUCONF, No. 845582. We are grateful to Martin Tappler, the team at AVL, especially Elisabeth Jöbstl, and the anonymous reviewers for their valuable inputs.

References

1. Aichernig, B.K., Schumi, R.: Property-based testing with FsCheck by deriving properties from business rule models. In: ICSTW, pp. 219–228. IEEE (2016)
2. Aichernig, B.K., Schumi, R.: Towards integrating statistical model checking into property-based testing. In: MEMOCODE, pp. 71–76. IEEE (2016)
3. Aichernig, B.K., Schumi, R.: Statistical model checking meets property-based testing. In: ICST, pp. 390–400. IEEE (2017)
4. Alur, R., Dill, D.L.: A theory of timed automata. Theor. Comput. Sci. **126**(2), 183–235 (1994)
5. Arts, T.: On shrinking randomly generated load tests. In: Erlang 2014, pp. 25–31. ACM (2014)
6. Ballarini, P., Bertrand, N., Horváth, A., Paolieri, M., Vicario, E.: Transient analysis of networks of stochastic timed automata using stochastic state classes. In: Joshi, K., Siegle, M., Stoelinga, M., D'Argenio, P.R. (eds.) QEST 2013. LNCS, vol. 8054, pp. 355–371. Springer, Heidelberg (2013). doi:10.1007/978-3-642-40196-1_30
7. Becker, S., Koziolek, H., Reussner, R.H.: The palladio component model for model-driven performance prediction. J. Syst. Softw. **82**(1), 3–22 (2009)
8. Blair, L., Jones, T., Blair, G.: Stochastically enhanced timed automata. In: Smith, S.F., Talcott, C.L. (eds.) FMOODS 2000. IAICT, vol. 49, pp. 327–347. Springer, Boston, MA (2000). doi:10.1007/978-0-387-35520-7_17
9. Book, M., Gruhn, V., Hülder, M., Köhler, A., Kriegel, A.: Cost and response time simulation for web-based applications on mobile channels. In: QSIC, pp. 83–90. IEEE (2005)
10. Bulychev, P.E., David, A., Larsen, K.G., Mikucionis, M., Poulsen, D.B., Legay, A., Wang, Z.: UPPAAL-SMC: statistical model checking for priced timed automata. In: QAPL. EPTCS, vol. 85, pp. 1–16. Open Publishing Association (2012). doi:10.4204/EPTCS.85.1

11. Chen, X., Mohapatra, P., Chen, H.: An admission control scheme for predictable server response time for web accesses. In: WWW, pp. 545–554. ACM (2001)
12. Claessen, K., Hughes, J.: QuickCheck: a lightweight tool for random testing of Haskell programs. In: ICFP, pp. 268–279. ACM (2000)
13. Claessen, K., Palka, M.H., Smallbone, N., Hughes, J., Svensson, H., Arts, T., Wiger, U.T.: Finding race conditions in Erlang with QuickCheck and PULSE. In: ICFP, pp. 149–160. ACM (2009)
14. Draheim, D., Grundy, J.C., Hosking, J.G., Lutteroth, C., Weber, G.: Realistic load testing of web applications. In: CSMR, pp. 57–70. IEEE (2006)
15. Govindarajulu, Z.: Sequential Statistics. World Scientific, Singapore (2004)
16. Grinchtein, O.: Learning of Timed Systems. Ph.D. thesis, Uppsala Univ. (2008)
17. Hastie, T., Tibshirani, R., Friedman, J.H.: The Elements of Statistical Learning: Data Mining, Inference, and Prediction. Springer Series in Statistics, 2nd edn. Springer, New York (2009). doi:10.1007/978-0-387-84858-7
18. Hoeffding, W.: Probability inequalities for sums of bounded random variables. J. Am. Statist. Assoc. **58**(301), 13–30 (1963)
19. Hughes, J.: QuickCheck testing for fun and profit. In: Hanus, M. (ed.) PADL 2007. LNCS, vol. 4354, pp. 1–32. Springer, Heidelberg (2006). doi:10.1007/978-3-540-69611-7_1
20. Hughes, J., Pierce, B.C., Arts, T., Norell, U.: Mysteries of dropbox: property-based testing of a distributed synchronization service. In: ICST, pp. 135–145. IEEE (2016)
21. Jaccard, J., Turrisi, R.: Interaction Effects in Multiple Regression. SAGE, Thousand Oaks (2003)
22. Kalaji, A.S., Hierons, R.M., Swift, S.: Generating feasible transition paths for testing from an extended finite state machine. In: ICST, pp. 230–239. IEEE (2009)
23. Kwiatkowska, M., Norman, G., Segala, R., Sproston, J.: Verifying quantitative properties of continuous probabilistic timed automata. In: Palamidessi, C. (ed.) CONCUR 2000. LNCS, vol. 1877, pp. 123–137. Springer, Heidelberg (2000). doi:10.1007/3-540-44618-4_11
24. Legay, A., Delahaye, B., Bensalem, S.: Statistical model checking: an overview. In: Barringer, H., Falcone, Y., Finkbeiner, B., Havelund, K., Lee, I., Pace, G., Roşu, G., Sokolsky, O., Tillmann, N. (eds.) RV 2010. LNCS, vol. 6418, pp. 122–135. Springer, Heidelberg (2010). doi:10.1007/978-3-642-16612-9_11
25. Legay, A., Sedwards, S.: On statistical model checking with PLASMA. In: TASE, pp. 139–145. IEEE (2014)
26. Lu, Y., Nolte, T., Bate, I., Cucu-Grosjean, L.: A statistical response-time analysis of real-time embedded systems. In: RTSS, pp. 351–362. IEEE (2012)
27. Nilsson, R.: ScalaCheck: The Definitive Guide. IT Pro, Artima Incorporated (2014)
28. Norell, U., Svensson, H., Arts, T.: Testing blocking operations with QuickCheck's component library. In: Erlang 2013, pp. 87–92. ACM (2013)
29. Papadakis, M., Sagonas, K.: A proper integration of types and function specifications with property-based testing. In: Erlang 2011, pp. 39–50. ACM (2011)
30. Rencher, A., Christensen, W.: Methods of Multivariate Analysis. Wiley, New York (2012)
31. Rina, T.S.: A comparative study of performance testing tools. Intern. J. Adv. Res. Comput. Sci. Softw. Eng. IJARCSSE **3**(5), 1300–1307 (2013)
32. Tang, J., Alelyani, S., Liu, H.: Feature selection for classification: a review. In: Data Classification: Algorithms and Applications, pp. 37–64. CRC Press (2014)

33. Verwer, S., Weerdt, M., Witteveen, C.: A likelihood-ratio test for identifying probabilistic deterministic real-time automata from positive data. In: Sempere, J.M., García, P. (eds.) ICGI 2010. LNCS (LNAI), vol. 6339, pp. 203–216. Springer, Heidelberg (2010). doi:10.1007/978-3-642-15488-1_17
34. Wald, A.: Sequential Analysis. Courier Corporation, New York City (1973)
35. West, B., Welch, K., Galecki, A.: Linear Mixed Models. CRC Press, Boca Raton (2006)

Short Contributions

Ongoing Work on Automated Verification of Noisy Nonlinear Systems with ARIADNE

Luca Geretti[1], Davide Bresolin[2], Pieter Collins[3],
Sanja Zivanovic Gonzalez[4], and Tiziano Villa[1(✉)]

[1] Universitá di Verona, Verona, Italy
{luca.geretti,tiziano.villa}@univr.it
[2] Universitá di Padova, Padova, Italy
davide.bresolin@unipd.it
[3] Maastricht University, Maastricht, The Netherlands
pieter.collins@maastrichtuniversity.nl
[4] Barry University, Miami, FL, USA
SZivanovic@barry.edu

Abstract. *Cyber-physical systems* (CPS) are *hybrid systems* that commonly consist of a discrete control part that operates in a continuous environment. Hybrid automata are a convenient model for CPS suitable for formal verification. The latter is based on *reachability analysis* of the system to trace its hybrid evolution and consequently verify its properties. However, when computing reachable states, a challenging task especially for nonlinear noisy systems is to control automatically the numerical precision to obtain meaningful approximations of the reached set. This paper presents the ongoing work and open issues in the automated computation of system evolution when the dynamics is described by differential inclusions. Differential inclusions allow to model noise for hybrid systems and also to decouple the components in a complex system, in order to simplify model-based design and verification. The proposed work aims to extend the capabilities of ARIADNE, a C++ library to perform formal verification of nonlinear hybrid systems.

1 Introduction

Formal verification is concerned with the identification of system properties that are guaranteed to hold for every possible behavior of the system itself. Such guarantee is based on the rigorous methodology underlying the computation or deduction of the desired properties. As a consequence, formal verification represents a powerful tool for evaluation of a system, compared to simulation techniques.

In this paper we focus on *hybrid systems*, i.e., dynamical systems that exhibit both a discrete and a continuous behavior. In order to model and specify hybrid systems in a formal way, the notion of *hybrid automaton* has been introduced [1]. Intuitively, a hybrid automaton is a "finite-state automaton" with continuous

© IFIP International Federation for Information Processing 2017
Published by Springer International Publishing AG 2017. All Rights Reserved
N. Yevtushenko et al. (Eds.): ICTSS 2017, LNCS 10533, pp. 313–319, 2017.
DOI: 10.1007/978-3-319-67549-7_19

variables that evolve according to dynamics characterizing each discrete state (called a *location*).

Of particular importance in the analysis of hybrid automata is the computation of the *reachable set*, i.e., the set of all states that can be reached under the dynamical evolution starting from a given initial state set. Many approximation techniques and tools to estimate the reachable set have been proposed in the literature (see [16] for a comprehensive analysis). We recently proposed a development environment for the verification of nonlinear compositional hybrid systems, called ARIADNE [4], which differs from existing tools by being based on the theory of computable analysis [8]. Such theory provides a rigorous mathematical semantics for the numerical analysis of dynamical systems, suitable for implementing formal verification algorithms. The tool has been applied mainly to the safety verification of robotic surgery tasks [6]. It also has been successfully used for dominance checking of controllers [3] and even for correct-by-construction code generation [7].

This paper discusses the ongoing work aimed at extending the dynamical model used in ARIADNE to *differential inclusions*, based on the work of [19], in order to perform reachability analysis in the presence of noisy inputs. While the most straightforward application of differential inclusions is for modeling system uncertainty, it is worth remarking that they can be used also to support *contract-based design* [16]: given a complex system, we can replace the actual input of an automaton with an input having *partially defined behavior*. The resulting decoupling of automata ultimately allows to analyze subsystems in isolation, thus trading-off system complexity for precision.

Unfortunately, the introduction of differential inclusions to a nonlinear system represents a challenge in terms of controlling the quality of the computed reachable sets. Such control can be exercised using a number of precision parameters, which should be tuned dynamically for maximum effectiveness. In other words, the successful verification of a noisy system cannot disregard a thorough analysis of such precision parameters and the identification of a proper set of policies for their automated control.

In the following, in Sect. 2 we start by presenting the approach used by ARIADNE for verification, in order to better understand how differential inclusions are a valuable addition to the framework. Then, a discussion on differential inclusions is provided in Sect. 3, followed by open issues related to automation aspects in Sect. 4.

2   Formal Verification in the Ariadne Framework

In this Section some insight on the approach used in ARIADNE is provided, in order to understand the impact of the introduction of differential inclusions. Detailed technical information on the framework can be found in [9] about functional calculus and [3] regarding the reachability routines.

Suppose we wish to verify that a safety property φ holds for a hybrid automaton H; i.e., that φ remains true for all possible executions starting from a set

X_0 of initial states, allowing to answer if a system operates within safe operating conditions expressed as a set. If this objective is cast as a reachability analysis problem, then it is necessary to prove that $ReachSet_H(X_0) \subseteq Sat(\varphi)$, where $ReachSet_H(X_0)$ is the set of states reached by H (also called the *reachable set*) and $Sat(\varphi)$ is the set of states where φ is true. Unfortunately, the reachability problem is not decidable in general [1]. Nevertheless, formal verification methods can be applied to hybrid automata: suppose we can compute an *outer* approximation $\bar{S}$ such that $\bar{S} \supseteq ReachSet_H(X_0)$. If $\bar{S} \subseteq Sat(\varphi)$ holds, then also $ReachSet_H(X_0) \subseteq Sat(\varphi)$ holds, i.e., the automaton H respects the property, or in other terms we *proved* the property. Conversely, if we can compute an *inner* approximation $\underline{S}$ such that $\underline{S} \subseteq ReachSet_H(X_0)$ that turns out to contain at least one point outside $Sat(\varphi)$, we have proved that H does not respect the safety property φ, i.e., we *disproved* the property.

Clearly, any approximation to the reachable set is bound to the numerical precision used, hence a given quality of approximation may not allow to prove or disprove the property. Computable analysis defines the conditions to construct approximations such that if the precision is progressively increased, a sequence of approximations converging to the reachable set is obtained.

For a given precision, an approximation is obtained by identifying the reached region resulting from the evolution of the system over time. Such evolution is obtained through a sequence of continuous and discrete steps. A continuous step represents time advancement and relies on the integration of a vector field $\dot{X} = f(X)$ for a chosen step size Δt, where f is nonlinear in general. A discrete step represents a transition, which changes the *hybrid state*, i.e., the pairing of the continuous state and the discrete state, without any time advancement.

At a first glance, evolution may appear to return results similar to those of simulative tools like MathWorks SIMULINK®. Instead, ARIADNE is designed to include all the possible behaviors that result from evolving sets rather than single points. The underlying engine relies on results from *interval analysis*, which supports the definition of constants over intervals (among other things). Analyzing a system in this case is equivalent to the simultaneous analysis of the set of singleton instances of the system, each corresponding to a distinct valuation of all constants. In particular, if a given constant represents a design parameter, parametric analysis [11] is able to identify subintervals where the constant yields optimal behavior of the system with respect to some metrics.

Since intervals only model a set of constant behaviors, differential inclusions represent the most natural extension to the tool: by using them it is possible to analyze a system in which arbitrary *variations* of quantities within bounded intervals occur. The resulting over-approximation of behaviors covered by the noisy model can consequently compensate for an inaccurate system definition, which is a common problem when modelling real systems.

3   Differential Inclusions

The seminal paper [19] that we are working to implement in ARIADNE considers a system with dynamics

$$\dot{x}(t) = f(x(t), v(t)), \ x(t) \in \mathbb{R}^n, \ v(t) \in V \subset \mathbb{R}^m \tag{1}$$

where $f : \mathbb{R}^n \times \mathbb{R}^m \to \mathbb{R}^n$ is a smooth function, V is a compact set and $v(t)$ is a measurable function known as the disturbance input. In particular, [19] discusses how to compute the reachable set for nonlinear control systems which are affine with respect to noisy inputs. Also, a reasonable assumption in practice is that noisy inputs are elements of a box whose vector components are intervals.

The numerical approach focuses on (a) using an auxiliary function system to account for the input during a continuous step of evolution, then (b) adding the high-order theoretical error between the given system and the auxiliary one. Such approach is formally correct since it yields an over-approximation of the reachable set. However, the higher the order one desires, the greater the number of parameters for the auxiliary system required for each continuous step, which clearly affects the efficiency of the algorithm. The question remains if the auxiliary system approach yields the best trade-off between precision and efficiency for computing reachable sets. The answer is not straightforward and most likely depends on the system itself.

Designing numerical algorithms for computing solutions of differential inclusions, both efficiently and with high precision, remains a point of current research. Different techniques and various types of numerical methods have been proposed as approximations to the solution set of a differential inclusion in the past. For example, ellipsoidal calculus was used in [15], a Lohner-type algorithm in [14], grid-based methods in [5,17], optimal control in [2], discrete approximations in [10,12], and optimal control and support vector machines with grids in [18]. However, these algorithms either do not give rigorous over-approximations and so they cannot be used to validate the system, or are low-order approximations, e.g., Euler approximations with a first-order single-step truncation error.

Essentially, the only algorithms mentioned above that could give arbitrarily accurate error estimates are the ones that use grids. However, higher-order discretization of a state space greatly affects the efficiency of the algorithm. In fact, it was noted in [5] that if one tries to obtain higher-order error estimates on the solution set of differential inclusions then grid methods should be avoided.

A recent publication [13] proposes a method for computing outer approximations of reachable sets for nonlinear control systems by constructing convex polyhedral enclosures of reachable sets; it produces upper and lower bounds via polyhedra and demonstrates the efficiency of the proposed algorithm through several examples. Since all the examples are input-affine systems, we plan to compare this approach to the implementation of [19] within ARIADNE.

Finally, in terms of theoretical extensions of the current approach, a desirable objective is to explore even higher-order error estimates. Additionally, we plan to use constraints for set representation, which allow for pseudo-affine inputs and inputs defined via more general convex sets. The ultimate goal however is the ability to handle differential inclusions which are nonlinear in the inputs.

4   Open Issues for Automation

The presence of differential inclusions introduces additional issues for continuous evolution, which require specific operations to be performed:

- **Reduction of auxiliary parameters.** Each continuous step increases the number of parameters by $2m$, where m is the dimension of the noise space. Consequently it is important to identify when some parameters can be lumped into a uniform error term δ, in order to reduce the dimensionality of the problem.
- **Reconditioning of the set.** When the uniform error term of the representation of the set becomes too large in respect to the set radius, it is beneficial to convert it into an additional parameter for the representation itself. Again, it is necessary to lump periodically one or more parameters into δ for scalability purposes. While reconditioning is a necessary operation in general, differential inclusions make its automation even more critical.
- **Splitting and recombining sets.** Additional precision can be obtained by splitting a large set over one parameter and evolving the split parts separately. However, the problem of identifying the conditions for an effective splitting is not trivial. Additionally, it is ultimately necessary to recombine split sets periodically to avoid an exponential explosion of the number of evolved sets. The problem is that recombination should introduce a small over-approximation error, in order to justify splitting in the first place.
- **Tuning of the continuous step size.** There is a trade-off to investigate between a large step size, which is unable to provide an accurate reachable set, and a small step size, which results in high complexity of the evolved set along with longer verification time.

In general, it is clear that local dynamics greatly affect the approximation error introduced in a single continuous step. As a consequence, a manual tuning phase at the beginning of the reachability routine has a very limited capability to identify a (sub)optimal strategy for evolution.

A reasonable approach relies on a *pre-analysis* of the system using *point-based simulation*. In this case, we drop the guarantees given by set-based evolution with the objective of gaining valuable local information on the system evolution in a significantly shorter verification time. The resulting information necessarily comes with no guarantees of correctness, meaning that the obtained evolution may include spurious transitions or miss some transitions. Still, for sufficiently well-behaved dynamics this approach is able to identify reached regions where evolution is critical from the numerical viewpoint. Given such pre-analysis of the system, preemptive policies can be enacted to tune numerical parameters in order to trade between precision and verification time.

Summarizing, it appears that dealing with noisy nonlinear systems requires both local and global strategies in order to allow evolution to progress with bounded over-approximation error and reasonable efficiency of computation. Future work will focus on improving such strategies, with the objective of providing as much automation as possible regardless of the dynamics involved.

References

1. Alur, R., Courcoubetis, C., Henzinger, T.A., Ho, P.-H.: Hybrid automata: an algorithmic approach to the specification and verification of hybrid systems. In: Grossman, R.L., Nerode, A., Ravn, A.P., Rischel, H. (eds.) HS 1991-1992. LNCS, vol. 736, pp. 209–229. Springer, Heidelberg (1993). doi:10.1007/3-540-57318-6_30
2. Baier, R., Gerdts, M.: A computational method for non-convex reachable sets using optimal control. In: Proceedings of the European Control Conference 2009, Budapest, HU, pp. 97–102. IEEE (2009)
3. Benvenuti, L., Bresolin, D., Collins, P., Ferrari, A., Geretti, L., Villa, T.: Ariadne: dominance checking of nonlinear hybrid automata using reachability analysis. In: Finkel, A., Leroux, J., Potapov, I. (eds.) RP 2012. LNCS, vol. 7550, pp. 79–91. Springer, Heidelberg (2012). doi:10.1007/978-3-642-33512-9_8
4. Benvenuti, L., Bresolin, D., Collins, P., Ferrari, A., Geretti, L., Villa, T.: Assume-guarantee verification of nonlinear hybrid systems with Ariadne. Int. J. Robust. Nonlinear Control 24(4), 699–724 (2014)
5. Beyn, W.-J., Rieger, J.: Numerical fixed grid methods for differential inclusions. Computing 81(1), 91–106 (2007)
6. Bresolin, D., Di Guglielmo, L., Geretti, L., Muradore, R., Fiorini, P., Villa, T.: Open problems in verification and refinement of autonomous robotic systems. In: 15th Euromicro Conference on Digital System Design (DSD), pp. 469–476, September 2012
7. Bresolin, D., Di Guglielmo, L., Geretti, L., Villa, T.: Correct-by-construction code generation from hybrid automata specification. In: 7th International Wireless Communications and Mobile Computing Conference (IWCMC), pp. 1660–1665, July 2011
8. Collins, P.: Semantics and computability of the evolution of hybrid systems. SIAM J. Control Optim. 49, 890–925 (2011)
9. Collins, P., Bresolin, D., Geretti, L., Villa, T.: Computing the evolution of hybrid systems using rigorous function calculus. In: Proceedings of the 4th IFAC Conference on Analysis and Design of Hybrid Systems (ADHS 2012), pp. 284–290, Eindhoven, The Netherlands, June 2012
10. Dontchev, T.: Euler approximation of nonconvex discontinuous differential inclusions. An. Stiint. Univ. Ovidius Constanta Ser. Mat. 10(1), 73–86 (2002)
11. Geretti, L., Muradore, R., Bresolin, D., Fiorini, P., Villa, T.: Parametric formal verification: the robotic paint spraying case study. In: Proceedings of the 20th IFAC World Congress, pp. 9658–9663, July 2017
12. Grammel, G.: Towards fully discretized differential inclusions. Set Valued Anal. 11(3), 1–8 (2003)
13. Harwood, S., Barton, P.: Efficient polyhedral enclosures for the reachable set of nonlinear control systems. Math. Control Signals Syst. 28(8) (2016)
14. Kapela, T.A., Zgliczynski, P.: A lohner-type algorithm for control systems and ordinary differential inclusions. Discrete Contin. Dyn. Syst. Ser. B 11(2), 365–385 (2009)

15. Kurzhanski, A., Valyi, I.: Ellipsoidal Calculus for Estimation and Control. Systems & Control: Foundations & Applications. Birkhäuser Basel, New York (1997)
16. Nuzzo, P., Sangiovanni-Vincentelli, A.L., Bresolin, D., Geretti, L., Villa, T.: A platform-based design methodology with contracts and related tools for the design of cyber-physical systems. Proc. IEEE **103**(11), 2104–2132 (2015)
17. Puri, A., Borkar, V., Varaiya, P.: ϵ-approximation of differential inclusions. In: Proceedings of the 34th IEEE Conference on Decision and Control, New Orleans, LA, USA, pp. 2892–2897. IEEE (1995)
18. Rasmussen, M., Rieger, J., Webster, K.: Approximation of reachable sets using optimal control and support vector machines. J. Comput. Appl. Math. **311**, 68–83 (2017)
19. Zivanovic, S., Collins, P.: Numerical solutions to noisy systems. In: 49th IEEE Conference on Decision and Control (CDC), pp. 798–803, December 2010

Generating Checking Sequences
for User Defined Fault Models

Alexandre Petrenko[1]([✉]) and Adenilso Simao[2]

[1] CRIM, Centre de recherche informatique de Montréal,
405 Ogilvy Avenue, Suite 101, Montréal, QC H3N 1M3, Canada
petrenko@crim.ca
[2] Instituto de Ciencias Matematicas e de Computacao,
Universidade de Sao Paulo, Sao Carlos/Sao Paulo, Brazil
adenilso@icmc.usp.br

Abstract. In this paper, we investigate how a checking sequence can be generated from a Finite State Machine, with respect to a user-defined set of faults, modeled as a nondeterministic FSM, called Mutation Machine (MM). We propose an algorithm for generating a checking sequence in this scenario and demonstrate its correctness.

Keywords: FSM testing · Fault models · Checking sequence · Mutation machine

1 Introduction

Generation of checking sequence (CS) from a Finite State Machine (FSM) is a relevant problem, when the implementation may not be reset or when reset operation it prohibitively costly. There are methods which, given a distinguishing sequence, can generate a checking sequence in polynomial time [2, 3]. Other methods generate checking sequence from characterization sets instead of a distinguishing sequence [1], since the former is available for any minimal machine, while the latter may not exist. Those methods, however, rely on the repetition of the sequences in the characterization sets, resulting in an exponentially long sequence. These methods also consider the classical fault domain where the implementation may have arbitrary faults, except extra states.

In this paper, we investigate how a CS can be generated from an FSM, with respect to a subset of faults. The faults of interest are modeled as a nondeterministic FSM, called Mutation Machine (MM), such that any implementation is assumed to be a deterministic submachine of the MM. We propose an algorithm for generating a CS in this scenario. After demonstrating the correctness of the algorithm, we illustrate its application on a simple example.

2 Checking Sequence Construction

An FSM is a tuple $M = (S, S_0, X, O, h)$, where S is the set of states, $S_0 \subseteq S$ is the set of initial states, X is the set of inputs, O is the set of outputs, which satisfy the condition

Published by Springer International Publishing AG 2017. All Rights Reserved
N. Yevtushenko et al. (Eds.): ICTSS 2017, LNCS 10533, pp. 320–325, 2017.
DOI: 10.1007/978-3-319-67549-7_20

$I \cap O = \emptyset$, and $h \subseteq (S \times X \times O \times S)$ is the set of transitions. For state s and input x, let $h(s, x)$ be the set of transitions from state s with input x. The FSM M is *initialized* if $|S_0| = 1$ and is *deterministic* if for each $(s, x) \in S \times X$, $|h(s,x)| \leq 1$. For an initialized FSM, where $|S_0| = 1$, write s_0, instead of $\{s_0\}$.

The machine M is *completely specified* (complete FSM) if $|h(s, x)| \geq 1$ for each $(s,x) \in S \times X$; otherwise, it is *partially specified* (partial FSM).

A *path* of the FSM $M = (S, S_0, X, O, h)$ from state $s \in S$ is a sequence of transitions $(s_1, x_1, o_1, s_2) (s_2, x_2, o_2, s_3) \ldots (s_k, x_k, o_k, s_{k+1})$, such that $(s_i, x_i, o_i, s_{i+1}) \in h$, for $1 \leq i \leq k$. Notice that we also allow a path to be empty, represented by ε. The machine is *strongly connected*, if it has a path from each state to any other state. The input projection (output projection) of the path is $x_1 x_2 \ldots x_k$ $(o_1 o_2 \ldots o_k)$. Input sequence $\beta \in I^*$ is a *defined* input sequence in state s of M if it is an input projection of a path from state s. We use $\Omega(s)$ to denote the set of all input sequences defined in state s and $\Omega(M)$ for the states in S_0, i.e., for M. $\Omega(M) = X^*$ holds for any complete machine M, while for a partial FSM $\Omega(M) \subset X^*$.

Given a path p, let $trav(p)$ be the set of transitions of M which appear in p. For state s and input x, let $trans(p, (s, x))$ be the set of transitions from state s with input x in $trav$ (p), i.e., $trans(p, (s,x)) = trav(p) \cap h(s,x)$. For the FSM $M = (S, S_0, X, O, h)$, given a set of states $S' \subseteq S$ and an input sequence α, let $path(S', \alpha)$ be the set of paths of M from states of S' with input projection α. We denote $path(S_0, \alpha)$ by $path_M(\alpha)$. Let $\lambda(S', \alpha)$ be the set of output projections of the paths in $Path(S', \alpha)$; we denote $\lambda(S_0, \alpha)$ by $\lambda_M(\alpha)$. Unless stated otherwise, paths are assumed to be from an initial state.

Given states $s, t \in S$ of the deterministic FSM $M = (S, S_0, X, O, h)$, t is *quasi-equivalent* to s, if $\Omega(t) \supseteq \Omega(s)$ and $\lambda(t, \alpha) = \lambda(s, \alpha)$ for all $\alpha \in \Omega(s)$; moreover, in case $\Omega(t) \supseteq \Omega(s)$, states are *equivalent*. States $s, t \in S$ are *distinguishable*, if $\lambda(t, \alpha) \neq \lambda(s, \alpha)$ for some $\alpha \in \Omega(t) \cap \Omega(s)$. The machine is *reduced*, if any two states are distinguishable. The quasi-equivalence (equivalence) of two deterministic FSMs is the corresponding relation of their initial states.

Spec $= (S, s_0, X, O, h)$ is an initialized deterministic FSM specification. We assume that it is strongly-connected machine, not necessarily complete and reduced.

Given an FSM $M = (S, s_0, X, O, h)$ and $s \in S$, let M/s be the FSM (S, s, X, O, h), i.e., M initialized in state s. We let s-after-α denote the set of states reached by input sequence α from state s; if α is applied to the initial state of M then we write M-after-α instead of s_0-after-α; for deterministic machines, we write s-after-$\alpha = s'$ instead of s-after-$\alpha = \{s'\}$.

We use a so-called *mutation machine* $MM = (S', S_0', X, O, h')$ which is a completely specified possibly nondeterministic FSM.

FSM $M = (S, s_0, X, O, h)$ is a *submachine* of $MM = (S', S_0', X, O, h')$ iff $S \subseteq S'$, $s_0 \in S_0'$ and $h \subseteq h'$. Any complete deterministic submachine of MM is one of the *mutants* of *Spec*. The number of mutants is $|S_0'| \prod_{(s,x) \in S \times X} |h'(s,x)|$. For the sets of states S, inputs X and outputs O, we define the machine $Chaos(S, X, O) = (S, s_0, X, O, (S \times X \times O \times S))$ representing the universe of all FSMs with $|S|$ states.

Let *Prod* be the product of *Spec* and $MM = (S', S_0', X, O, h')$; the states of *Prod* is a subset of $(S \cup \{\Delta\}) \times S'$. A state (Δ, s) is a Δ-state. The product *Prod* $= (P, P_0, X, O,$

H), where $P_0 = \{(s_0, s')|s' \in S_0'\}$ is such that P and H are the smallest sets satisfying the following rules:

1. If $(s, s') \in P, (s, x, o, t) \in h, (s', x, o', t') \in h'$, and $o = o'$, then $(t, t') \in P$ and $((s, s'), x, o, (t, t')) \in H$.
2. If $(s, s') \in P, (s, x, o, t) \in h, (s', x, o', t') \in h'$, and $o \neq o'$, then $(\Delta, t') \in P$ and $((s, s'), x, o', (\Delta, t')) \in H$.

Notice that Δ-states are sink states. If the product has no Δ-states, then any mutant of MM is quasi-equivalent to $Spec$.

An input sequence $\omega = \Omega(Spec)$ is a *checking sequence* for $Spec$ w.r.t. MM, if for each deterministic submachine N of MM, if $\lambda_N(\omega) = \lambda_{Spec}(\omega)$, then N is quasi-equivalent to $Spec/s$, where $s \in S$.

Given a path $p = ((s_1, m_1), x_1, o_1, (s_2, m_2)) ((s_2, m_2), x_2, o_2, (s_3, m_3)) \ldots ((s_k, m_k), x_k, o_k, (s_{k+1}, m_{k+1}))$ of the product $Prod$ of $Spec$ and MM, let $p_{\downarrow MM}$ be the corresponding path in MM, i.e., $p_{\downarrow MM} = (m_1, x_1, o_1, m_2) (m_2, x_2, o_2, m_3) \ldots (m_k, x_k, o_k, m_{k+1})$.

A path of the product $Prod$ is *deterministic* (w.r.t. MM) if for every state s and input x, $|trans(p_{\downarrow MM}, (s, x))| \leq 1$. Given a set of paths Q of $Prod$, let $det(Q)$ be the set of paths of Q which are deterministic (w.r.t. MM) and $\Delta(Q)$ be the set of deterministic paths which leads to a Δ-state.

Algorithm for generating a CS for $Spec$ w.r.t. MM
Input: $Spec$ and MM
Output: A CS for $Spec$ w.r.t. MM
$\omega := \varepsilon$
Compute the product $Prod$ of $Spec$ and MM.
While there exists a nonempty shortest input sequence α, such that $\Delta(det(path_{MM}(\omega\alpha))) \neq \emptyset$ **do**
$\omega := \omega\alpha$
End While
Return ω

Lemma 1. Let ω be an input sequence such that for each input sequence α, we have that $\Delta(det(path_{MM}(\omega\alpha))) = \emptyset$. Then, ω is a checking sequence for $Spec$ w.r.t. MM.
Proof. Assume that ω is not a checking sequence for $Spec$ w.r.t. MM, but for each input sequence α, we have that $\Delta(det(path_{MM}(\omega\alpha))) = \emptyset$.

Thus, there exists a deterministic submachine N of MM, such that $\lambda_N(\omega) = \lambda_{Spec}(\omega)$, and for each $s \in S$, we have that N is not quasi-equivalent to $Spec/s$. This implies that state N-after-ω is not quasi-equivalent to any state $Spec/s$-after-ω. Then for each $s \in S$, there exists an input sequence $\beta \in \Omega(s)$ such that $\lambda_{N/N-\text{after}-\omega} \neq \lambda_{Spec/s-\text{after}-\omega}(\beta)$.

Let $p_{\omega\beta}$ be the path in N which has $\omega\beta$ as the input projection. It follows that $p_{\omega\beta} \in \Delta(det(path_{MM}(\omega\beta)))$, since N is deterministic; moreover, it leads to a Δ-state, since $\lambda_{N/N-\text{after}-\omega}(\beta) \neq \lambda_{Spec/s-\text{after}-\omega}(\beta)$, thus, $\Delta(det(path_{MM}(\omega\beta))) \neq \emptyset$, a contradiction. $\square$

Thus, by Lemma 1, if the algorithm stops, the resulting sequence ω is indeed a checking sequence. It remains to show that it will always stop for any specification and mutation machine.

Lemma 2. After a finite number of steps, the algorithm terminates.

Proof. First, notice that for a given deterministic submachine of MM, there is exactly one deterministic path with a given input sequence projection (many submachines can share the same path). Thus, the number of paths in $det(path_{MM}(\omega))$ is limited by the number of deterministic submachines of MM; as there are finitely many such submachines, there are finitely many paths in $det(path_{MM}(\omega))$. Let Sub_{ω} be the set of deterministic submachines for which correspond the paths in $det(path_{MM}(\omega))$. At least one path in $det(path_{MM}(\omega))$ leads to a Δ-state, since the algorithm updated ω in the previous iteration to $\omega\alpha$ and $\Delta(det(path_{MM}(\omega\alpha))) \neq \varnothing$.

Let α be a nonempty input sequence, such that $\Delta(det(path_{MM}(\omega\alpha))) \neq \varnothing$. Let $Sub_{\omega\alpha}$ be the set of deterministic submachines each which has a path in $det(path_{MM}(\omega\alpha))$. As Δ-states are sink states, any submachine in Sub_{ω} with a path to a Δ-state is not in $Sub_{\omega\alpha}$. Thus, there exists at least one submachine which is in Sub_{ω} but not in $Sub_{\omega\alpha}$. The set of submachines with paths in $det(path_{MM}(\omega))$ is thus reduced each time ω is updated by the algorithm. As the set of submachines is finite, eventually after a finite number of steps the set Sub_{ω} has no more machines distinguishable from the specification machine $Spec$, which means that for any input sequence α, it holds that $\Delta(det(path_{MM}(\omega\alpha))) \neq \varnothing$, and the algorithm terminates. $\square$

We now illustrate the application of the algorithm. Consider the FSM in Fig. 1a. Observe first that it has no distinguishing sequence. In Fig. 1b, we include a mutation machine for which we will generate a checking sequence.

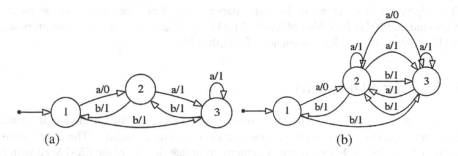

Fig. 1. (a) Specification FSM. (b) The Mutation Machine MM

Notice that there are twelve deterministic complete submachines of MM. One possibility to obtain a checking sequence for $Spec$ is to use any of the applicable methods [2, 3], ignoring MM. However, the resulting checking sequence would be unnecessarily long.

The algorithm starts by building the product of $Spec$ and MM, as well as initializing ω with the empty sequence. The nonempty input sequence $\alpha = aa$ is such that $\omega\alpha$ reaches a Δ-state in the product, since $det(path_{MM}(\omega\alpha)) = \{((1, a, 0, 2), (2, a, 1, 3)),$

$((1, a, 0, 2) (2, a, 0, \Delta))$, $((1, a, 0, 2), (2, a, 1, 2)))\}$, i.e.,$\Delta(det(path_{MM}(\omega\alpha))) \neq \varnothing$. We append α to ω, so that now $\omega = aa$. In the next iteration, the nonempty input sequence $\alpha = ba$ is selected, since $det(path_{MM}(\omega\alpha)) = \{((1, a, 0, 2), (2, a, 1, 3), (3, b, 1, 2), (2, a, 1, 3)), ((1, a, 0, 2), (2, a, 1, 2), (2, b, 1, 1), (1, a, 0, \Delta)), ((1, a, 0, 2), (2, a, 1, 2), (2, b, 1, 3), (3, a, 1, 3))), ((1, a, 0, 2), (2, a, 1, 2), (2, b, 1, 3), (3, a, 1, 2)))\}$, i.e., $\Delta(det(path_{MM}(\omega\alpha))) \neq \varnothing$. We append α to ω, so that now $\omega = aaba$. In the next iteration, the nonempty input sequence $\alpha = aba$ is selected, since $det(path_{MM}(\omega\alpha)) = \{((1, a, 0, 2), (2, a, 1, 3), (3, b, 1, 2), (2, a, 1, 3), (3, a, 1, 3), (3, b, 1, 2), (2, a, 1, 3)), ((1, a, 0, 2), (2, a, 1, 3), (3, b, 1, 2), (2, a, 1, 3), (3, a, 1, 2), (2, b, 1, 1), (1, a, 0, \Delta)), ((1, a, 0, 2), (2, a, 1, 3), (3, b, 1, 2), (2, a, 1, 3), (3, a, 1, 2), (2, b, 1, 3), (3, a, 1, 2)), ((1, a, 0, 2), (2, a, 1, 2), (2, b, 1, 3), (3, a, 1, 3), (3, a, 1, 3), (3, b, 1, 2), (2, a, 1, 2)), ((1, a, 0, 2), (2, a, 1, 2), (2, b, 1, 3), (3, a, 1, 2), (2, a, 1, 2), (2, b, 1, 3), (3, a, 1, 2)))\}$, i.e., $\Delta(det(path_{MM}(\omega\alpha))) \neq \varnothing$. We append α to ω, so that now $\omega = aabaaba$. In the next iteration, the nonempty input sequence $\alpha = bba$ is selected, since $det(path_{MM}(\omega\alpha)) = \{((1, a, 0, 2), (2, a, 1, 3), (3, b, 1, 2), (2, a, 1, 3), (3, a, 1, 3), (3, b, 1, 2), (2, a, 1, 3), (3, b, 1, 2), (2, b, 1, 1), (1, a, 0, 2)), ((1, a, 0, 2), (2, a, 1, 3), (3, b, 1, 2), (2, a, 1, 3), (3, a, 1, 3), (3, b, 1, 2), (2, a, 1, 3), (3, b, 1, 2), (2, b, 1, 3), (3, a, 1, \Delta)), ((1, a, 0, 2), (2, a, 1, 3), (3, b, 1, 2), (2, a, 1, 3), (3, a, 1, 2), (2, b, 1, 3), (3, a, 1, 2), (2, b, 1, 3), (3, b, 1, 2), (2, a, 1, \Delta)), ((1, a, 0, 2), (2, a, 1, 2), (2, b, 1, 3), (3, a, 1, 3), (3, a, 1, 3), (3, b, 1, 2), (2, a, 1, 2), (2, b, 1, 3), (3, b, 1, 2), (2, a, 1, \Delta)), ((1, a, 0, 2), (2, a, 1, 2), (2, b, 1, 3), (3, a, 1, 2), (2, a, 1, 2), (2, b, 1, 3), (3, a, 1, 2), (2, b, 1, 3), (3, b, 1, 2), (2, a, 1, \Delta)))\}$, i.e., $\Delta(det(path_{MM}(\omega\alpha))) \neq \varnothing$. We append α to ω, so that $\omega = aabaababba$. There is no nonempty input sequence such that $\Delta(det(path_{MM}(\omega\alpha))) \neq \varnothing$. Thus, by Lemma 1, $aabaababba$ is a checking sequence for $Spec$ with respect to MM.

Consider now the $Spec$ in Fig. 1(a) and the corresponding $Chaos(S, X, O)$ which represents a traditional fault domain, the universe of all FSMs with up to three states. The algorithm we propose in this paper generates the checking sequence $aaaabaabababbabbabbabbbba$, of length 24. On the other hand, the algorithm proposed in [1], generates a checking sequence of length 130.

3   Experimental Results

In this section we present some preliminary experimental results on the length of the checking sequence obtained for various size of a mutation machine. The experiments are set up as follows. For each run, a random complete deterministic FSM $Spec$ with 5 states, 2 inputs and 2 outputs is generated, as proposed in [4]. Then, increasingly bigger mutation machines are generated from $Spec$ by adding transitions to it. The size of the mutation machine is the number of its transitions; the smallest mutation machine is the specification itself, which the biggest one is the Chaos machine with that a given number of states, inputs and outputs. We executed 30 runs and collected the length of the obtained checking sequence. Figure 2 shows the result of the experiments. We note that, as expected, the length of the checking sequence increases with the size of the mutation machine. However, the increment tends to be smaller, as the number of transitions approaches the maximum.

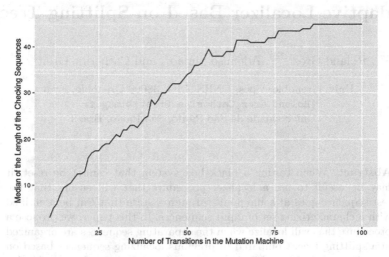

Fig. 2. Variation of the length of the checking sequence with respect to the number of transitions in the mutation machine.

4 Conclusion

In this paper, we proposed an algorithm for generating a checking sequence with respect to a user-defined fault model. In the forthcoming steps of this research, we plan to characterize scenarios when the algorithm can be effectively applied as well as its scalability.

Acknowledgement. This work was partially supported by MESI (Ministère de l'Économie, Science et Innovation) of Gouvernement du Québec and NSERC of Canada, and by Brazilian Funding Agency FAPESP, Grant 2013/07375-0.

References

1. Rezaki, A., Ural, H.: Construction of checking sequences based on characterization sets. Comput. Commun. **18**(12), 911–920 (1995)
2. da Silva Simão, A., Petrenko, A.: Generating checking sequences for partial reduced finite state machines. In: TestCom/FATES, pp. 153–168 (2008)
3. Hierons, R.M., Ural, H.: Optimizing the length of checking sequences. IEEE Trans. Comput. **55**(5), 618–629 (2006)
4. da Silva Simão, A., Petrenko, A.: Checking completeness of tests for finite state machines. IEEE Trans. Comput. **59**(8), 1023–1032 (2010)

Adaptive Localizer Based on Splitting Trees

Roland Groz[1(✉)], Adenilso Simao[2], and Catherine Oriat[1]

[1] Univ. Grenoble Alpes, CNRS, LIG, 38000 Grenoble, France
{Roland.Groz,Catherine.Oriat}@imag.fr
[2] Universidade de São Paulo, São Paulo, Brazil

Abstract. When testing a black box system that cannot be reset, it may be useful to use a localizer procedure that will ensure that the test sequence goes at some point through a state that can be identified with a characterizing set of input sequences. In this paper, we propose a procedure that will localize when the separating sequences are organized in a splitting tree. Compared to previous localizing sequences based on characterization sets, using the tree structure one can define an adaptive localizer, and the complexity of localizing depends on the height of the tree instead of the number of states.

1 Introduction

In testing methods based on FSM models, it is important to ensure that the black box implementation under test is in a known state at key points after applying some prefix input sequence, and before applying a trailing sequence. The same is also true when the test is used to retrieve some kind of state model information from a black box, as in the inference problem.

Hennie [2] and Kohavi [4] introduced approaches based on locating sequences, to build checking sequences, that can test for conformance. More recently, we introduced a localizer procedure to infer a FSM model of a black box system which cannot be reset [1] with two key assumptions: first, an upper bound n on the number of states, and second a characterization set (aka W-set) for the system. Whatever the initial state of the system, the application of the localizer will make it possible to ascertain the state reached at the end of it, or more precisely before applying the last characterizing sequence. For $W = \{w_1, w_2, w_3\}$, the localizer's input sequence is $(w_1^{2n-1}w_2)^{2n-1}(w_1^{2n-1}w_3)$. The core trick, as already suggested by Hennie, is that after applying at most $n + 1$ times a sequence, the machine must have entered a cycle, and we proved [1] that another $n - 2$ applications were enough (in worst case) to identify where the machine is in the cycle, so as to predict the next application. After w_1^{2n-1} the answer of the machine to w_1 can be predicted, so by applying w_2 we can know its answers to both w_1 and w_2. Similarly, after $(w_1^{2n-1}w_2)^{2n-1}$ we know what its answers would be to w_1 AND w_2 after applying w_1^{2n-1}, so we now substitute w_3 and therefore we identify the state reached after $(w_1^{2n-1}w_2)^{2n-1}w_1^{2n-1}$. The length of the sequence is exponential in the cardinal of the characterization set.

Published by Springer International Publishing AG 2017. All Rights Reserved
N. Yevtushenko et al. (Eds.): ICTSS 2017, LNCS 10533, pp. 326–332, 2017.
DOI: 10.1007/978-3-319-67549-7_21

In this paper, we propose an improved localizer when the characterizing sequences are organized in a splitting tree [5]. In that case, the length of the localizing sequence is exponential in the height of the tree, so it would reduce to linear in the number of sequences when the tree is balanced. The main difficulty lies in the fact that each input sequence from the W-set must be applied after repeating a fixed number of times $(2n - 1)$ a fixed sub-localizing sequence to ensure that the next iteration would be a repeated situation identifiable from the previous observations. The localizer procedure from [1] uses a fixed order of input sequences from the W-set to ensure that the same sequence is repeated at each level. With a splitting tree, the sequence to repeat may not be fixed. In this paper, we show that it is possible to combine variable sequences with predictability: differing from [3], we allow cycles that hop through different states and levels up and down the tree. Our new localizer is adaptive, and it does not produce a fixed input sequence, but an adaptive one.

2 Definitions

In this paper, a FSM is assumed to be a *strongly connected* complete deterministic Mealy machine $M = (Q, I, O, \delta, \lambda)$, with finite state, input and output sets Q, I, O; δ and λ as transition and output mappings.

Two states $q, q' \in Q$ are distinguishable by a set $H \subset I^*$ if there exists a *separating sequence* $\gamma \in H$ such that $\lambda(q, \gamma) \neq \lambda(q', \gamma)$. An FSM is *minimal* if all states are pairwise distinguishable. A set W of sequences of inputs (therefore conventionally called a W-set) is a *characterization set* for an FSM M if each pair of states is distinguishable by W.

Figure 1 shows an FSM M_0, taken from [5], with 6 states, 2 inputs (a, b) and two outputs $(0, 1)$. $W = \{b, aab, ab, aaab\}$ is a characterization set for M_0.

A *localizer* w.r.t. a set $H \subset I^*$ and $n \in \mathbb{N}$ is a procedure that applies an input sequence $\Xi\gamma$ to an *unknown* machine with at most n states such that $\gamma \in H$ and the output responses to each sequence in H can be ascertained in the state reached after applying Ξ. Note that H is not required to be a characterization set, and we only assume we know a bound on the number of states.

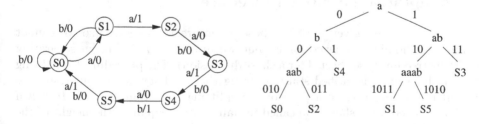

Fig. 1. FSM M_0 and a splitting tree T for it

Following [5], we now define splitting trees. A *splitting tree* for an FSM $M = (Q, I, O, \delta, \lambda)$ is a rooted tree T with a finite set of nodes such that:

- each non-leaf node N is labelled by a non-empty sequence of inputs $\gamma \in I^+$;
- each edge $e : N_1 \to N_2$ is labelled by a non-empty output sequence of outputs $\theta \in O^+$ of the same length as the label of the source node N_1.

A splitting tree T is separating for M if each node can be associated with a class of a partition of its states, such that:

- the root of T is associated with the full set of states Q of the machine M;
- let $e : N_1 \to N_2$ be an edge of T such that N_1 is labelled by $\gamma \in I^+$, e is labelled by $\theta \in O^+$. If N_1 is associated with $Q_1 \subseteq Q$, then N_2 is associated with $Q_2 = \{q \in Q_1 \; ; \; \lambda(q, \gamma) = \theta\}$.

A splitting tree is *fully separating* if each leaf node is associated with a single state. In that case, the input sequences from the root of the tree to a leaf separate the state on this leaf from all other states. The advantage of structuring a W-set as a splitting tree is that a state can be identified by applying less input sequences: with a W-set, we potentially have to apply Card W sequences, while with a splitting tree, we only have to apply $\log(\mathrm{Card}\,W)$ sequences, if the tree is balanced. As the localizer algorithm is exponential in Card W, the gain from using splitting trees rather than W-sets is crucial. In Fig. 1, we choose an initial sequence $a \notin W$ that better balances the tree and splits on a short sequence.

Given a splitting tree T, and a node N of T, we will use the following notations:

- We denote the subtree rooted at node N also by N.
- $\mathrm{root}(T)$ is the root node of T. Following the previous notation, this root node could also be denoted by T.
- $I(N)$ is the input sequence that labels node N.
- $\Lambda(N)$ is the output sequence that labels the edge *leading* to node N.
- Given a child node N' of N, $T(N \leftarrow N')$ is the modified tree where N has been replaced by the tree rooted at N'. In other words, the subtree rooted at N' is grafted one level upwards.

3   Adaptative Localizer Procedure

We assume we are given a FSM whose structure is unknown (so we cannot compute a homing sequence for it) but we are given T, a known separating splitting tree for it (see Sect. 4 for a short discussion). The procedure L will bring the machine to an identified state, meaning that we know its output responses for all input sequences in a path of the splitting tree from the root to a leaf N. The procedure L should be called initially with d equal to the height of the splitting tree T.

The boolean function Predictable(**in** i, **in** Nt, **out** $N1$) returns true when we can be sure that the next (i-th) application of $L(d-1, T)$ would return a node $N1$. Nt is an array of nodes from the tree indexed from 0 to $i - 1$.

```
 1  procedure L(d, T) return Node N                    // d is max-depth to use
 2
 3      if d = 0 then
 4          |   return root(T)
 5      else if d = 1 then
 6          |   apply I(root(T)), observe some Λ(N)
 7          |   return N
 8      else
 9          |   i := 0
10          |   repeat
11          |       |   Nt[i] := L(d − 1, T)
12          |       |   if Nt[i] is a leaf then
13          |       |       |   return Nt[i]      // a leaf will be returned through all
                                                   // recursive calls as we are now localized
14          |       |   end
15          |       |   i := i + 1
16          |   until Predictable(i, Nt, N1)
17          |   N := L(d − 1, T(parent(N1) ← N1))
18          |   return N
19      end
20  end
```

We now illustrate the algorithm on the example FSM M_0 and its associated splitting tree T. In the following, we will denote a node N of the tree T by the path from the root of T to N. For instance, the node associated with $S3$ will be denoted by $\langle a/1, ab/11 \rangle$. We use primes to differentiate inner values of variables in recursive calls. We suppose we start in the state $S0$. The depth of the splitting tree T is 3, so the first call to the adaptive localizer is $L(3, T)$.

$L(3, T)$
    $i := 0$
    $Nt[0] := L(2, T)$
        $i' := 0$
        $Nt'[0] := L(1, T)$
            apply a, observe 0 // we are now in $S1$
        $Nt'[0] = \langle a/0 \rangle$
        $i' := i' + 1 = 1$
        $Nt'[1] := L(1, T)$
            apply a, observe 1 // we are now in $S2$
        $Nt'[1] = \langle a/1 \rangle$
            . . .

After five more iterations, we are in $S1$ and $Nt' = [\langle a/0 \rangle, \langle a/1 \rangle, \langle a/0 \rangle, \langle a/1 \rangle, \langle a/0 \rangle, \langle a/1 \rangle, \langle a/0 \rangle]$ It is predictable that if we applied a, we would observe 1. Predictable($i, Nt', N1$) is true and $N1 = \langle a/1 \rangle$.

```
1  procedure Predictable(i, Nt, out N1) return boolean
2  │  r := 0                                              // repetition factor
3  │  Ns := empty_set            // set of states in last r elements of Nt
4  │  repeat
5  │  │    r := r + 1
6  │  │    Ns := Ns ∪ leaves(Nt[i − r])              // set of all leaf nodes
7  │  │    s := card(Ns)
8  │  until r = i or s ≤ r
9  │  if s > r then
10 │  │    return false
11 │  else
                              // we have entered a loop, can we predict N1?
12 │  │    while leaves(Nt[i − r − 1]) ⊆ Ns and r ≤ i − 1 do
13 │  │    │    r := r + 1
14 │  │    end
15 │  │    find greatest j such that
16 │  │        i − r ≤ j < i − 1 and ∀m ∈ [0, r − s − 1], Nt[j − m] = Nt[i − 1 − m]
17 │  │    N1 := Nt[j + 1]
18 │  │    while j > i − s do
19 │  │    │    j := j − 1
20 │  │    │    if ∀m ∈ [0, r − s − 1], Nt[j − m] = Nt[i − 1 − m] and Nt[j + 1] ≠ N1
       │  │    │    then
21 │  │    │    │    return false
22 │  │    │    end
23 │  │    end
24 │  │    return true
25 │  end
26 end
```

$$N := L(1, T(root(T) \leftarrow \langle a/1 \rangle))$$
$$\text{apply } ab, \text{ observe } 10 \text{ // we are now in } S3$$
$$\text{return } \langle a/1, ab/10 \rangle$$
$$Nt[0] = \langle a/1, ab/10 \rangle$$
$$i := i + 1 = 1$$
$$Nt[0] := L(2, T)$$
$$i' := 0$$
$$Nt'[0] := L(1, T)$$
$$\text{apply } a, \text{ observe } 1 \text{ // we are now in } S4$$
$$Nt'[0] = \langle a/1 \rangle$$
$$\dots$$

After 6 iterations, we are in $S4$ and $Nt' = [\langle a/1 \rangle, \langle a/0 \rangle, \langle a/1 \rangle, \langle a/0 \rangle, \langle a/1 \rangle, \langle a/0 \rangle, \langle a/1 \rangle]$ It is predictable that if we applied a, we would observe 0. Predictable(i, Nt', $N1$) is true and $N1 = \langle a/0 \rangle$.

$$N := L(1, T(root(T) \leftarrow \langle a/0 \rangle)$$
        apply b, observe 1 `// we are now in` $S5$
      return $\langle a/0, b/1 \rangle$
      `// We have fully identified` $S4$`, and we are in` $S5$
    $Nt[1] = \langle a/0, b/1 \rangle$

The whole localizing sequence has $7 + 2 + 7 + 1 = 17$ inputs as follows (here decorated with landmark steps S', S''):

$$a/0 \ a/1 \ a/0 \ a/1 \ a/0 \ a/1 \ a/0 \ S' \ ab/10 \ a/1 \ a/0 \ a/1 \ a/0 \ a/1 \ a/0 \ a/1 \ S'' \ b/1$$

Let us recap: in the state S', we know that if we applied a, we would get 1. We thus apply the input sequence associated with node $\langle a/1 \rangle$, which is ab, and get 10. In the state S'', we know that if we applied a, we would get 0. We thus apply the input sequence associated with node $\langle a/0 \rangle$, which is b and get 1. We thus have fully identified the state S'' in the trace, which is $S4 = \langle a/0 \, b/1 \rangle$.

If the procedure is started from $S1$, it localizes in 17 steps also. From $S2, S3, S4$ and $S5$ the length of the sequences yielded by the procedure are 9, 8, 26 and 25 respectively. The non-adaptive localizer with optimal ordering (by increasing size) of $W = \{b, ab, aab, aaab\}$ would yield $((b^{11}ab)^{11}b^{11}aab)^{11}(b^{11}ab)^{11}b^{11}aaab)$ requiring 1885 inputs. Even when the tree is not balanced the gain is huge, because only the worst case will require the full height of the tree.

4 Perspectives

An adaptive localizer as presented here lowers the complexity of localizing, from an exponential in the number of sequences to an exponential in the height of the splitting tree. This paves the way for new applications of localizing, in conformance testing or inference for non-resettable machines. In particular, it is possible to consider adapting an inference algorithm [1] so that the sequences separating subsets of states are discovered instead of being given. Thus it would be possible to infer incrementally with just a bound on the number of states, and with no initial knowledge of separating sequences for a black box system.

Acknowledgments. The authors acknowledge feedback from A. Petrenko.

References

1. Groz, R., Simao, A., Petrenko, A., Oriat, C.: Inferring finite state machines without reset using state identification sequences. In: Proceedings of the International Conference on Testing Software and Systems, ICTSS 2015, Dubai, November 2015
2. Hennie, F.C.: Fault-detecting experiments for sequential circuits. In: Proceeding of Fifth Annual Symposium on Circuit Theory and Logical Design, pp. 95–110 (1965)
3. Jourdan, G.-V., Ural, H., Yenigun, H.: Reducing locating sequences for testing from finite state machines. In: ACM-SAC 2016, pp. 1654–1659 (2016)

4. Kohavi, Z., Rivierre, J.A., Kohavi, I.: Checking experiments for sequential machines. Inf. Sci. **7**, 11–28 (1974)
5. Smetsers, R., Moerman, J., Jansen, D.N.: Minimal separating sequences for all pairs of states. In: Dediu, A.-H., Janoušek, J., Martín-Vide, C., Truthe, B. (eds.) LATA 2016. LNCS, vol. 9618, pp. 181–193. Springer, Cham (2016). doi:10.1007/978-3-319-30000-9_14

Refining the Specification FSM When Deriving Test Suites w.r.t. the Reduction Relation

Aleksandr Tvardovskii[✉]

National Research Tomsk State University, 36 Lenin Street, Tomsk, Russia
tvardal@mail.ru

Abstract. Finite State Machines (FSMs) are widely used when deriving tests for components of discrete event systems. In general, the specification FSM can be nondeterministic and in this case, a test suite with the guaranteed fault coverage is derived with respect to the reduction relation. However, when deriving such tests for nondeterministic FSMs, the existing methods return rather long test suites which cannot be used for real systems. In order to shorten a test suite, the set of possible implementation FSMs can be reduced. We present an approach for deriving shorter test suites for nondeterministic FSMs with respect to the reduction relation via refining the specification FSM.

Keywords: Finite state machines (FSM) · Nondeterministic FSM · Test derivation

1   Introduction

Finite State Machine (FSM) based test derivation is an active research area that has a long history [1, 2]. The well-known method is the W-method [2] and many derivatives of this method have been developed including those for FSMs with the nondeterministic behaviour (see, for example, [3–5]). In FSM based testing, the specification behaviour and the behaviour of an implementation under test (IUT) are described by FSMs and by applying input sequences to the IUT and observing the produced outputs a tester should conclude whether the IUT conforms to its specification. Best known conformance relations are the equivalence and reduction relations [4]. In the former case, the IUT has to have the same behaviour as the specification FSM; in the latter case, the behaviour of the IUT has to be contained in the behaviour of the specification FSM.

In this paper, we propose to refine the FSM specification via deleting some transitions in such a way that the refined specification has an (adaptive) distinguishing sequence that distinguishes every two different states and all the states are definitely reachable from the initial state [5], i.e., each state is (adaptively) reachable from the initial state. Under such conditions, the length of a test suite against nondeterministic FSMs is comparable with that for deterministic FSMs.

The rest of the paper has the following structure. Section 2 contains the preliminaries. A procedure for deriving complete test suites against nondeterministic FSMs with

N. Yevtushenko et al. (Eds.): ICTSS 2017, LNCS 10533, pp. 333–339, 2017.
DOI: 10.1007/978-3-319-67549-7_22

respect to the reduction relation is presented in Sect. 3. Section 4 contains a proposed procedure for reducing the specification FSM. Section 5 concludes the paper.

2 Preliminaries

In this section, we introduce necessary definitions and notations which are mainly taken from the paper [5].

A *finite state machine* (FSM), or simply a *machine*, is a 5-tuple $S = \langle S, I, O, h_S, s_0 \rangle$ where S is a finite nonempty set of states with the designated state s_0, I and O are finite input and output alphabets, and $h_S \subseteq S \times I \times O \times S$ is a *transition (behavior) relation*. FSM S is *nondeterministic* if for some pair $(s, i) \in S \times I$, there can exist several pairs $(o, s') \in O \times S$ such that $(s, i, o, s') \in h_S$; otherwise, the FSM is deterministic. FSM S is *complete* if for each pair $(s, i) \in S \times I$ there exists $(o, s') \in O \times S$ such that $(s, i, o, s') \in h_S$; otherwise, the FSM is *partial*. FSM S is *observable* if for every two transitions (s, i, o, s_1), $(s, i, o, s_2) \in h_S$ it holds that $s_1 = s_2$. In the following, we consider complete observable possibly nondeterministic FSM specifications, while an implementation is a complete deterministic FSM.

Figure 1 shows a FSM A for which $I = \{i_1, i_2, i_3\}$, $O = \{o_1, o_2, o_3\}$, $S = \{1, 2, 3\}$ and 1 is the initial state. Suppose that input i_1 is applied to this FSM at the state 1. After applying input i_1 the FSM can remain at state 1 and produce an output o_1. However, the FSM can also stay at state 1 while producing output o_2.

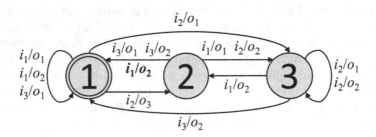

Fig. 1. FSM A

A *trace* of FSM S at state s is a sequence of input/output pairs $\alpha = i_1/o_1 \ldots i_l/o_l$ of consecutive transitions starting from state s. A sequence of inputs $i_1 \ldots i_l$ is an *input sequence*, a sequence of outputs $o_1 \ldots o_l$ is an *output* sequence.

Given an input alphabet I and an output alphabet O, a *test case* TC(I, O) is an initially connected observable FSM $T = (T, I, O, h_T, t_0)$ with an acyclic transition graph such that at each state only one input with all possible outputs is defined. Given a complete FSM S over alphabets I and O, a test case TC(I, O) represents an adaptive experiment with the FSM S. If $|I| > 1$ then a test case is a partial FSM. A state $t \in T$ is a *deadlock* state of the FSM T if there are no defined inputs at this state. The notion of a test case can be used for representing an adaptive input sequence when the next input depends on the output to the previous input. In general, given a test case T, the *length (height)* of the test case T is defined as the length of a longest trace from the initial state to a deadlock state of T and it specifies the length of the longest input sequence that can be applied to an FSM S during the experiment.

A test case T is a *distinguishing* test case (DTC) for an FSM S if for every trace γ of T from the initial state to a deadlock state, γ is trace at most at one state of S. Sometimes, a distinguishing test case is called an *adaptive distinguishing sequence*. A distinguishing test case for a submachine of FSM A in Fig. 1 without the bold transition $(2, i_1, o_2, 1)$ is shown in Fig. 2.

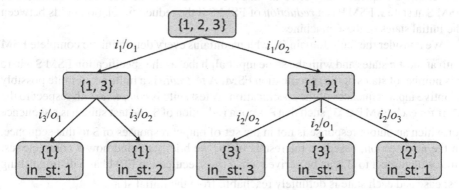

Fig. 2. A distinguishing test case for a submachine of FSM A without the bold transition $(2, i_1, o_2, 1)$

A test case T represents an (*adaptive*) *transfer* sequence from the initial state to state s if every trace of T from the initial state to a deadlock state takes the FSM from the initial state to state s. According to [5], if there exists an (*adaptive*) *transfer* sequence from the initial state to state s then state s is *definitely reachable* from the initial state and must be implemented in a conforming implementation [5]. Adaptive transfer sequences to states 2 and 3 for FSM A in Fig. 1 is shown in Fig. 3. For a deterministic FSM, a transfer sequence is simply an input sequence.

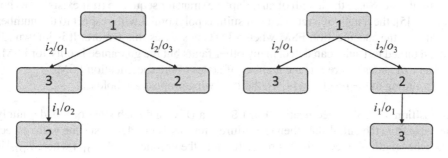

Fig. 3. Transfer test cases for FSM A

Test cases are (adaptive) input sequences which are derived against the given FSM specification to determine whether a given black-box implementation under test (IUT), which is also assumed to have the FSM behavior, conforms to the given specification. In this paper, an IUT *conforms* to the specification if an implementation FSM is a reduction of the specification FSM. In other words, an IUT conforms to the specification FSM if for each input sequence the output response of the IUT is contained in the set of output responses of the specification FSM to this input sequence. If the observed outputs do not match, then the implementation has a fault, i.e., it is a *nonconforming* implementation.

Given states s and p of complete FSMs S and P, state p is a *reduction* of s, $p \leq s$, if the set of I/O sequences of FSM P at state p is contained in the set of I/O sequences of FSM S at state s. FSM P is a *reduction* of FSM S if the reduction relation holds between the initial states of these machines.

We consider the fault domain $\mathfrak{I}_n$ which contains every deterministic complete FSM with at most n states and with the same input alphabet as the specification FSM S where n is number of states of the specification FSM. A *test suite* is a finite set of finite possibly adaptive input sequences of the specification. A test suite is *complete* with respect to the $\mathfrak{I}_n$ if for each FSM P $\in \mathfrak{I}_n$ such that P is not a reduction of S, the test suite has a sequence for which an output response is not in the set of output responses of S to this sequence. In the next section, based on the results of [4] we briefly remind how a complete test suite with respect to $\mathfrak{I}_n$ can be derived when the specification FSM has a distinguishing test case and each state is definitely reachable from the initial state.

3   Deriving a Complete Test

Methods for deriving tests with respect to the reduction relation are based on (adaptive) distinguishing and transfer sequences. A test suite of polynomial length can be derived under the following conditions: (1) an IUT is deterministic and does not have more states than the specification FSM; (2) the specification FSM has an (adaptive) distinguishing test case of polynomial length and each state is definitely reachable from the initial state.

An algorithm below returns a complete test suite with respect to the $\mathfrak{I}_n$ if the specification FSM has a distinguishing test case and each state is definitely reachable from the initial state. Since the length of an (adaptive) transfer sequence (if it exists) does not exceed n [5], the length of a returned test suite is polynomial with respect to the number of states of the specification FSM when a DTC possesses this feature. It is known [3] that a returned test suite can detect many other faults but the guarantee is only for FSMs with up to n states where n is the number of states of the specification FSM.

According to the results in [4, 5], the following proposition holds.

Proposition 1. If the specification FSM S has a DTC and each state of S is definitely reachable from the initial state then Procedure 1 returns a complete test suite with respect to $\mathfrak{I}_n$; the length of a test suite is proportional to the product $|S|\,|I|\,|L_{\mathrm{DTC}}|$ where L_{DTC} is the length of the distinguishing test case DTC.

Procedure 1 **Deriving a complete test suite w.r.t. the fault domain** $\mathfrak{I}_n$
Input: A complete possibly nondeterministic observable specification FSM S with n states
Output: A complete test suite *TS* with respect to $\mathfrak{I}_n$
Step-1: **If** some state of S is not definitely reachable from the initial state or the FSM has no DTC
Then Return the message "The specification FSM does not possess the necessary features"
Else Step-2
Step-2: Derive a state cover of the FSM using (adaptive) transfer sequences;
Append every sequence of the state cover with a DTC;
Append every sequence of the state cover with all possible inputs which in turn, are appended with a DTC;
Denote *TS* the obtained set of (adaptive) input sequences;
Return the obtained set *TS* of input sequences.

4   Refining the Specification FSM

If the specification FSM S has no DTC or some state is not definitely reachable from the initial state then we could find a maximal submachine of S (i.e. a submachine with maximum number of transition) that possesses this feature, however, this is not always possible. For example, there is no such submachine if there are at least two states where transitions under the every input are deterministic and the FSM is taken to the same state with the same output. Nevertheless, if this is possible then we could delete some transitions from the specification FSM in order to have an FSM where each state is definitely reachable and there is a DTC of polynomial length. For example, a submachine of the FSM in Fig. 1 without the bold transition $(2, i_1, o_2, 1)$ has a DTC of length 2 and each state is definitely reachable from the initial state.

Given the specification FSM S, let S^{red} be its maximal complete submachine where each state is definitely reachable and there is a DTC of polynomial length. If $S = S^{red}$ then a test suite returned by Procedure 1 is *complete* with respect to the fault domain $\mathfrak{I}_n$. If S is not equal to S^{red} then Procedure 1 is used for deriving a test suite *TS* for FSM S^{red} and the following proposition holds.

Proposition 2. If for each input sequence of *TS* the output response of an IUT P is in the set of output responses of S^{red}, then the IUT is a reduction of the FSM S. If the output response of the IUT to some sequence of *TS* is not contained in the corresponding set of output responses of the specification FSM S to this input sequence, then the IUT is not a reduction of S.

If the output response of the IUT to some sequence of *TS* is not contained in the corresponding set of output responses of S^{red} but is contained in the set of output responses of S, then we cannot conclude whether the IUT conforms to its specification. i.e., the verdict is *inconclusive*.

When deriving distinguishing test cases, merging-free FSMs are often considered. An FSM S is *merging-free* if for every two transitions (s_1, i, o, s) and (s_2, i, o, s) it holds that states s_1 and s_2 coincide. In [6] it is shown, that a merging-free FSM S has a DTC if and only if for each pair of state of S there exists a DTC and moreover, if there exists a DTC then there exists a DTC with the length that is polynomial with respect to the number of states of S. However, in this paper, we do not derive a maximal merging-free submachine of the specification FSM. Another way to find a maximal submachine of S that possesses necessary features could be the enumeration of all submachines of the specification FSM. However, as this number is big enough, we further propose to consider only deterministic submachines of the specification FSM. Another reason for considering deterministic submachines is that if a complete deterministic FSM has an adaptive distinguishing sequence then the length of such sequence is $O(n^2)$ [7].

Procedure 2 Refining the specification FSM

Input: a complete possibly nondeterministic observable specification FSM S with n states

Output: a complete submachine S^{red} of FSM S where each state is definitely reachable and there is a DTC of reasonable length or the message "The specification FSM cannot be reduced"

Step-1: Find a set of all complete deterministic submachines of FSM S, determine a submachine S' which has a DTC.

If such FSM does not exist

Then Return the message "The specification FSM cannot be reduced";

Else derive a DTC and a transfer sequence for each state of S'

Step-2: For each transfer sequence α from the initial state to state s of S', remove from S each transition tr such that tr is executed by S when α is applied, and transition tr breaks the property of α to be a transfer sequence to state s in S.

Step-3: For a DTC of S', remove from S each transition tr such that tr is executed by S when any sequence α from TC is applied and transition tr breaks the property of TC to be DTC for S.

Denote S^{red} the FSM obtained from S after removing transitions.

If Procedure 2 returns FSM S^{red} then S^{red} has DTC and each state is definitely reachable from the initial state, i.e., for each state of S^{red} there exists an (adaptive) transfer sequence, then a test suite returned by Procedure 1 for S^{red} has the fault coverage defined by Proposition 2.

5   Conclusions

In this paper, an approach for deriving test suites of reasonable length for nondeterministic FSMs with respect to the reduction relation has been proposed. A proposed method is based on deriving a submachine of the initial FSM specification that has a distinguishing test case of polynomial length and each state is definitely reachable from the initial state can be derived. Derived for refined specification test is not always complete, but can be used for checking an appropriate subset of implementations.

Acknowledgement. This work is partly supported by RSF Project No. 16-49-03012.

References

1. Gill, A.: Introduction to the Theory of Finite-State Machines, 272 p (1964)
2. Chow, T.S.: Test design modeled by finite-state machines. IEEE Trans. Software Eng. **4**(3), 178–187 (1978)
3. Dorofeeva, R., El-Fakih, K., Maag, S., Cavalli, A.R., Yevtushenko, N.: FSM-based conformance testing methods: a survey annotated with experimental evaluation. Inf. Software Technol. **52**, 1286–1297 (2010)
4. Petrenko, A., Yevtushenko, N.: Conformance tests as checking experiments for partial nondeterministic FSM. In: Grieskamp, W., Weise, C. (eds.) FATES 2005. LNCS, vol. 3997, pp. 118–133. Springer, Heidelberg (2006). doi:10.1007/11759744_9
5. Petrenko, A., Yevtushenko, N.: Adaptive testing of deterministic implementations specified by nondeterministic FSMs. In: Wolff, B., Zaïdi, F. (eds.) ICTSS 2011. LNCS, vol. 7019, pp. 162–178. Springer, Heidelberg (2011). doi:10.1007/978-3-642-24580-0_12
6. Yevtushenko, N., Kushik, N.: Nondeterministic merging-free finite state machines. In: Proceedings of IEEE East-West Design & Test Symposium (EWDTS), pp. 338–341 (2015)
7. Lee, D., Yannakakis, M.: Testing finite-state machines: state identification and verification. IEEE Trans. Comput. **43**(3), 306–320 (1994)

Author Index

Printed in the United States
By Bookmasters